P9-DMH-246

HOWARD ABADINSKY
New York State Department of Correctional Services

Probation and Parole

Theory and Practice

Prentice-Hall, Inc., *Englewood Cliffs, New Jersey 07632*

Library of Congress Cataloging in Publication Data

ABADINSKY, HOWARD
Probation and parole.

Includes bibliographical references and index.
1. Probation—United States. 2. Parole—United States. I. Title.
HV9278.A2 364.6′3′0973 76-48730
ISBN 0-13-715953-6

Printed in the United States of America

10 9 8 7 6 5 4 3 2 1

Prentice-Hall International, Inc., *London*
Prentice-Hall of Australia Pty. Limited, *Sydney*
Prentice-Hall of Canada, Ltd., *Toronto*
Prentice-Hall of India Private Limited, *New Delhi*
Prentice-Hall of Japan, Inc., *Tokyo*
Prentice-Hall of Southeast Asia Pte. Ltd., *Singapore*
Whitehall Books Limited, *Wellington, New Zealand*

To all of my girls:

Donna, Alisa, and Sandi

And to the memory of
Barry M. Sutherland

Contents

PART TWO
Parole History and Administration

Acknowledgements

Ann Abadinsky
Anthony Ariola
Jean Burke
Frank Carroll
Robert Kaplan
Lawrence Ptalis
George Savastano
Donald Wunderlich

A special thanks to **Robert Billings** for the use of his M.A. thesis, "The Impact of the *Menechino Decision* on New York State Parole."

Preface

There are several currents running through the waters of criminal justice these days, and to paraphrase a line from a Bob Dylan song, "You *have* to be a weatherman to know which way the wind is blowing." Riding on one current is James Q. Wilson, who, in an article adapted from his book and appropriately entitled "Lock 'Em Up,"* argues that the rate of serious crime can be significantly reduced by imprisonment; rehabilitation, he states, is at best of questionable value, while imprisonment definitely incapacitates offenders for their period of incarceration.

Other critics of the present criminal justice system and its rehabilitative efforts, such as Paul Lerman and Robert Martinson, generally conclude that "with few isolated exceptions, the rehabilitative efforts that have been reported so far have had no appreciable effect on recidivism."**

These criticisms challenge the basic philosophy which underlies probation and parole practice. Probation and parole are based on the belief that offenders can be rehabilitated and that there are treatment

*James Q. Wilson, "Lock 'Em Up," *New York Times Magazine*, March 9, 1975.

**Robert Martinson, "What Works? Questions and Answers About Prison Reform," *The Public Interest* (Spring 1974), p. 25.

methods available to carry out the task of rehabilitation. This is embodied in the so-called *treatment model,* which takes its strength from the proposition that to a large extent crime is the result of individual pathology—a deviance that can be dealt with through the use of psychosocial treatment methods. These methods are described and their strengths and weaknesses are presented.

Harlow, Weber and Wilkins, while not challenging the negative findings concerning rehabilitation, note that "a large number of offenders who are candidates for incarceration may instead be retained in the community as safely, as effectively, and at much less expense."* This expense currently is estimated in New York, for example, at between $13,000 and $26,000 per year per inmate. Thus, probation and parole, as part of the criminal justice system, exist for economic as well as philosophical reasons.

This book is concerned with the study of probation and parole as parts of the criminal justice system. In order to discuss this topic, it is necessary to consider the impact that probation and parole have on the system as a whole. For example, when probation is understaffed, judges tend to send "marginal" cases to prison instead of placing these offenders on probation. This results in an increase in the prison population, and pressure on the parole board to release more inmates on parole. Severe overcrowding in Southern prisons has resulted in judges giving lighter sentences and parole boards accelerating their release of inmates.**

These are only a few examples of the need to deal with any part of criminal justice in terms of how it affects and is affected by the rest of the system. In probation and parole we are most concerned with the impact on the offender. United States Attorney General Edward H. Levi has stated that "The whole criminal justice system must be viewed in light of its effect on the offender after he is released from prison."†

Another current running through the waters of criminal justice is generally referred to as *community-based treatment.* Community-based treatment is viewed as an alternative to incarceration in traditional correctional institutions. Harlow, Weber and Wilkins note that community-based treatment is often used as "a code

*Quoted in Edward Edelfonso, ed., *Issues in Corrections* (Beverly Hills: Glencoe Press, 1974), p. 369.

**Wayne King, "Six States in South Move to Ease Prison Crowding," *New York Times,* January 5, 1976, p. 1.

†Speech before the Governor's Conference on Employment and the Prevention of Crime, Milwaukee, February 2, 1976.

word with connotations of 'advanced correctional thinking' and implied value judgments against the 'locking up' and isolation of offenders."* It has three basic advantages:

1. It avoids the isolation of the offender from his family and makes community reintegration easier.
2. It allows access to educational, vocational, and employment programs not available in correctional institutions.
3. It is usually less costly than traditional imprisonment.

Community-based treatment includes:

probation
parole
juvenile aftercare
halfway houses
minimum security community-based correctional institutions
foster care, group homes, and a wide variety of juvenile treatment programs

The use of community-based treatment is a response to the disillusionment with traditional correctional institutions, and by far the largest areas within this approach are encompassed in probation and parole services.

Probation and parole are becoming increasingly popular for many reasons, not the least of which is the increasing cost of maintaining offenders in correctional institutions. Probation and parole have also come under the increasing scrutiny of the courts and various public and private agencies and organizations. Colleges and universities are reflecting this interest by offering courses in probation and parole.

Parole in particular is being criticized from within and without the field of criminal justice. David Fogel, Executive Director of the Illinois Law Enforcement Commission, proposes that traditional parole be abolished by automatically releasing all inmates after they have served 50% of their sentence. Fogel would also limit a judge's sentencing alternatives and require that they explain each sentencing decision in a written memorandum.** David Gilman, Counsel to the National Council on Crime and Delinquency, has called for abolishing parole.

*Edelfonso, p. 338.

**Remarks delivered at the American Society of Criminology Annual Meeting, Toronto, November 1, 1975.

He suggests that sentences be limited, and that offenders be required to serve the entire time without benefit of early release on parole.* This book should help the reader understand the basis for such criticism.

Also coming under increasing scrutiny is the treatment of juvenile offenders. There is a movement to remove *status offenses* from the jurisdiction of the juvenile court. At the same time, there is support for increased sanctions for juvenile offenders. This book will discuss both issues.

Obviously, you have to be a *weatherman* to know which way the wind is blowing—because in criminal justice it can blow in more than one direction at the same time. This book is designed to help the reader analyze, chart, and navigate the winds and currents that affect modern probation and parole practices and services.

*David Gilman, "The Sanction of Imprisonment; for Whom, for What, and How," *Crime and Delinquency* (Oct. 1975), pp. 346–47.

Introduction

Probation and Parole in the Criminal Justice System

> The system of criminal justice America uses . . . is not a monolithic, or even consistent system. Every village, town, county, city, and State has its own criminal justice system, and there is a Federal one as well.*

The recognition of probation and parole as integral parts of the criminal justice system is intertwined with the evolution of changing attitudes toward crime and the criminal. Probation and parole are part of a pattern of reform in society's response to the problem of crime and the criminal. However, as Jack D. Douglas notes, the organizations and systems created to carry out reforms in one era, often become viewed as reactionary in the next.[1]

The problem of crime and the criminal is a complicated one, covering many areas and beginning with the definition of "crime."

WHAT IS CRIME?

Quite simply, crime is any violation of criminal law. However, this definition leaves much unstated. For example, criminal laws are rela-

*President's Commission on Law Enforcement and Administration of Justice.

[1] Jack D. Douglas, ed., *Crime and Justice in American Society* (Indianapolis: Bobbs-Merrill Co., 1971), pp. 4–5.

tive to time and place. Before the Harrison Act was passed in 1914, heroin and other derivatives of opium were freely available in the United States. After 1914, the possession of heroin became a crime. In 1919, with the passage of the Volstead Act, possession of most alcoholic beverages becamc illegal. In 1933, the law was repealed and possession was no longer a crime (if proper taxes were paid). Currently, in the United States, each state has its own laws regulating the possession of marijuana. These laws differ greatly; one state may impose severe penalities, while another may not.

Packer presents the following definition of crime: "A crime is not merely any conduct forbidden by law; it is forbidden conduct for which punishment is prescribed and which is formally described as a crime by an agency of government having the power to do so." [2] Gibbons notes several elements that must be present if an act is to be defined as a crime under law: [3]

The behavior must constitute a "harm;" it must result in clearly visible, external consequences detrimental to the general interests of society.

The behavior must be legally forbidden before it has been committed, and it must clearly fit within an existing category of forbidden conduct.

There must be *mens rea*, literally "evil mind," or criminal intent as opposed to accidental behavior.

A crime must carry a legally prescribed penalty.

Crime is often viewed as being either *mala in se* or *mala prohibita*. *Mala in se* refers to acts that are intrinsically evil—murder, for example. *Mala prohibita* refers to acts that are merely defined by a given society as unlawful—restraint of trade, for example. Somewhere between these two categories fall numerous laws that cover acts sometimes defined as "victimless crimes." Included in this category are prostitution, drug abuse, homosexuality, and gambling. With respect to laws against such behavior, Schur states that they are part of society's tendency to overlegislate and thereby create crime out of deviance.[4]

[2] Herbert L. Packer, *The Limits of the Criminal Sanction* (Stanford: Stanford University Press, 1968), p. 18.

[3] Don C. Gibbons, *Society, Crime and Criminal Careers* (Englewood Cliffs, N.J.: Prentice-Hall, Inc., 1973), pp. 21–22.

[4] *See* Edwin M. Schur, *Our Criminal Society* (Englewood Cliffs, N.J.: Prentice-Hall, Inc., 1968).

WHO IS A CRIMINAL?

Quite simply, a criminal is a person who has been convicted of a crime. However, like the definition of crime, it raises important questions. Is a person who commits criminal acts a criminal if he is never apprehended and/or convicted? This question becomes even more perplexing when we consider the fact that most reported crimes do not result in an arrest and conviction. In addition, studies indicate that many crimes are not reported. This problem becomes important when we consider the question of recidivism. Has the offender been rehabilitated, or has he merely become more successful at avoiding detection?

Perhaps it is more important to study who actually becomes identified as a criminal. Later in this book, a composite sketch of the "average" prison inmate indicates that he is usually young, poor, and from a minority group. However, such a composite does not reveal some of the dynamic aspects of this question. Studies have indicated that the law is simply not enforced on an equal basis. Blumberg notes that society cannot enforce every law and punish every lawbreaker without causing mass paranoia, violent conflict, and savage repression.[5] If not all laws are enforced, and not all lawbreakers arrested, how is enforcement decided? Douglas states that the policeman arrests those who are most easily convicted; those least likely to be able to defend themselves adequately, and who are least likely to file a suit over such matters as false arrest or brutality—the poor. He concludes that these "organizational" factors reinforce the criminal law's bias against the poor.[6]

Differential legal treatment of the poor has resulted in a growing discrepency between the different classes of our society. While one class can afford an "F. Lee Bailey," another class must settle for public legal aid. This has caused a profound sense of injustice and alienation among the urban poor.

There have been studies which indicate that the law is not enforced in the same manner in different areas of the same jurisdiction. In an urban ghetto, for example, the police may not view a crime against a minority person as serious. The same crime against a white person, however, may bring a vigorous response, especially if the perpetrator was not white.[7]

[5] Abraham Blumberg, "Criminal Justice in America," in Douglas, p. 46.

[6] Douglas, p. 28.

[7] *See* Wayne R. LaFave, *Arrest: The Decision To Take a Suspect Into Custody* (Boston: Little, Brown, and Co., 1965).

Offenders who have already been convicted of a crime become part of the official records of law enforcement agencies. This increases their susceptibility to arrest, a fact of life with which all probation and parole officers must deal. Some offenders are given the opportunity to avoid being put through the criminal justice process. Later in this book we shall study the use of programs that seek to "divert" offenders out of the criminal justice process and into some other method of being handled. These programs can easily become another method for providing differential treatment whereby the middle-class can avoid the stigma and severity of the criminal process, while the poor are made to face the full force and fury of criminal sanctions.

In response to the question of "who" is a criminal, there are some observors who state that a criminal is a *victim* of society. Quinney, for example, states that "Criminal law is used by the state and the ruling class to secure the survival of the capitalist system, and, as capitalist society is further threatened by its own contradictions, criminal law will be increasingly used in the attempt to maintain domestic order." [8]

Criminal Punishment

Let us focus in on views of punishment, since probation and parole are viewed as two methods of ameliorating punishment. Let us look at the views of Quinney and the "radical school," as well as the others who have an important position on the problem of crime and the criminal. Packer, based on the arguments of H. L. A. Hart, presents five characteristics of punishment:

1. It must involve pain or other consequences normally considered unpleasant.
2. It must be for an offense against legal rules.
3. It must be imposed on an actual or supposed offender for his offense.
4. It must be intentionally administered by human beings other than the offender.
5. It must be imposed and administered by an authority constituted by a legal system against which the offense is committed.[9]

[8] Richard Quinney, *Critique of the Legal Order* (Boston: Little, Brown and Co., 1974), p. 16.

[9] Packer, p. 21.

EARLY RESPONSES

Early responses to deviant behavior ranged from the payment of fines, to trial by combat, banishment, and death by torture. A primitive system of vengence, *lex talionis,* an eye for an eye, was passed down from generation to generation as each family, tribe, or society sought to preserve its own existence without recourse to a written code of laws. Hammurabi, King of Babylonia, finally set down a written code of law about 4000 years ago. Although now in written form, his law continued the harsh tradition of *lex talionis.* A reading of the Code of Hammurabi today impresses one with the severity of the sentences imposed—a wide range of crimes carried the death penalty.[10]

At a later time, the Hebrews adopted the concept of an eye for an eye—but under the law of the Old Testament, this was interpreted to mean financial compensation for the victims of crime or negligence. A perpetrator who was unable to pay was placed into involuntary servitude, a limited and moderate form of slavery. The ancient Hebrews used fines extensively for a variety of offenses including robbery and burglary, while the death penalty was reserved for murder and theological offenses such as Sabbath violations and adultery. Due to the various procedural restrictions with respect to capital punishment, its actual use by the Hebrews was limited.

The Romans derided the use of fines for such offenses as robbery and burglary, and utilized the death penalty extensively in ways that have become etched in history. The fall of the Roman Empire resulted in there being very little "rule of law" throughout Europe. When law was gradually restored, fines and restitution became an important form of punishment as those in power sought to increase their wealth. When the offender was unable to pay, he was often subjected to mutilation. Trial by combat also began to flourish, in part because of the difficulty in proving criminal allegations. However, with the spread of Christianity, trial by combat was replaced with trial by ordeal. This involved various forms of torture which the accused was made to undergo.

Throughout the Middle Ages in Europe there was a continuation of the extensive use of execution, often accompanied by torture, as a deterrent to deviant behavior. (Much of this type of behavior involved

[10] Joseph W. Swain and William H. Armstrong, *The Peoples of the Ancient World* (New York: Harper and Brothers, Publishers, 1959), p. 31.

theological offenses such as heresy and witchcraft.) The prevailing belief was that the more brutal the punishment, the better its deterrent effect.

However, there existed for many centuries a disparity in the manner in which punishment was meted out. The rich and the influential often received little or no punishment for offenses that resulted in torture and death for the less fortunate. This was forcefully challenged in the eighteenth century with the advent of the Classical School.

CLASSICAL SCHOOL

The Classical School flourished in the last half of the eighteenth century, and was greatly influenced by Jean Jacques Rousseau's concept of the "social contract": "as each gives himself absolutely, the conditions are the same for all." [11] Rousseau commented that a society may use the death penalty: "it is in order that we may not fall victims to an assassin that we consent to die if we ourselves turn assassins. In this treaty, so far from dispensing of our own lives, we think only of securing them, and it is not to be assumed that any of the parties then expects to get hanged." [12] Rousseau states that a criminal makes war on society and is thus deserving of death. However, there was a great deal of compassion within the Classical School, and Rousseau stated that the "State has no right to put to death, even for the sake of making an example, any one whom it can leave alive without danger." [13]

Eighteenth century Europe experienced a revolt against the abuses in criminal justice, including being "examined" in secret, with torture freely applied in order to gain confessions. This revolt was given prominence by Cesare Beccaria (1738-94) who in 1764 wrote *An Essay On Crimes and Punishments* in which he stated: "Let the laws be clear and simple; let the entire force of the nation be united in their defense; let them be intended to favor every individual, than particular classes of men . . ." Beccaria believed that the law should stipulate a particular penalty for a specific crime, and that judges should mete out identical sentences for each occurrence of the same offense.

[11] Columbia University Staff, eds., *Introduction to Contemporary Civilization in the West* (New York: Columbia University Press, 1957), 1, p. 1151.

[12] Jean J. Rousseau, "The Social Contract," in Frederich A. Olafson, ed., *Society, Law, and Morality* (Englewood Cliffs, N.J.: Prentice-Hall, Inc., 1961), p. 211.

[13] *Ibid.*, p. 212.

As a result of Beccaria's work, there were great changes in the legal system. The French Code of 1791, for example, left only the question of guilt to the judgment of the court. Punishment was in accord with the severity of the offense. The influence of Beccaria was spread by others: William Blackstone, Jeremy Bentham, and Samuel Romilly. As a result of their work, the English criminal law was coded by 1800.

Basic to Classical thought was the concept of "free will." Man was viewed as endowed with the ability to choose between right and wrong. All persons, it was argued, tend to seek pleasure and avoid pain; punishment, therefore, was a deterrent to crime. Laws were coded and published. Each offense stipulated a particular penalty, and judges were to mete out identical sentences for each occurrence of the same offense. Since every man was endowed with free will, punishment was not to be varied to suit the personality or circumstances of the offender. Taylor, Walton, and Young sum up Classical thought as a theory of social control: "it delimits first, the manner in which the state should react to criminals, second, those deviations which permit individuals to be labeled as criminals, and third, the social basis of criminal law." [14] They note that the Classical theory, like contract theories in general, found important support amongst the rising middle-class. Classical theory, however, was unrealistic insofar as it could only be operational in a society where property and wealth were equally distributed and where everyone had an equal and identical stake in "the system." [15]

The obvious shortcomings of Classical theory soon became apparent. It was unrealistic to ignore any and all mitigating circumstances. Even Beccaria believed that certain persons, the insane and incompetent, should be treated in a special manner. In an attempt to apply the law without consideration of circumstances, the court became faced with meting out identical punishment to first offenders and repeaters. Taylor, et al., note that "It was impossible in practice to ignore the determinants of human action and to proceed as if punishment and incarceration could be easily measured on some kind of universal calculus." [16] It was against this background that what has been called the Neo-Classical School arose.

[14] Ian Taylor, et al., *The New Criminology* (New York: Harper and Row Publishers, 1973), pp. 2–3.

[15] *Ibid.* p. 6.

[16] *Ibid.*, p. 7.

NEO-CLASSICAL SCHOOL

Fox notes that the Neo-Classical School was characterized by: [17]

1. modification of the doctrine of free will, which could be affected by pathology, incompetence, insanity, or other conditions, as well as premeditation;
2. acceptance of the validity of mitigating circumstances;
3. modification of the doctrine of responsibility to provide mitigation of punishments with partial responsibility in such cases as insanity, age, and other conditions that would affect "knowledge and intent of man at the time of the crime;"
4. admission into court procedures of expert testimony on the question of degree of responsibility.

Taylor, et al., state that the Neo-Classical model is, with some modifications, the prevailing model for criminal justice in the western world. [18]

THE POSITIVE SCHOOL

Fox notes that the Positive School is so named because of its view that legal determinations are to be based on proof and evidence as opposed to speculation and philosophy. [19] A founder of this "school" was Cesare Lombroso (1835-1909), who is best remembered for his faulty research into the physical characteristics of criminals. However, his major contribution to criminal justice, and that of the Positive School, is the concept that "There is no crime that does not have its roots in numerous causes." The Positive School set the stage for studying crime according to scientific principles.

Basic to the positive approach was a denial of the concept of free will. Instead, the positivists substituted a "chain of interrelated causes," and a deterministic basis for criminal acts. Positivism became mingled with Darwinism, and punishment, therefore, became viewed not as retribution, but as part of a natural selection process for safeguarding society. Accordingly, the Positive School did not necessarily favor

[17] Vernon Fox, *Introduction to Criminology* (Englewood Cliffs, N.J.: Prentice-Hall, Inc., 1976), p. 37.

[18] Taylor, pp. 9–10.

[19] Fox, p. 38.

gentleness toward offenders. Raffaele Garofalo, a student of Lombroso, for example, suggested death for those who committed criminal acts as a result of a permanent psychological impairment that made them unfit to live in society. The positivists also recommended castration for sex offenders as part of their bent toward the "survival of the species" ideology.

The views of the Classical, Neo-Classical, and Positive Schools are important because they transcend their own time and continue to be applicable to contemporary issues in the criminal justice system of the twentieth century. The question is still being asked, "Do we judge the crime or the criminal?"

CRIMINAL PUNISHMENT IN THE TWENTIETH CENTURY

Punishment in modern criminal justice has five purposes:

1. revenge or retribution
2. protection of society
3. general deterrence
4. individual deterrence
5. rehabilitation

Retribution, as we have seen, is an inheritance from earlier and more primitive responses to deviant behavior. The degree to which it remains a salient factor in the imposition of criminal punishment is the degree to which we continue to retain the concept of *lex talionis.* There is a generally held notion that somehow a criminal is to be "made to pay" for his actions. This sometimes leads to incongruous situations: a condemned prisoner is provided with medical treatment in order to insure that he is healthy enough to be executed. Should he die before his scheduled execution, it is said that he "escaped" the gallows, the electric chair, etc.

Within this first purpose of punishment is a theological concept—*expiation* (some might rightfully argue that expiation should be considered under category five). Under Hebrew law, various forms of corporal punsihment, ranging from thirty-nine lashes to death by stoning, are viewed not as punishment, but as providing the "sinner" with an opportunity to atone for his acts. In an interesting article on this concept, Else and Stephenson state that expiation "is a clear passage from enmity to harmony."[20] They note that "At the foundation of our legal-moral system, allegedly, is the assumption that when a person or corporate entity is judged responsible for an offense he must *ipso facto* offer expiation for that offense." [21] The authors note that much of sociological theory places the cause of crime on a socio-economic basis, and thus society shares in the cause of crime; however, at the same time, society refuses to accept the burden of expiation that is laid heavily on the individual offender.[22]

Protection of society refers to the physical restraints placed on the criminal as a result of being found guilty of a crime. Obviously, while an offender is incarcerated, society is protected from his potential criminal activities. However, this span of time is usually limited since most offenders sent to prison are at some time released back into the community. To the extent that incarceration is physically debilitating, additional protection may be afforded. To the extent that prison "ages" an offender, and the proclivity to recidivate is related to an offender's age, community protection may be further enhanced. Some critics argue that these advantages are more than offset because prison often provides a "school" for learning new criminal activities while the men it releases are more embittered than before imprisonment.

General deterrence has been referred to as "intimidation" by Herbert Packer, who states that while it has considerable appeal, general deterrence does not suffice as a justification for punishment because its effect has not been determined.[23] Erik Wright views the concept of general deterrence within the context of utilitarianism: its purpose is to create "a significant risk factor in the commission of crime."[24] It is not what happens to specific persons who actually receive punishment that is important, but the effect on the general population that does not. While Wright presents this concept within the context of the *Politics of Punishment*, which he views as essentially aimed against the poor, a Freudian view presents a different perspective: "if anti-social actions are not punished by the outside world the power of the Superego is weakened, and the danger arises that our own antisocial impulses may break out in action." [25] Wright offers an alternative to this view by

[20] J. F. Else and K. D. Stephenson, "Expiation: A Theory of Reform," *Crime and Delinquency* (October 1974), p. 360.

[21] *Ibid.*, p. 363.

[22] *Ibid.*, p. 364.

[23] Packer, p. 39.

[24] Erik Olin Wright, *The Politics of Punishment* (New York: Harper and Row, 1973), p. 34.

[25] Robert Foren and Royston Bailey, *Authority in Social Casework* (Oxford: Pergamon Press, 1968), p. 9.

noting that the development of social systems that would strengthen the internal sanctions of the superego is superior to depending upon stiffer penalties and more law enforcement officers.[26]

If it were determined that man, as a person endowed with free will, made decisions on the basis of some utilitarian process, the impact of general deterrence would conceivably by quite significant. However, as case studies indicate, criminal behavior is often impulsive and defies a logical causal examination. Perhaps this lack of a rational basis for much of our society's criminal behavior merely reflects a society that, while fearful of injury by criminals, seems relatively impervious to the massive annual slaughter of thousands of persons by automobiles. Additionally, as we noted earlier, most crimes are not resolved by an arrest and punishment and this tends to undermine the impact of deterrence.

Individual deterrence refers to the effect of the imposition of punishment on the individual offender. This concept rests on a hedonistic foundation—that men seek pleasure and avoid pain. As in general deterrence, this concept implies a rational, deliberate basis for crime. Within the framework of individual deterrence, once a person is punished for a criminal act he will be reluctant to engage in further criminal activity. The logical extension or limit to this train of thought is that the more severe the punishment, the greater the individual deterrence. Short of execution, this concept has yet to be proven as empirically sound. Of course, within a constitutional framework that prohibits "cruel and unusual punishment" an empirical test may be impossible.

Rehabilitation is a relatively late arrival on the criminal justice scene. Some critics state that rehabilitation has opened the door for the development of a host of questionable schemes for dealing with offenders under the guise of treatment and "for their own good." The American Friends Committee notes: "Retribution and revenge necessarily imply punishment, but it does not necessarily follow that punishment is eliminated under rehabilitative regimes."[27]

Probably the most significant question raised about rehabilitation pertains to its effectiveness. Some critics maintain that it does not work, while others maintain that rehabilitation has not really been tried. Another group of critics, among them Richard Quinney, states that rehabilitation is actually irrelevant. They view crime as being a product of capitalism and their solutions are essentially political with a

[26] Wright, p. 35.

[27] American Friends Committee, *Struggle for Justice* (New York: Hill and Wang, 1971), p. 20.

Marxian bent. Thus, "crime is not caused by the mugger, but by the social, economic and political structure that deprives him of a decent standard of living." [28]

However, the concept of rehabilitation has been a cornerstone of probation and parole—it will be a major focus of this book.

PROBATION, PAROLE, AND REHABILITATION

As noted, probation and parole emanated from a reformist trend to ameliorate the severity of punishment. When this reform blended with positivist thinking, probation and parole began to evolve as distinct methods for helping offenders to better adjust to their social and economic situations. The full impact of this approach to crime and the criminal was realized with the advent of the Freudian "revolution."

Freud, and those who followed him, incorporated a *medical model* approach into the way non-physiological problems were dealt with. Accordingly, criminals were "sick" persons in need of "treatment." The offender's behavior was viewed as the manifestation of individual pathology, to be treated as any other illness would be handled—through diagnosis and the application of scientific principles of human growth and behavior. To an important extent, psychoanalytic theory (which will be discussed in greater detail later in this book) substituted psychological determinism for the biological determinism of Lombroso. The treatment expert soon became an important person within the criminal justice system.

PROBATION, PAROLE, AND CRIMINAL JUSTICE

In the following chapters we will be reviewing the development of probation and parole, current operations and practices, and trends and directions, in addition to gaining an understanding of how these two facets of criminal justice fit into the total system.

Before turning to a schematic overview of probation and parole in the modern criminal justice system, a word of caution about the word "system." *Webster's New World Dictionary* defines a "system." as an arrangement of things so related or connected as to form a unity or organic whole. Using this definition, neither the casual observer nor

[28] Amitai Etzioni, *Social Problems* (Englewood Cliffs, N.J.: Prentice-Hall, Inc., 1976), p. 10.

the serious student would view criminal justice as a system. Instead, what we see is a collection of agencies that expend billions of dollars annually and employ over a million people. Coffey, Eldefonso, and Hartinger describe a "system as simply a chain of causes and effects." They state that the high degree of fragmentation often causes unfavorable effects and they note that "A system that produces *unfavorable* effects may continue to work but with little or no *effective* impact on the problem for which it was intended." They further state that "consistent effective impact is the measure of the success of any system."[29] The authors note that the criminal justice system must respond and adjust to social and legal change since these often impinge directly upon police, courts, prosecution, defense, and corrections. While this may provide "mitigating" circumstances for the "system's" shortcoming as a system, this author prefers not to refer to criminal justice in terms of a system. Instead, he suggests that Edwin Schur provides a more adequate and descriptive term: "the criminal justice sequence."

The following excerpt from a report on the criminal justice system in New York City provides a vivid example of the problem that is endemic to criminal justice, not just in New York but throughout the country, particularly in urban areas.[30]

> Criminal justice agencies are rarely treated in fact as constituting a system. Indeed, to call it a system is really more in the wish than in the fact. In New York City there is no system-wide planning and, of course, no system-wide budget. Instead each agency (or in some cases groups of agencies) presses its own interests without regard to any overall plan. This often results in a misallocation of resources with those agencies in the criminal justice system having the most public visibility (primarily the police) tending to receive a disproportionate share of the funds available for criminal justice purposes.
>
> This misallocation of resources has been directly responsible for two of the gravest problems found in the criminal justice system—adminstrative plea bargaining and inappropriate sentencing. Thus agencies responsible for processing cases—e.g., the courts and the district attorneys —were found to be starved for funds, while at the same time the funding for police increased to the extent that there were even more patrol cars than police officers available to man them.
>
> This lack of funding and the concomitant lack of staff for non-police agencies has forced these agencies to concentrate on the number of

[29] Alan Coffey, et al., *Introduction to the Criminal Justice System* (Englewood Cliffs, N.J.: Prentice-Hall, Inc., 1974), p. 6.

[30] New York State Commission of Investigation, *The Criminal Justice System in the City of New York:* (Albany: State of New York, November 1974).

dispositions in order to prevent the backlog of cases from becoming totally unmanageable. The result of this pressure to somehow clear the court calendar is that defendants are given lighter sentences than they would receive if their individual cases were judged solely on their merits. As a result, criminal activity is not adequately deterred and the revolving door of the criminal justice system continues to spin.

Probation and Parole in the Criminal Justice System

(A General Schematic)

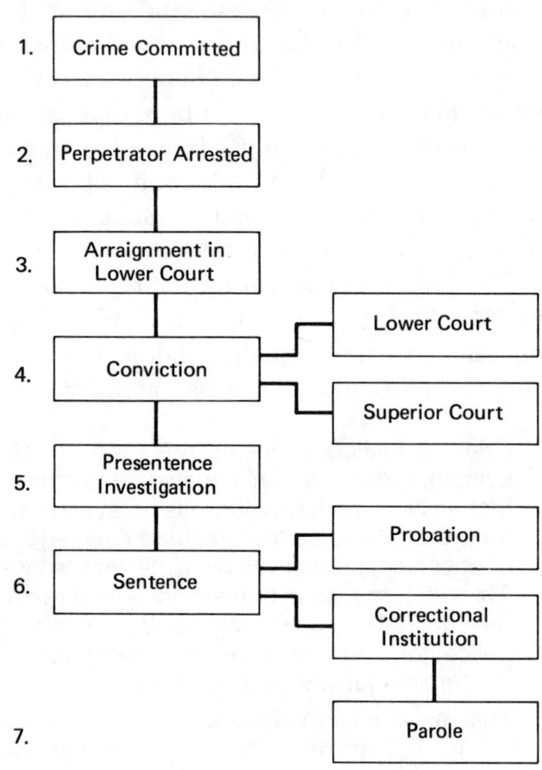

TABLE 1. Percent Distribution of Total Criminal Justice Expenditure from Own Sources of State and Local Governments, by State, Fiscal Year 1974!

(Amounts in thousands of dollars)

Item	*Expenditures from own sources*			*Percent distribution*	
	Total State-local	*State*	*Local*	*State*	*Local*
United States, Total	11 900 140	3 725 706	8 174 434	31.3	68.7
Alabama	107 500	37 586	69 914	35.0	65.0
Alaska	45 149	37 406	7 743	82.9	17.1
Arizona	135 615	43 444	92 171	32.0	68.0
Arkansas	43 981	19 988	23 993	45.4	54.6
California	1 826 838	485 081	1 341 757	26.6	73.4
Colorado	130 100	52 451	77 649	40.3	59.7
Connecticut	167 527	83 113	84 414	49.6	50.4
Delaware	33 706	24 293	9 413	72.1	27.9
District of Columbia	171 601	—	171 601	—	100.0
Florida	480 707	168 848	311 859	35.1	64.9
Georgia	211 825	78 839	132 986	37.2	62.8
Hawaii	52 753	16 270	36 483	30.8	69.2
Idaho	29 133	13 106	16 027	45.0	55.0
Illinois	669 479	176 005	493 474	26.3	73.7
Indiana	179 599	63 129	116 470	35.1	64.9
Iowa	95 339	33 310	62 029	34.9	65.1
Kansas	92 211	41 212	50 999	44.7	55.3
Kentucky	100 963	43 885	57 078	43.5	56.5
Louisiana	176 375	63 902	112 473	36.2	63.8
Maine	37 202	19 827	17 375	53.3	46.7
Maryland	280 901	153 076	127 825	54.5	45.5
Massachusetts	355 088	104 073	251 015	29.3	70.7
Michigan	546 413	129 609	416 804	23.7	76.3
Minnesota	159 920	45 119	114 801	28.2	71.8
Mississippi	64 708	29 508	35 200	45.6	54.4
Missouri	210 607	53 273	157 334	25.3	74.7
Montana	28 431	11 873	16 558	41.8	58.2
Nebraska	55 426	20 126	35 300	36.3	63.7
Nevada	54 349	14 454	39 895	26.6	73.4
New Hampshire	27 170	9 907	17 263	36.5	63.5
New Jersey	493 284	134 948	358 336	27.4	72.6
New Mexico	47 528	22 702	24 826	47.8	52.2
New York	1 786 995	370 995	1 416 000	20.8	79.2
North Carolina	221 599	125 991	95 608	56.9	43.1
North Dakota	17 722	6 085	11 637	34.3	65.7

Ohio	450 540	147 193	303 347	32.7	67.3
Oklahoma	85 936	34 395	51 541	40.0	60.0
Oregon	122 579	47 135	75 444	38.5	61.5
Pennsylvania	597 843	192 271	405 572	32.2	67.8
Rhode Island	42 939	23 951	18 988	55.8	44.2
South Carolina	95 510	45 023	50 487	47.1	52.9
South Dakota	20 556	8 896	11 660	43.3	56.7
Tennessee	157 831	51 348	106 483	32.5	67.5
Texas	442 588	124 272	318 316	28.1	71.9
Utah	39 750	19 002	20 748	47.8	52.2
Vermont	22 817	17 065	5 752	74.8	25.2
Virginia	220 358	104 844	115 514	47.6	52.4
Washington	188 794	70 654	118 140	37.4	62.6
West Virginia	46 929	22 246	24 683	47.4	52.6
Wisconsin	212 194	76 934	135 260	36.3	63.7
Wyoming	15 232	7 043	8 189	46.2	53.8

— Represents zero or rounds to zero.

*U.S. Law Enforcement Administration and U.S. Bureau of the Census, *Expenditure and Employment Data for the Criminal Justice System: 1974* (Washington, D.C.: U.S. Government Printing Office, 1975), p. 15.

A Comparison of Expenditures for Probation and Parole Services in the Fiscal Year 1974*

(Amounts in thousands of dollars)

Alabama	3,320
Alaska	1,490
Arizona	5,628
Arkansas	716
California	146,914
Colorado	5,562
Connecticut	5,325
Delaware	636
District of Columbia	5,133
Florida	26,355
Georgia	11,101
Hawaii	1,134
Idaho	720
Illinois	13,693
Indiana	3,913
Iowa	3,023
Kansas	1,284
Kentucky	3,043
Louisiana	5,440
Maine	847
Maryland	14,232
Massachusetts	14,873
Michigan	14,427

Minnesota	4,937
Mississippi	1,268
Missouri	7,697
Montana	835
Nebraska	1,653
Nevada	2,730
New Hampshire	1,002
New Jersey	19,648
New Mexico	1,845
New York	59,358
North Carolina	7,292
North Dakota	290
Ohio	16,200
Oklahoma	2,797
Oregon	5,492
Pennsylvania	23,710
Rhode Island	1,903
South Carolina	2,101
South Dakota	317
Tennessee	4,136
Texas	14,146
Utah	2,386
Vermont	799
Virginia	6,811
Washington	13,431
West Virginia	1,301
Wisconsin	7,636
Wyoming	245

*Based on direct current expenditures for probation, parole, and pardon by state governments, 384 large city governments, and 312 large county governments. *Source:* U.S. Law Enforcement Administration and U.S. Bureau of the Census, *Expenditure and Employment Data for the Criminal Justice System: 1973–74* (Washington, D.C.: U.S. Government Printing Office, 1976).

PART ONE

Probation History and Administration

Chapter 1

Historical Antecedents

While a dictionary can provide a definition of probation, only careful study can lead to an understanding of the variety of services provided by a modern probation agency. Although these services have their origins in recent history, probation has historical antecedents that reach back into the twelfth century.

Pardons developed in the twelfth century as one aspect of the king's authority to determine the punishment to be imposed for various offenses. The pardon included the power to commute or remit the prescribed penalty in individual cases, and was often used to induce criminals to inform on their confederates or to join the military.[1]

Benefit of clergy has its origin in the pious regard in which the Christian church was held by heads of state. It dates back to the thirteenth century, a time when most serious crimes in England, and elsewhere, were punishable by death.[2] Based on ecclesiastical rules against answering to serious charges in secular courts, clerical defendants were entitled to be tried in "court Christian"[3] where they were

[1] Naomi D. Hurnard, *The King's Pardon for Homicide* (Oxford: Oxford University Press, 1969), pp. vii, 1, and 327.

[2] Walter Hartinger, Edward Eldefonso, and Alan Coffey, *Corrections: A Component of the Criminal Justice System* (Pacific Palisades, Cal.: Goodyear Publishing Co., 1973), p. 101.

[3] Hurnard, pp. 375–78.

most often treated leniently.[4] Benefit of clergy was later extended to nonclerics who were able to prove their literacy by quoting a passage from the psalm *Miserere me* (Have mercy on me . . .) . Illiterates soon began to memorize the passage and the practice lost any real meaning.[5] Henry VIII did away with all but the name, and replaced the probation aspect of benefit of clergy with such practices as the burning of a defendant's palms, branding, and transporting to America.[6]

Benefit of clergy was officially abolished in England in 1827 for commoners, and in 1841 for the aristocracy. It was practiced briefly in the American colonies, but was abolished after the Revolution.[7]

Judicial reprieve was used in the English courts to serve as a temporary suspension of sentence to allow the defendant to appeal to the crown for a pardon. Although it was originally meant to be only a temporary postponement, it eventually developed into a judicial reprieve whereby sentences were often never actually imposed.[8]

JOHN AUGUSTUS (1784-1859)

This pioneer of modern probation was born in Woburn, Massachusetts and became a successful shoemaker in Boston.[9] In 1852 *A Report of The Labors of John Augustus* was published at the request of his friends, and in it Augustus wrote: "I was in court one morning . . . in which the man was charged with being a common drunkard. He told me that if he could be saved from the House of Correction, he never again would taste intoxicating liquors: I bailed him, by permission of the Court." [10] Thus began the work of the nation's first probation officer, a volunteer who worked without pay.

Augustus would appear in court and offer to bail a defendant. If the judge agreed, and they usually did, the defendant would become Augustus' charge. Augustus would assist the person in finding work or

[4] Hartinger, Eldefonso, and Coffey, p. 101.

[5] Louis P. Carney, *Introduction to Correctional Science* (New York: McGraw-Hill, 1974), p. 298.

[6] Hartinger, Eldefonso, and Coffey, p. 101.

[7] Carney, p. 298.

[8] *Ibid.*, p. 299.

[9] See *John Augustus, First Probation Officer*, originally published in 1939 by the National Probation Officers Association, and reprinted in 1972 by Patterson Smith Publishers, Montclair, N.J.

[10] *Ibid.*, pp. 4–5.

a residence; Augustus' own house was literally filled with people he had bailed. When the defendant returned to court, Augustus would report on his progress toward rehabilitation and recommend a disposition in the case. These recommendations were usually accepted.

His first experience with a drunkard led to an interest in helping others charged with the same offense. During the first year of his efforts he assisted ten drunkards who, because of his work, received small fines instead of imprisonment. He later helped other types of offenders, young and old, men and women, and was able to report only 10 absconders out of 2000 cases.

The work of John Augustus received support from the judges and the newspapers which reported on his efforts. However, prosecutors viewed him as an interloper who kept court calendars crowded by preventing cases from being disposed of quickly. Policemen and court clerks opposed his work because they received money for each case disposed of by a commitment to the House of Correction. Because of his voluntary work, Augustus neglected his business and eventually experienced financial ruin. He required the help of friends for his support.

His work was apparently very effective and the people he helped were able to remain free of alcohol and gainfully employed. Augustus thoroughly investigated each person he considered helping, taking account of "the previous character of the person, his age and the influences by which in the future he would likely be surrounded. . . ."[11] Augustus kept a careful record of every case in which he intervened and was able to provide statistics on the persons he had helped.

ORIGINS OF MODERN PROBATION

The origins of modern probation in the United States following Augustus date back to the middle of the 19th century and the establishment of prisoners aid societies and childrens aid societies. The work of these groups had an important effect on the courts because many employed paid agents. These agents worked in the criminal courts primarily to rescue children for whom there were no special courts. Although their work, like that of John Augustus, was unofficial, it was similar in practice and results to probation. The agents investigated and placed

[11] *Ibid.*, p. 34.

children in homes or with child-care institutions. Later, under the authority of new laws, they conducted investigations for the court and acted as guardians of neglected children and young offenders.[12]

In 1869, Massachusetts provided for a Visiting Agent of the Board of Charities to investigate and be present when a child was being tried in court. The agent was also responsible for child placement. In 1873 a Michigan law authorized a County Agent to investigate, place out, and visit, delinquent children. For adult offenders, at that time anyone over 16, the suspended sentence, an extension of English common law, was used in many states. Some states authorized the fixing of conditions to the suspended sentence, and these were the forerunners of probation regulations.[13]

Probation Begins in Massachusetts

In 1878 Massachusetts passed a law which authorized the Mayor of Boston to hire a probation officer who would be supervised by the Superintendent of Police. The Massachusetts courts had been using "bailing on probation," as noted in the work of John Augustus. A case would be adjourned before the imposition of sentence and the defendant would be released on bail. The person acting in the capacity of a probation officer would guarantee the return of the defendant to court at the end of the adjournment period. This became the period of supervision and the court had the power to extend it, discharge the defendant, fine him or imprison him. In most other states probation developed out of the suspended sentence and did not involve the fixing of bail.

Maryland, in 1894, authorized its courts to suspend sentence generally or for a specific time, and they could "make such orders to enforce such terms as to costs, recognizance for appearance, or matters relating to the residence or conduct of the convicts as may be deemed proper." The Baltimore courts also began using agents of the Prisoner's Aid Society and later appointed salaried probation officers. Missouri, in 1897, enacted a "Bench Parole Law" which authorized the courts to suspend sentence under certain conditions. The courts also appointed officers, misnamed "parole officers," to carry out this probation work.[14]

[12] Sheldon Glueck, ed., *Probation and Criminal Justice* (New York: The Macmillan Co., 1933), pp. 226–27.

[13] *Ibid.*

[14] *Ibid.*, pp. 227–28.

The 1878 Massachusetts law, the first of its kind, authorized a probation officer to investigate cases and recommend probation when appropriate.[15] The second state to adopt a probation law was Vermont, twenty years later. The twenty year lapse between probation laws in Massachusetts and Vermont is probably the result of the poor communications of that period. In 1898 Vermont authorized the appointment of a probation officer by the courts in each county, each probation officer serving all of the courts in his particular county. Another New England state, Rhode Island, soon followed with a probation law that was novel. It placed restrictions on who could be granted probation. These included persons convicted of treason, murder, robbery, arson, rape, and burglary. This violated one of the basic principles of modern corrections: judge the offender and not just the offense. The restrictive aspects of Rhode Island's probation law were copied by many other states. The Rhode Island probation law, which applied to children and adults, also introduced the concept of a state administered probation system. The State Board of Charities and Correction appointed a state probation officer and his deputies, "at least one of whom should be a woman." [16]

THE TURN OF THE CENTURY

The spread of probation was accelerated by the juvenile court movement,[17] which started in the Midwest and developed quite rapidly. In 1899 Minnesota enacted a law which authorized the appointment of county probation officers, but the granting of probation was limited to those under 18. Four years later this was changed to 21. In April 1899, Illinois enacted the historical Juvenile Court Act which authorized the world's first juvenile court.[18] The law also provided for the hiring of probation officers to investigate cases referred by the courts, but it made no provision for the probation officers to be paid.

However, charitable organizations and private philanthropists provided the funds to pay the probation officers. At the end of the first year Chicago had six probation officers who were supported by the Juvenile

[15] *Ibid.*

[16] *Ibid.*, pp. 229–31.

[17] President's Commission on Crime and Administration of Justice, *Task Force Report: Corrections* (Washington, D.C.: Government Printing Office, 1966), p. 27.

[18] Glueck, p. 231.

Court Committee of the Chicago Women's Club. In addition, in each police district a policeman spent part of his time out of uniform performing the duties of a probation officer. On July 1, 1899 Illinois' first juvenile court judge addressed the captains of Chicago's police districts: "You are so situated that you, even more than the justices, can get at the underlying facts in each particular case brought before you by the officers of your command. I shall want you to select some good reliable officers from each district for the work of investigating juvenile cases." [19]

In 1899, Colorado enacted a compulsory education law which enabled the development of a juvenile court using truant officers as probation officers.[20] By 1925 probation was available for juveniles in every state. Availability of probation for adults followed, becoming fact in every state by 1956.[21]

The first directory of probation officers in the United States, published in 1907, identified 795 probation officers working mainly in the juvenile courts. Like the first probation officer in Illinois, Mrs. Alzina Stevens,[22] many were volunteers, and some who were paid worked only part-time. By 1937, there were more than 3,800 persons described as probation officers,[23] and by 1965 there were 6,336 probation officers for juveniles and 2,940 probation officers supervising adult felons.[24]

[19] J. Lawrence Schultz, "The Cycle of Juvenile Court History," *Crime and Delinquency* (Oct. 1973), p. 465.

[20] Glueck, p. 232.

[21] *Task Force Report,* p. 27.

[22] Schultz, p. 465.

[23] George Killinger and Paul F. Cromwell, eds., *Corrections in the Community* (St. Paul, Minn.: West Publishing Co., 1974), p. 171.

[24] *Task Force Report,* p. 30.

Chapter 2

The Court System

A probation agency provides three basic services to the courts:

1. juvenile services
2. presentence investigation
3. supervision of probationers

The administration of these services may be under the auspices of the courts, or they may be administered by a separate agency. Before looking at these services it is necessary to look first at the court systems, both federal and state.

THE FEDERAL COURT SYSTEM

The federal courts were established under the Constitution or laws of the United States, and they are concerned primarily with the judicial administration of federal law. There are 480 district judges operating out of 92 district courts. The largest is the Southern District of New York which has 27 judges operating out of Foley Square in New York City. The second largest is Boston. Federal courts have exclusive jurisdiction in only a relatively few types of cases; most of their jurisdiction is shared with the state courts when dealing with criminal law. For example, bank robbery is both a federal and state crime.

The most important aspect of the federal courts in criminal matters is their appellate responsibilities; that is, the reviewing of state cases on appeal. This process begins in the district courts, may move up to the Court of Appeals and, if taken all the way, will conclude with the United States Supreme Court. Also, in the federal system, the district courts maintain jurisdiction over criminal cases involving the violation of federal statutes.

Organization of Federal Courts For Criminal Cases

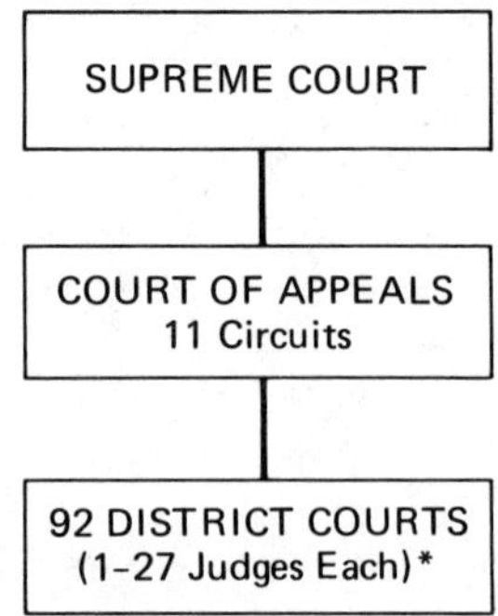

*The Southern District of New York is the largest with 27 judges. It includes the Borough of Manhattan in New York City.

THE STATE COURT SYSTEM[1]

State court systems are organized in three basic levels of jurisdiction: appellate, general, and limited. Courts at each of these levels may further be classified by the type of cases that they are authorized to hear—criminal, civil, or a combination of both.

At the first level are courts of limited jurisdiction. These courts represent 77% of the total number of courts in the United States and are where the vast majority of legal actions, predominantly misdemeanor and traffic cases, begin and usually end. At this level is the greatest amount of variation in patterns of organization within the court system in general. Two states have no courts of limited jurisdiction, a

[1] Law Enforcement Assistance Administration, *National Survey of Court Organization* (Washington, D.C.: Government Printing Office), pp. 1–3.

few have single statewide systems of limited courts, and the majority have several different types of limited courts covering the same geographic area. Thus, residents of a particular area may have to go to different courts in order to pay a traffic fine, be tried for a misdemeanor, or for juvenile proceedings.

At the next level are the courts of general jurisdiction, also called major trial courts. Most states are divided into judicial districts for the organization of the general jurisdiction courts, with each circuit or district consisting of one or more counties. Other states may have general jurisdiction courts organized along county lines, and some states have more than one type of general jurisdiction court—either two circuit type systems or a mixture of circuit system with a county-based system.

General jurisdiction courts are unlimited in the civil and/or criminal cases they are authorized to hear. A majority of serious criminal cases are tried in these courts. In most states there is some overlapping of jurisdiction between courts at the general and limited levels, and often among courts at the same level. In addition to hearing original actions, three-fourths of the courts of general jurisdiction hear cases on appeal from the courts of limited jurisdiction.

Courts of appellate jurisdiction are at the top of the judicial organizational structure. They are further grouped into courts of last resort and intermediate appellate courts (in the 23 states where they have been established). Intermediate courts hear appeals from courts of original jurisdiction. Courts of last resort have jurisdiction over final appeals from either courts of original jurisdiction or intermediate appellate courts. They may also have other responsibilities (e.g., administrative authority over some or all of the courts in the state).

Juvenile Courts

The juvenile court system differs from state to state and even within states. Jurisdiction over juveniles may be located in the court of general jurisdiction, in a separate juvenile court, or in various types of limited jurisdiction courts. It is possible that within one state juvenile jurisdictions are located in two or more different types of courts. In 15 states and the District of Columbia, juvenile jurisdiction is exercised exclusively by the court of general jurisdiction. In 5 other states, the court of general jurisdiction handles juvenile matters except for a few counties where a separate juvenile court has been established or juvenile jurisdiction has been vested in a court of limited jurisdiction.

Where the court of general jurisdiction acts as the juvenile court, a separate division often handles juvenile proceedings. Eight states have established a statewide system of juvenile or family courts with exclusive jurisdiction of juvenile cases. In six states, juvenile jurisdiction is exercised by a single court of limited jurisdiction. In the remaining 16 states, jurisdiction is shared among courts of general jurisdiction, separate juvenile courts, and courts of limited jurisdiction.

There are two other topics that require discussion before we turn our attention to probation itself—plea bargaining and sentence disparity. These two current problems in the judicial system are often interrelated, and nearly always affect probation services.

General Organization of a State Court System For Criminal Cases

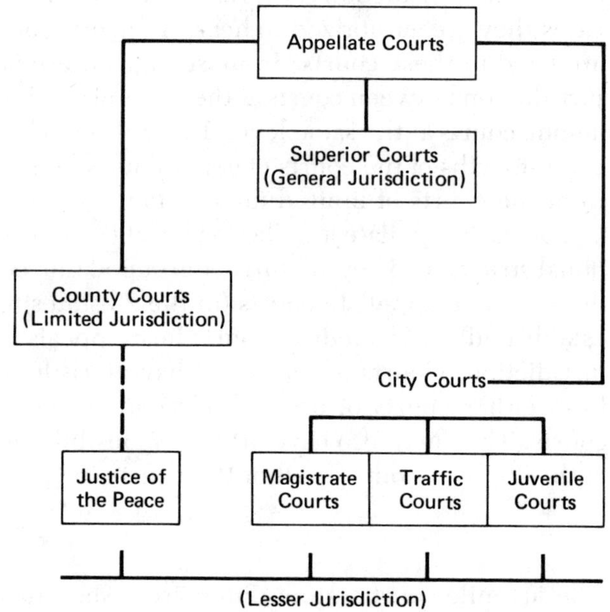

PLEA BARGAINING

Plea bargaining is an informal process whereby the prosecution negotiates with the defense until an agreement is reached in which the defendant pleads guilty in exchange for a reduction in the criminal charges against him. The extensive use of this practice, which accounts for about 80-90% of all convictions in the United States, is the result of overcrowded court calendars and a need to dispose of cases quickly. Plea bargaining saves the state the time and costs involved in a trial, and results in the defendant receiving a lesser sentence than he would if convicted after a trial. The willingness of the prosecution to accept a lesser plea depends on such matters as the seriousness of the offense, the evidence against the defendant, and the caseload of the prosecutor's office.

Although plea bargaining has been extensively criticized, it continues as the major method of resolving criminal cases. Lewis Katz states that "The pressures of too many cases and too little time cause the emphasis of plea bargaining to be upon settlement regardless of whether there is a relationship between the settlement and the facts of the case."[2] Guilty defendants will often hold out and appear to dictate their own punishment (or rather lack of it), while innocent persons may plead guilty to avoid remaining in jail while awaiting trial, or because they fear being convicted for a more serious crime.

Because of the increased use of plea bargaining, the role of the judge and the presentence report in sentencing has diminished. In view of the diminished sentencing role of the judge, Czajkoski suggests that the probation officer counsel the prosecutor on the rehabilitative potential of the defendant prior to agreeing to accept a lesser plea.[3] In such cases a presentence report could be ordered prior to the plea bargaining. This approach is supported by a recent New York Court of Appeals decision which states that any sentence promised during plea bargaining is conditional on it being appropriate in light of information contained in the subsequent presentence report.[4]

SENTENCE DISPARITY

Whenever two defendants who committed the same crime receive quite different sentences, there is by definition a disparity. Willard Gaylin states that "When serious criminals go unpunished, when minor offenses are excessively punished, when a chosen group receives lesser punishment or a despised group more punishment . . . It corrodes the basic structural prop of equity that supports our

[2] Lewis Katz, *Justice is the Crime* (Cleveland. Press of Case Western Reserve University, 1972), p. 197.

[3] Eugene H. Czajkoski, "Exposing the Quasi-Judicial Role of the Probation Officer," *Federal Probation* (Sept. 1973), pp. 9–10.

[4] *People v. Selikoff* (35 N.Y. 2d 227), 1974.

sense of justice. An excessive disparity in sentencing threatens that kind of breakdown."[5]

A recent survey in New York State revealed that even for the crime of homicide there was a great deal of disparity between the sentences imposed in New York County (Manhattan) and elsewhere in the state.[6] Former Attorney General Ramsey Clark notes that "Some judges sentence long, some short. Illustrations of the inequality in sentencing occur every day, often in different courtrooms in the same courthouse."[7]

Sentence disparity is now receiving more attention both in and out of the criminal justice system. It is often defended by referring to the modern correctional philosophy of making the sentence fit the offender and not merely having it reflect the crime.

Attorney General Edward H. Levi has commented that "If the imposition of punishment appears to be fickle—a matter of chance—or if it appears to be unequal with respect to socioeconomic groups, offenders who do suffer punishment for crimes may be left with an emotional scar that itself makes reunification very difficult." The Attorney General went on to say that "Today there is an accidental quality to the imposition of punishment."[8] The National Advisory Commission has noted that "An offender who believes he has been sentenced unfairly in relation to other offenders will not be receptive to reformative efforts on his behalf."[9]

The Commission reports that various techniques have been developed to reduce disparate and irrational sentencing. In some jurisdictions, where there is more than one judge passing sentence for the same level of offenses (e.g. felonies), the judges meet in a sentencing council and discuss the sentences of individual offenders. The council acts as a check on the attitudes and practices of the single sentencing judge. Other jurisdictions conduct sentencing institutes to consider broad principles and methods of sentencing offenders.[10]

Another method of reducing disparate sentencing is to have appel-

[5] Willard Gaylin, *Partial Justice* (New York: Alfred A. Knopf, 1974), p. 5.

[6] *See* "Plea Bargains Resolve 8 of 10 Homocide Cases," *New York Times* (Jan. 27, 1975), p. 1.

[7] Ramsey Clark, *Crime in America* (New York: Simon and Schuster, 1970), p. 224.

[8] Speech before the Governor's Conference on Employment and the Prevention of Crime, Milwaukee (Feb. 2, 1976).

[9] National Advisory Commission on Criminal Justice Standards and Goals (NACCJSG), *Corrections* (Washington, D.C.: Government Printing Office, 1973), p. 178.

[10] *Ibid.*

late review of sentences. Under this system, a judge is required to state his reasons for imposing a particular sentence, which then become the subject of appellate review. Imlay and Reid state that "One of the expected advantages of this review is to contribute to an offender's rehabilitation by enhancing his belief that the system is fair and not subject to the unchecked caprice of one official." [11] They also note that "One of the immediate effects on the probation officer of the provision for appellate review of sentencing is the possibility that an appellate court may find that a sentencing record is so incomplete as to require remand." [12] In such an event, the probation department would be required to provide further presentence investigation information including an update on certain information already submitted. This would be especially applicable in cases where a lengthy period had elapsed since the time of original sentencing.[13]

Imlay and Reid make an important observation relative to modern correctional policy: "Uniformity in sentencing would, of course, thereby be promoted by appellate review of sentences, in derogation of the notion of individualized sentencing." [14]

In a report on *Sentencing of California Felony Offenders*, Carl Pope presents some of the dynamic aspects of the problem.[15]

> For years, many critics have charged that the criminal justice system operates in a biased manner toward certain disadvantaged members of society. According to this perspective, those underprivileged segments of society such as the poor, the black, and other minorities are overrepresented in official crime records and often receive more severe treatment than other similarly situated offenders. In a recent monograph, Schrag points out:
>
> Criminal sanctions also vary according to other characteristics of the offender, and for any given offense they tend to be most frequent and most severe among males, the young (excepting juveniles handled in civil courts), the unemployed or underemployed, the poorly educated, members of the lower classes, members of minority groups, transients, residents of deteriorated urban areas. These are precisely the population segments that continued to have the highest rates for most criminal offenses. (1971:90)

[11] Carl H. Imlay and Elsie L. Reid, "The Probation Officer, Sentencing and the Winds of Change," *Federal Probation* (Dec. 1975), p. 15.

[12] *Ibid.*, p. 16.

[13] *Ibid.*

[14] *Ibid.*

[15] Carl E. Pope, *Sentencing of California Felony Offenders* (Washington, D.C.: U.S. Government Printing Office, 1975), pp. 10–11.

More forcibly, Quinney (1970:142) observes that "perhaps the most obvious example of judicial discretion occurs in the handling of cases of persons from minority groups. Negroes in comparison to whites, are convicted with lesser evidence and sentenced to more severe punishment."

While observations such as those noted above invoked intuitive reactions, adequate empirical data bearing on the issue is sparse at best. Although a number of social researchers have attempted to measure the degree to which discrimination is operative in sentence dispositions, the findings of these endeavors have often proven to be contradictory.

One of the earliest empirical assessments of differential sentencing practices covering the period from 1930 to 1940 was conducted by Johnson (1941). Studying the court records of 645 adult homicide offenders in North Carolina, Georgia, and Virginia, Johnson concluded that sentencing practices were highly biased against blacks, especially those who were charged with killing whites. Garfinkel (1949), in a replication of Johnson's study, reached a similar conclusion—that blacks were treated more severely than white offenders. Both studies, however, were methodologically unsophisticated in their failure to utilize control variables. Neither, for example, considered the effects of prior record on sentence outcome. It is quite possible that those with a more serious prior record were treated more severely, and if blacks had more extensive prior histories of criminal involvement, they would have received more severe sentences.

Bensing and Schroeder (1960), controlling for seriousness of offense, analyzed 662 homicides that occurred in Cleveland from 1947 to 1954. Their findings proved opposite to those noted by Garfinkle and Johnson in that they found no evidence of racial discrimination once seriousness of offense was introduced as a control variable. Whereas blacks who killed whites were generally treated more severely than whites who killed blacks, the former group were also more apt to have faced more serious charges, such as homicide while perpetrating robbery or rape.

Bullock (1961) also studied the sentence length of 3,644 cases of homicide, rape and burglary for the year 1958. Using the chi square test of independence, while controlling for type of offense, type of plea, prior record, region of State and urbanization, Bullock's findings generally supported the existence of differential sentencing practices. Blacks were frequently sentenced to longer periods of confinement for burglary than whites and shorter periods of confinement for murder. Bullock further concluded that those pleading guilty received shorter sentences than did those who pled not guilty.

In two methodologically more rigorous studies conducted by Green (1961 and 1964), a significant relationship was found to exist between sentence severity and race. Although bivariate tables indicated that blacks were treated more severely than whites, Green found that when severity of offense and prior record were employed as control variables, these relationships disappeared. He concluded that whereas there were sentencing differences among blacks and whites, they resulted not from racial discrimination, but from actual legal differences in the cases of apprehended offenders. Green's analysis demonstrated that blacks who had robbed whites, for example, were significantly more likely to have been armed than were blacks who had robbed other blacks. Vines and Jacobs (1963), however, in examining over 4,000 court cases from New Orleans Parish, Louisiana, for the years 1954, 1958, and 1969, discovered that blacks received significantly longer sentence than whites, even when they controlled for severity of the offense committed.

The findings of these studies are indeed puzzling. The evidence accumulated so far seems to be contradictory and sheds little light on the issue of differential sentencing practices. Hindelang (1969), in reviewing these discrepant results, suggested that they may be accounted for by certain peculiarities in the studies themselves. Hindelang observed that those studies that found evidence of differential sentencing practices utilized data from Southern regions of the country and were, on the average, approximately 10 years older than those studies finding no evidence of discrimination. Furthermore, these studies were generally limited to the single offense of homicide and failed to utilize control variables. Hindelang's analysis, however, was limited to studies conducted before 1965. Since that time a number of additional studies have also explored the problem of sentencing discrimination. Although these recent investigations are generally more methodologically rigorous, use more recent data, and include a wider variety of offenses, their findings are still contradictory.

A partial explanation for these contrary findings may lie in the nature of the data and the strategy often used to explore the issue of differential sentencing. A major shortcoming of many studies in this area is that generally only one indicator of possible severity is employed—that most often being the length of confinement imposed by the trial judge (or jury). Keeping in mind, however, the fact that criminal processing is dynamic rather than static, it would seem worthwhile to employ additional indicators of severity. Decisions made at one stage, for example, may be strengthened, diluted, or left unchanged by those occurring at a later point in time. For example, sentence lengths imposed by trial judges may later be altered by decisions of parole boards. Further, it is quite possible that although certain groups of offenders are more likely to receive longer sentences than others when confined, it may also be the case that these groups are less likely to actually be confined. The failure of many previous research efforts to incorporate this dynamic perspective into their designs is probably more a reflection of the inadequacy of available data than poor methodological strategy.

A corollary point is the fact that a majority of those studies noted above focused on offenses of a very serious nature (e.g., homicide) in which offenders were thought likely to receive prison commitments. As a result the focus of inquiry was on those offenders adjudicated in superior court or its equivalent (e.g., Federal district court), thus omitting analysis at the lower or municipal court level, where a substantial proportion of all felony cases is actually adjudicated. It is true that superior court convictions and resulting sentences are generally more severe than those occurring at the lower court, but it would seem worthwhile to investigate sentencing patterns at both stages. Again, adequate data reflecting both stages of processing have not been widely available. Transactional data, however, provide a longitudinal perspective, thus furnishing a stronger analytic foundation for investigating the dynamic aspects of sentencing.

ADMINISTRATION OF PROBATION

"Probation in the United States is administered by hundreds of independent agencies operating under a different law in each State and under widely varying philosophies, often within the same State." [16] There is a continuing debate as to whether probation services should be administered by the judiciary or by an executive agency autonomous from the courts.

Those who favor judicial administration of probation maintain that it is more responsive to court direction, that there is better feedback, and that judges have more confidence in probation which they administer. Those who oppose judicial administration and favor a separate administration, usually part of a larger correctional agency, point out that judges are not equipped to administer probation services. They note that when judges do administer probation, a disproportionate amount of time is spent on presentence investigations for the judge, forcing some neglect of the supervision of offenders. It is also noted that all other subsystems for carrying out the dispositions of the court, such as prisons and parole, are already under a separate state-wide jurisdiction. Proponents of this system maintain that a separate state agency for probation allows for better coordination with other correctional services.

For purposes of study we will divide probation systems into six categories:

1. *Juvenile.* Separate probation services for juveniles administered on a county or local level, or on a statewide basis. In either case, the administration of juvenile probation is effectively separated from probation services that are provided for adults.

[16] *Task Force Report,* p. 28.

2. *Municipal.* Independent probation units usually administered by the lower courts.

3. *County.* Under laws and guidelines established by the state, a county operates its own probation agency; this system is similar to the municipal system.

4. *State.* One agency administers a central probation system which provides services throughout the state.

5. *State Combined.* Probation and parole are administered on a statewide basis by one agency.

6. *Federal.* Probation is administered as an arm of the courts, but its probation officers are authorized to supervise parolees released from criminal and military institutions.

This list is by no means exhaustive. For example, in Fulton County, Georgia, there is a separate system that provides probation services for all courts in the county. In the rest of Georgia, however, probation services are provided by the Department of Offender Rehabilitation, which also administers prisons and parole.[17] In Wisconsin the Division of Corrections administers probation for adults, except in Milwaukee County, where juvenile and adult probation is administered by the local courts.[18]

The Advisory Commission on Intergovernmental Relations reports the following:[19]

Probation Administration

Adult:

a. local—11
b. state and local—13
c. state—26

Juvenile:

a. local—13
b. state and local—20
c. state—6

[17] Personal Interviews with Georgia probation/parole staff.

[18] Robert Carter and Leslie T. Wilkins, eds., *Probation and Parole* (New York: John Wiley and Sons, 1970), p. 317.

[19] Advisory Commission on Intergovernmental Relations, *State-Local Relations in the Criminal Justice System* (Washington, D.C.: Government Printing Office, 1971), pp. 282–86.

Some states separate misdemeanor probation cases from their other adult cases for administrative purposes.

Adult Misdemeanor:

a. local—13
b. state and local—11
c. state—16

Twenty-one states combine probation and parole in the same agency, always on a state basis.

*DEFINITIONS**

Court System. A judicial agency established or authorized by constitutional or statutory law. A court system may consist of a single court or a group of two or more courts in the same judicial district.

Court. Each geographically separate locality at which a court system holds sessions (sits) and which operates independently.

Federal Court. A court established under the Constitution or laws of the United States and concerned primarily with the judicial administration of Federal law.

State Court. A court established or authorized under the constitution or laws of a State and concerned primarily with the judicial administration of State and local government laws; viz., all courts other than Federal courts.

Judicial district, circuit, or precinct. One of the geographic areas into which a State is commonly divided for judicial purposes. A district may include two or more counties having separate court locations and presided over by the same judge or judges.

Jurisdiction. Refers to subject-matter jurisdiction, i.e., the authority of courts or judicial officers over a particular class of cases.

Court of appellate jurisdiction. A court having jurisdiction of appeal and review, with original jurisdiction conferred only in special cases; includes both courts of last resort and intermediate appellate courts.

Court of last resort. An appellate court which has jurisdiction over final appeals in a State.

Court of intermediate appeals. An appellate court which is limited in its appellate jurisdiction by State law or at the discretion of the court of last resort in the State.

*Source: Law Enforcement Assistance Administration.

Court of original jurisdiction. A court having jurisdiction in the first instance to try and pass judgment upon the law and facts, as distinguished from a court of appellate jurisdiction; includes both courts of general jurisdiction and courts of limited or special jurisdiction; also referred to as "trial court."

Court of general jurisdiction. A trial court of unlimited original jurisdiction in civil and/or criminal cases, also called "major trial court."

Court of limited or special jurisdiction. A trial court whose legal jurisdiction covers only a particular class of cases, e.g., probate, juvenile, traffic, or cases where the amount in controversy is below a prescribed sum or which is subject to specific expections; e.g., courts limited to hearing civil cases with a maximum of $500 in controversy or criminal cases wth a maximum penalty of $500 fine or 6-months sentence. Certain courts with unlimited civil jurisdiction but limited criminal jurisdiction are in this category.

Criminal jurisdiction. Includes jurisdiction of criminal felonies, felony preliminary hearings, misdemeanors, traffic, and municipal or county ordinance violations.

Civil jurisdiction. Includes both actions at law and pleadings in equity; also probate (wills and estates), mental competence, guardianship, and domestic relations proceedings.

Juvenile jurisdiction. Refers to special jurisdiction over delinquent and neglected children (minors).

Trial de novo. A completely new trial in a court with appellate jurisdiction conducted as if no trial had been had in the court below.

Other judicial personnel. Personnel, other than judges, who participate in the "judging process" such as commissioners, masters, referees, etc. These personnel usually hear only certain types of cases or carry proceedings to a certain point. Does not include judges pro tem, visiting judges, or any type of reserve judges. Also known as "para-judicial" personnel.

Chancery/Equity courts. A court which has jurisdiction in equity, and which administers justice and decides controversies in accordance with the rules, principles, and precedents of equity; as distinguished from a court having the jurisdiction, rules, principles, and practice of the common law.

Probate court. A court which has jurisdiction over the following civil matters:

a. Administering estates of deceased persons, minor children of deceased persons, and incompetents.
b. Administering trusts.
c. Administering the affairs or determining the guardians of orphans, mental defectives, and incompetents.
d. Setting disputes over wills.

Chapter 3

Juvenile Services

Of the three basic services that a probation agency provides to the court, juvenile services is probably the most trying. This is because the juvenile court has not lived up to its expectations, despite good intentions. This in part is due to the shortage of trained staff and the problems encountered in juvenile court. Smith and Rubin note that investigations in juvenile cases are often cursory, with children receiving hurried and arbitrary hearings, and probation supervision is usually inadequate.[1]

THE JUVENILE COURT

Following the Illinois Juvenile Court Act of 1899 there was a rapid proliferation of juvenile courts.[2] The foundation for the creation of separate courts for juveniles was the result of the efforts of the "child saving movement" headed by feminist reformers of the late 19th century. The juvenile court was designed to remove children from the

[1] Ted Rubin and Jack F. Smith, *The Future of the Juvenile Court* (College Park, Md.: American Correctional Association, 1971), p. 2.

[2] Schultz, p. 457.

criminal process by creating programs for delinquent, dependent, and neglected young persons. The underlying concept was that of *parens patriae*, whereby the child was not accused of a crime, but instead given guidance and assistance. Young persons charged with offenses, and "status offenders" (incorrigibles and truants, for example) came under the jurisdiction of the juvenile court.

A book on the juvenile court published in 1927[3] presents an important insight into the prevailing concepts on which the juvenile court was founded:

> These principals upon which the juvenile court acts are radically different from those of the criminal courts. In place of judicial tribunals, restrained by antiquated procedure, saturated in an atmosphere of hostility, trying cases for determining guilt and inflicting punishment according to inflexible rules of law, we have now juvenile courts, in which the relations of the child to his parents or other adults and to the state or society are defined and are adjusted summarily according to the scientific findings about the child and his environments. In place of magistrates, limited by the outgrown custom and compelled to walk in the paths fixed by the law of the realm, we have now socially-minded judges, who hear and adjust cases according not to rigid rules of law but to what the interests of society and the interests of the child or good conscience demand. In the place of juries, prosecutors, and lawyers, trained in the old conception of law and staging dramatically, but often amusingly, legal battles, as the necessary paraphernalia of a criminal court, we have now probation officers, physicians, psychologists, and psychiatrists, who search for the social, physiological, psychological, and mental backgrounds of the child in order to arrive at reasonable and just solutions of individual cases.

Because of the non-criminal concept, the usual safeguards of due process which were applicable in adult courts, were absent in juvenile court proceedings. The right to counsel, to confront and cross-examine witnesses, to avoid self-incrimination, were some of the basic rights denied to juveniles. Because the focus of the juvenile court was to provide treatment, procedures were often vague, and the judge, with the assistance of the probation department, was given broad powers over young persons.

There was increasing concern over the operation of the juvenile court just prior to the monumental *Gault Decision*. Various organizations and individuals in law and education pressed for changes which would guarantee fairness in the juvenile court. In 1967, the United

[3] Herbert H. Lou, *Juvenile Courts in the United States*, (Chapel Hill: University of North Carolina Press, 1927).

States Supreme Court decided the case of Gerald Gault, a fifteen-year-old who had been committed to a state training school in Arizona. The Court ordered procedural safeguards which guaranteed a minimum of due process in all juvenile courts (*see In Re Gault,* Chapter 7).

Not all states have separate juvenile courts. Florida, for example, abolished its juvenile courts in 1973, and juvenile cases are assigned to judges sitting in adult courts. Several European countries do not have juvenile courts. In Sweden, a child welfare council performs the function of the juvenile court. The council consists of five members, including a lawyer, a clergyman, and a school teacher. Norway and Denmark have a similar system.[4] Belgium has Committees for the Protection of Youth which provide help for families who are unable to cope with the problems presented by their children.[5] Scotland has abolished its juvenile court system and now has Children's Panels for all but the most serious offenses, which are reserved for formal court proceedings.[6]

PROCEDURES IN JUVENILE COURT

There is a lack of uniformity among juvenile (sometimes called "family") courts throughout the United States. In more than half the states, juvenile probation services are administered by the juvenile court; in the remainder, welfare, corrections, or other agencies administer these services. In some jurisdictions, certain violations of law are handled by the adult criminal courts no matter what the age of the offender (for example, murder, kidnapping, and armed robbery). The legal age of a juvenile varies from state to state (from 16 to 21), although it is usually eighteen. The juvenile court is usually closed to the general public and its records are confidential. In most jurisdictions a juvenile is not routinely fingerprinted or photographed by the police.

INTAKE SCREENING

Cases are referred to the juvenile court by the police, parents, school officials or other public and private agencies. The case is first reviewed

[4] Martin R. Haskill and Lewis Yablonsky, *Juvenile Delinquency* (Chicago: Rand McNally, 1974), p. 48.

[5] J. Lenoir, "Modern Juvenile Codes: Belgium," *International Journal of Offender Therapy and Comparative Criminology* (No. 2, 1973), p. 178.

[6] Andrew Wilson, "New Approaches in the Handling of Juvenile Delinquents in Scotland," *International Journal of Offender Therapy and Comparative Criminology* (No. 3, 1974), p. 252.

by an intake officer, usually a member of the probation staff. This officer interviews the young person, the policeman or agency representative, and the child's parent(s) in an effort to determine if the juvenile court has jurisdiction. If the answer is in the affirmative, the officer must determine if the case is appropriate for formal court processing, or can be handled as an *unofficial case.* This responsibility is similar to that exercised in adult criminal courts by the prosecutor who decides which cases are to be presented to the court for prosecution.[7] Roughly one-half of all cases are disposed of without the filing of a petition.[8] (The filing of a petition parallels the filing of a complaint in adult criminal courts.)

Unofficial Cases

When the intake officer believes that it is possible to assist the young person without formal action, it is an *unofficial case.* Haskill and Yablonsky state that the term *unofficial* refers to cases that are too trivial to warrant court action or alleged but not proven cases of delinquency where the intake officer believes that social casework rather than legal action is needed.[9]

If the child and his parents or guardians are agreeable to the informal processing, the young person can be placed under the supervision of a probation officer for a period of up to 90 days. The use of this informal probation accounts for about 20% of the cases disposed of at intake.[10] Dawson is critical of the process used in unofficial cases: "Because informal adjustment normally has substantial advantages for the juvenile, the incentive to confess is great." These advantages cast a doubt on the voluntariness and truth of admissions of guilt.[11]

The period of informal probation can be a crucial time in the life of a young person. If successful, the youngster may avoid further juvenile court processing; if unsuccessful, he will face the labyrinth that is the criminal justice system. No one is more aware of this than the probation officer, who, using all of the skills and resources at his command, attempts to assist the youngster and the youngster's parents through the crisis. Counseling, group therapy, tutoring, vocational guidance,

[7] Czajkoski, pp. 10–11.

[8] Edward Eldefonso and Alan R. Coffey, *Process and Impact of the Juvenile Justice System* (Beverly Hills: Glencoe Press, 1976), p. 17.

[9] Haskill and Yablonsky, p. 31.

[10] Paul Lerman, ed., *Delinquency and Social Policy* (New York: Praeger Publishers, 1970), p. 40.

[11] Dawson quoted in Banjamin Frank, ed. *Contemporary Corrections* (Reston, Va.: Reston Publishing Co., 1973), p. 56.

and recreational services are all put to use in order to help the young person (if all of these services are available). If these efforts are unsuccessful, the probation officer can then file a formal petition which will make the case an official one.

Official Cases

The decision to file a petition is based on the following:

1. The child or his parents deny the allegations
2. Unofficial handling does not seem appropriate in view of the seriousness of the case
3. Informal probation has failed.

In some juvenile courts the same probation officer may handle the case from intake through termination, while in others probation officers or other staff persons are involved in different stages of the court process. Smith and Rubin maintain that it is desirable to utilize a non-professional to present a case to the court. After adjudication the case should be referred to a probation officer for study prior to dispositional hearing. They believe that such a system would provide for better use of the probation officer's time by freeing him (or her) from what are often clerical-type duties, such as serving notice upon the parties and having the case placed on the court calendar, relative to the filing of a petition. The authors also believe that this will prevent the probation officer, who is essentially the helping agent of the court, from being identified as a "prosecuting agent." [12]

Hearings. The filing of a petition results in a hearing. Hearings in juvenile court are less formal than in adult courts. Judges usually do not wear robes and they sit at a desk instead of the high bench that is characteristic of the adult courts.

There are several types of hearings in juvenile court. A judge may hold a *detention hearing* to determine if the young person, called a *respondent* (instead of a defendant), should be held in a juvenile detention facility pending further court action. If the judge determines that the respondant's behavior is a danger to himself or the safety of others, or that he will probably not return to court voluntarily, the young person can be held in detention.

The *adjudication hearing* is held to review the allegations contained

[12] Rubin and Smith, p. 29.

in the petition. If the allegations are sustained, the judge makes a *finding of fact* (which parallels the verdict in criminal court), then orders a predisposition report. Afterwards, at the *dispositional hearing* the judge reviews the contents of the report and decides on a program of treatment for the young person.

Probation in the Juvenile Court

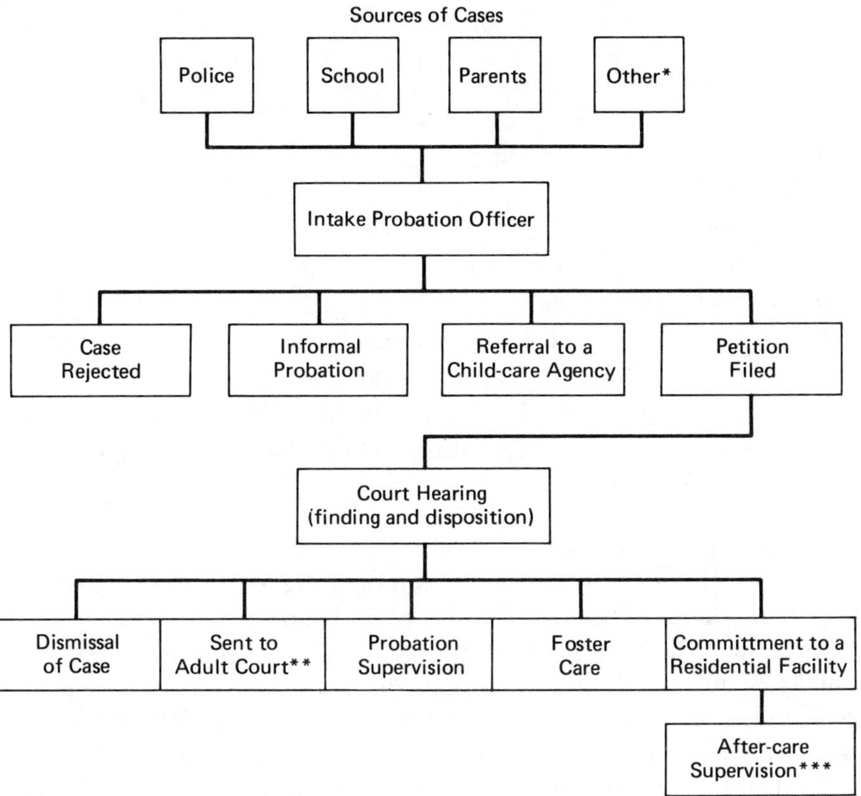

*Public and private agencies.

**Juveniles who commit serious offenses may be sent to adult courts for trial.

***Supervision provided by the probation department or a juvenile after-care (parole) agency.

PREDISPOSITION REPORT

The goal of the juvenile court is to provide treatment. In order to do so on the basis of the best information available, the judge orders a predisposition investigation. The probation officer who conducts the investigation will present a report that includes the sociocultural and psychodynamic factors which influenced the juvenile's delinquent activities,[13] providing a *social history* that is used by the judge to determine the disposition of the case. The judge's decision may be influenced to a considerable degree by the contents of the report. It therefore must be a factual and objective statement concerning the child's family, social and educational history, and any previous involvement with public or private agencies. It should also indicate the physical and mental health of the child as reported by the court psychiatrist and psychologist.

The report will include the following:

1. a review of school records
2. a review of court records
3. a review of police records
4. interviews with family members
5. interviews with teachers
6. interviews with any employers or youth workers
7. interviews with any complaining witnesses
8. any psychiatric, psychological, and medical exams
9. a recommendation which should include the treatment alternatives available in the case.

The probation officer must present his findings with supportive statements as to the actual situation surrounding the case. Other than in his recommendation, suppositions or opinions are to be avoided. Cohn reports that although the recommendation of the probation officer is usually requested by the judge in juvenile court, it is not always included as a formal part of the predisposition report.[14] The completed report should enable the judge to make a disposition based on the individual merits of the case and the rehabilitative needs of the young person.

Gross reports that a study of Minnesota probation officers handling juvenile cases indicated that the items they considered most important in the report were the child's attitude toward the offense, family data, and previous delinquency. However, these same probation officers reported that the judges considered the present offense data the most

[13] Peter G. Garabedian and Don C. Gibbons, *Becoming Delinquent: Young Offenders and the Correctional System* (Chicago: Aldine Publishing Co., 1970), p. 183.

[14] Cited in Garabedian and Gibbons, p. 190.

important item, followed by previous delinquency and the child's attitude toward the offense.[15]

Another study of probation officers' recommendations in the Bronx (New York City) Children's Court indicated that the primary considerations were the child's personality, family background and general social background, with the seriousness of the delinquent act of secondary importance.[16]

The Office of Children's Services conducted a survey of 431 cases handled in New York City in 1972-73. It revealed that probation officers recommended probation in 54.2% of the cases, and the judges ordered probation in 53.5% of the cases. Probation officers recommended a training school in 9.2% of the cases and judges sent 8% of the youngsters to training schools. (There was no determination made as to whether the probation officer's recommendations and the judge's dispositions related to the same specific juveniles of the 431 surveyed.)[17]

Juvenile Court Judge John P. Steketee (Kent County, Michigan) is critical of the standard predisposition report, which he characterizes as a static life-history document. Steketee proposes instead an effort to secure an immediate commitment from children, parents, and school officials to deal with specific behavior problems. In Judge Steketee's court, the probation officer initiates an immediate treatment program, using behavior modification techniques, and the results of treatment are reported to the judge in the predisposition report.[18] This adds a new and important dimension which the judge can consider when making his disposition decision.

---

*IN THE JUVENILE COURT

THE JUVENILE DIVISION OF THE CIRCUIT COURT

THE CITY OF ST. LOUIS

PRESIDING JUDGE: HONORABLE Gary M. Gaertner

SOCIAL INVESTIGATION

[15] Cited in *Ibid.*, p. 186.

[16] *Ibid.*, p. 204.

[17] Office of Children's Services, *Juvenile Injustice* (New York: Judicial Conference of the State of New York, 1973), pp. 44–45.

[18] John P. Steketee, "Community and Behavioral Approaches to Delinquency," *Juvenile Justice* (Nov. 1973), p. 22.

**Source:* Law Enforcement Assistance Administration.

IN THE INTEREST OF:

Timothy Wells

BIRTHDATE:

July 22, 1962 (verified)

DATE OF REPORT:

June 17, 1976

CASE NO: 50550

JUVENILE OFFICER:

William Russell

PREVIOUS POLICE AND/OR COURT HISTORY:

5-26-75 Unauthorized use of Fire Hydrant. Worker Russell. Timothy Wells was taken into custody at 12:30 p.m. at 3124 Hoffman on 5-18-75 by Officer Purcell. The arrest occurred after the officer observed Timothy with a fire hydrant wrench in his hand, turning on the fire hydrant at 3124 Hoffman. The officer turned off the above hydrant and the one on the next corner east at Lake and 15th Avenues. Case serviced and closed on 7-29-75.

5-10-76 Trespassing and Peace Disturbance. Worker Russell. Timothy Wells was taken into custody at his home, 3201 Octavia, at 8:30 a.m., on 4-17-76 by Officers Moore and Keller. The arrest occurred following a complaint filed on 4-15-76 by Bruce Kelly, Assistant Principal at Hawthorne School. Mr. Kelly reported that an ex-student at Hawthorne, Timothy Wells, came into the school yard and created a disturbance. When asked to leave, Timothy used profanity and threatened Mr. Kelly with bodily harm. Sufficient evidence, warrant refused; case referred to probation department for informal adjustment. The worker closed the case of 5-27-76 by referring the family to the St. Louis Speech and Hearing Center.

5-24-76 Common Assault. Worker Russell. Timothy Wells was taken into custody at 3038 Douglass at 6:45 p.m., on 5-21-76 by Officers Flynn and Burger. The arrest occurred following a complaint by one John Bullen of 3827 Broadway (on official court supervision on a suspended commitment to MSTS). Bullen reported that he was struck on the head with a baseball bat by Timothy Wells during a fight with Timothy and his brothers, Earl and William, and a sister, Dolores.

Following an investigation, Timothy Wells, Earl Wells, and John Bullen were all conveyed to the Juvenile Court and booked for common assault. All warrants were refused for insufficient evidence, and the matter was referred to the probation department for an informal adjustment. The case was closed on 5-27-76 after enrolling Timothy (Earl and William) in the Work Restitution Program for four weeks and referring Timothy to the St. Louis Speech and Hearing Center. On the following day, the worker learned of the petition for the present offense.

REASON FOR HEARING:

Timothy was referred to the Court on 5-20-76 by the St. Louis County Juvenile Court. On 5-10-76, Timothy allegedly attempted to steal three pairs of sunglasses from the Kresge's Store, 7800 Kingston Road in St. Louis, Missouri.

Timothy has remained in the home since the alleged offense on 5-10-76. He has since received one subsequent referral for common assault. He has also been present and worked well on three Saturday mornings of the Work Program for Probationers.

COLLATERAL CONTACTS:

INFORMANTS: The child's parents, Florence and Marvin Wells, were interviewed in their home on 6-5-76. Numerous other contacts have been made with them since two other children, Earl and William, were assigned to the supervision of this worker on 2-20-76. Both parents seem interested and have been cooperative with this court representative.

CONTACTS WITH OTHER AGENCIES:

St. Louis Speech and Hearing Center. The Center was contacted by telephone on 6-8-76 to verify Timothy's appointment for a hearing evaluation. Timothy has such an appointment scheduled for 2:30 on 6-26-76. The Center is capable of providing diagnostic and treatment services for an apparent hearing and speech disorder.

FAMILY HISTORY:

HOME: Timothy resides with both parents, four sisters, two brothers and a nephew at 3201 Octavia. The residence is a one story brick home with includes three bedrooms, living room, kitchen and an ample basement which has been partially converted for additional living quarters for Timothy, Earl and William. A home visit made on 6-5-76 revealed that the residence is nicely furnished and was neat and orderly. Mr. and Mrs. Wells are purchasing the residence and make monthly installment payments of $106.00. The family moved to their present location in 1966.

FATHER: Marvin Wells was born in St. Louis on 12-1-36. He was the youngest of eight children. Mr. Wells reports that he finished high school and two years of business college before beginning employment as a machinist at Weiss Welding Works. He was employed there between 1960 and 1971. With the promise of a higher salary, he worked for the Kramer Tool Co., from 1971 to 1974 but returned to his former employer. He currently works from 3:30 p.m. to midnight Monday through Friday and grosses approximately nine hundred dollars per month.

MOTHER: Florence Wells was born in St. Louis on 2-21-38. She was the fourth of eight children. She reports that she has completed high school and began work about three years ago when her youngest child, Christine, started school. Mrs. Wells has been working as a nurse's aid at the Laurel Heights Nursing Home. She works from 6:30 a.m. to 3:00 p.m. Sunday through Friday and earns approximately three hundred dollars per month. Mrs. Wells has stated that she has been suffering from hypertension for the past sixteen years.

PARENTS' ATTITUDE: Marvin and Florence Wells blame Timothy for the present offense. He has admitted that he tried to steal the sunglasses. His parents feel that they are capable of discipline supervision and care for Timothy but they also admit that he has problems in which they need assistance. They feel that Timothy is angry and depressed because of an apparent hearing handicap. They are willing to seek help with this problem.

OTHER FAMILY INFORMATION:

The other children are Andrea (BD: 9-2-57), Alicia (BD: 12-11-59), Dolores (BD: 1-14-60), Earl (BD: 8-15-62), William (BD: 12-1-65) and Christine (BD: 5-16-70). Dolores, Earl, and William are also known to the Court. Dolores received a referral on 9-6-75 for peace disturbance and loitering (a group demonstration at Westside High School), serviced and closed on 1-27-76. Dolores is a student at Westside High School, and has a preschool age son, Michael who also lives with the family. Earl has three referrals and William has one referral. At a hearing held on 1-21-76, Earl and William were found to have committed a common assault and were both placed on official court supervision on a suspended commitment to Missouri Hills. They have been cooperative in keeping weekly appointments with the worker and following my instructions. There seem to be no special problems between Timothy and his siblings. However Timothy is most argumentative with William.

PERSONAL HISTORY:

EARLY DEVELOPMENT: Timothy was a full term baby born without complications. Mrs. Wells stated that Timothy was unusually prone to illness in his childhood. He seemed to catch everything. She went so far as to state that the family moved to their present home in 1966 because the family physician recommended gas heat for Timothy over the coal burning furnace which they had in their last residence.

HEALTH:

Timothy is a black male who is five feet four inches tall and weighs one hundred pounds. He is of medium complexion with brown eyes and black hair. Mrs. Wells reports that Timothy gets sick when he becomes overly excited.

Timothy has an apparent hearing and speech disorder. The problem reportedly was initially diagnosed by the school doctor at Northridge School who stated that Timothy would be totally deaf in his left ear by age seventeen.

SCHOOL:

No direct school contact can be made during the summer vacation. However Mr. and Mrs. Wells stated that Timothy was suspended from Hawthorne School in 1975 for behavior problems. He began school at Northridge School in September of 1975 and continued there until around January of 1976. Mrs. Wells reported that Timothy enjoyed school there and did well because he liked his teacher, Sister Frances. However when Sister Frances left the school, Timothy's school problems resumed. Mrs. Wells stated that she then stopped sending Timothy to the school because they could no longer afford it. She attempted to enroll Timothy in the public schools but could not make the arrangements. Thus Timothy did not attend any school for the second semester of the past school year.

EMPLOYMENT: None.

LEISURE TIME ACTIVITIES:

Timothy enjoys boxing, basketball and football. However his parents won't permit him to participate because of health reasons. Timothy and his parents report that he has no close friends.

RELIGION:

Timothy is Baptist but is inactive in Church.

GENERAL PERSONALITY:

When asked, Timothy said he didn't think about himself. He said he has no problems and gets along with people. However he also said that he has no friends, nor does he need them.

CHILD'S ATTITUDE:

Timothy admits and accepts responsibility for his behavior. He stated that he doesn't know why he tried to steal the sunglasses. He said he had three dollars in his pocket at the time.

Timothy has a very negative attitude. He appears sullen and angry and his verbal responses are generally short and gruff, especially if you must ask him to repeat himself. He also has a short temper.

PSYCHOLOGICAL OR PSYCHIATRIC EVALUATION:

Timothy was given a psychological evaluation on 7-2-75 by the Rev. Raymond A. Hampe, Ph.D., Associate Director, Department of Special Education, Archdiocese of St. Louis. A battery of three tests was administered. Timothy was referred by Malcolm Bliss Mental Health Center for placement in special class due to behavior problems at school (Hawthorne).

Timothy was seen as functioning in the borderline to slow range of mental ability with probable higher potential which is unavailable due to emotional factors and major weakness in his grasp of lanaguage concepts. "Timothy is an immature, willful, anxious, sensitive boy who has strong achievement motivation and desires to be accepted. He does not see himself as being successful and accepted and therefore is greatly frustrated." Timothy projected hostility toward the examiner but cooperated. No obvious sensory or motor impairments were noted.

In summary, Timothy was seen as being anxious for success but expecting failure. Recommendations were for the parents to offer additional responsibilities and privileges marked by confidence in his ability to succeed. A special school placement was offered to eliminate the normal school's constant source of negative self evaluation.

SUMMARY AND EVALUATION:

This is the matter of Timothy Wells who will be fourteen years old on 7-22-76. Timothy is before the court for stealing three pairs of sunglasses from the Kresge's Store in St. Louis, Missouri on 5-10-76. He admits doing so but offers no explanation. Timothy has a total of four referrals to the court, three of which occurred in June of this year.

Timothy's home situation is satisfactory. The parents are responsible working people who are purchasing a home. They express interest in their children and have demonstrated cooperation with this worker in connection with Earl and William who are currently under supervision. The parents acknowledge that Timothy is a "problem child" and Mrs. Wells brought Timothy to my attention even before he officially came to the attention of the court.

Timothy is seen as an angry and frustrated youth. He has a low tolerance for frustration and a short temper which displays it. Timothy is sensitive to failure and has come to expect it of himself. He professes no problems which require correction but seems capable of following advice and instructions.

Timothy apparently has some form of hearing and speech disorder. Mrs. Wells feels that his hearing is poor and speculates that Timothy has learned to compensate somewhat by learning to read lips. His speech is characterized by brief, to-the-point statements which are rather unclear. Timothy's scheduled for a thorough hearing evaluation on 6-26-76.

Timothy is seen as an appropriate candidate for rehabilitation within the community. His three referrals in June of 1976 seem to indicate that his need to act out has reached a peak level. Although angry and frustrated at the world around him, Timothy's referrals are not of a serious nature. He is therefore not regarded as a serious threat to persons or property although his unstable emotional characteristics might indicate some further form of striking back. However a strong incentive can be offered to curb recidivism.

The plan for Timothy involves a thorough hearing and speech evaluation and follow-up on recommendations made for therapy. Timothy should also undergo psychiatric therapy, most realistically at the Child Guidance Center. Further, Timothy should be enrolled in a special school setting where teaching is individualized and tutorial in nature and where the program is stimulating and rewarding for appropriate behavior. Such programs are offered at Providence School and Project Door. No firm recommendation can be made in regard to a specific school, as the referral procedure is still under way. Furthermore, Timothy should have a regular weekly appointment with his Deputy Juvenile Officer for further counseling and to coordinate plans.

ALTERNATIVE PLANS:

Placement in either a community group home or at Missouri Hills. Placement outside of the home has been ruled out because Timothy's problems do not include poor parental supervision. Rather, his problem involves insecurity which can best be treated in his home.

RESTITUTION:

The Victim Assistance Program report states that there was no loss suffered by the Kresge's Store, as the three pair of sunglasses involved were recovered. Therefore there is no monetary reimbursement indicated. Furthermore, Timothy has worked well the past three Saturdays in the Work Program for Probationers. He has one more Saturday left in the original enrollment from the informal adjustment, so it is felt that he has made ample service restitution to the community.

PLAN:

It is therefore recommended that Timothy Wells be committed to the Division of Children's Service for placement at Missouri Hills. Further that the commitment be held in abeyance and said minor remain in the home of his parents on Official Court Supervision and subject to the following special rules. That said minor cooperate in prescribed hearing and speech therapy. To cooperate in prescribed psychiatric therapy. To keep a weekly appointment with the Deputy Juvenile Officer through September of 1976. And further that the Deputy Juvenile Officer investigate an appropriate school setting for said minor for the fall term of 1976.

RESPECTFULLY SUBMITTED:

William Russell

William Russell
Deputy Juvenile Officer

APPROVED BY:

Susan Davidson

Susan Davidson
Acting Supervisor

STATUS OFFENDERS

In addition to having jurisdiction over children who have been arrested and charged with committing an offense, the juvenile court has authority over status offenders. These are children who have not committed any offense for which an adult could be prosecuted. They are sometimes referred to as *persons in need of supervision* (PINS) or *children in need of supervision* (CHINS), and they may be habitual truants or incorrigibles who are "out of control of lawful authority."

The National Council on Crime and Delinquency (NCCD) reports that 23% of all boys and 70% of all girls held in juvenile institutions are not guilty of an offense which, if committed by an adult, would be prosecuted as a crime.[19] While awaiting court action, status offenders can be detained under conditions that are deplorable. In some jurisdictions juvenile detention facilities are merely separate quarters or cells within adult institutions. Sarri reports that while it is difficult to determine the percentage of status offenders held in local jails, a survey by the NCCD in upstate New York indicated that 43% of the children held in local jails were there for status offenses.[20] Sarri further states that female status offenders are more likely to be detained, and for longer periods of time, than males.[21] In juvenile detention facilities, status offenders are often mixed with youngsters who are awaiting adjudication for criminal acts.

A considerable number, if not a majority, of PINS petitions are filed by the children's mothers, ostensibly because these youngsters are beyond their control. However, Rector has stated that children often become status offenders by running away from home because of brutal or alcoholic parents. He notes that "One of the major reasons for girls running away is to avoid sexual abuse from their fathers, stepfathers, or mother's boyfriends." [22]

The child who is found to be a status offender is usually placed on probation during his initial encounter with the juvenile court. His probation status may include placement in foster care or a group home. However, if the youngster fails to cooperate with the treatment program, or if he runs away, he is returned to court for a further disposition. This can result in a training school placement. Probation supervision in the juvenile court tends to be inadequate because of a shortage of staff, and the Office of Children's Services states that "One must wonder how many of these (PINS) children might have remained in their own homes if the probation officers had had more time for each child." [23]

The NCCD and the American Society of Criminology are in favor of removing status offenses from the jurisdiction of the juvenile court. This would avoid stigmatizing children who have not committed any offense, and it would allow the juvenile court to concentrate its efforts

[19] "It Has Come to Our Attention," *Federal Probation* (June 1975), p. 77.

[20] Rosemary Sarri, "The Detention of Youths in Jails and Juvenile Detention Facilities," *Juvenile Justice* (Nov. 1973), p. 4.

[21] *Ibid.*

[22] Milton Rector, *PINS Cases: An American Scandal* (Hackensack, N.J.: National Council on Crime and Delinquency, 1973), p. 3.

[23] Office of Children's Services, *The PINS Child: A Plethora of Problems* (New York: Judicial Conference of the State of New York, 1974), p. 71.

on those who have. However, Judge Lindsay Arthur, reflecting the position of many of his juvenile court colleagues, maintains that the court's legal use of sanctions in the case of status offenders must be preserved. He states that it is often necessary to force children into treatment. He is candid enough to admit that the juvenile court stigmatizes children, and he makes "no pretense that a juvenile record is confidential because we know it is not." [24] Judge Arthur believes that "The stigma may be less important than the need for treatment." [25] Judge Alan Couch maintains that the stigma of the juvenile court aggravates the problems of the status offender. He notes that although status offenses are not applicable to criminal laws, the public and the juvenile view the dispositions of the juvenile court as criminal sentences.[26]

The public view of a juvenile court disposition and the stigma that it creates, has been a subject of concern and study. In fact, the concern with stigmatization extends beyond the area of the juvenile court, and its study has often been referred to as the *labeling* or *societal reaction* perspective.

THE LABELING/SOCIETAL REACTION PERSPECTIVE

According to this approach, society creates deviance by setting up certain social and/or legal boundaries, and then labels as "deviants" those who transgress these boundaries: homosexuals, psychotics, delinquents, addicts, criminals, etc.

The labeling perspective stresses the importance of studying the affects of society's reaction to rule-breaking, as opposed to ascertaining the causes of rule-breaking. Labeling "theorists" point out that society's reaction may lead to a series of counter-actions and reactions, often leading to what is referred to as *secondary deviance*. Thus, for example, a youngster labeled a "juvenile delinquent" may find it difficult or impossible to make or maintain non-delinquent peer group associations and friendships. As a result, he is forced to associate with others similarly labeled, and eventually assumes a delinquent self-image and life-style.

[24] Lindsay Arthur, "Status Offenders Need Help Too," *Juvenile Justice* (Feb. 1975), pp. 5–6.

[25] *Ibid.*, p. 6.

[26] Alan Couch, "Diverting the Status Offender from the Juvenile Court," *Juvenile Justice* (Nov. 1974), p. 21.

The impact of stigma, and the application of the labeling perspective can also be seen when the problem of offender employment is discussed later in this book. For more information on labeling, see the following: Edwin M. Schur, 1971. *Labeling Deviant Behavior: Its Sociological Implications.* New York: Harper and Row. Howard S. Becker, 1963. *Outsiders: Studies in the Sociology of Deviance.* New York: The Free Press. Kai T. Erikson, 1966. *Wayward Puritans.* New York: John Wiley and Sons.

DISPOSITION

There are two basic alternatives available to the juvenile court judge: community-based treatment or institutional treatment. Within each of these alternatives is a variety of categories of treatment, ranging from probation supervision to a state training school commitment.

Probation

Probation is used in about half of the adjudicated delinquent cases.[27] A juvenile on probation is supervised in the community by a probation officer trained in providing guidance and counseling. The probation officer works toward modifying the attitudes of the young person under his supervision in order to help him relate to society in a law-abiding manner.

At the root of antisocial behavior in many juveniles is a difficulty in relating to authority. Parents and others who have represented authority to the young person have caused him to develop a negative, even hostile, attitude toward all authority. This leads to rebellion at home and at school, or against society in general.[28] The probation officer must help the young person revise his ideas about people in authority over him. The p.o. may do this by providing a role model for the youngster, or may help to develop a healthy attitude toward others who can provide a desirable role model. These persons may be teachers, athletic coaches, or perhaps a recreation leader in the community.

The juvenile probation officer must accept the young person and be

[27] Lerman, p. 40.

[28] Charles H. Shireman, "How Can the Correctional School Correct?" *Crime and Delinquency,* (July 1960), p. 268.

able to demonstrate respect and caring for him or her. The officer must be honest with the youngster, while setting realistic limits for him —something his parents are usually unable to do. Misbehavior or antisocial activities, cannot be accepted but the client must be.

In the course of this work, the p.o. will involve the family in the helping process and meet with the young person on a regular basis. He (or she) may use a variety of methods, including casework and group counseling. If necessary, the officer will seek placement in a foster home for the client.

Scarpetti and Stephenson state that, for the most part, juveniles who are placed on probation, as opposed to being committed to an institution, "are not seriously delinquent and probably not in need of intensive rehabilitative efforts." [29] However, the New York State Judicial Conference notes that youngsters with severe behavior problems are often placed on probation, not because it is the best response, but because it is the only treatment available.[30] While violent juvenile crime has increased at an alarming rate (up 52.6% from 1968–1973),[31] there continues to be a lack of facilities to treat violent juvenile offenders.[32]

Disposition Hearing*

William Price and his mother sat uneasily before the Judge. The allegations of the amended petition had been sustained on the basis of a full admission. The Judge was looking through the probation officer's report for information on which to base his disposition. His eye was drawn to the psychologist's report attached to the court report. The courtroom was silent, all eyes on the Judge.

In the report William was described as "fairly handsome" and "athletically built." The Judge glanced up and looked directly at the boy. William turned his eyes away. The Judge decided that

[29] Scarpetti and Stephenson quoted in Garabedian and Gibbons, p. 219.

[30] Office of Children's Services, *The PINS Child,* p. 71.

[31] Data from the U.S. Senate Subcommittee to Investigate Juvenile Delinquency.

[32] Ted Morgan, "They Think, 'I can kill because I'm 14,' " *New York Times Magazine* (Jan. 19, 1975), p. 22.

*From Lawrence E. Cohen, *New Directions in Processing of Juvenile Offenders: The Denver Model* (Washington, D.C.: U.S. Government Printing Office, 1975).

the boy might be called handsome despite his "waterfall" haircut and a slight case of acne, but he was certainly not sufficiently robust to be dubbed "athletic."

The psychologist's report indicated that William might or might not be aggressive to girls in the future. "That's not much help," the Judge thought, "it could apply to most young men. Chances are the boy feels worse about the situation than the girl. At least he *looks* remorseful."

"William, do you realize you could have seriously injured that girl?"

"I didn't mean to hurt her. I thought it was what she wanted."

"That was a dangerous supposition, young man. I hope you realize by now that any use of violence in any circumstances can have the most serious consequences. Society doesn't regard such things lightly."

"Yes, sir."

"Besides the offense with the girl, you also ran away from the officer who was trying to arrest you."

"I'm sorry about that. I guess I lost my head."

"Are you in the habit of losing your head?"

"No, sir. I just wasn't thinking."

"William," the Judge said sternly, "I have serious doubts about allowing you to remain in the community. How do I know you won't lose your head again and really hurt someone the next time?"

"I promise, Judge. I won't do anything foolish again."

The Judge turned to Mrs. Price and said sympathetically, "I know it has been very difficult for you to raise William by yourself. It would be a pity for all that effort to go to waste."

Tears welled up in Mrs. Price's eyes. "Yes, your Honor. Please let William come home. I know he'll be good. And I've changed my job now so I can be with him more," she said in a trembling voice.

William's eyes were focused on his mother while she talked. The Judge noted that concern for her was mirrored in his face.

"How has Bill been doing since he came home from Juvenile Hall, Mrs. Price?"

"Just like always, Judge. He's a good boy."

"William," the Judge said, "what would you do with yourself if I allowed you to remain in your home?"

"Go to school."

"I see you are one year behind in your school grade. Do you plan to finish high school?"

"Yes, sir." William's face noticeably brightened.

"And then what do you plan to do?"

"I guess I'll go in the service."

The Judge looked at the probation officer. "Mr. Clarke, I'm going to follow your recommendation and make William a ward of the court and place him on probation. If he stays out of trouble during the next year, I want him brought back to court so we can terminate his case. By my calculation he could be off probation about nine or ten months before he graduates. This should be long enough so that his record will not hinder him from entering the service."

The Judge turned back to William. "I hope you've learned a lesson from this, Son. You stay out of trouble and you should have a good opportunity to make something of yourself. The burden is on you. Don't spoil your chances for a career and for a decent life for yourself and your mother."

"Thank you, Judge," Mrs. Price said. "William is a good boy. I don't think he'll make any more trouble for anyone."

She and her son left the room, the boy with his arm around her shoulders.

AN EXAMPLE OF THE JUVENILE COURT PROCESS: DENVER*

The juvenile court which was authorized by the Colorado State Legislature in 1903 has two full-time judges and two full-time referees who preside over hearings. As the flow chart indicates, the juvenile case process is quite involved. A juvenile—a person under the age of eighteen in Colorado—who is arrested by the police is brought to the Delinquency Control Division (DCD) of the Denver Police Department. His parents or guardians are immediately notified and re-

* Lawrence E. Cohen, *New Directions in Processing of Juvenile Offenders: The Denver Model* (Washington, D.C.: U.S. Government Printing Office, 1976).

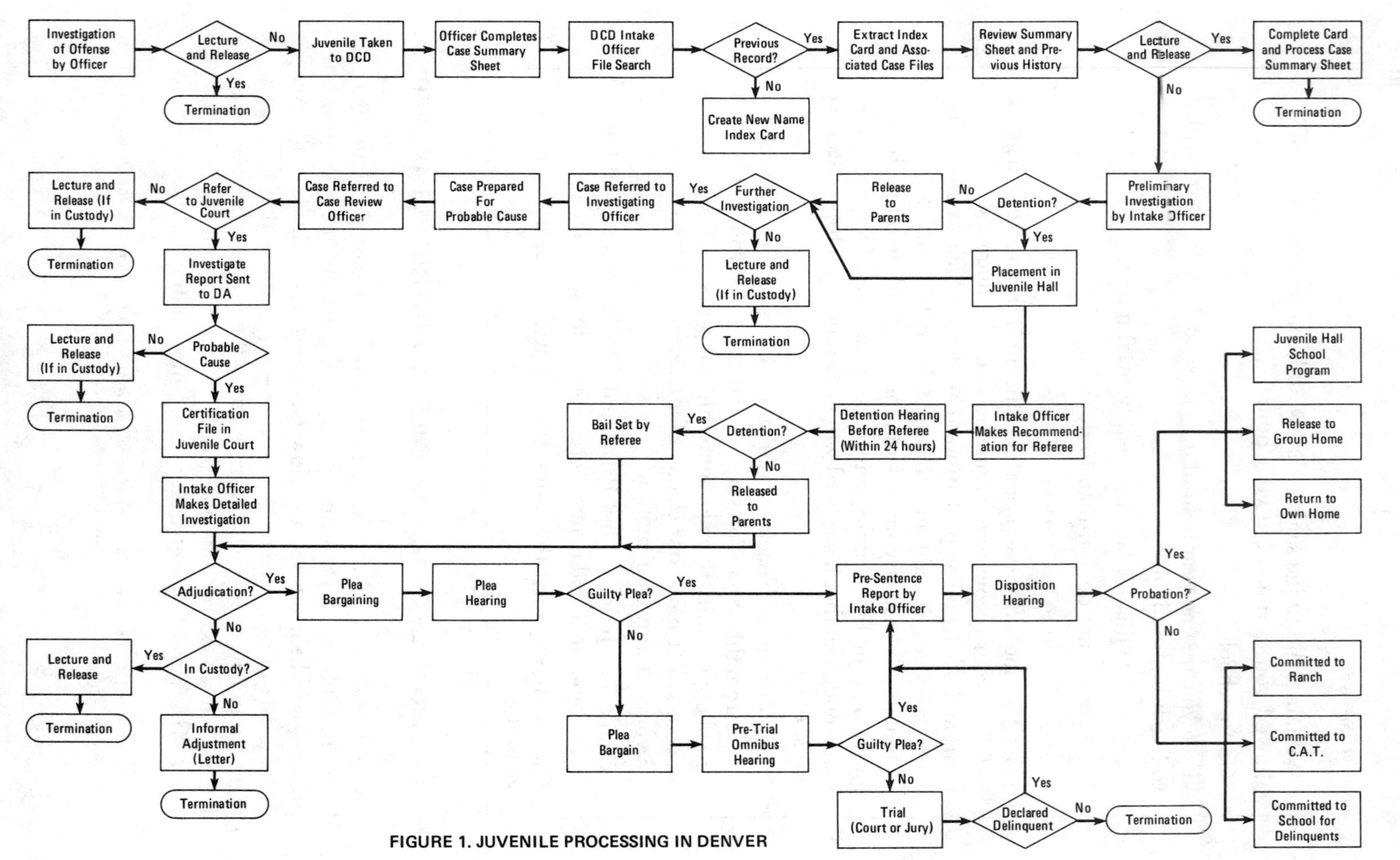

FIGURE 1. JUVENILE PROCESSING IN DENVER

quested to appear. The youngster is advised of his rights in the presence of his parents and/or attorney.

The arresting officer completes a case summary sheet which is reviewed by a DCD intake officer. The intake officer has the option of releasing the child for a non-court treatment program or of instigating a preliminary investigation for possible court adjudication. The criteria he is to use in making this determination includes:

1. the severity of the offense;
2. prior record;
3. apparent risk to the community; and
4. the expressed wishes of the complainant.

If the youngster is released, the intake officer assumes the responsibility for making a referral to an appropriate treatment agency. If the youngster or his parents do not agree to this arrangement, or if the child fails to complete his treatment program, he will be referred to the juvenile court. If the youngster completes the treatment program successfully his case is terminated without further legal action. If, on the other hand, the intake officer refers the case to juvenile court, his responsibility ends. The police intake officer also has the responsibility of deciding if detention is necessary pending any court adjudication. The criteria to be used in making this determination are similar to the preceding list.

Probation Intake

When the DCD intake officer decides to refer a child to the juvenile court, he files a complaint and transfers the case to the probation intake unit. The intake probation officer conducts a preliminary investigation and submits his findings with a recommendation to the District Attorney. In Denver, it is the District Attorney who decides if the filing of a petition is warranted. If the answer is yes, a petition is returned to the intake probation officer. If the answer is no, the District Attorney will refer the matter back to the probation department, thus delegating the responsibility for deciding on a disposition to the probation intake unit.

Hearings

In a case that is set for adjudication, the first phase is a *plea hearing* at which the child, his parents, attorney, the probation officer, and a court referee are in attendance. If the child's plea is guilty, the probation officer prepares a further, and more detailed, report—social investigation—that is made available to the court and the child's attorney at least 48 hours before the *dispositional hearing.*

At the end of the dispositional hearing, the court referee makes a determination, at which point the case is transferred to the field probation division which will continue any neçessary processing or supervision, depending on the nature of the disposition.

If the child pleads not guilty, he is provided with an *omnibus hearing* which may be presided over by a referee or a judge. The purpose of this hearing is to:

1. hear attorney's motions;
2. determine proper jurisdiction;
3. assure full-disclosure of evidence;
4. allow for changes in plea and plea bargaining; and
5. determine the appropriateness of a jury trial.

If a child's family is unable to afford an attorney, he is represented by the Public Defender's Office. If at the conclusion of the trial, the youngster is found guilty, a disposition hearing is set, and the Public Defender continues to represent him in an effort to gain the most favorable treatment for his client.

Judges and Referees

All Colorado juvenile court judges serve full-time and are appointed by the Governor from a list of nominees submitted by a special panel. After their two-year appointed term has expired, they must run on their records at the time of the general election. If they are elected it is for a six-year term. The qualifications for a juvenile court judge are:

1. graduation from an accredited law school;
2. membership in the Colorado State Bar; and
3. engagement in the practice of law for at least 5 years.

Referees generally act as judicial officers and preside over hearings that occur at the early stages of the juvenile court process in Denver, thus freeing judges for trials. They have the same qualifications as judges, but are not appointed by the Governor, although when a vacancy occurs, the Governor will frequently fill it from a list of current court referees.

****Standards for the Education and Training of Juvenile Probation Officers, by State, 1973 (continued)**

State	*State Standards Exist*	*Counties Determine Standards*	*Minimum Educational Requirements (Entry Level)*	*Training Programs Offered*
Alabama		Varies by county	Bachelor's degree in social or behavioral sciences plus 6 months experience in probation or parole	Varies by county
Alaska	Mandatory		Bachelor's degree with minimum of 20 hours in behavioral sciences	
Arizona			Bachelor's degree in behavioral sciences	
Arkansas		Varies by county		Varies by county
California	Advisory only	Counties allowed free choice in adherence to standards	Bachelor's degree in social science; master's degree preferred	No uniformity; varies by county from none to highly organized
Colorado	Mandatory		Bachelor's degree in behavioral sciences	

** From Richard W. Kobetz and Betty B. Bosarge, *Juvenile Justice Administration* (Gaithersburg, Md.: International Association of Chiefs of Police, 1973), pp. 374–78. Reprinted with permission of the publisher.

Standards for the Education and Training of Juvenile Probation Officers, by State, 1973 (continued)

State	*State Standards Exist*	*Counties Determine Standards*	*Minimum Educational Requirements (Entry Level)*	*Training Programs Offered*
Connecticut	Mandatory		Bachelor's degree in social sciences; state civil service examination required of all applicants	
Delaware	Mandatory		Bachelor's degree in social sciences (master's degree requirement under consideration)	Mandatory by statute
District of Columbia	Mandatory Federal standards		Bachelor's degree	
Florida	Mandatory		Bachelor's degree in behavioral sciences	State conducts mandatory training programs
Georgia	Standards for state-employed juvenile probation officers only	Set own standards for county-employed juvenile probation officers	State-employed officers must possess bachelor's degree; one year experience; and pass examination	Varies by counties; consultation on training provided by State Council of Juvenile Court Judges

Hawaii	Mandatory		Bachelor's degree in social sciences	Pre-service training mandatory
Idaho		Varies by county		
Illinois	Permissive state standards	Counties allowed free choice in adherence to standards	Bachelor's degree	Varies by county
Indiana	Mandatory	Some counties also have additional standards for juvenile probation officers	Bachelor's degree in psychology, sociology or in a related field; state probation officer examination required	Varies by county court
Iowa	Mandatory		Bachelor's degree in social sciences	
Kansas		Varies by county	Some counties require bachelor's degree	Varies by county
Kentucky	Mandatory		Bachelor's degree plus merit examination	
Louisiana	Standards for state-employed probation officers only	Each parish sets own standards	State-employed officers must possess bachelor's degree and pass civil service examination; many parishes adhere to state standards	Varies by parish

Standards for the Education and Training of Juvenile Probation Officers, by State, 1973 (continued)

State	*State Standards Exist*	*Counties Determine Standards*	*Minimum Educational Requirements (Entry Level)*	*Training Programs Offered*
Maine	Mandatory		Bachelor's degree	In-service training required; conducted by State Bureau of Probation and Parole
Maryland	Mandatory		Bachelor's degree plus merit examination	State conducts in-service training; provides stipends for outside training plus educational leaves with full salary; pre-service training mandatory
Massachusetts	Mandatory		Bachelor's degree plus one year experience in social work OR one year of graduate work	
Michigan		Varies by county	Some counties require a bachelor's degree in human development or a related field; civil service test required in some counties	Required in some counties

Minnesota	Mandatory for state-employed probation officers and all counties except Ramsey, Hennepin and St. Louis	Ramsey, Hennepin and St. Louis Counties set own standards	Bachelor's degree in behavioral sciences required in all counties and for state employment	Varies by county
Mississippi		Varies by county	None; statewide merit test only	Varies by county
Missouri	Mandatory		Bachelor's degree OR four years' experience in social work	Varies by county
Montana	Mandatory		Bachelor's degree in social sciences OR bachelor's degree in other field plus three years' experience in social work	
Nebraska	State sets standards in 10 judicial districts only	Omaha, Lincoln and several other communities set own standards		

Standards for the Education and Training of Juvenile Probation Officers, by State, 1973 (continued)

State	*State Standards Exist*	*Counties Determine Standards*	*Minimum Educational Requirements (Entry Level)*	*Training Programs Offered*
Nevada		Established by district court judges		Varies by judicial district
New Hampshire	Standards vary from candidate to candidate			State requires on-the-job training
New Jersey	Mandatory		Bachelor's degree in behavioral sciences	Scholarships offered for education and training; pre-service and in-service training mandatory
New Mexico	Mandatory		No college degree required at entry level, but bachelor's degree mandatory for promotion	Varies by judicial district
New York	Mandatory except for New York City and Monroe County	New York City and Monroe County set own standards	State requires bachelor's degree plus written examination; in addition, Chautaugua, Niagara, Onondaga, Erie, Nassau and Westchester Counties require graduate work	Varies by county

North Carolina	Mandatory in 14 of 30 judicial districts		Bachelor's degree plus related experience	In-service training optional
North Dakota		Varies by county		Varies by county
Ohio	Standards exist only for counties receiving subsidies	Counties not receiving state subsidies set own standards	Most counties require bachelor's degree in social sciences; state standards require bachelor's degree OR experience in social work	Varies by county
Oklahoma	Mandatory for counties with population of 100,000	Varies by county (population less than 100,000)	Bachelor's degree in social sciences; no experience necessary	Varies by county
Oregon		Varies by county		In-service training conducted by state; optional
Pennsylvania	Mandatory		Bachelor's degree in social sciences	In-service training mandatory; conducted by state
Rhode Island	Mandatory		Bachelor's degree plus experience in social work	In-service training mandatory; conducted by state

Standards for the Education and Training of Juvenile Probation Officers, by State, 1973 (continued)

State	*State Standards Exist*	*Counties Determine Standards*	*Minimum Educational Requirements (Entry Level)*	*Training Programs Offered*
South Carolina	Mandatory		Bachelor's degree in social sciences	
South Dakota		Varies by court district	Some courts require bachelor's degree	In-service training optional
Tennessee	Mandatory		Bachelor's degree in psychology or related field; state civil service examination.	Optional
Texas		Varies by county		Varies by county
Utah	Mandatory		Bachelor's degree in social sciences or related field; no experience necessary	Mandatory for all juvenile probation officers
Vermont	Mandatory for all correctional officers		Bachelor's degree in social sciences	In-service training mandatory for all correctional officers

Virginia	Mandatory		Bachelor's degree in related field; state merit examination for social workers; experience not necessary	Optional
Washington	Mandatory for state-employed juvenile probation officers	Varies for county employees	Bachelor's degree in social sciences plus written examination for state employees; most counties have same requirements	Mandatory training for state employees; most counties conduct in-service training
West Virginia		Varies by county	Some counties require bachelor's degree in social sciences or related field	Varies by county
Wisconsin	Mandatory for employees of the State Department of Health and Social Services	Standards vary for county employees	State requires bachelor's degree in social sciences; merit examination, and one year work experience in social welfare (females must possess master's degree in social work); most counties adhere to state standards	Pre-service training mandatory for state employees; 15 hours graduate work must also be accumulated; most counties provide in-service training

Standards for the Education and Training of Juvenile Probation Officers, by State, 1973 (continued)

State	*State Standards Exist*	*Counties Determine Standards*	*Minimum Educational Requirements (Entry Level)*	*Training Programs Offered*
Wyoming	State Board of Pardons administers probation programs in districts; no standards exist			

The two charts that follow present a summary of the various decisions available to the juvenile court as well as the goals that should be considered when making a disposition.

Institutional Care

There are several types of facilities to which juveniles are sent by the juvenile court. The training school is a public institution which accepts all youngsters sent by the courts. Each training school is usually set up to handle particular categories of juveniles. They may be assigned on the basis of age, aggressiveness, or delinquent history. This is done to avoid mixing younger juveniles with older ones, adjudicated delinquents with status offenders, or more disturbed youngsters with those having less serious problems. The training school usually provides a degree of security not available in other types of juvenile institutions. Juveniles are committed to training schools based on the following considerations:

1. there is *finding of fact* that the child has committed an offense which would be punishable by imprisonment if committed by an adult;
2. the parents are unable to control their child or provide for his or her social, emotional and educational needs;
3. there is no other child welfare service available that is sufficient;
4. the child needs the services available at the training school.

The establishment of the Massachusetts Lyman School for Boys in 1847 began an era of providing separate facilities for juvenile offenders. The training, or reform, schools were patterned after adult prisons. They were regimented, with large impersonal dormitories. They provided some basic medical and dental treatment, and limited education and vocational training. Over the years there has been an increased emphasis on vocational training, remedial education, and rehabilitation through the use of social workers, teachers, psychiatrists, psychologists, and recreation workers.[33]

One training school, *The Warwick School for Boys,* is located 55 miles from New York City. It is one of six training schools operated by the New York State Division for Youth. The school is a pleasant-looking institution with 700 acres of lawns and trees, and houses about 170

[33] Herb C. Willman, Jr. and Ron Y. F. Chun, "Homeward Bound," *Federal Probation* (Sept. 1973), pp. 52–53.

Figure 2
GOALS IN DECISIONS

<table>
<tr><th></th><th>1) DISMISS</th><th>INFORMAL
2) ADJUSTMENT</th><th>3) CONSENT DECREE</th><th>4) PROBATION</th><th>5) COMMITMENT/PLACEMENT</th></tr>
<tr><td>Exposure of Youngster to System</td><td>Terminate contact as soon as possible</td><td>Need for brief contact by community agency or probation office</td><td>Adjudication not required to provide necessary services</td><td>Adjudication required to provide necessary services</td><td>Maximum Contact needed to provide external controls</td></tr>
<tr><td>Mobilization of Individual and Family Resources</td><td>Not indicated at present</td><td>Need for brief external assistance to family</td><td colspan="2">Need for external assistance to family</td><td>Substitute for family required at present</td></tr>
<tr><td>Intervention in School Adjustment</td><td>Not indicated at present</td><td>If required can be accomplished by minimum intervention</td><td colspan="2">Need to provide intervention to the degree necessary</td><td>Need to provide specialized education and training</td></tr>
<tr><td>Distributive Justice</td><td>Prior behavior demands dismissal (offense seen as accidental, minor incident)</td><td>Prior behavior demands informal adjustment</td><td>Prior behavior demand consent decree</td><td>Prior behavior demand probation</td><td>Need to arrest continuing delinquent behavior</td></tr>
<tr><td>Protection of Community and/or self</td><td>Not indicated at present</td><td>Minimum risk but intervention required</td><td colspan="2">Potential risk requiring active intervention</td><td>Obvious risk requiring removal from community</td></tr>
<tr><td>Intervention in Emotional Adjustment and Control</td><td>Not indicated at present</td><td>Need to provide brief intervention to assist child and family in stabilizing emotional adjustment and control</td><td colspan="2">Need to provide necessary intervention to assist child and family in stabilizing emotional adjustment and control</td><td>Need to provide specialized environment and/or services to improve emotional adjustment and control</td></tr>
<tr><td>Intervention in Peer Relationships</td><td>Not indicated at present</td><td>Not indicated at present</td><td colspan="2">Need to modify, encourage, and/or control peer relationships</td><td>Need to remove or extricate from specific negative peer relationships</td></tr>
</table>

Figure 3

CONSIDERATIONS FOR DECISIONS

	1) DISMISS	INFORMAL 2) ADJUSTMENT	3) CONSENT DECREE	4) PROBATION	5) COMMITMENT/PLACEMENT
Delinquent Behavior	First substantiated complaint	First substantiated complaint	Prior contact on minor offenses	Prior contact on serious offenses.	Several prior contacts on serious offenses
Family Structure	Observed family strength and support	Indications of need for improvement of family structure	Questionable family strength and support needing active intervention		Weak and/or harmful family relationships
School Adjustment	Acceptable school report	Marginal school adjustment	Questionable or unfavorable school adjustment needing active intervention		Unacceptable school adjustment with little potential for improvement
Nature of Offense	Minor	Minor	Prior Minor offense or more serious first offense	Serious prior offense or offenses	Serious and chronic offender
Threat to self and/or family	No apparent threat	No apparent threat	Questionable threat		Obvious threat
Emotional adjustment and control	Apparently good	Perhaps adequate but indicative of needing positive assistance	Questionable or inadequate but with potential for effective intervention		Inadequate with no apparent potential improvement
Attitude towards current situation	Realistic responsible	Realistic but somewhat irresponsible	Perhaps realistic but somewhat irresponsible		Unrealistic and irresponsible
Peer-Group Relationship	Apparently positive	Questionable	Questionable		Unacceptable with no apparent potential for improvement
Clients Response	Accepting	Accepting	Perhaps reluctant but capable of utilizing court services		Inability to utilize court services

residents in several dormitories. There are also some individual rooms which are assigned on a "merit" basis. The school's annual budget is about 2½ million dollars, and it has a staff of 180 persons. There is a ratio of better than one staff member dealing directly with every two residents.

The daily schedule calls for two hours of compulsory academic instruction and two hours of physical education, with additional services for those who require more help. Both individual and group counseling are provided. Vocational training in such areas as mechanical drawing, woodworking, electricity, painting and kitchen work is available and optional.

The residents are all adjudicated delinquents who have committed offenses ranging from petty larceny to rape and murder, all before their sixteenth birthday. There are no walls or gates around the school, and security is maintained through the use of supervised activities. Nevertheless, counselors report that there is fear in the surrounding community because some residents have become involved in criminal acts while outside the school. Despite the extensive services offered, some residents complain of too much idle time and poor food.[34]

The cost of training schools is high, as expensive as $20,000 per resident per year in some states. The cost of Warwick is in excess of $15,000 per resident annually. Yet Willman and Chun report that training schools are turning out an increasing amount of youngsters who are going on to further criminal activities.[35] The United States Senate Subcommittee to Investigate Juvenile Delinquency reports that the training schools are expensive and do not prevent recidivism.[36] The recidivism rate of delinquents who are sent to training schools is estimated at 80%.[37]

In an effort to offer alternatives to the training school for youngsters in need of some type of institutional care, various programs have been developed. Massachusetts, a pioneer in the treatment of juveniles, has dismantled virtually all of its training schools. Under Jerome Miller, the Commissioner of the Department of Youth Services, all but one of the Massachusetts training schools were closed and replaced with community-based group homes and other treatment programs oper-

[34] Enid Nemy, "Parents of Young Offenders Meet and Ask 'What Went Wrong?' " *New York Times* (Feb. 25, 1975), p. 40.

[35] Willman and Chun, p. 53.

[36] *Report of the Senate Subcommittee to Investigate Juvenile Delinquency* (Dec. 19, 1974), pp. 2–3.

[37] "The Crime Wave," *Time* (June 30, 1975), p. 24.

ated largely by private agencies.[38] Massachusetts had operated five large training schools, including the Lyman School, all of which were plagued by poor and yet expensive programs. There were inadequate educational and vocational programs, and the institutions were "at best custodial, and at worst punitive and repressive." [39] Dr. Miller reorganized juvenile treatment in Massachusetts with an approach that has three main thrusts:[40]

1. to provide therapeutic and humane homes instead of custodial and punitive institutions;
2. to use small community-based residential and nonresidential schools instead of large training schools; and
3. to purchase juvenile services from private agencies rather than having the state operate all programs.

One of the more widely-discussed and copied residential institutions, Highfields, continues in operation in the State of New Jersey.

Highfields[41] was established in New Jersey in 1950 as a short-term, non-custodial, residential treatment center. The residents were 20 boys who had been adjudicated as delinquents and placed on probation. The maximum stay at Highfields was four months. It was believed that, through the use of intensive methods, youngsters who were not deeply disturbed or mentally deficient could be rehabilitated in this four-month period.

The founders of Highfields, Lloyd W. McCorkle and F. Lovell Bixby, had a research evaluation design built into the program, a feature unique to this institution. The evaluation involved a control group from a nearby reform school, the Annandale Reformatory. The research goal was to see if a short-term, non-custodial treatment center would have a more positive effect on residents than the conventional juvenile institution represented by Annandale.

Highfields had no guards or locked doors. There was an absence of authoritarian leadership. During the day residents worked at the New Jersey Neuro-Psychiatric Institute, and in the evening they met in

[38] Yitzhak Bakal, *Closing Correctional Institutions* (Lexington, Mass.: D.C. Heath, 1974), p. 151.

[39] *Ibid.*, p. 154.

[40] *Ibid.*, p. 162.

[41] *See* Lloyd W. McCorkle, Albert Elias, and F. Lovell Bixby, *The Highfields Story* (New York: Henry Holt and Co., 1958), 182 pp; H. Ashley Weeks, *Youthful Offenders at Highfields* (Ann Arbor: University of Michigan Press, 1966), 208 pp.; and Leslie T. Wilkins, *Evaluation of Penal Measures* (New York: Random House, Inc., 1969), pp. 87–89.

groups of ten for a daily therapy session. Family and friends were encouraged to visit, and residents were given passes to visit a nearby town, and sometimes to go home for a visit.

The treatment objective was to give delinquent boys an opportunity for self-rehabilitation by achieving a series of preliminary and prerequisite goals. There were few formal rules, since the purpose was to enable the child to develop a non-delinquent orientation through "guided group interaction." Control was exercised through the development of a healthy peer-centered informal therapy situation.

The differences between Highfields and the control group at Annandale were essentially as follows:

Highfields' residents came from somewhat "higher status" homes.

Annandale boys began their delinquent patterns earlier than Highfields' boys.

Annandale boys appear to have had "more intense" delinquent careers.

Annandale boys were older.

Annandale had a higher number of blacks in the sample group.

It must also be noted that boys sent to Highfields who were found to be "unsuitable" or who ran away were usually sent back to court for further disposition. Most were subsequently sent to training schools which did not have the luxury of being able to reject their residents.

Despite the differences in the experimental group and the control, and the fact that some Highfields residents ran away, with a few committing serious offenses, the researchers concluded that Highfields was a success. They concluded that Highfields accomplished better results than Annandale in a shorter time and at considerably less expense. For example, 63% of the boys who completed treatment at Highfields were in no further serious difficulty for one year after their release. In contrast, the figure for Annandale was 47%. Further evaluation indicated that there appeared to be little difference in outcome for white boys sent to both institutions. However, black boys did significantly better at Highfields than those at Annandale.

In criticizing the findings and conclusions at Highfields, Lerman states that the results were not impressive in view of the more "advantaged" population at Highfields. He concludes that "treatment programs have not yet been proved to have an appreciable impact on failure rates." [42]

Highfields has been replicated with the same or a better rate of "success" in other states (several other "Highfields-type schools" were also opened in New Jersey). One such school was opened in Kentucky and, true to its origins, was named *Southfields*. The residents of Southfields were compared to a control group at a nearby training school, Kentucky Village. Statistical results indicated that Southfields obtained results similar to, if not better than, Highfields. Like Highfields, residents rejected from Southfields were referred back to court and usually committed to a training school.[43]

One persistent problem for the juvenile court in providing alternative institutional care for youngsters is the ability of private treatment institutions and agencies to refuse to accept children who do not "fit in" with their programs. These private institutions benefit from receiving a great deal of public funding, while they retain the privilege of screening their residents. Probation officers and judges are often frustrated in their attempt to find suitable placement for a youngster because of this situation. The probation officer makes an evaluation based on his professional judgment. This is transmitted to the judge in the form of a recommendation. However, in the final stage the private institution can decide that the child is incompatible with their program. The court is then faced with the alternatives of probation or a training school.

The Group Home

Another type of facility used to treat youngsters referred by the juvenile court is the group home. The New York State Division for Youth utilizes such facilities as part of its *Urban Home Program.* These relatively small facilities usually house about 7 youngsters in a home with several bedrooms, a bath, living room, kitchen, dining area, and basement recreation area. The Division attempts to place its homes in residential areas that are in proximity to public transportation, public schools, and recreation facilities. The interior of the home approximates that of a large single-family dwelling.

The residents range in age from 13 to 17 years. They must possess

[42] Lerman, p. 326.

[43] Lovick C. Miller, "Southfields," *Crime and Delinquency* (July 1970), pp. 305–16.

sufficient strengths and stability to be maintained in this type of facility. The program is designed to help youths who:

1. are in unresolvable conflict with their parents, but are not seriously disturbed or psychotic;
2. have inadequate homes and need to develop skills for independent living;
3. need to deal with community social adjustment problems in a therapeutic family environment;
4. need to deal with individual adjustment problems and to learn about themselves in relation to others; and
5. need to develop self-confidence through successful experiences.

Each resident has daily chores such as doing dishes, making the bed, and mowing the lawn. The houseparents perform the surrogate parent role by preparation of meals, ensurance of a curfew, help with homework, and other tasks usually handled by parents in healthy families. The youngsters attend local schools on a full-time basis, or they have a schedule which incorporates both school and employment.

There are regular group counseling sessions conducted by trained social workers. The sessions are geared to help youths understand and overcome problems which have led to the placement, and to define goals consistent with their individual ability. There are also individual counseling programs for those residents who need to be helped to live independently and for those who need assistance in improving their family relationships. Day-to-day counseling and conflict resolution are handled by the houseparents.

The program is geared to gain as much community acceptance and participation as possible. The first part of this concept is the small number of residents in each home. However, there have been incidents involving group home residents, some of a serious nature. In order to overcome community resistance, Citizen's Advisory Committees have been formed from the group home areas. An attempt is made to stress the success of the program and the relatively few incidents compared to the number of youngsters helped.[44]

Providence Educational Center (PEC)[45]

The PEC in St. Louis, Missouri, a community-based alternative to the training school, provides intensive remedial education and counseling

[44] Various publications of the New York State Division for Youth.

[45] Law Enforcement Assistance Administration, *Providence Educational Center* (Washington, D.C. Government Publishing Office), pp. 1–90.

services to 75 adjudicated youngsters aged 12-16 years, who have a history of school failure. Thirty-one percent are "status offenders" and the rest have committed crimes ranging from shoplifting to armed robbery to homicide. The center, which became operational in 1972, is based on the premise that the long term rehabilitation of this type of delinquent is contingent on the development of skills needed to enhance educational ability, employment skills, and family and social relationships. Gerald Caplan, Director of the National Institute on Law Enforcement and Criminal Justice, reports that the PEC has decreased the incidence of recidivism among the youths it has serviced, while improving their ability to function in public school and employment.

PEC utilizes teams of professionally-trained counselors, educators and social workers. There is an individualized program for each student utilizing three program components:

1. EDUCATION: consists of a highly individualized approach to providing instruction and remedial assistance in reading, mathematics, and other academic subjects. Classes are ungraded and the student-teacher ratio is approximately 6 to 1.
2. SOCIAL SERVICES: performs diagnostic assessments, provides regular group and individual counseling, as well as counseling and assistance to families, and acts as liaison with the juvenile court on each case.
3. AFTERCARE: is responsible for easing the transition back into the community—the public schools, a job, or various training programs.

PEC is basically a school whose students live at home while they are being helped to prepare for return to public school or employment. However, it provides more intensive and comprehensive services than most youths on probation could receive from the public schools and other community agencies. Because it is nonresidential, it provides services at a lower cost per student than other institutional treating alternatives available to the Juvenile Court in St. Louis.

PEC's overall educational and social objectives are organized into five basic areas, each representing a "system" or "milieu" in which the youth functions. The five systems are:

1. The *Individual:* objectives in this area relate to self-image and self-assessment.

2. The *Peer Group:* objectives in this area focus both on the ability to relate to and the kinds of relationships formed with delinquent peers, and on the content of such relationships.

3. The *Family:* objectives related to this area refer to relationships with other family members, especially parents, and to the ability to function within and productively contribute to the family unit.

4. The *Community:* objectives related to this area focus on the avoidance of further juvenile and adult offenses, stability in public school attendance and performance, or stability in employment.

5. The *Educational System:* objectives in this area relate to the student's performance at PEC, including attendance, classroom behavior, and performance and achievement in subject areas (reading, math, language arts, social studies, arts and crafts, shop, and science).

The major unit for delivering services is the classroom, staffed by a team composed of at least 2 teachers and a social worker. Their efforts are supported by various staff specialists in curriculum, reading, and counseling. The classes average 12 students and are ungraded, with an emphasis on the development of fundamental skills using individualized instruction.

Referral to PEC is both informal and formal, usually beginning with a preliminary discussion of a proposed referral with a Deputy Juvenile Officer and other court officials. Subsequently, a case write-up is prepared by the court and sent along with an admission application to intake at PEC. Eligibility is based on the following:

1. He (or she*) must have had prior involvement with the Juvenile Court and be under the active supervision of a Deputy Juvenile Officer and/or caseworker;

2. must be between 12 and 16 years of age;

3. cannot be seriously emotionally disturbed, retarded, or severely handicapped;

4. must be functioning on a "pre-high school achievement level" (less than eighth grade) in reading; and

5. the referring agent, parent, and child must agree to an on-going and active involvement with the program.

*PEC began accepting girls in 1974.

The eligibility determination is made by PEC staff, and there is some flexibility built into the intake process on an individualized case basis.

PEC attempted to use a behavior modification approach to discipline but was forced to abandon it because, while the use of rewards was useful with younger students, it was impossible to provide meaningful rewards for older youths. In addition, PEC staff did not have the time or training necessary to apply the approach in an efficient manner. A more conventional approach is now used, involving the Deputy Juvenile Officer under whose supervision the youngster remains as a result of his probation status.

The Homeward Bound Program[46]

Homeward Bound is an outdoor-adventure model of treatment patterned after a British program to train merchant seamen. In addition to physical conditioning and outdoor activity, it provides for structured and stressful situations geared to unify groups of youngsters toward a common goal. It allows the participants to achieve "hard-won success in establishing confidence and a more positive self-image."

The Massachusetts Department of Youth Services operates a Homeward Bound School in the Colorado Rockies. Their program includes backpacking, high altitude camping, solo survival, and rock climbing. Its participants are adjudicated delinquents referred by the courts and accepted on a "space available basis" only. The program is in two phases and lasts six weeks. It is voluntary, and prior to coming to Homeward Bound, the program is carefully explained to each referred youngster. Every successful participant is released directly home, thus avoiding other types of institutional care.

The school has no locks, fences, or secure rooms. Following an initial orientation at the school, the 32 boys are divided into brigades of eight each. During the day they work on community service projects, take short hikes, run some obstacle courses, and do calisthenics as part of a conditioning program. A few hours are also spent with a counselor developing an aftercare plan. In the evening there are classes in ecology, survival, search and rescue, overnight expeditions, and ropes and knots. Most of the youngsters do not pay attention. However, they soon discover that they are unable to manage on their first overnight expedition; packs are not in order, some gear is left behind, and the wrong food is taken along. The youngsters' first experience with not

[46] Willman and Chun, pp. 53–57.

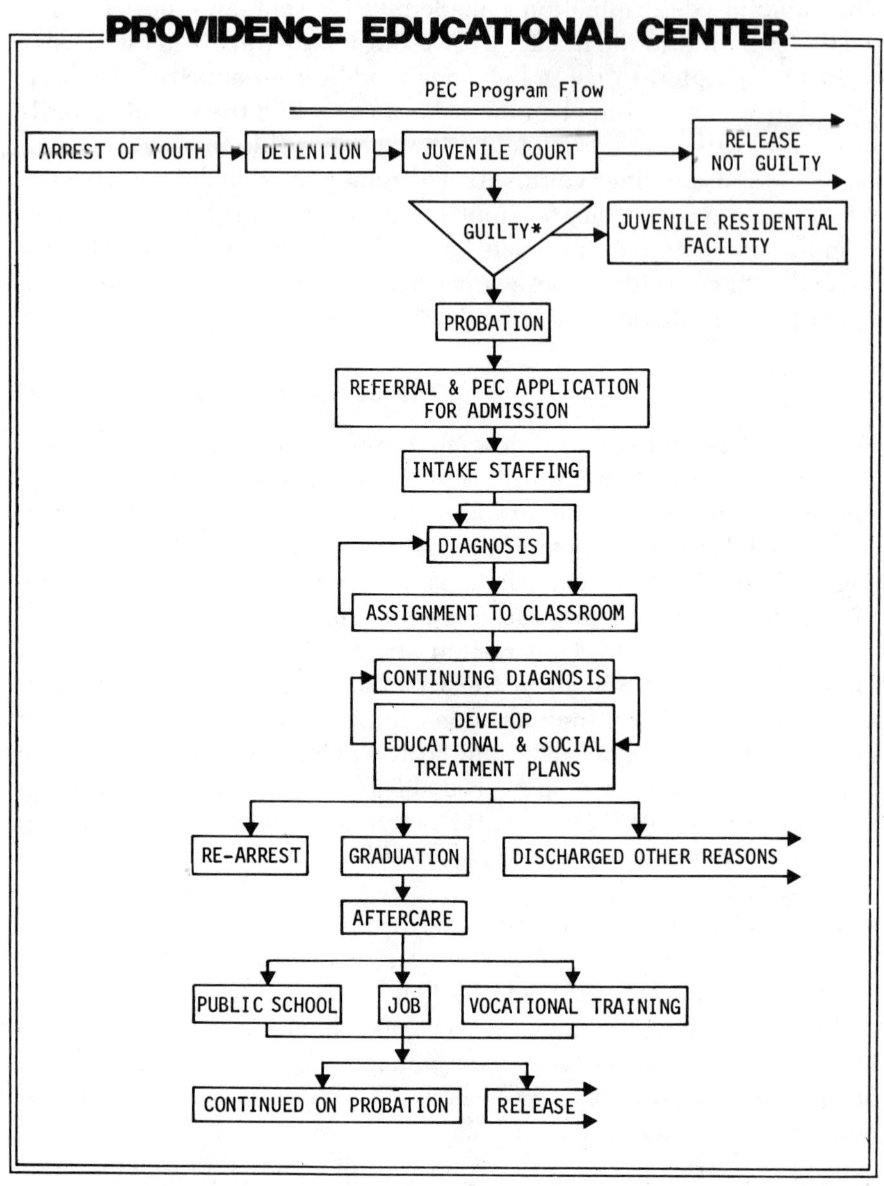

*Case adjudicated: juvenile delinquent

paying attention is a cold, wet, and hungry night. In subsequent classes, the youngsters are quite attentive and responsive.

The second phase of the program entails a cross-country trot through swamps, woods, and rivers, beginning at 5 A.M. and lasting until darkness, that leaves the participants exhausted. Each participant is then immediately asked to sign an agreement to continue in the program. Because of peer pressure and the challenge, it is unusual for a boy not to sign-up. From then on, his time is taken up learning the intricacies of survival, navigation and logistics, first aid, etc. Overnight and then three-day expeditions are held, all leading to a ten-day course across the Appalachian Trail in several feet of snow. Slow youngsters are helped by their peers and group interaction is intensified. There is excitement and danger, and personal skill and cooperation take on new importance.

The final test is a three-day solo survival experience; no peers, instructors, or supervision. All of the youngster's learning and experience are put to the test on this trip—alone for 3 days and nights, far from comfort and civilization. On the final evening, each boy receives a certificate and an emblem indicating his successful completion of the program.

The program proves to its participants the point that workers often try to make to their clients: "You are far more capable than you think you are." The need for discipline and restraint, as well as perseverance, is the important lesson taught at HB. A study of the program revealed that only 20.8% of the participants recidivated, compared to 42.7% of a control group. Massachusetts has closed all but one of its training schools and has increased its referrals to HB, exchanging a six-week program for the traditional six to nine month training school experience.

AFTERCARE

The NCCD defines juvenile aftercare as "the release of a child from an institution at the time when he can best benefit from release and from life in the community under the supervision of a counselor." [47] Following the institutional stay, a juvenile may continue under probation supervision, or may be supervised by other aftercare (parole) workers. The NCCD reports that in 34 states the department that administers the juvenile institutions also provdes aftercare services.[48] The author, for example, worked for the New York State Department of Social Welfare, which used to operate the state training schools. He was

[47] Lerman, p. 296.

[48] *Ibid.*, p. 297.

employed with the title of "Youth Parole Worker" and his responsibilities included the supervision of juveniles released from training schools. Arnold reports that, in fact, about 80% of the juveniles released from training schools are supervised by aftercare workers connected with the institutions. The rest are supervised by probation officers or personnel from other social service agencies.[49]

The first responsibility of the aftercare worker is to plan for the release and placement of the young person. Placement plans include where the juvenile will live, whether he or she is to work or attend school, or both, and arrangements for any supportive services which may be available in the community. The children may be returned to their own homes or, if it is desirable, be placed in an alternate setting such as a foster home, group home, or halfway house. The aftercare worker usually investigates placement alternatives and finalizes a program which is submitted to the training school officials responsible for release decision-making.

The release plans are evaluated at the institution, along with the child's social history and adjustment while in the training school. The decision to send a child home is based on the conditions in the home, the attitude of the parents and their concern for the child's welfare. If the home situation is considered unsatisfactory, the child may be placed with a relative, in a group home, or in a foster home. When a child is placed in a group home or foster care, the worker will spend time with the foster parents or the home staff as well as with the child, to help the adjustment to the new surroundings. The worker will also continue to work with the natural parents in order to help them accept the placement outside their home, and to assist them in preparing for the child's eventual return to his or her own home.

JUVENILE COURT JUDGES

In addition to a knowledge of the law, a juvenile court judge must have a basic understanding of the social sciences. Winslade states, however, that "The role of the juvenile court judge as the synthesizer of law, social science, and morality in addition to being a kindly father figure, proved to be too demanding."[50] Rubin and Smith note that many

[49] William R. Arnold, *Juveniles on Parole* (New York: Random House, 1970), p. 23.

[50] William J. Winslade, "The Juvenile Courts: From Idealism to Hypocracy," *Social Theory and Practice* (Fall 1974), p. 189.

juvenile judges come to the court from general law practice and have little knowledge of the philosophy and procedures of the juvenile court. They further observe that the judges also have little knowledge of child welfare agencies and other resources, and most have had no experience with children of lower-class groups, the most likely segment to be in the juvenile court.[51]

In 1967, the President's Commission noted that a survey of juvenile court judges revealed:

1. that half had not received undergraduate degrees,
2. another fifth had no college education at all, and
3. another fifth were not members of the bar.[52]

A more recent survey of juvenile court judges indicates an improvement in education and experience levels.[53]

A survey conducted by the International Association of Chiefs of Police revealed that, of the 42 states responding, none had written statewide standards governing the selection, education, and training of juvenile court judges. The IACP found that the standards for selection of juvenile court judges vary so greatly from state to state, and even within states, that it is extremely difficult to develop a comparative summary for the states.[54] Five of the 42 states do not require all judges who handle juvenile cases to be qualified attorneys, and most states do not require judges to attend pre-service or in-service training courses on juvenile procedures. The IACP concludes that "It is folly to assume that anyone licensed to practice law can be a judge in a juvenile court; yet this is the way the system operates."[55] The juvenile court should no longer serve as "a training camp for new judges who aspire to the bench of a more 'prestigious' court."[56]

In order to overcome some of the difficulties encountered by juvenile court judges, some states have now mandated that they attend various training programs.[57] The National Council of Juvenile Court

[51] Rubin and Smith, p. 19.

[52] President's Commission on Law Enforcement and Administration of Justice, *The Challenge of Crime in a Free Society* (New York: Avon Books, 1972), p. 217.

[53] Kenneth C. Smith, "A Profile of Juvenile Court Judges in the United States," *Juvenile Justice* (Aug. 1974), pp. 28–33.

[54] Richard W. Kobetz and Betty B. Bosarge, *Juvenile Justice Administration* (Gaithersburg, Md.: Internation Association of Chiefs of Police, 1973), p. 299.

[55] *Ibid.*, p. 310.

[56] *Ibid.*, p. 316.

[57] William C. Gordon, "The Family Court: Advantages and Problems," *Juvenile Justice* (Nov. 1974), p. 13.

Judges sponsors a National College located on the campus of the University of Nevada at Reno. Since 1969 the college has been training juvenile and family court judges to keep abreast of the laws and behavioral approaches related to the problems of delinquency, neglect, and child abuse. The standard two-week sessions for juvenile court and family court judges offer equal focus on legal and behavioral aspects of juvenile court practice.

Typical topics include a review of Supreme Court and other court decisions related to juveniles, procedural matters (such as intake), dispositional hearings, and adjudication, child neglect and abuse. Other topics are drug abuse, juvenile institutions and their alternatives, waiver of cases, transfer to adult courts, and evidence, in addition to behavioral science applications in the court.

Special one-week courses are also offered to graduates of the standard two-week programs. These sessions usually deal with specific topics and are "issue-oriented." The topics include such items as children with learning disabilities, status offenders, and drug treatment programs. The college also conducts from 25 to 55 other yearly training programs in other locations. These courses are directed to a variety of disciplines, including court administrators, probation and aftercare personnel.[58] Other programs for training juvenile court judges and personnel are sponsored by state councils of juvenile court judges, and The National Council on Crime and Delinquency has developed various manuals for juvenile and family court judges.

Some jurisdictions are also using *referees* (or *masters*), legally trained officials who can hold hearings on behalf of the judge and recommend findings and dispositions to him. The referee must be familiar with community resources and be trained in the behavioral sciences, in addition to having a legal background. The use of such specialized and skilled personnel in the juvenile court is another improvement toward the original ideals that first caused the juvenile court to come into existence.

Definitions*

Detention Center. A facility that provides temporary care in a physically restricting environment for juveniles in custody pending court disposition and

[58] Gerald P. Wittman, "A College For Juvenile and Family Court Judges," *Target* (Mar. 1975), p. 5.

*Law Enforcement Assistance Administration.

often for juveniles who have been adjudicated delinquent or are awaiting return to another jurisdiction.

Shelter. A facility that provides temporary care similar to that of a detention center, but in a physically unrestricting environment.

Reception and Diagnostic Center. A facility that screens juvenile court commitments and assigns them to appropriate treatment facilities.

Training School. A specialized institution serving delinquent juveniles committed directly to it by juvenile court or placed in it by an agency having such authority.

Ranch, Forestry Camp, Farm. A residential treatment facility for juveniles whose behavior does not necessitate the strict confinement of a training school, often allowing them greater contact with the community.

Halfway House. A facility where 50 percent or more of the resident juveniles are on probation or aftercare/parole, allowing them extensive contact with the community, such as through jobs and schools.

Group Home. A facility where juveniles are allowed extensive contact with the community, such as through jobs and schools, but none or less than half are placed there on probation or aftercare/parole.

Juvenile. A person charged with a criminal offense or juvenile offense, over whom the juvenile court has original jurisdication. The juvenile court's jurisdiction is determined by the age of the person who must, in most States, be under 18 years of age.

Juveniles Adjudicated Delinquent. Juveniles who through formal judicial proceedings have been adjudged delinquent.

Juveniles in Need of Supervision. Juveniles who have been declared in need of supervision by juvenile court (such as PINS, CHINS—person or child in need of supervision) under special statutes for juvenile "status offenders."

Juveniles Held Pending Disposition by Court. Juveniles held for delinquency who have not had any hearing or who have had only a preliminary hearing or screening and who are awaiting further court action.

Voluntary Commitments. Juveniles who committed themselves or were referred to the facility for treatment by parent, court, school, social agency, etc., without being adjudged delinquent or declared in need of supervision by a court.

Dependent and Neglected Children. Juveniles held as a result of the inability or unwillingness of their parents to care for them. Juveniles held on delinquency charges, adjudicated delinquent, or declared in need of supervision may also be dependent and neglected.

Chapter 4

Presentence Investigation

The second basic service provided by a probation agency is the presentence investigation which, when reduced to writing, becomes the presentence report. The presentence report is usually made after the conviction of a defendant in a criminal case, and it has five purposes:

1. The primary purpose is to help the court make an appropriate disposition of the case. The report should help in deciding for or against probation, in determining the conditions of probation, in deciding among available institutions and in determining the appropriate length of sentence. The American Bar Association notes that "The primary purpose of the presentence report is to provide the sentencing court with succinct and precise information upon which to base a rational sentencing decision." [1]

2. The presentence report serves as a basis for a plan of probation or parole supervision and treatment. The report indicates problem areas

[1] American Bar Association, *Standards Relating to Probation* (New York: American Bar Association, 1970), p. 11. (The ABA Standards are printed in 18 volumes. Price is $3.25 for a single volume; bulk order prices are $2.50 each for 10–24 of the same title, and $2.00 each for 25 or more of the same title. They may be ordered from ABA Circulation Dept., 1155 E. 60th Street, Chicago, Ill. 60637)

in the defendant's life, his or her capacity for using help, and the opportunities available to him in his environment and in the community. During the investigation the offender usually begins to relate to the probation department, learning how probation officers work and getting some understanding of the nature of the agency.

3. The presentence report assists prison personnel in their classification and treatment programs. Institutions depend heavily upon the report, particularly during the early part of the inmate's stay when the institution is trying to understand and plan a program for the individual. The report can provide valuable material that will help in planning for the care, custody and rehabilitation of the inmate. This includes everything from the type of custody required and the care of physical needs, to the planning of the various phases of the institutional program. Many institutions will have very little, if any, background or social information material other than that provided by the presentence report. This means that the report will have a marked effect on the way in which an inmate is approached and viewed by the institution since they will take the word of the probation officer over that of the inmate. The ideal report can give focus and initial direction to institution authorities for treatment and training as well as care and management.

4. The presentence report serves to furnish parole authorities with information pertinent to release planning and consideration for parole, and determination of any special conditions of parole.

5. The report serves as a source of information for research in corrections and criminal justice. Unfortunately, because of a lack of uniformity in form and content of the reports, their usefulness is somewhat limited.

In the report the probation officer attempts "to focus light on the character and personality of the defendant, and to offer insight into his problems and needs, to help understand the world in which he lives, to learn about his relationships with people, and to discover salient factors that underlie his specific offense and conduct in general, and "to suggest alternatives in the rehabilitation process." [2] The report is not expected to show guilt or innocence, only to relate the facts which the probation officer has been able to gather during the course of the

[2] Division of Probation, "The Selective Presentence Investigation Report," *Federal Probation* (Dec. 1974), p. 48.

investigation. Keve states that the presentence report typifies the philosophy of modern corrections; the report provides the court with a plan "that is corrective in intent, whereas without such knowledge the disposition can only be punitive." [3]

The presentence investigation is usually initiated after a defendant is found guilty. However, the National Advisory Commission recommends the preparing of a report in advance "since it may allow the defendant to obtain a sentence of nonincarceration or community supervision shortly after his guilt is adjudicated. This avoids the unseemly final rush to avoid removing the offender from the community (detention) for the few days between adjudication and sentence." [4]

The Florida Presentence Investigation Law

CHAPTER 74-112, Section 921.23, Florida Statutes, reads: Pre-sentence investigation reports.—

(1) Any court of the state having original jurisdiction of criminal actions, where the defendant in a criminal felony case has been found guilty or has entered a plea of nolo contendere or guilty shall refer, and in misdemeanor cases in its discretion may refer, the case to the parole and probation commission for investigation and recommendation. It shall be the duty of the commission to make a report in writing to the court prior to sentencing at a specified time depending upon the circumstances of the offender and the offense. Said report shall include the following:

(a) A complete description of the situation surrounding the criminal activity with which the offender has been charged, including a synopsis of the trial transcript, if one has been made, and, at the offender's discretion, his version and explanation of the act;

(b) The offender's educational background;

(c) The offender's employment background, including any military record, his present employment status and his occupational capabilities;

(d) The social history of the offender, including his family relationships, marital status, interests, and related activities;

[3] Paul W. Keve, "The Professional Character of the Presentence Report," *Federal Probation* (June 1962), p. 51.

[4] National Advisory Commission, p. 187.

(e) Residence history of the offender;

(f) The offender's medical history and, as appropriate, a psychological or psychiatric evaluation;

(g) Information about environments to which the offender might return or to which he could be sent should a sentence of non-incarceration or community supervision be imposed by the court;

(h) Information about any resources available to assist the offender such as treatment centers, residential facilities, vocational training programs, special education programs or services that may preclude or supplement commitment to the division of corrections;

(i) Views of the person preparing the report as to the offender's motivations and ambitions and an assessment of the offender's explanations for his criminal activity;

(j) An explanation of the offender's criminal record, if any, including his version and explanation of any previous offenses;

(k) A recommendation as to disposition by the court.

It shall be the duty of the commission to make a written determination as to the reasons for its recommendation. The commission shall include an evaluation of the following factors:

1. The appropriateness or inappropriateness of community facilities, programs, or services for treatment or supervision;
2. The ability or inability of the commission to provide an adequate level of supervision for the offender in the community and a statement of what constitutes an adequate level of supervision;
3. The existence of other treatment modalities which the offender could use but which do not exist at present in the community.

The preparation of a presentence report requires a basic expertise in the following:

1. interviewing,
2. understanding and interpreting reports, and
3. reporting information in a clear and concise manner.

The Interview

In probation and parole, much of the necessary information is received directly from people. In the presentence report, most of the information is gained by interviewing. These interviews are conducted in all types of surroundings; from hot and noisy detention pens, where dozens of people may be awaiting arraignment, to the relative quiet of the probation office.

Obviously, a quiet, comfortable setting with a maximum of privacy is the best environment for an interview. A place that lacks privacy or has numerous distractions will adversely affect the productivity of the interview. Sometimes interviews are conducted in the defendant's home. This provides an opportunity to observe the offender's home situation, and adds an additional and sometimes vital dimension to the report.

The interview is an anxiety-producing situation for the defendant. Previous experiences in similar situations, such as questioning by the police, may have been quite unpleasant. The probation officer tries to lower this anxiety by cordially introducing him or herself and explaining the purpose of the interview and the presentence report. This is especially important for the defendant who is not familiar with the court process.

The probation officer may try to deal with matters of concern to the defendant. A married male defendant may be engaged in a discussion of how his wife and children can secure public assistance in the event that he is imprisoned. The p.o. might offer to write a letter of referral for the wife to take with her to the Department of Welfare. In some way, the officer must show genuine concern and interest in the defendant, at the same time being realistic enough to expect many answers and statements from the defendant that will be self-serving. Since the p.o.'s contact with the defendant is limited, the officer cannot expect to probe deeply into the defendant's personality.

Some defendants will be overtly hostile, while others will mask their hostility with "wise-crack" answers. The p.o. must control both temper and temperament. He or she is the professional and must never lose sight of that fact during the interview. In questioning, open-ended queries, such as "What have you been doing?", should be avoided. Questions should be specific, but require an explanation rather than a simple answer of "yes" or "no." The p.o. must avoid putting answers into the defendant's mouth with such questions as, "Did you quit that job because it was too hard?"

When the investigation is complete, the defendant should be reinterviewed in order to give him an opportunity to refute certain information, or clarify any aspects of the report which are in conflict.

Review of Records and Reports

The probation officer will be reviewing several records and reports in the course of his investigation. The first is the arrest record of the defendant. This record will take the form of an arrest sheet from the Federal Bureau of Investigation or another law enforcement agency, such as the state police. These forms usually contain numerous abbreviations that must be deciphered by the probation officer if the record is to be useful. The arrest sheet does not describe the offense; it contains only the official charge, for example, *Burglary 3rd.* There is no mention of the type of premises that were burgled and what was taken. In addition, the sheet often omits the disposition of the arrest. The probation officer may not be able to determine from the report what happened to the case. Therefore, it is necessary for the p.o. to check with the agency that made the arrest and the court that processed the case.

The nature of the defendant's prior record is extremely important. The law of many jurisdictions provides for a harsher sentence if the defendant has a prior felony conviction. In addition, the defendant's eligibility for probation and a variety of treatment programs, such as drug rehabilitation, may be affected by his prior record.

The p.o. will review the reports concerning the current offense, in addition to interviewing the arresting officer. He will look for information that was omitted during the trial, possibly including mitigating or aggravating circumstances, and perhaps giving a different perspective of the offense. He will review any previous presentence reports as well as reports of other correctional agencies which have had contact with the defendant. These might include training schools or residential treatment centers, and prison and parole agencies. The p.o. will also review the school records of the defendant.

If there are any psychiatric or psychological reports available, the p.o. will review and analyze them. To do this, the p.o. must understand the nomenclature used by psychiatrists and psychologists, and the meaning of any tests administered by the latter.

Preparing the Report

When the probation officer prepares the presentence report he places all of his information under various topical headings. For example:[5]

OFFENSE
- Official version
- Statement of codefendants
- Statement of witnesses, complainants, and victims

DEFENDANT'S VERSION OF OFFENSE

PRIOR RECORD

FAMILY HISTORY
- Defendant
- Parents and siblings

MARITAL HISTORY

HOME AND NEIGHBORHOOD

EDUCATION

RELIGION

INTERESTS AND LEISURE-TIME ACTIVITIES

HEALTH
- Physical
- Mental and emotional

EMPLOYMENT

MILITARY SERVICE

FINANCIAL CONDITION
- Assets
- Financial obligations

EVALUATIVE SUMMARY

RECOMMENDATION

The probation officer should make a judgement as to whether a psychiatric and/or psychological referral should be made during the probation investigation. Indiscriminate referrals to mental health clinics or court psychiatrists are wasteful, since delinquency and crime are not necessarily symptomatic of an internalized conflict. In those cases where symptoms of mental disorder are obvious, and in those

[5] Robert M. Carter, "It is Respectfully Recommended . . . ," *Federal Probation* (June 1966), p. 41.

situations where the offender may benefit from an exploration of his problems, a referral should be made. If no referral is made, or there is a lack of psychiatric and psychological information, the p.o. should present his or her own observations concerning the defendant's intellectual capacity and personality. This will include such things as the offender's contact with reality and ability to express thoughts.

If the p.o. has received conflicting information about the defendant, and is unable to reconcile the discrepancies, this should be pointed out in the report and not left up to the reader to discover (or *not* discover).

Of crucial importance in any presentence report are the sections entitled *Evaluative Summary* and *Recommendation.* Nothing should appear in either of these sections that is not supported by the rest of the report. The summary contains the highlights of the total report, and should serve as a reminder to the reader of the information that has already been presented. The recommendation is a carefully thought-out statement, based on the officer's best professional judgment. It contains the alternatives that are available in the case, and reflects the individualized attention that each case received.[6]

Carter notes that the probation officer is in a unique position with respect to making a recommendation to the judge. "The officer has had an opportunity to observe the defendant in the community, not only from a legal-judicial, investigative perspective, but also from the viewpoint of a general life-style." [7] In order to present a meaningful recommendation, the p.o. must have knowledge of the resources and programs that are available. Unfortunately, a p.o. sometimes submits a recommendation for a treatment program that is not available either in the community or at a correctional institution.

One question that the p.o. must decide in the recommendation is whether or not to recommend probation. In many jurisdictions a conviction for certain crimes, or a previous felony conviction, precludes a sentence of probation. The p.o. must know the statutes of the applicable jurisdiction. The officer must also weigh the potential danger of the defendant to the community; must evaluate the defendant's rehabilitation potential and ability to conform to probation regulations; and must consider whether probation will be construed by the community as too lenient in view of the offense committed, or as "getting away with it" by the defendant.

In an effort to assist workers in making sentence recommendations,

[6] *Ibid.*

[7] *Ibid.*

the Vera Institute of Justice in New York, devised a scoring system based on three factors:

1. the defendant's prior criminal record,
2. the defendant's employment record, and
3. the defendant's family relationships.

These three factors were considered the ones that judges relied upon most in making their sentencing determinations.[8]

Vera Institute of Justice
Bronx Sentencing Project
Sentencing Recommendation Guidelines

Family Ties

+3 Lives with spouse.

+2 Lives with children, with or without another family member.

+2 Supports spouse or children, with or without supporting another family member.

+2 Supports one or more family members voluntarily.

+1 Supports a non-family person voluntarily.

+1 Has been living with a family member other than spouse or children.

+1 Has been living with a non-family person for the past six months.

0 None of the above.

NOTE: "Spouse" includes a legal spouse, or any person of the opposite sex with whom the defendant has lived in a conjugal relationship continuously for at least six months. "Family member" includes any person related to the defendant by blood or adoption, including half and step relatives.

Employment

+4 Present job three months or more.

+3 Present and prior jobs six months or more.

[8] Joel B. Lieberman, S. Andrew Schaffer, and John M. Martin, *The Bronx Project of the Institute of Justice* (Washington, D.C.: Government Printing Office, 1972), pp. 1–53.

+3 Person at home caring for children.

+2 Present and prior jobs three months or more.

+2 Present job less than three months.

+2 Attending school, or receiving a pension or social security, or unemployed due to a medical disability.

+2 Prior job three months or more which terminated upon arrest.

+1 Receiving unemployment, or woman supported by husband.

+1 Job commitment.

0 None of the above.

NOTE: In order to be able to add present and prior jobs, there must be no more than a two-week hiatus between each job. "Present job" means one to which the defendant's employer has stated he can return if he is in custody during the pendency of the case.

Prior Record

+4 No arrests ever.

+2 No convictions within 8 years.

If at least one felony or misdemeanor conviction occurred within the last eight years, use the following chart:

Number of felonies in total prior record	*Number of misdemeanors in total prior record*					
	0	*1*	*2*	*3*	*4 or more*	*At least 4, all within 12 years*
0		0	−1	−2	−3	−4
1	−1	−1	−2	−3	−4	−4
2 or more	−3	−3	−4	−4	−4	−4
At least 2, both within 12 years	−4	−4	−4	−4	−4	−4

NOTE: If the arrest date of the last prior case occurred within 6 months of the conviction date of the present case, deduct 1 point from whatever score appears in the chart.

A. −5 to 0 Points—*For Information Only* (tantamount to recommending prison).

B. 0 to 1 Point—*Discretion* (either putting in "For Information Only," or "Supervised Release;" in either the worker must indicate why he chose one over the other).

C. 1 to 7 Points—*Supervised Release* (probation).

D. 8 to 11 Points—*Optional* (from four possibilities: 1. fine, 2. conditional discharge, 3. unconditional discharge, and 4. probation).

E. Worker is unable to complete verification of defendant's information.

CRITICISM OF THE PRESENTENCE REPORT

The presentence report is not without its critics. Blumberg, for example, maintains that some judges do not read the presentence report, while others carefully select passages condemning the defendant to read aloud in the courtroom in order to justify their sentences.[9] While the United States Supreme Court has expressed confidence in the presentence report (*see Williams v. New York* in Chapter 6), Blumberg maintains that many judges discount the reports because of the hearsay nature of the information.[10] In a reversal of Blumberg's criticism, Gaylin states that "the enormous dependence on the probation officer and the presentence report which is his product," makes the p.o. rather than the judge the sentencer.[11] Czajkoski notes that studies do indeed indicate a high correlation (95%) between the probation officer's recommendation and the judge's decision.[12] However, Dawson states that the probation officer may write into the presentence report the recommendation that he thinks will be well-received by the judge.[13]

In some jurisdictions, the probation officer is overburdened with presentence reports, or the size of his supervision caseload, and may

[9] Abraham S. Blumberg, *Criminal Justice* (Chicago: Quadrangle Books, 1970), p. 157.

[10] *Ibid.*, pp. 160–61.

[11] Gaylin, p. 13.

[12] Czajkoski, pp. 9–10.

[13] Robert O. Dawson, *Sentencing* (Boston: Little, Brown, and Co., 1969), p. xi.

not have the time to do an adequate investigation and prepare a useful presentence report. In courts where the judge usually pays little attention to the contents of the report, the p.o. will not be inclined to pursue necessary information and prepare well-written reports.

REQUIRING A PRESENTENCE REPORT

The President's Commission on Law Enforcement and Administration of Justice reported that about one-fourth of the states require a presentence report for crimes punishable by more than one year of imprisonment. In the federal government and the great majority of states the judge retains the discretion to order a presentence report.[14] The American Bar Association (ABA) recommends that all "courts should be supplied with sufficient resources to call for a presentence investigation and a written report in every criminal case, including misdemeanors." [15] The President's Commission recommended that "all courts should require presentence reports for all offenders, whether reports result from a full field investigation by probation officers or, in the case of minor offenders, from the use of short forms." [16]

CONFIDENTIALITY OF THE PRESENTENCE REPORT

There is a controversy over whether or not the contents of the presentence report should be disclosed to the defendant. Judge James B. Parsons (U.S. District Court of Northern Illinois) believes that sources of information must be protected or they will hesitate to provide information. Family members or employers may fear retribution from the defendant if they provide negative information. The police may be reluctant to provide information if the defendant will be privy to it.[17]

Judge Roszel C. Thomsen (Chief Judge, U.S. District Court of Maryland) notes that Maryland is one of the federal districts (there are 92) which customarily reveals the contents of the presentence report to

[14] *The Challenge of Crime in a Free Society*, p. 355.

[15] American Bar Association, p. 4.

[16] *The Challenge of Crime in a Free Society*, p. 355.

[17] James B. Parsons, "The Presentence Report Must Be Preserved as a Confidential Document," *Federal Probation* (Mar. 1964), pp. 3–7.

the defendant's attorney. However, the probation officer's recommendation and other confidential information are withheld. Judge Thomsen reports that probation officers have not found that this practice affects their ability to gather information.[18]

States, like federal districts, vary in their approach to confidentiality. In the County of Milwaukee, Wisconsin, the judge customarily discusses the presentence report with the prosecutor, the probation officer, and the defendant's attorney before passing sentence. However, this is not the practice throughout Wisconsin, where state law gives the trial judge the option of disclosing the report to the defendant's attorney.[19] In Michigan, a neighboring state, the report is confidential by law.[20] In Illinois, where the presentence report is not explicitly authorized by statute, the report is routinely given to the defendant's attorney for comment.[21]

The American Bar Association recommends that all information which adversely affects the defendant should be discussed with the defendant or his attorney.[22] The President's Commission stated that "In the absence of impelling reasons for non-disclosure of specific information, the defendant and his counsel should be permitted to examine the entire presentence report." [23]

The National Advisory Commission recommends that the presentence report "be available to defense counsel and the prosecution." [24] The Commission rejects the argument that sources of information will "dry up;" the Commission states that "(1) those jurisdictions which have required disclosure have not experienced this phenomenon; and (2) more importantly, if the same evidence were given as testimony at trial, there would be no protection or confidentiality." [25]

Certainly it would seem that the "doctrine of fair play" would require a system whereby the defendant would be protected from the effects of unfounded information contained in the presentence report.

[18] Roszel C. Thomsen, "Confidentiality of the Presentence Report: A Middle Position," *Federal Probation* (Mar. 1964), pp. 8–10.

[19] Dawson, pp. 18, 64.

[20] *Ibid.*, p. 63.

[21] David W. Neubauer, *Criminal Justice in Middle America* (Princeton, N.J.: General Learning Press, 1974), p. 239.

[22] American Bar Association, p. 41.

[23] *The Challenge of Crime in a Free Society*, p. 356.

[24] National Advisory Commission on Criminal Justice Standards and Goals, *Corrections* (Washington, D.C.: Government Printing Office, 1973), p. 188.

[25] *Ibid.*, p. 189.

The minimum safeguard should enable the defendant to have an opportunity to refute any derogatory information, or to offer mitigating circumstances.

According to Norm Larkins, a probation officer in Alberta, Canada, "Disclosure of information has led probation officers to develop techniques whereby the information obtained by them and presented in the report is more objective and accurate (with less reliance on heresay information)." [26] He reports that before the initial interview with the defendant is conducted "it is explained that a copy of the report will be made available to the offender or his legal counsel prior to sentencing. It is the duty of the offender to bring to the judge's attention any mistakes or omissions which he feels would be important in influencing the sentencing." [27]

Target, a periodical dealing with criminal justice, reported the following innovation by the Legal Aid Society:

> In 1974, with Law Enforcement Assistance Administration funding, the New York Legal Aid Society established the Presentence Service Group to provide in-house social services to clients convicted of a felony and to prepare Presentence Memoranda on their behalf, in accordance with the New York State Criminal Procedure Act.
>
> The Presentence Service Group evaluates the accuracy of presentence reports prepared by New York City's Department of Probation. The New York laws were amended in September, 1975, to make these reports available to defense counsel. The Group's legal services also include: (1) short term counseling; (2) referrals to community resources; (3) educational and/or vocational opportunities; (4) diagnostic assessment of clients; and (5) verification of information provided by the client for the Group's preparation of a presentence memorandum.
>
> The memoranda, which are submitted to the court prior to sentencing, are prepared by the Group with the cooperation of staff attorneys who represent each client on the Group's caseload. A memorandum includes an indepth analysis of the client's background and social history; letters of recommendation and other forms of documentation relevant to the client's past accomplishments and present endeavors; diagnostic assessments of the client; and recommendations based on the Group's evaluation of the client.
>
> Although in an advocacy position, the Presentence Group strives to make its reports reflect an honest, realistic portrayal of the client that is supported by valid documentation. The reports become part of the official court record.

[26] Norm Larkins, "Presentence Investigation Report Disclosure in Alberta," *Federal Probation* (Dec. 1972), p. 59.

[27] *Ibid.*

In New York, access to probation reports is now viewed by the legal profession as an integral part of the presentencing procedure. Defense counsel may use the provision to protect his/her client from unfair sentencing by contradicting inaccurate, biased, or unsubstantiated material that is presented to the court prior to sentencing.

The Presentence Group is an important addition for the Society's staff attorneys, most of whom have neither the resources nor training to assess the social and psychological aspects of probation reports. The Group is comprised of social workers and field counselors. Many of the counselors are ex-offenders who bring to the Group additional insight into the motivation and life styles of clients.[28]

LONG FORM AND SHORT FORM REPORTS

There are two types of presentence reports, the long form and the short form. The long form is usually more exhaustive and time-consuming than the short form. Increasing pressures on probation agencies for more presentence reports have resulted in the short form gaining popularity. Following are examples of both these forms, short form first.

UNITED STATES DISTRICT COURT
Central District of New York

PRESENTENCE REPORT*

NAME John Jones

ADDRESS
1234 Astoria Blvd.
New York City

LEGAL RESIDENCE
Same

AGE 33 DATE OF BIRTH 2–8–40
New York City

SEX Male RACE Caucasian

CITIZENSHIP U.S. (Birth)

EDUCATION 10th grade

DATE January 4, 1974

DOCKET NO. 74–103

OFFENSE Theft of Mail by Postal Employee (18 U.S.C. Sec. 1709) 2 cts.

PENALTY Ct. 2–5 years and/or $2,000 fine

PLEA Guilty on 12–16–73 to Ct. 2
Ct. 1 pending

VERDICT

CUSTODY Released on own

[28] "New York Indigents Receive Pre-Sentencing Assistance," *Target* Mar. 1976), p. 4.

*Division of Probation, "The Selective Presentence Investigation Report," *Federal Probation* (Dec. 1974), pp. 53-54.

MARITAL STATUS Married

DEPENDENTS Three (wife and 2 children)

SOC. SEC. NO. 112–03–9559

FBI NO. 256 1126

DETAINERS OR CHARGES PENDING: None

CODEFENDANTS *(Disposition)* *None*

recognizance. No time in custody.

ASST. U.S. ATTY Samuel Hayman

DEFENSE COUNSEL Thomas Lincoln Federal Public Defender

DRUG/ALCOHOL INVOLVEMENT: Attributes offense to need for drinking money

---

DISPOSITION

DATE

SENTENCING JUDGE

Offense: Official Version. Official sources reveal that during the course of routine observations on December 4, 1973, within the Postal Office Center, Long Island, New York, postal inspectors observed the defendant paying particular attention to various packages. Since the defendant was seen to mishandle and tamper with several parcels, test parcels, were prepared for his handling on December 5, 1973. The defendant was observed to mishandle one of the test parcels by tossing it to one side into a canvas tub. He then placed his jacket into the tub and leaned over the tub for a period of time. At this time the defendant left the area and went to the men's room. While he was gone the inspectors examined the mail tub and found that the test parcel had been rifled and that the contents, a watch, was missing.

The defendant returned to his work area and picked up his jacket. He then left the building. The defendant was stopped by the inspectors across the street from the post office. He was questioned about his activities and on his person he had the wristwatch from the test parcel. He was taken to the postal inspector's office where he admitted the offense.

Defendant's Version of Offense. The defendant admits that he rifled the package in question and took the watch. He states that he intended to sell the watch at a later date. He admits that he has been drinking too much lately and needed extra cash for "drinking money." He exhibits remorse and is concerned about the possibility of incarceration and the effect that it would have on his family.

Prior Record

Date	Offense	Place	Disposition
5-7-66 (age 26)	Possession of Policy Slips	Manhattan CR. CT. N.Y., N.Y.	$25.00 Fine 7-11-66
3-21-72 (age 32)	Intoxication	Manhattan CR. CT. N.Y., N.Y.	4-17-72 Nolle

Personal History. The defendant was born in New York City on February 8, 1940, the oldest of three children. He attended the public school, completed the 10th grade and left school to go to work. He was rated as an average student and was active in sports, especially basketball and baseball.

The defendant's father, John, died of a heart attack in 1968, at the age of 53 years. He had an elementary school education and worked as a construction laborer most of his life.

The defendant's mother, Mary Smith Jones, is 55 years of age and is employed as a seamstress. She had an elementary school education and married defendant's father when she was 20 years of age. Three sons were issue of the marriage. She presently resides in New York City, and is in good health.

Defendant's brother, Paul, age 32 years, completed 2½ years of high school. He is employed as a bus driver and resides with his wife and two children in New York City.

Defendant's brother, Lawrence, age 30 years, completed three semesters of college. He is employed as a New York City firefighter. He resides with his wife and one child in Dutch Point, Long Island.

The defendant after leaving high school worked as a delivery boy for a retail supermarket chain then served 2 years in the U.S. Army as an infantryman (ASN 123 456 78). He received an honorable discharge and attained the rank of corporal serving from 2-10-58 to 2-1-60. After service he held a number of jobs of the laboring type.

The defendant was employed as a truck driver for the City of New York when he married Ann Sweeny on 6-15-63. Two children were issue of this marriage, John, age 8, and Mary, age 6. The family has resided at the same address (which is a four-room apartment) since their marriage.

The defendant has been in good health all of his life but he admits he has been drinking to excess the past 18 months which has resulted in some domestic strife. The wife stated that she loved her husband and will stand by him. She is amenable to a referral for family counseling.

Defendant has worked for the Postal Service since 12-1-65 and resigned on 12-5-73 as a result of the present arrest. His work ratings by his supervisors were always "excellent."

Evaluative Summary. The defendant is a 33-year-old male who entered a plea of guilty to mail theft. While an employee of the U.S. Postal Service he rifled and stole a watch from a test package. He admitted that he planned on selling the watch to finance his drinking which has become a problem resulting in domestic strife.

Defendant is a married man with two children with no prior serious record. He completed 10 years of schooling, had an honorable military record, and has a good work history. He expresses remorse for his present offense and is concerned over the loss of his job and the shame to his family.

Recommendation. It is respectfully recommended that the defendant be admitted to probation. If placed on probation the defendant expresses willingness to seek counseling for his domestic problems. He will require increased motivation if there is to be a significant change in his drinking pattern.

Respectfully submitted,

Donald M. Fredericks
U.S. Probation Officer

SOMERSET COUNTY PROBATION DEPARTMENT
STATE OF NEW JERSEY
Adult Presentence Report

NAME: Howard Peter Williams BORN: June 2, 1950 SEX: Male

ALIAS: None PLACE OF BIRTH: New Brunswick, N.J.

ADDRESS: 409 Franklin Boulevard
Franklin Township, N.J.

INDICTMENT No. 128-71-M

ORIGINAL CHARGE(S): Armed Robbery; Assault With Intent to Rape

---

FINAL CHARGE(S): Armed Robbery N.J.S. 2A:141-1 & 2A:151-5
Plea Bargain: Second count of indictment dismissed.

CONVICTION: PLEA: X DATE: Dec. 13, 1972

SENTENCE DATE: Feb. 9, 1973 JUDGE: Paul E. Martin

ASSIGNED: X (Public Defender) Paul P. Morgan RETAINED:

DATE OF ARREST: May 12, 1972

CUSTODIAL STATUS: ROR: (date)

BAIL: $500 (revoked 10/16/72); 150 days jail time

CODEFENDANT(S): Allan Murray, Y.C.I., Pending Sentencing

DISPOSITION: On Robbery charge, 7-10 years State Prison, Trenton, and on charge of Being Armed, additional term 3-5 years State Prison, Trenton; consecutive to sentence imposed on charge Robbery. 150 days jail time credit.

CIRCUMSTANCES OF OFFENSE:

OFFICIAL VERSION: On May 12, 1972 at 8:05 p.m., police responded to the report of an armed robber at Glenn's Discount Center, 1450 Hamilton St., Franklin Twp., N.J. The perpetrators were described as two males, one of whom was armed with a shotgun. They had threatened the woman manager with the weapon, and had gotten away with several cartons of cigarettes. The getaway vehicle was observed almost immediately, and a high speed chase ensued, lasting 20 minutes. The suspects vehicle ran through several road blocks, but was eventually halted with assistance from the New Brunswick Pol. Dept. after a collision with a parked car. Three subjects, including the defendant were taken into custody. A 12 gauge shotgun, five (5) buckshot shells and eight (8) cartons of cigarettes were found in the car.

DEFENDANT'S VERSION: Defendant related that he was approached by Allan, a codefendant, who told him he knew of a place they could rob, and that it would be "an easy touch." Allan also supplied the shotgun and getaway car. Defendant admitted to holding the shotgun on the manager, while Allan went to the cash register.

REMARKS OF COMPLAINANT, VICTIMS, WITNESSES: The victim was interviewed, but stated that she was so shaken by the incident, that she preferred not to make a statement for the record.

COMMENTS: Police reports indicate that after the defendant forced the victim into the bathroom at gunpoint, he demanded that she remove her clothing and lay on the floor. When she refused to comply, the defendant threatened her, and said "I'll blow your head off." Defendant then placed his hand on her genital area and when she pushed his hand away, defendant slapped her face. The victim escaped when the defendant's attention was diverted by Allan, a codefendant.

OFFENSE HISTORY:

JUVENILE: YES ** NO____
SEE ATTACHED
ADULT: YES ** NO____

DETAINERS: None

AGE OF FIRST CONVICTION: 19 Years

OFFENSE: Disorderly Person (Trespassing)

EXPLAIN: Police investigating a reported breaking and entering, found the defendant near a tire company warehouse at 11:22 p.m. Defendant admitted to trespassing and was fined $50.00 plus $10.00 Costs.

PREVIOUS PROBATION, INSTITUTIONALIZATION, PAROLE: Defendant's brief exposure to juvenile probationary supervision by this department ended with incarceration following two violations within ten days of each other. Since then, defendant has been returned to the institution as a parole violator. He has been at Annandale and Bordentown, where his overall adjustment could be considered as fair at best. Defendant's conduct and attitude while on parole were poor. Since being placed on probation in Middlesex County on March 6, 1972, defendant has been convicted of Armed Robbery twice.

EVALUATION OF PAST RECORD AND COMMENTS: Records indicate that defendant's rejection of any form of authority accounts for his juvenile record. Defendant has been using heroin for the past six years. This, together with his many previous and continuing problems has seen him become involved in more aggressive acting out against society. Defendant has thus far failed to respond to probation or parole supervision, and did not avail himself of an opportunity to complete a drug rehabilitation program.

RESIDENCE:

How Long Has Defendant Lived in the Present:

Town or City:	22 Years
County:	22 Years
State:	22 Years

COMMENTS: Except for periods of incarceration, defendant has resided at one of two addresses on Franklin Boulevard, Franklin Township, N.Y. for all of his life.

FAMILY HISTORY:

Parental:

Def. is the younger of 2 sons born of his parents marriage. Defendant's father deserted the family in 1958, and his mother moved to Elizabeth, N.J., where she entered a paramour relationship which produced 3 children. Def. was raised by his maternal grandparents, but has been on his own since his grandmother died in 1968. Def. expressed affection for his grandmother, but admitted that she was unable to give him the necessary supervision and guidance.

Marital:

Def. married one Geraldine (nee Wilson Williams on Nov. 25, 1969 at Franklin Twp., N.J. Two children were born of this marriage, which ended in divorce on Feb. 18, 1972. Defendant's children are Caroline, age 2½; and Howard, Jr., age 16 months. Def. indicated that his marital breakup was the result of his continued use of heroin and involvement in criminal activities. Def. related that his wife has since moved from this area, and her present whereabouts are unknown. Efforts by this department to locate defendant's wife have been unsuccessful.

COMMUNITY INVOLVEMENT AND TIES: Def. is a life long area resident, and has several relatives residing in Franklin Twp., N.J.

MILITARY HISTORY: Not applicable.

Branch of Service: ______________

Length of Service: ______________

Type of Discharge: ______________

Military Discipline: ______________

Service No.

COMMENTS: Def. was classified 4-F on May 15, 1970 by Local Board No.40, Somerville, N.J.

EDUCATIONAL ACHIEVEMENT:

In school now: Yes__________ No____**____

If yes, name of school:

Grade:______________

If no, highest grade completed:______eighth______

Age left school:______17 years______

Reason for leaving:

Incarceration (See Juvenile Record).

COMMENTS ON EDUCATIONAL BACKGROUND:

It appears that defendant received a social promotion to the ninth grade, as he had failed all but one of his previous courses. Records indicate that defendant was a chronic discipline problem, in that he constantly challenged school authorities, and projected an image of belligerence. Defendant was tested at Annandale in 1965, and found to have I.Q. of 88.

PHYSICAL INFORMATION:

HEIGHT:____5′7″____ WEIGHT:____150 lbs.____

Distinguishing marks and discussion of physical appearance:

Abdominal scar (appendectomy)

3″ scar upper right arm (knife wound)

HEALTH:
Physical:
No problems: ______________________________
Previous or existing problems:
Defendant related that he has had a kidney infection since April, 1972.

Mental:
No problems: See Below
Previous or existing problems:

COMMENTS: Def. was examined at the N.J. State Diagnostic Center at Menlo Park on July 8, 1965. Def. was a patient at the N.J. State Hospital, Vroom Building, Trenton, N.J. from Jan. 3, 1973 to Jan. 25, 1973. Def. entered the Discovery House drug program on March 6, 1972 and was ejected by the staff on May 3, 1972 due to ". . . an unwillingness on his part to conform to house regulations, despite numerous opportunities to correct his attitude"

HISTORY OF DRUG AND/OR ALCOHOL USAGE: Def. admitted to a 6 year history of heroin addiction. He related that his last habit was 15 "bags" per day. Def. refused to comment on how he supported his habit. Def. stated that he drinks alcoholic beverages in moderation.

DRUG AND/OR ALCOHOL RELEVANCE TO PRESENT OFFENSE: Considering defendant's drug history, it appears that his motivation was to obtain money for drugs.

EMPLOYMENT:
Social Security No. 163-24-6197

PRESENT EMPLOYMENT: Unemployed

Employer:
Address:

Nature of Work:

Employment Started: ______________________

Earnings: ______________________

Employer Comments:

COMMENT OF PAST EMPLOYMENTS:

If Unemployable, Explain:
Presently incarcerated.

Means of Subsistence during periods of unemployment:
Lived with relatives and friends

Occupational Skills, Ambitions and Interests:
Def. has no occupational skills or interests, and voiced no ambitions for the future.

COMMENTS ON EMPLOYMENT HISTORY: Def. has been unemployed since Sept., 1971. His longest period of employment was with Revlon, Inc., Edison Twp., N.J. where he worked from Aug., 1969 to March, 1970, as a Porter. Defendant's other periods of employment were generally for less than one month.

FINANCIAL STATUS:

Assets:
None.

Liabilities:
None.

ANALYSIS

ASSESSMENT OF FACTORS CONTRIBUTING TO PRESENT OFFENSE:
It appears that the codefendant Allan assembled a "team" to execute the present offense. Allan supplied the car and shotgun, as well as suggesting the place for the armed robbery. Murray was chosen to drive the car, while the def. handled the shotgun and threatened the woman manager. All three participants were heroin users, and it would seem that their motivation was to obtain money for drugs.

ASSESSMENT OF DEFENDANT'S PERSONALITY, PROBLEMS AND POTENTIALS AS RELATED TO ADJUSTMENT:
Defendant's involvement in the present offense is seen as the last in a series of offenses against society which have become more aggressive and violent with the passage of time. He is the product of a broken home, and was never afforded the supervision and discipline necessary in his formative years. Defendant's marriage ended in divorce as the result of his drug abuse and criminal activity. Def. was a problem in school, and has never developed work habits. His heroin addiction has compounded the preexisting problems. Def. has failed to "make it" on probation, parole or in a drug rehabilitation program. He appears to be unready to deal with his problems at the present time.

COMMUNITY RESOURCES OF POTENTIAL ASSISTANCE IN THIS CASE.
Not relevant.

SIGNATURE OF OFFICER:

____

PRIOR RECORD:

Juvenile

4/2/65	Franklin Twp., N.J.	Intoxicated (found unconscious while being carried by two companions)	6/18/65 Juv. & Dom. Rel. Ct. of Som. Cty. N.J. one day exam at N.J. Diagnostic Center.
Between 4/19/65 and 4/27/65	Franklin Twp., N.J.	Larceny of 4 motor vehicles (Subject admitted to taking 7 different cars)	
5/24/65	New Brunswick, N.J.	Larceny of Motor Vehicle	
6/6/65	Franklin Twp., N.J.	Open Lewdness (Entered girls locker room in high school and exposed himself to a girl in the nude by holding his penis)	7/29/65 Juv. & Dom. Rel. Ct. of Somerset County. Indet. term at Annandale Reformatory on all four complaints. Service of said sentences to run concurrently with each other. Paroled on 10/21/66
6/26/67	Franklin Twp., N.J.	Idly Roaming Streets at night	12/8/67 Juv. & Dom. Rel. Ct. of Som. Cty. one year probation.
1/18/68	Franklin Twp., N.J.	Violation of Probation (Idly Roaming Streets at night)	1/19/68 Juv. & Dom. Rel. Ct. of Som. County cont. on prob.; 8:00 p.m. curfew.
1/28/68	Franklin Twp., N.J.	Unlawful Possession of Narcotics (Heroin) Violation of Probation (Curfew Violation)	2/9/68 Juv. & Dom. Rel. Ct. of Som. Cty. Ind. term N.J. Reformatory, to be delivered to the Y.R.C.C. at Yardvill on each complaint service of said sentences to run concurrently with each other. 2/20/68 Transferred to Bordentown Unit. Paroled 7/3/69. Returned as Parole Violator 3/26/70. Discharged 2/11/71.
7/15/69	New Brunswick, N.J.	Disorderly Person (Trespassing)	$50.00 Fine, $10.00 Costs.
8/4/69	Clark Twp., N.J.	1. Carrying Concealed Weapon	1. 2/19/70 Indictment dismissed prior to trial.

		2. Disorderly Person (Possession of Narcotic Paraphernalia)	2. 1/28/71 $15.00 fine, $10.00 Costs.
2/25/70	Franklin Twp., N.J.	Disorderly Person (Use of Narcotics—Heroin, as amended from original charge of Possession of Heroin)	3/16/70 6 months Somerset County Jail suspended. 18 mos. probation.
3/10/71	New Brunswick, N.J.	1. Carrying Concealed Weapon 2. Assault and Battery Upon a Police Officer	3/6/72 Middlesex Cty Court. Indictment dismissed as a result of Plea Bargaining
5/13/71	Franklin Twp., N.J.	Disorderly Person (Failure to Give a Good Account and Failure to Register as a Narcotics User)	5/17/71 10 days Somerset County Jail
5/23/71	New Brunswick, N.J.	Breaking and Entering Petty Larceny	3/6/72 Middlesex Cty. Ct., Ind. term at the Y.C.I., to be dél. to the Y.R.C.C. at Yardville, susp., 5 years probation. Concurrent.
11/1/71	New Brunswick, N.J.	Possession of Revolver in Motor Vehicle Without Requisite Permit to Carry Same	
7/10/72	New Brunswick, N.J.	Armed Robbery	12/5/72 Middlesex County Court. Found Guilty after Trial. Awaiting sentencing.

PRE-SENTENCE DIAGNOSIS [29]

California criminal courts have the option of sending, prior to sentencing, an individual convicted of a felony to the Department of Corrections for the purpose of obtaining a diagnostic evaluation and a recommendation for an appropriate sentence.

Felons are referred for up to 90 days of study and observation within which period a report is made back to the court recommending a disposition in the case.

In arriving at the recommendations for each case referred by the courts, the Reception Center staff (of the Department of Corrections) performs a complete work-up utilizing both interviews and testing. Information on the life history, experiences, attitudes, psychiatric problems, etc., of the individual is compiled in the Cumulative Sum-

[29] Information from the California Department of Corrections.

mary which is returned to the court along with the statement recommending either sentencing to prison or supervision in the community. In either event, RC staff have followed the practice of specifying the reasons for their recommendations.

Alternatives recommended for dealing with cases at the community level have included straight probation and probation with jail. Originally, the county referring a case for a diagnostic observation was to reimburse the state for the service. In 1965, the statute was modified to eliminate this requirement. The immediate effect was a marked increase in the utilization of the program. While there were only 271 cases referred in 1964, in 1974 the figure was 2,940.

Chapter 5

Granting Probation

The President's Commission reported that only fifteen states have no restrictions on who may be granted probation in felony cases. Other states restrict probation for persons convicted of serious crimes, such as rape and murder, and some restrict probation for persons with prior felony convictions.[1] New York prohibits probation for anyone convicted of certain felony crimes.[2] Michigan restricts probation for third felony offenders. Kansas does not exclude anyone from probation eligibility.[3] This lack of consistency has moved the ABA to recommend that probation be available in every case, and if limited it should be for only the most serious offenses.[4]

DISCRETIONARY ASPECTS

Judges differ in their approach to granting probation when it is a statutory alternative. Some seek the advice of the police, the pro-

[1] *Task Force Report,* p. 34.

[2] *New York State Penal Law,* Article 2, Sec. 65.00.

[3] Dawson, p. 72.

[4] ABA, pp. 2–3.

secutor, and/or the probation department.[5] The geographic area where the court is situated may also affect the granting of probation. When court calendars are crowded, as they are in most urban areas, plea bargaining is more likely to result in probation being granted. The judge's feelings toward the particular offense or the offender may also enter into the sentencing decision. The many factors which decide if a defendant is granted probation contribute to the continuing controversy over "differential punishment."

However, there are factors which, to a greater or lesser extent, are considered in all cases relative to the granting of probation: the age and rehabilitation potential of the defendant; the defendant's criminal record, including indications of professional criminality and crimes of violence; the defendant's relationship with his or her family; evidence of any deviant behavior such as drug abuse or sex offenses; and the attitude of the community toward the particular offense and the particular offender. There are also other questions which may be considered in determining whether or not probation is granted. Does the defendant's attitude toward the offense indicate genuine remorse? Was probation promised to the defendant in order to induce him to plead guilty? Will being placed on probation enable the defendant to provide the victim with restitution? Will being placed on probation enable the defendant to provide support and care for his or her family?[6]

The quality of service provided by a probation agency must also be considered by the trial judge. Unfortunately, in some jurisdictions probation is nothing more than a suspending of sentence, since little or no supervision is actually provided.

The ABA presents the advantages of probation rather than imprisonment:

1. The liberty of the individual is maximized by such a sentence; at the same time the authority of the law is vindicated and the public effectively protected from further violations of the law.

2. The rehabilitation of the offender is affirmatively promoted by continuing normal community contacts.

3. The negative and frequently stultifying effects of confinement are avoided, thus removing a factor that often complicates the reintegration of the offender into the community.

[5] Dawson, p. 76.

[6] *Ibid.*, pp. 79–99.

4. The financial costs of crime control to the public treasury are greatly reduced by reliance on probation as an important part of the correctional system.[7]

5. Probation minimizes the impact on innocent dependents of the offender.[8]

The ABA sets three conditions for a sentence of imprisonment rather than probation:

1. When confinement is necessary to protect the public from further criminal activity by the defendant.
2. When the offender is in need of correctional treatment which can effectively be provided if he is confined.
3. When the seriousness of the offense would be unduly depreciated if a sentence of probation were imposed.[9]

CONDITIONS OF PROBATION

Although the President's Commission observed that "Differential treatment requires that the rules be tailored to the needs of the case and of the individual offender,"[10] this suggestion is often not put into practice. Probation departments require a defendant to sign a standard form which usually contains a variety of regulations that may or may not reflect the client's individual needs. There are also special conditions that can be imposed by the judge or the probation department, such as fines and restitution. When a fine or restitution is beyond the ability of a defendant to pay, it may severely handicap the supervision process.

Sutherland and Cressey caution that when conditions of probation are too restrictive, the probation officer is inclined to overlook their violation. This can result in the probation officer losing the respect of the probationer.[11] The ABA recommends that the conditions of probation be spelled-out by the court at the time of sentencing, and em-

[7] Imprisonment costs from ten to thirteen times as much as probation, according to most estimates.

[8] ABA, pp. 3–4.

[9] *Ibid.*

[10] *Task Force Report,* p. 34.

[11] Edwin Sutherland and Donald R. Cressey, *Principles of Criminology* (New York: Lippincott Co., 1966), p. 488.

phasizes that they should be appropriate for the offender.[12] However, probation regulations in different probation agencies tend to be markedly similar. They exhort the probationer to live a law-abiding and productive life, to work, and to support his or her dependents. They require that the offender inform the probation officer of his or her residence and that permission be secured before leaving the jurisdiction of the court. Some require that the probationer obtain permission before getting married, applying for a motor vehicle license, or contracting any indebtedness.

The *New York State Penal Law* enumerates some of the conditions of probation that a court may impose:

1. Avoid injurious or vicious habits
2. Refraining from frequenting unlawful or disreputable places or consorting with disreputable persons
3. Work faithfully at a suitable employment or faithfully pursue a course of study or vocational training that will equip him for suitable employment
4. Undergo available medical or psychiatric treatment and remain in a specified institution, when required for that purpose
5. Support his dependents and meet other family responsibilities
6. Make restitution of the fruits of his offense or make reparation, in an amount he can afford to pay, for the loss or damage therby. When restitution is a condition of the sentence, the court shall fix the amount thereof and the manner of payment
7. Satisfy any other conditions reasonably related to his rehabilitation

The *New York State Penal Law* also enumerates conditions relating to supervision:

1. Report to a probation officer as directed by the court or the probation officer and permit the probation officer to visit him at his place of abode or elsewhere
2. Remain within the jurisdiction of the court unless granted permission to leave by the court or the probation officer
3. Answer all reasonable inquiries by the probation officer and

[12] ABA, p. 9.

promptly notify the probation officer of any change in address or employment[13]

In juvenile cases the conditions of probation usually include such items as "obedience of the child to his parents, regular attendance at school, being home at an early hour in the evening, and avoiding disreputable companions and places."[14]

Fifth Judicial District Department of Court Services
Terms and Conditions of Probation[15]

Probation Number ______
Division Sentence ______

TO WHOM THESE PRESENTS BRING:

I, ______________________________, having been granted (probation) (deferred sentence) on the ______ day of ___________, 19______, by the District Court, Polk County, Iowa for the offense of _______________ for which the Court allowed me supervision under the authority of the Department of Court Services. If sentence was deferred, the Court further ordered that I be returned to the above named Court for further disposition on the ______ day of ___________ 19______.

I do hereby agree to abide by the following terms and conditions as set forth by the Court and Department of Court Services:

---

1. I will secure and maintain lawful employment as approved by my Probation Officer and I agree to contact same, within twenty-four (24) hours, if I lose such employment.
2. I will support my dependents and fulfill all my financial obligations to the best of my ability.
3. I will obey all laws and conduct myself honestly and responsibly in my associations with others.
4. I will reside in Polk County, State of Iowa unless otherwise granted permission by my Probation Officer.

[13] *New York State Penal Law*, Article 2, Sec. 65.10.

[14] Ruth Shonle Cavan, *Juvenile Delinquency* (New York: Lippincott Co., 1969), p. 441.

[15] From the Law Enforcement Assistance Administration.

5. I shall secure from my Probation Officer written and/or oral permission before:

a. changing employment
b. borrowing money, going into debt, or buying on credit
c. opening or using a checking account
d. traveling outside my county of residence
f. purchasing or operating a motor vehicle which shall be adequately covered by liability insurance
g. changing place of residence

6. I will contact my Probation Officer as frequently as he may direct, by oral/or written report.

7. I will not own, possess, carry or use a firearm or weapon of any kind.

8. I agree:

a. to (completely abstain from) (limit) the use of alcoholic beverages
b. to completely abstain from use of narcotic drugs, stimulants, hallucinogenics, or marijuana, except those prescribed to me by a licensed physician
c. that upon request of my Probation Officer, I will submit to Toxicology testing
d. to contact my Probation Officer immediately if I have any contact with Law Enforcement authorities
e. that any information I have under my control, I will make available to my Probation Officer

9. I expressly agree and consent that should I leave the State of Iowa and be arrested in another state, I do hereby waive extradition to the State of Iowa from any state in which I may be found, and also agree that I will not contest any efforts by any jurisdiction to return me to the State of Iowa.

10. Special conditions:

____

____

____

11. I understand that I am under the Supervision of the Fifth Judicial District Department of Court Services, and that any violation, of the above conditions, may be cause for a Report of

Violation to be submitted to the Court which could lead to revocation of my probation privileges.

I hereby certify that I have had read to me the above stipulations, and I agree to co-operate fully with this Agreement until discharge by the Court. I further certify that I have received a copy of the Probation Agreement.

Signed and witnessed this _____ day of __________, 19 _____.

_______________________ _______________________

Intake Agent Signature

____

Supervising Agent

LENGTH OF SUPERVISION

The length of probation terms vary from state to state. The ABA recommends that the term should be two years for a misdemeanor conviction and five years for a felony conviction.[16] Some states allow for the termination of probation prior to the end of the term, allowing the judge some needed flexibility since it is difficult to determine, at the time of sentencing, how long the term should be.[17] A number of states authorize early termination of probation without actually having statutory guidelines as to when it is to be exercised. A larger number have specific guidelines or procedures for termination.[18] New York statutes allow for early termination except for conviction for a Class III felony, for which life-time probation is mandated.[19] In juvenile cases most jurisdictions provide for early termination by the judge upon a recommendation from the probation officer.[20]

Alexander Rheiner notes that "Excessively long periods of probation appear to have little value. By far the most violations occur within the first year of probation." [21] Probation officers in New York City report that they have a high early termination rate as a result of the need to

[16] ABA, p. 3.

[17] Carter and Wilkins, p. 172.

[18] ABA, p. 3.

[19] *New York State Penal Law,* Article 2, Sec. 65.00.

[20] Cavan, p. 442.

[21] Rheiner quoted from Carter and Wilkins, *Probation and Parole,* p. 170.

keep caseloads down. Information from other jurisdictions in other states indicates that this is not an unusual situation.[22] This means that probationers may be discharged even though they should remain under supervision. Sutherland and Cressey point out that "Some individuals can get along satisfactorily in the community as long as they have the supervision and guidance of a probation officer, but return to crime if that assistance is withdrawn too soon." [23]

PROBATION VIOLATION

When any of the conditions of probation have been violated, there exists a "technical violation." When a violation involves a new crime, it is a non-technical or new arrest violation. The probation agency response to a violation is a matter of discretion, and this discretion has been subjected to criticism. Czajkoski maintains that technical violations are often ignored by probation agencies until it is believed that the probationer has committed a new crime. "Invoking the technical violation thus becomes the result of the probation officer making the adjudication that a crime has been committed. The probationer has a hearing on the technical violation, but is denied a trial on the suspected crime which triggered the technical violation." [24]

The revocation process originates with the probation officer, and he exercises what Czajkoski refers to as a "quasi-judicial role" in that he decides whether or not to seek revocation. The probation officer's attitude toward the probationer and the violation will influence whether or not revocation action is initiated. The probation officer will usually confer with his superiors and, if the violation is considered serious enough, a notice of violation will be filed with the court. The case will then be placed on the court calendar, and the probationer will be given a copy of the alleged violations and directed to appear in court for a preliminary hearing.

Preliminary Hearing

The following flow chart indicates the possibilities presented at each stage of the probation revocation process. At the preliminary hearing the probationer can deny the charges of probation violation or plead

[22] Personal interviews with probation staff throughout the country.

[23] Sutherland and Cressey, p. 488.

[24] Czajkoski, pp. 11–13.

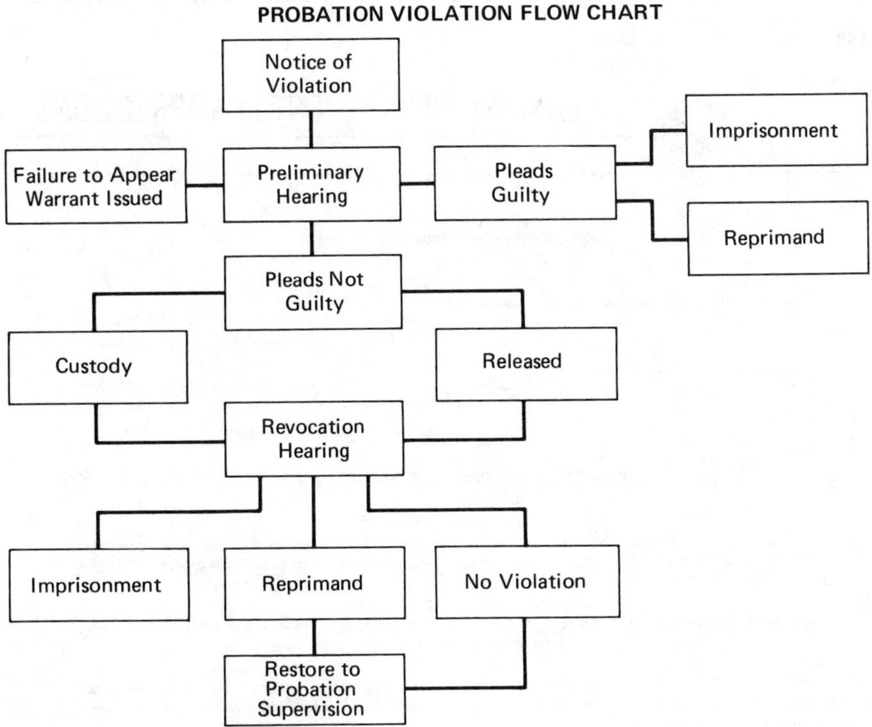

guilty to them. If the plea is guilty the judge may deal with the case at once. If the probationer denies the charges a revocation hearing is scheduled. The judge may remand the probationer to custody pending the hearing, or can release him on bail or on his own recognizance. The probation department will subsequently prepare a full violation of probation report detailing the charges and providing a summary of the probationer's adjustment to supervision. This report is presented to the judge prior to the revocation hearing.

Revocation Hearing

At the revocation hearing the probationer will have an opportunity to testify and present witnesses. There may be an attorney present to represent him or her (according to the provisions outlined in the "Gagnon" and "Mempa" decisions in Chapter 6). A representative of the probation department will also be present. If the judge finds no violations, the probationer is restored to supervision. If the judge sustains any of the charges brought by the probation officer, the probationer can be reprimanded and restored to supervision, or the

DF–6

LOUISIANA DEPARTMENT of CORRECTIONS

NOTICE OF PRELIMINARY HEARING

TO: ____________________

LSP NO.: ____________________ DATE: ____________________

DOCKET NO.: ____________________

SECTION I

RIGHTS OF THE PAROLEE/PROBATIONER

An alleged violator shall be afforded a preliminary hearing conducted by an independent hearing officer, to determine if there is probable cause to believe there has been a violation of the conditions of his parole/probation.

The alleged violator shall be given written notice as to the time and place of the preliminary hearing and the specific violation (s) he is alleged to have committed.

The alleged violator shall have the right to be represented by retained counsel, to speak in his own behalf, and/or bring documents or individuals who can give relevant information to the hearing officer.

The offender shall have the right to cross-examine adverse witnesses unless the hearing officer determines that this would subject them to risk or harm.

If an alleged parole/probation violator is indigent and unable to employ counsel, he has the right to request appointed counsel to represent him at the preliminary hearing. If such a request is made, the offender's eligibility for appointed counsel shall be made in compliance with the Supreme Court's Guidelines.

The preliminary hearing will be held as soon as possible after the arrest and detention of an alleged violator. The preliminary hearing is for the resolution of factual, not legal issues. Legal issues may, of coure, be dealt with in other forums.

Based on the information before him, the hearing officer should determine if there is probable cause to hold the offender for the final decision of the Parole Board/Court on a revocation. The hearing officer shall make a summary, or digest indicating the reasons for his decision and the evidence on which it was based.

The alleged violator shall be given a written copy of the hearing officer's decision and a summary of the proceedings.

If held more than sixty (60) days on a violation detainer, the alleged violator has a right to a revocation hearing before the board/court on his written request.

probation can be revoked and imprisonment ordered. In some probation cases the defendant is actually sentenced at the time of conviction, but the imposition of sentence is suspended in favor of probation. In other cases, the defendant is placed directly on probation without being sentenced. In the latter case, if a violation is sustained, the judge can revoke probation and sentence the probationer to a term of imprisonment. The sentence, however, must be in accordance with the penalty provided by law for the crime for which the probationer was originally convicted.

Probation violation procedures may vary slightly in different jurisdictions. They are also being subjected to new court tests which may result in revisions. However, the basic method will probably remain relatively stable as compared to parole violation procedures, which are in a state of flux.

One question which varies from state-to-state is the matter of "street time." Some jurisdictions credit a probation violator with the time spent under supervision, while others do not. The following table gives a state-by-state breakdown. For a full discussion of "street time" turn to page 190.

Credit for "Street Time"—Probation*

Alabama	No	Montana	Yes
Alaska	No	Nebraska	No
Arizona	No	Nevada	No
Arkansas	No	New Hampshire	Discretionary
California	No	New Jersey	No
Colorado	No	New Mexico	Yes
Connecticut	Yes	New York	No
Delaware	No	North Carolina	No
District of Columbia	No	North Dakota	No
Florida	No	Ohio	No
Georgia	Yes	Oklahoma	No
Hawaii	No	Oregon	No
Idaho	No	Pennsylvania	No
Illinois	Yes	Rhode Island	Discretionary
Indiana	No	South Carolina	No
Iowa	No	South Dakota	Discretionary
Kansas	In part	Tennessee	No
Kentucky	No	Texas	No
Louisiana	In part	Utah	Discretionary
Maine	No	Vermont	No
Maryland	No	Virginia	No
Massachusetts	No	Washington	Yes
Michigan	No	West Virginia	No
Minnesota	No	Wisconsin	No
Mississippi	No	Wyoming	No
Missouri	Discretionary	Federal	No

**Source:* Richard C. Hand and Richard G. Singer, *Sentencing Computation Laws and Practice: A Preliminary Survey* (Washington, D.C.: American Bar Association, 1974).

Chapter 6

Legal Decisions Affecting Probation

Legal decisions that affect probation usually affect parole also and *vice versa.* However, for purposes of study the significant legal decisions in probation and parole have been divided according to the primary thrust of the case.

THREE THEORIES OF PROBATION

Traditionally an individual on probation has not been considered a free man, despite the fact that he is not incarcerated. The basis for imposing restrictions on his freedom is contained in three theories:

1. GRACE Theory—probation is a conditional privilege, an act of mercy by the judge. If any condition of this privilege is violated, then it can be revoked.
2. CONTRACT Theory—the probationer signs a stipulation agreeing to certain terms in return for conditional freedom. As in any contractual situation, a breach of contract can result in penalties, in this case revocation of probation.

3. CUSTODY Theory—the probationer is in the legal custody of the court and is thus a quasi-prisoner with his or her constitutional rights being limited accordingly.

The legal decisions that are discussed in this chapter often challenge the above theories.[1]

The legal decisions discussed here and in Chapter 11 should be viewed within their historical context. In 1966, the United States Supreme Court rendered the famous *Miranda Decision*[2] which mandated that accused criminals be informed of certain rights (to remain silent, to have counsel). In 1967, in another Arizona case, the Supreme Court rendered the *Gault Decision* which gave certain rights to juveniles. In that same year came the *Mempa Decision*, which gave probationers the right to have counsel in certain instances of probation violation. Five years later, the Court continued to show an "interest" in the rights of certain "status" persons (juveniles, probationers, welfare recipients, the mentally ill) when it handed down the *Morrissey Decision*. The following year, 1973, the Court handed down the *Gagnon Decision*.

Juvenile Court—In Re Gault, *387, U.S. 1, S. Ct. (1967)*

The primary result of the *Gault Decision* was to provide juveniles with procedural safeguards in the juvenile court. Since the juvenile court is a "treatment" court, in which the treatment professional is the probation officer, the decision had a significant impact on probation practice in that court.

Gerald Gault, age 15, was on probation in Arizona. On the basis of a verbal complaint that he had made an obscene phone call, he was arrested by the police. Gerald was held in the Children's Detention Home, which is run by the probation department. The probation officer filed a petition and a hearing was scheduled in juvenile court for the following day. No copy of the petition or the charges contained therein was given to Gerald or his parents. At the hearing Gerald's mother and two probation officers appeared before a juvenile court judge in the judge's chambers. No one was sworn and no transcript was made of the proceedings. Following this hearing Gerald was held in detention for several more days and then released to his parents with a

[1] *See* H. Richmond Fisher, "Probation and Parole Revocation: The Anomaly of Divergent Procedures," *Federal Probation* (Sept. 1974), pp. 23–29.

[2] *Miranda v. Arizona*, 384, U.S. 436, S. Ct. (1966).

note from the probation officer stating that another hearing had been scheduled.

At the second hearing there was conflict over what transpired at the first hearing. For the second time the complainant was not present. The judge ruled that her presence was not necessary. At the conclusion of the hearing, Gerald was committed to the State Industrial School as a juvenile delinquent. Arizona law did not permit any appeal in juvenile cases. However, on a writ of *habeas corpus*, the case made its way up to the United States Supreme Court.

The Supreme Court ruled that Gerald had been denied due process of law. The Court ordered that in juvenile cases the respondent (equivalent to the defendant in adult cases) is entitled to:

1. written notice of charges
2. right to counsel
3. right to confront and cross-examine witnesses
4. privilege against self-incrimination

Presentence Report—Williams v. New York, *337 U.S. 241, 69 S. Ct (1949)*

Williams was convicted of murder and the jury recommended life imprisonment. However the judge, based on the presentence report, imposed the death sentence. The presentence report revealed that the defendant was a suspect in thirty burglaries. While the defendant had not been convicted of these crimes, the report indicated that he had confessed to some and had been identified as the perpetrator of some of the others. The judge also referred to parts of the report which indicated the defendant was "a menace to society."

Williams appealed the death sentence, arguing that the sentencing procedure violated due process of law "in that the sentence of death was based upon information supplied by witnesses with whom the accused had not been confronted and as to whom he had no opportunity for cross-examination or rebuttal." The court rejected this argument, stating: "Under the practice of individualizing punishments, investigational techniques have been given an important role. Probation workers making reports of their investigations have not been trained to prosecute but to aid offenders. Their reports have been given a high value by conscientious judges who want to sentence persons on the best available information rather than on guesswork and inadequate information. To deprive sentencing judges of this kind of information would undermine modern procedural policies that have been cautiously adopted throughout the nation after careful consideration and experimentation. We must recognize that most of the information now relied upon by judges to guide them in the intelligent imposition of sentences would be unavailable if information were restricted to that given in open court by witnesses subject to cross-examination. And the modern probation report draws on information concerning every aspect of a defendant's life. The types and extent of this information make totally impractical if not impossible open court testimony with cross-examination. Such a procedure could endlessly delay criminal administration in a re-trial of collateral issues."

A recent New York decision which cited *Williams v. New York* upheld the right of a trial judge to deny the defense attorney an opportunity to review the presentence report. The New York Appeals Court in this case rejected the argument that the refusal to disclose the presentence report violated due process. However, the court did note "the trend favoring disclosure." [3]

Probation Revocation—Mempa v. Rhay, *389 U.S. 128, 88 S. Ct. (1967)*

Mempa was convicted of "joy-riding" in a stolen car and placed on probation for two years. Four months later Mempa's probation was revoked on the ground that he had been involved in a burglary. A court hearing was held several weeks later during which the probation officer was the sole prosecution witness. The probationer was not represented by counsel, nor was he asked if he wished to have counsel appointed for him. Probation was revoked and a ten year sentence imposed. Mempa appealed on the grounds that he was entitled to counsel at his revocation hearing. His petition was denied, and it worked its way up the appeals process to the United States Supreme Court.

The Supreme Court ruled that some rights could be lost if counsel were not present at a probation revocation hearing. It was noted that counsel can aid in "marshalling facts." The Court further stated that counsel is required "at every stage of a criminal proceeding where substantial rights of a criminal accused may be affected." Sentencing is a critical stage of the criminal procedure and since Mempa was sentenced at his revocation hearing, he was entitled to an attorney.

[3] Court of Appeals, "Criminal Law-Presentence Report-Disclosure Refused," *New York Law Journal* (Mar. 3, 1975), p. 1.

Probation Revocation—Gagnon v. Scarpelli, *411 U.S. 778, 93 S. Ct. (1973)*

Scarpelli pleaded guilty to armed robbery in Wisconsin and was sentenced to fifteen years imprisonment, but the sentence was suspended and he was placed on probation for seven years.

He was given permission to reside in Illinois under the Interstate Compact (discussed in Chapter 17). Shortly thereafter he was arrested with a codefendant while burglarizing a house in Illinois. Probation was revoked by Wisconsin without a hearing, and Scarpelli was incarcerated in a state reformatory to serve the original fifteen year sentence.

Three years later, although already on parole from the reformatory, Scarpelli appealed on the basis that probation revocation without a hearing and counsel is a denial of due process. The case eventually reached the United States Supreme Court. The Court denied the need for counsel in this case because Scarpelli already had counsel when he was sentenced to fifteen years, although at that time the imposition of sentence was suspended in favor of probation. However, the Court, citing guidelines established in *Morrissey v. Brewer* (see parole legal decisions in Chapter 11), held that the probationer is entitled to a notice of the alleged violations, a preliminary hearing to decide if there is sufficient cause to believe that probation was violated (in order to remand the probationer to custody), and a revocation hearing which is "a somewhat more comprehensive hearing prior to the making of the final revocation decision."

The Court stated that at these hearings the probationer will have the opportunity to appear and present witnesses and evidence in his own behalf, and a conditional right to confront adverse witnesses. The Court determined that:

> Probation revocation, like parole revocation, is not a stage of a criminal prosecution, but does result in loss of liberty. Accordingly, we hold that a probationer, like a parolee, is entitled to a preliminary hearing and a final revocation hearing in the conditions specified in *Morrissey v. Brewer.*

The Court indicated that under certain circumstances relating to the peculiarities of a particular case, counsel must be provided for probationers and parolees at their preliminary and revocation hearings. The court set up the following criteria:

> . . . Counsel should be provided in cases where, after being informed of his right to request counsel the probationer or parolee makes such a request based on a timely or colorable claim:
>
> (i) that he has not committed the alleged violation of the conditions upon which he is at liberty or
>
> (ii) that, even if the violation is a matter of public record or is uncontested, there are substantial reasons which justified or mitigated the violation and made revocation inappropriate and that the reasons are complex or otherwise difficult to develop or present.

The court went on to note:

> In passing on a request for the appointment of counsel, the responsible agency also should consider, especially in doubtful cases, whether the probationer appears to be capable of speaking effectively for himself. In every case in which a request for counsel at a preliminary or final hearing is refused the grounds for refusal should be stated succinctly and for the record.

It should be noted that the United States Supreme Court, by setting up some sort of criteria for right of counsel, was attempting to stem the tide of litigation on this very point.

PART ONE—DISCUSSION TOPICS

1. Compare the historical antecedents of probation to current probation practices.
2. Analyze the different court systems used in the United States.
3. Examine the problem of plea bargaining and provide alternatives to its use.
4. Explore the problem of sentence disparity.
5. Compare the different options available for the administration of probation.
6. Discuss the concept of *parens patriae*.
7. Explore alternatives to the juvenile court.
8. Compare procedures in the juvenile court with those of the adult criminal court.
9. Compare the predisposition report to the presentence report.

10. Defend or criticize juvenile court jurisdiction over status offenses.

11. Account for the apparent lack of success of most juvenile institutional programs.

12. Discuss improvements that have been suggested for raising the quality of juvenile court judges.

13. Examine the type of education and experience that is relevant for being able to write a presentence report.

14. Analyze the criticisms of the presentence report.

15. Discuss the question of confidentiality of the presentence report.

16. Discuss the criteria that should be used in considering the granting of probation.

17. Examine the conditions of probation, and draft a "model" set of conditions.

18. Compare the *Gault Decision* to the *Gagnon Decision*.

19. Discuss the concept of "street time" in probation.

PART TWO

Parole History and Administration

PARALLEL SERVICES

Probation	Parole
Presentence Report	Pre-parole Report
Court	Board
Probation Supervision	Parole Supervision

Chapter 7

Prisons

The old system was designed to make good inmates. The new penology is designed to make inmates ready for re-entry to society.*

Just as a study of probation requires some knowledge of the courts, a study of parole requires some knowledge of prisons. In this chapter the author will be referring to institutions of imprisonment by their traditional name, rather than by the more modern euphemism, "correctional institutions."

ORIGINS OF THE AMERICAN PRISON SYSTEM

The use of imprisonment rather than corporal punishment and execution is the result of the influence of classical philosophers of the 18th century, particularly Beccaria.[1] Despite its European philosophical origins, the extensive use of prisons as places of confinement (as opposed to detention) is uniquely American.[2] However, prisons built

* Benjamin Ward, New York State Commissioner of Correctional Services, quoted in the *New York Times*, April 19, 1975.

[1] Thorston Sellin, "A Look At Prison History," *Federal Probation* (Sept. 1967), p. 19.

[2] Jessica Mitford, *Kind and Usual Punishment* (New York: Alfred A. Knopf, 1973), p. 30.

in the United States did inherit the European philosophy of penal servitude, requiring inmates to perform labor of the "most harsh and servile kind." [3]

The early places of imprisonment ranged from large wooden houses in cities, where escapes were common, to abandoned mines, such as the one used by Connecticut in 1790. These early prisons were places for punishment and not rehabilitation, although they were considered a humane improvement over whippings and hangings.[4]

Walnut Street Jail

The Walnut Street Jail in Philadelphia was built as the result of efforts by Quaker reformers in Pennsylvania. Construction began before the Revolution, and in 1790 the jail began receiving felons from all parts of the state. Walnut Street featured a Bible, hard work, and isolation for each inmate. A convict was blindfolded upon arrival and remained in his cell until released, at which time he was blindfolded again. He never saw another inmate. In this manner he was saved from the corrupting influence of his peers while he concentrated on studying in his cell. It was believed that through this system a criminal would learn faith and the good habits of work and moderation.[5] However, many went mad and died as a result of their solitary confinement.[6]

Many firsts occurred here, including several historic events, as well as innovations in the prison system. The Walnut Street Jail provided for a rudimentary classification system, including segregation of the sexes, separation of debtors and witnesses from felons, and a special cell block known as the "penitentiary house." for hard-core criminals. From the main yard of this jail a balloonist was given the first "air-mail" letter by George Washington. In 1793, when the agent (warden) died of yellow fever, Mrs. Mary Weed, his widow, became the first woman prison administrator in the United States, remaining in the position until 1800.[7]

While the system attracted scholars from abroad, its poor architec-

[3] Sellin, p. 21.

[4] New York State Special Commission on Attica, *Attica* (New York: Praeger Publishers, 1972), p. 7.

[5] W. David Lewis, *From Newgate to Dannemora* (Ithaca, N.Y.: Cornell University Press, 1965), pp. 2–3.

[6] Mitford, p. 31.

[7] Carney, Introduction to Correctional Science, p. 82.

ture, overcrowding, and lack of productive work led to its eventual demise.[8]

Newgate

Thomas Eddy (1758–1827), a Tory who was briefly imprisoned during the Revolution, became interested in prisons through his own experience as a prisoner. Eddy was influenced by the Quaker prison in Pennsylvania and the Classical philosophers. In 1796 he accomplished the building of New York's first penitentiary, located in Greenwich Village. It was named after the famous English penal institution, Newgate, and Eddy became its first agent. Consistent with the prevailing belief of prison reformers of that day, Eddy maintained that the goal of deterrence required inflicting pain on criminal offenders.[9]

While there was a great deal of similarity between the Walnut Street Jail and Newgate, the latter, unlike Walnut Street, was constructed for felons and did not have accommodations for vagrants, witnesses, and debtors. Eddy also discarded the idea that it was necessary to keep inmates in solitary all day. Instead, convicts slept in apartments measuring 12 feet x 18 feet and housing eight inmates.

Eddy encouraged religious worship, established a night school, and approved of provisions in the law which prohibited corporal punishment at Newgate. Despite improvements in treatment at the prison, Newgate experienced several riots. Eddy was eventually removed because of political considerations, and politics was to continue to have an unsettling effect on Newgate.[10]

When difficulties increased at Newgate, a return to flogging was legislated in 1819.[11] In 1828, Newgate was abandoned in favor of a newly completed prison at Sing Sing.[12]

Pennsylvania After Walnut Street

After the demise of Walnut Street, reformers were successful in having two penitentiaries built, Western in Pittsburgh, 1826, and Eastern in Philadelphia, 1829. Hard labor was enforced and the policy of

[8] *Ibid.*

[9] Lewis, pp. 4–6.

[10] *Ibid.*, pp. 30–37.

[11] *Ibid.*, p. 46.

[12] Department of Correctional Services, *Corrections in New York State* (Albany: New York State Department of Correctional Services, 1970), p. 9.

solitary confinement was retained. Each cell had a private exercise yard, and the inmate slept and worked in his cell without any contact with other prisoners.[13]

AUBURN PRISON

The next great milestone in American prison history is Auburn Prison, which became the world's most frequently copied prison. Designed by its first agent, William Brittin, it featured a center that was comprised of tiers of cell blocks surrounded by a vacant area, with a high wall around the entire institution. The cells measured seven by three and one-half feet and were seven feet high.

As a result of an increase in prison discipline problems in New York, it was decided to divide Auburn's inmates into three classes. The most hardened inmates were placed in solitary; a less dangerous group spent part of the day in solitude and the rest of the time working in groups; and the "least guilty" worked together all day and were separated only at night. It was obvious that the Auburn officials had failed to learn from past experiences with solitary confinement. Inmates in the first group jumped off tiers, cut their veins, and smashed their heads against walls; over half of the deaths in the first year were among persons in solitary. As a result, solitary confinement was discontinued except as punishment for violations of prison rules.[14]

With solitary confinement abandoned, a new system that would become world-famous was instituted at Auburn. Inmates left their cells each day and worked together in "congregate style." However, total silence was strictly enforced. (Prisoners weren't even allowed to communicate with their families except through the prison chaplain.) Inmates had a common dining area and a common work area, and they ate and worked in complete silence. The Auburn system was an unrelenting routine of hard work, moderate meals and solitary evenings in individual cells. Inmates were awakened early and marched to work before breakfast. They were marched back and forth from work to breakfast and lunch, and finally marched to dinner and from there back to their cells. They followed this routine six days a week. On Sundays,

[13] Carney, p. 83.

[14] Lewis, pp. 67–70.

when there was no work, they were addressed by the prison chaplain, who stressed the American virtues of simple faith and hard work.[15]

The administrators of Auburn believed that their most important task was the breaking of an inmate's spirit in order to drive him into a state of submission. There was some difference of opinion about what to do after the "breaking" process. One school of thought stressed deterrence as its goal and was determined to derive as much economic benefit as possible from inmate labor. (In fact, in the early days of its existence, Auburn actually made a profit.) Another school of thought held that rehabilitation was the ultimate goal and that, after breaking, an inmate should be helped through education and religion so that he could return to society a better man.[16]

Auburn, which became the prototype for other prisons in the United States, developed the infamous lockstep shuffle, and dressed its inmates in grotesque and ridiculous- looking black and white striped uniforms. For a fee, free citizens could come to the prison and view the inmates, an act that was encouraged in order to further degrade its inhabitants. One of Auburn's most noted administrators, Elam Lynds, was proud of his record of ruling the prison with the lash.

Most American prisons patterned themselves after Auburn. The fortress-like buildings sprouted up throughout the country. They were bleak and silent factories with labor pools of broken people, stressing discipline and silence. Soon, the very punishment that prisons had been created to eliminate became widely used in the institutions themselves, and continued to be used into the 20th century. By the end of the 19th century the concept of rehabilitation had virtually disappeared and prisons were viewed simply as places to keep criminals incarcerated. This was reflected even in the name of the warden's first assistant, the "principal keeper." [17]

The Auburn-style prisons built throughout the country were not without their critics. In 1870, a new generation of prison reformers organized the National Prison Association (NPA). They declared that rehabilitation, not punishment, was the primary goal of prisons. There were scattered efforts made to implement the principles of the NPA. One of the most famous was the founding of the Elmira Reformatory [18] which eventually led to the use of parole in the United States.

[15] N.Y.S. Comm. on Attica, pp. 8–9.

[16] Lewis, p. 84.

[17] N.Y.S. Spec. Comm. on Attica, pp. 10–11.

[18] *Ibid.*, p. 12.

THE TWENTIETH CENTURY

By the turn of the century prison authorities everywhere were turning away from the old silent discipline. Industrial upheaval resulted in opposition, especially by labor unions, to the sale of prison-made goods. New sanitary arrangements, showers and dining halls, as well as outdoor exercise facilities were built. The lockstep, striped uniforms, and the shaved head disappeared. There was separate treatment for the insane and the tubercular. Organized sports were introduced and there was an attempt to "re-create the man in prison." The theory that imprisonment was to be meted out to fit the crime disappeared from the statute books, and the limited rights of the convict and the need to rehabilitate him gradually took its place.

The "new era" of prisons, however, saw reduced work opportunities create idleness, and overcrowding increase while prison discipline decreased. While a new type of official, steeped in sociological and psychological theory, took the place of the old, new problems were also encountered.[19]

MODERN AMERICAN PRISONS

Erik Wright has noted that contemporary American prisons, while maintaining totalitarian control over inmates, have adopted the goal of rehabilitation. Retribution is no longer a formal goal of prisons.[20] However, despite the avowed goal of rehabilitation, approximately 95% of all expenditures in the entire corrections effort is for custody, while only 5% is for health services, education, and vocational training, the mainstays of rehabilitation.[21]

The poor state of the American prison system in the 20th century is reflected in both professional and popular writings. Smith and Fried state that "day-to-day prison conditions are horrid, squalid and inhuman." [22] Karl Menninger describes prisons as "unhealthy, filthy,

[19] See Blake McKelvey, *American Prisons* (Montclair, N.J.: 1972), pp. 219–32.

[20] Erik Olin Wright, *The Politics of Punishment* (New York: Harper and Row, 1973), pp. 152–54.

[21] Ramsey Clark, *Crime in America* (New York: Simon and Schuster, 1970), p. 213.

[22] Joan Smith and William Fried, *The Uses of the American Prison* (Lexington, Mass.: D.C. Heath and Co., 1974), p. 140.

dangerous, immoral, indecent crime-breeding dens of iniquity." [23] In a series on violence in the New York *Daily News*, Kitty Hanson wrote that "the men who come out of our prisons are rarely made better by the system. Most of them come out worse, and often more dangerous." [24] Ed Tromanhauser, one of the convict authors of *An Eye For An Eye*, writes that "While all the talk about rehabilitation goes on and on, the whole system keeps right on doing what it has been doing for a century—demeaning, degrading, dehumanizing, and punishing." [25] This situation is compounded by the fact that the United States uses imprisonment more than any other developed country.[26]

Congressman Herman Badillo of New York maintains that prisons are rife with racism and reports that the situation is intensified by a prison population that is half black while only 8% of correctional workers are black.[27] Another frequently mentioned problem is the lack of adequate vocational training in American prisons, despite the obvious need. Most prisons are located in rural areas, far from the cities that are the homes of most of the inmates. While rural prisons help provide employment for local residents, their location is a hardship for visiting families of prison inmates, and it makes work-release more difficult.

There are a few bright spots. Most states have instituted work-release programs that permit inmates to leave the prison during the day for employment. Many have high school equivalency courses and in a few areas college level courses are available to inmates. Furloughs are available in some jurisdictions, allowing inmates to go home for visits, usually for a week or less. Recent court decisions have helped to curtail the absolute and often arbitrary exercise of authority by prison officials. However, the American Correctional Association states: "The theory of rehabilitation has made some changes in the prison: terminology has changed, there are more programs, sweeping floors is now work therapy: . . . The theory of rehabilitation has merely been imposed upon the theories of punishment and control." [28]

[23] Karl Menninger, *The Crime of Punishment* (New York: Viking Press, 1968), p. 143.

[24] Kitty Hanson, "U.S. Prisons: breeding ground for brutality," *New York Daily News*, March 13, 1975, p. 76.

[25] H. Jack Griswold, Mike Misenheimer, Art Powers, and Ed Tromanhauser, *An Eye For An Eye* (New York: Holt, Rinehart and Winston, 1970), p. 24.

[26] "The Use of Imprisonment," *VIP Examiner*, NCCD, Spring 1975, p. 1.

[27] Herman Badillo and Milton Haynes, *A Bill of No Rights: Attica and the American Prison System* (New York: Outerbridge and Lazard, Inc., 1972), p. 9.

[28] William Parker, *Parole* (College Park, Md.: American Correctional Assoc., 1975), p. 26.

SOCIETY'S FAILURES

Karl Menninger has observed that some prisoners want to be helped and some do not.[29] Russell G. Oswald, former Corrections Commissioner of the State of New York, stated that not all inmates want to improve themselves; "Some do and some do not." [30] Unfortunately, American prisons are usually unable to provide help for those who want it, or to motivate those who do not. As attractive as the goal of rehabilitation sounds, it is not a realistic expectation for many of the inmates of our nation's prisons. Our prisons are inhabited by the most discriminated-against racial, cultural, and economic groups. The prison population is itself a minority of the minorities. New York State provides the picture of a *typical offender:*[31]

> If we were to generalize, we would say that today's offender is between the ages of 16 and 30; that he is likely to be unskilled, a school dropout and that he is inclined to be unrealistically optimistic about his future, despite these deficiencies.
>
> He is more inclined to suspicion of others' motives than is the average, he tends to project blame for his failures on others, but his IQ is usually every bit as high as his counterpart on the street. His unhappy experiences with those in authority from childhood on have left him resentful of anything having the aura of authority; yet he respects, and responds to, directness. He prefers to "hear it like it is," but he is not above deviousness in his dealings with those who can be of use to him.
>
> He has difficulty in forming close and lasting relationships with others and he is much more impressed with actions than with words. He may speak scornfully of the "square world" but chances are he would like to have full membership in it. He has the same need for love, security, and for happiness that we all have and he is prey to the same fears and worries that plague us all. He is capable of change if he can be motivated to desire it and to work for it.
>
> If confined in a New York State correctional facility, he has a history of having had at least two, if not more, previous encounters with the law. He is one of a total of 14,000 offenders incarcerated throughout the State in a variety of facilities ranging from 2,000 bed maximum security high-walled prisons to the 35 bed community-based urban treatment center. If

[29] Menninger, p. 262.

[30] Oswald cited in Leonard Orland and Harold R. Tyler, eds., *Justice In Sentencing* (Mineola, N.Y.: Foundation Press, 1974), p. 142.

[31] Volunteer Service Program Staff, *Guidelines for Volunteers Services* (Albany, N.Y.: N.Y.S. Dept. of Correctional Services, 1974), pp. 17–19.

a new arrival in a State prison, he can anticipate a stay of approximately 22 months (this is of course an average). If the offender is a woman she is one in a total of fewer than 500 incarcerated adults. Male or female, there is a 70% chance that today's offender is black or Puerto Rican, and a 78% chance that he or she was reared in a large urban center where there was little touch with the so called "good life" of American society.

The California Inmate.[32]

About 14 percent of all persons convicted of felonies are sent to state prison. Mainly, these are serious offenders. A large proportion have a prior history of violence.

While their crimes cover the entire range of felony misconduct, most of the men in state prison are sent there by the courts for these offenses—15.5 percent for homicide, 27.4 percent for robbery, 14.5 percent for burglary, 7.5 percent for assault, and 15.4 percent for drug crimes.

About 70 percent of the male inmates were either sent to prison for a crime of violence or have a prior history of violent behavior.

The median age of male inmates is 30.1 years, somewhat lower than in the past. The age median has been declining in recent years. About 24 percent of the male inmates are less than 25 years old.

Nearly half of the men in prison are native Californians. Three-fourths have lived in this state for at least 10 years. A total of 53 percent are minorities—18 percent Mexican, 33 percent Black, and two percent other minorities.

The typical male inmate possesses average intelligence, and the median achievement level for newly received prisoners is just under eighth grade.

Although the median figures for prison time served fluctuate from year to year, a typical California inmate will spend about 36 to 40 months in prison prior to first parole, a period often said to be longer than in most other states. Typically, a California parolee will be in that status from about 20 to 30 months, although great individual variation is possible.

TOTAL INSTITUTIONS

Many of the problems that exist in a prison are characteristic of a "total institution," which Erving Goffman defines as "a place of residence and work where a large number of like-situated individuals, cut

[32] Information from the California Department of Corrections.

off from the wider society for an appreciable period of time, together lead an enclosed, formally administered round of life." [33] Total institutions include mental hospitals, convents, monasteries, boarding schools, and military posts, as well as prisons. They have a tendency to "mold" persons into compliant and often shapeless forms in order to maintain discipline and a sound working order, or for other less utilitarian reasons. Prisons, and other total institutions, provide a dreary uniformity—clothing, sleeping quarters, food, etc. Depersonalization and dehumanization pervade these institutions.

Total institutions encompass much of an inmate's life, and they leave him little room for self-assertion and individual decision-making. Thus, when he leaves the institution he is often ill-prepared for life on the outside. Cut off from the real world, offenders often feel lost upon release. When the trauma of release is more than a parolee is able to tolerate, he may wish to return "home" to prison. A parole officer has to deal with many difficult situations; one of the most difficult, however, is when a client requests to be placed back in prison because he is unable to "make it on the street."

Goffman notes, however, that the impact of total institutions is usually of limited duration; after release, both the negative and positive experiences are soon left behind with no lasting effect. (This raises questions about the theory of *individual deterrence*).

In a review of prison conditions, Morris and Jacobs state that "there is no doubt that the prison population is, for the most part, a more serious offender group than in the past because less serious offenders are selected for such programs" as diversion and probation.[34]

Reasons and Kaplan note that because about two-thirds of most prison populations have been incarcerated before, it is sometimes erroneously concluded that the failure rate is about 70%. However, the authors point out that prisons are continuously receiving their own failures who populate and re-populate the prison and who become disproportionately represented in prison populations.[35] The kind of vigorous studies necessary to determine the extent to which released offenders actually return to prison has not been done, and so Morris and Hawkins caution that "it is unwise to dismiss prisons as complete

[33] Erving Goffman, *Asylums: Essays on the Social Situation of Mental Patients and Other Inmates* (Garden City, N.Y.: Doubleday, 1961), p. xiii.

[34] Norval Morris and James Jacobs, *Proposals for Prison Reform* (New York: Public Affairs Committee, 1974), p. 27.

[35] C. E. Reasons and R. L. Kaplan, "Functions of Prisons," *Crime and Delinquency* (Oct. 1975), p. 365.

failures." [36] Reasons and Kaplan state that studies of commitment rates suggest that about two-thirds of those released from prison do not in fact return.[37]

Vocational Training in Institutions.[38] Prisons have historically stressed the need for inmates to perform work as part of their "rehabilitation." However, prison work was usually of the most servile kind, and did not provide an inmate with useful skills for his post-incarceration adjustment. There was very little vocational training, and where it existed it was usually informal.

> Formal systems of vocational training began to expand in the United States in the late nineteenth century as a response not only to the educational needs of a rapidly growing high school population but also to industrial demand for skilled workers not being met through apprenticeship or immigration. Vocational training in correctional institutions began with the opening of the Elmira Reformatory in 1876.
>
> Vocational training was designed, if not as a substitute for apprenticeship, at least with the same types of crafts or trades in mind. Modern industrial and service jobs are so different from the traditional crafts and trades that it is not surprising that pre-employment classroom training has not been the most successful means of preparing individuals for work.
>
> Recognition that a large proportion of inmates is unskilled has provided the impetus for vocational training in prisons, even though there are serious obstacles in the way of success.
>
> *Extent and Content.* Unfortunately, most estimates of the extent of training lump together formal training courses and informal on-the-job training in prison industries. The latter frequently lack variety and relevance, and while some inmates undoubtedly benefit from the training aspects of their prison employment, it is difficult to assess the effect of such informal training in the aggregate.
>
> The scope of vocational training programs varies, depending on the size and financial capability of the correctional system. The Federal Bureau of Prisons reported that in fiscal 1973 over 5,000 inmates completed vocational training. According to Pownall, training programs in Federal prisons are concentrated in the institutions that have the youngest inmates.[2]

[36] Morris and Hawkins quoted from Benjamin Frank, ed., *Contemorary Corrections* (Reston, Va.: Reston Publishing Co., 1973), p. 106.

[37] Reasons and Kaplan, p. 365.

[38] From Phyllis Groom McCreary and John M. McCreary, *Job Training and Placement for Offenders and Ex-Offenders* (Washington, D.C.: Government Printing Office, 1975), pp. 8–9.

[1] George A. Pownall, *Employment Problems of Released Prisoners* (Washington, D.C.: U.S. Department of Labor, 1969), p. 12.

[2] Pownall, *Employment Problems of Released Prisoners*, p. 12.

A 1972 survey of vocational training in correctional institutions recorded 12,868 trainees enrolled in 855 vocational education programs in state and Federal institutions.[3] This represents less than 10 percent of the 130,800 population of the responding institutions. More than half of the institutions offered five or fewer vocational programs. The most common programs, representing 53 percent of the programs reported, were: auto mechanics, arc and acetylene welding, machine shop, masonry, radio and TV repair, auto body repair, carpentry, barbering, baking and cooking, architectural and mechanical drafting, air conditioning and refrigeration, and small engine repair.

Evaluation of vocational training in institutions has been confined for the most part to informal observation, but Far West Laboratory recently sifted reports on 1,000 programs and came up with only 66 that the staff considered were effective enough to be described in their Sourcebook.[4] They found that a traditional mixture of classroom chalk-and-talk and shop-area experience in manipulating tools of the trade are the most common methods used in institutional training. Some demonstration and pilot programs are using innovative approaches.

Frequently, courses are tied to prison maintenance, either because it is necessary in order to run the institution, or because it is the only feasible way to obtain the materials and experience needed for the course. The danger is that priorities may become confused as the administration of the institution begins to view the course as existing primarily to provide food services, barbering, upholstery of prison furniture, or repair of institution vehicles.[5] Often a reverse process takes place, with institutional maintenance courses evolving into vocational training programs, which may or may not have relevance to the job market the offender will face or to his training preferences.

Enrollment in a single vocational program ranged from one trainee to 102 trainees, according to the 1972 survey. Sixty-eight percent had 6 hours or more instruction time a day. Seventeen percent had between 3 and 4 hours of instruction time. Over half of the vocational programs included 1 to 2 hours of related instruction a day in such matters as theory or related mathematics.

[3] Donald Richard Neff, "Summary, Conclusions and Recommendations of Vocational Education in State and Federal Adult Correctional Institutions in the United States" (from a doctoral research study, August, 1972).

There were 202 institutions that responded. This number represents 77.6 percent of those institutions which were contacted (Federal, state and local with over 100 male inmates and all those housing women). Texas and South Carolina provided division-wide responses that included all of the correctional institutions' vocational education programs for their respective states.

[4] *A Guide to Correctional Vocational Training: The First National Sourcebook,* July 1973, produced by New England Resource Center for Occupational Education, Newton, Massachusetts, and Far West Laboratory for Educational Research and Development, San Francisco, California.

[5] The continual struggle to keep training schedules from being washed away by production needs is reminiscent of the same struggle recounted by training directors in industry.

The most common length of vocational programs was 1 year, the next common was 6 months. Three-fourths of the programs were of the open entry/open exit type.

The teacher-trainee ratio was one teacher for every 12 trainees. There were 1,044 civilian teachers and 134 inmate teachers. Over 80 percent of the civilian teachers held vocational teaching certificates from their state.

Vocational education personnel had some responsibility for the selection and screening of the trainee for vocational programs in 93 percent of the responding institutions.

Seventy-four or 40 percent of the 185 institutions included in the survey had funds budgeted specifically for vocational education. Sixty-four percent of all the vocational programs were sponsored directly by the institution. Thirty-six percent of the programs were funded by outside sources.

A little more than half of the institutions with programs reported some form of job placement connected with their vocational education programs. This is in most cases extremely informal and likely to be haphazard.[6]

Criticism of Inmate Training. Criticism of inmate vocational training has been harsh. "In isolated settings, divorced from labor markets, working with second-rate materials and a highly disadvantaged clientele, vocational training alone seems to have minimal impact." [7] On the other hand, Wellford does say, ". . . for the minority who gain skills in prison at which they can find a post-release vocation, prison work experience and training is a major rehabilitative influence." [8]

A member of the Bureau of Prisons staff says that it is becoming increasingly difficult to provide meaningful vocational and industrial education inside a correctional facility.[9] She confirms that much of the training, whether under the guise of on-the-job training in institutional maintenance or prison industries, or whether in vocational training shops and in related classroom instruction, uses obsolete equipment and production standards that are much lower than those in private industry. As a result, she concludes that most prison occupational training programs have been ineffective in terms of preparation for specific post release employment.

[6] In one state institution for women visited for the research on this project, the two vocational counselors had no idea how many women had a job when they left the institution and no statistics were available. Interviews with corrections authorities indicate that this lack of basic information is common.

[7] Robert Taggart III, *The Prison of Unemployment, Manpower Programs for Offenders.* Policy Studies in Employment and Welfare 14, Gen'l. ed.: Sar A. Levitan and Garth L. Mangum, Baltimore and London: The Johns Hopkins University Press, 1972, p. 49.

[8] Charles Wellford, "Manpower and Recidivism," in *Proceedings: The National Workshop of Corrections and Parole Administration* (New Orleans: American Correctional Association, 1972), pp. 113–120.

[9] Sylvia G. McCollum, *The Potential of New Educational Delivery Systems for Correctional Treatment,* A Correctional Education Handbook, April 1973, pp. 7–8.

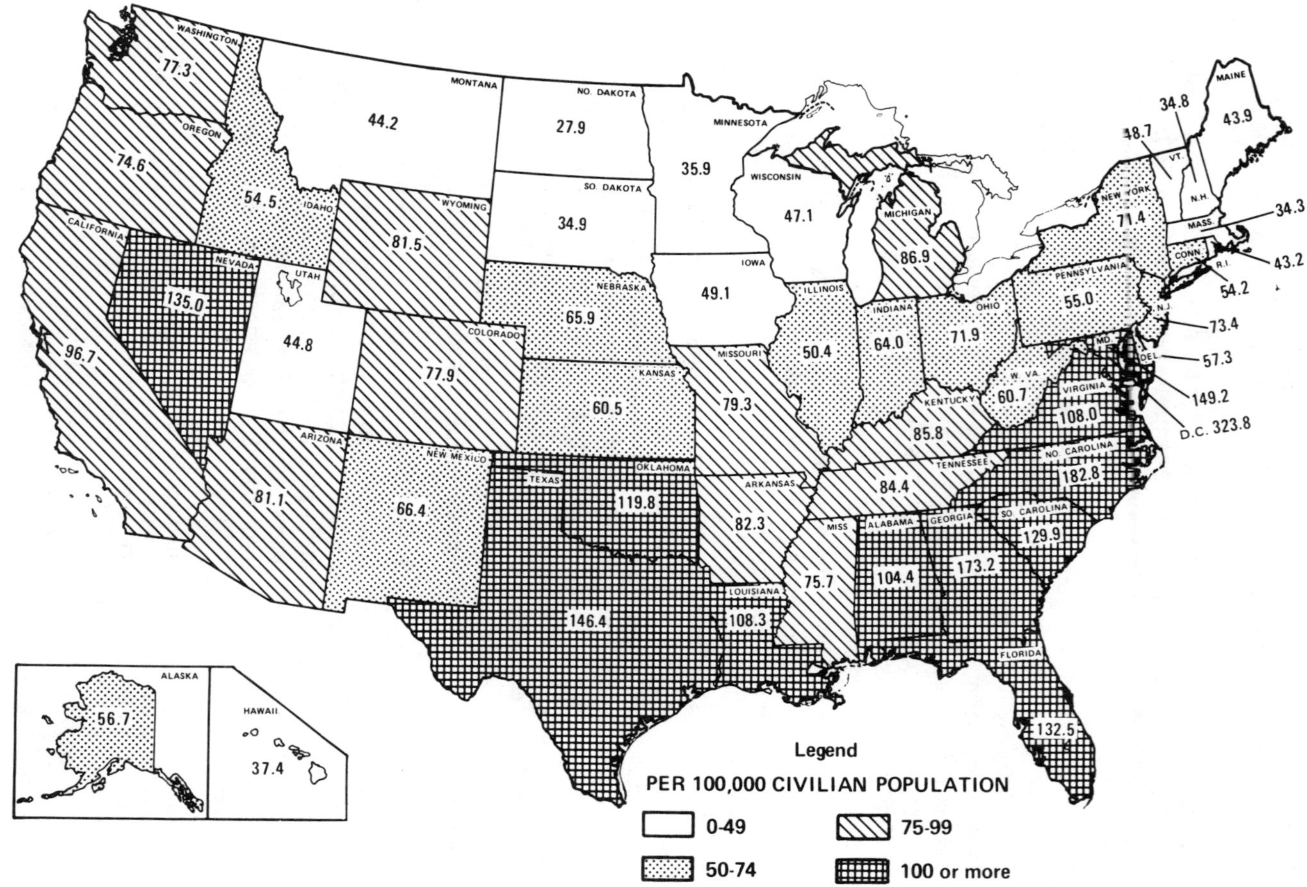

Prisoners in State institutions: number per 100,000 civilian population at yearend 1973

	1974 Provisional Population[1]	1974 Total Commitments	1974 Commitments per 100,000	1975 Estimated Population[2]	1975 Total Projected Commitments[3]	1975 Projected Commitments per 100,000	1975 Average Adult Inmate Population	1975 Inmates per 100,000
Alabama[6]	3,577,000	3,139	87.75	3,610,209	NA[4]	NA	4,794	132.79
Alaska	337,000	NA	NA	345,706	NA	NA	458	132.48
Arizona	2,153,000	1,174	54.52	2,248,129	1,564	69.56	2,101	93.45
Arkansas	2,062,000	1,367	66.29	2,096,669	1,572	74.97	2,211	105.45
California	20,907,000	12,024	57.51	21,145,466	11,566	54.69	21,922[5]	103.67
Colorado*	2,496,000	1,184	47.43	2,568,185	1,550	60.35	1,684	65.57
Connecticut*	3,088,000	1,883	60.97	3,101,945	2,280	73.50	1,707	55.02
Delaware*	573,000	NA	NA	579,224	NA	NA	NA	NA
Florida	8,090,000	7,788	92.26	8,415,139	10,776	128.05	14,030	166.72
Georgia*	4,882,000	7,074	144.89	4,955,106	8,128	164.03	7,249	146.29
Hawaii*	847,000	NA	NA	866,271	207	23.89	388	39.02
Idaho	799,000	513	64.20	820,498	599	73.00	562	68.49
Illinois*	11,131,000	3,220	28.92	11,135,256	6,207	55.74	6,817	61.50
Indiana*	5,330,000	6,455	121.10	5,364,082	8,342	155.51	3,964	73.89
Iowa	2,855,000	715	25.04	2,862,490	889	31.05	1,681	58.72
Kansas*	2,270,000	NA	NA	2,275,232	NA	NA	1,604	70.49
Kentucky[6]	3,357,000	2,398	71.43	3,391,422	NA	NA	3,091	91.14
Louisiana	3,764,000	NA	NA	3,794,205	NA	NA	4,965	130.85
Maine*	1,047,000	510	48.71	1,060,334	643	60.64	492	46.40
Maryland*	4,094,000	NA	NA	4,136,900	NA	NA	6,756	163.31
Massachusetts*	5,800,000	867	14.94	5,827,707	1,006	17.26	2,783	47.75
Michigan	9,098,000	5,299	58.24	9,153,729	6,139	67.06	9,230	100.83
Minnesota	3,917,000	430	10.97	3,944,982	NA	NA	1,387	35.15
Mississippi	2,324,000	1,940	83.47	2,350,772	2,276	96.81	2,228	94.77

	1974 Provisional Population[1]	1974 Total Commitments	1974 Commitments per 100,000	1975 Estimated Population[2]	1975 Total Projected Commitments[3]	1975 Projected Commitments per 100,000	1975 Average Adult Inmate Population	1975 Inmates per 100,000
Missouri	4,777,000	2,313	48.41	4,801,900	2,429	50.58	4,080	84.96
Montana	735,000	309	42.04	745,147	379	50.86	359	48.17
Nebraska	1,543,000	833	53.98	1,557,802	857	55.01	1,086	69.71
Nevada	573,000	423	73.82	594,065	512	86.18	882	148.46
New Hampshire	808,000	NA	NA	825,579	NA	NA	NA	NA
New Jersey*	7,330,000	5,073	69.20	7,370,459	5,489	74.47	5,094	69.11
New Mexico	1,122,000	1,045	93.13	1,148,500	1,230	107.09	1,097	95.51
New York*	18,111,000	8,356	46.13	18,078,434	9,494	50.30	15,283	84.53
North Carolina*	5,363,000	12,802	238.70	5,433,235	13,824	254.43	12,931	237.99
North Dakota[6]	637,000	208	32.65	641,809	NA	NA	174	27.11
Ohio	10,737,000	6,546	60.96	10,758,245	7,673	71.32	10,280	95.55
Oklahoma	2,709,000	1,924	71.02	2,746,436	2,196	79.95	3,102	112.94
Oregon	2,266,000	1,223	53.97	2,309,653	1,394	60.35	2,216	95.94
Pennsylvania*	11,835,000	4,018	33.95	11,845,272	NA	NA	6,616	55.85
Rhode Island*	937,000	NA	NA	933,820	NA	NA	442	47.33
South Carolina*	2,784,000	4,259	152.98	2,832,371	6,712	236.97	5,262	185.78
South Dakota	682,000	305	44.72	685,935	390	56.85	324	47.23
Tennessee	4,129,000	2,088	50.56	4,180,209	2,828	67.65	3,746	89.61
Texas	12,050,000	10,546	87.51	12,263,317	12,677	103.37	17,692	144.26
Utah	1,173,000	426	36.31	1,201,431	505	42.03	636	52.93
Vermont*	470,000	654	139.14	476,317	672	141.08	405	85.02
Virginia[6]*	4,908,000	3,857	78.58	4,972,876	NA	NA	5,847	117.57
Washington	3,476,000	2,373	68.26	3,492,707	1,878	53.76	2,906	83.20

	1974 Provisional Population[1]	1974 Total Commitments	1974 Commitments per 100,000	1975 Estimated Population[2]	1975 Total Projected Commitments[3]	1975 Projected Commitments per 100,000	1975 Average Adult Inmate Population	1975 Inmates per 100,000
West Virginia	1,791,000	286	15.96	1,802,690	NA	NA	945	52.42
Wisconsin	4,566,000	1,402	30.70	4,603,016	1,638	35.58	2,737	59.46
Wyoming	359,000	126	35.09	365,646	241	65.91	230	62.90

[1] The statistics of 1974 Provisional Populations were taken from the *Current Population Reports* of the Bureau of the Census, prepared under the auspices of the Federal-State Cooperative Program for Local Population Estimates. Estimates of populations are based upon certain indices which have been found to correlate highly with population level. Among these indices are: elementary school enrollment, the number of registered motor vehicles, voter registration; and a two-year average of resident births and deaths.

[2] Estimates of 1975 state population were derived by subtracting the 1970 census population from the provisional 1974 population, dividing the difference by four to get the mean rate of increase or decrease in this four-year span, and adding that mean to the provisional 1974 statistics.

[3] Projections of 1975 commitments for each state were determined by taking the average number of individuals committed monthly in the first 6–10 months of calendar year 1975 and using that number to project to years ahead.

[4] NA is used where the information was Not Available for comparative purposes.

[5] California's average adult inmate population was adjusted to exclude the civilly committed narcotics addicts, who average 2,103 of the total number incarcerated.

[6] The committment figures for these states are based on FY 1974–75 statistics. Figures were not available for 1975 projections of commitment.

* In addition to felons, these states incarcerate some misdemeanants at the state level. South Carolina does not make the distinction between misdemeanants and felons, but for comparative purposes they do incarcerate some inmates who could be defined as misdemeanants.

The only misdemeanants incarcerated at the state level in Kansas are women.

Chapter 8

Historical Antecedents[1] and Administration

Parole did not develop from any specific source or experiment, but is an outgrowth of a number of independent measures, including the conditional pardon, apprenticeship by indenture, the transportation of criminals to America and Australia, the English and Irish experiences with the system of Ticket of Leave, and the work of American prison reformers during the nineteenth century.

CONDITIONAL PARDONS AND TRANSPORTATION TO AMERICA

The transportation of criminals to the American Colonies began early in the seventeenth century. In the beginning no specific conditions were imposed upon those receiving these pardons. However, after a number of those pardoned had evaded transportation or had returned to England prior to the expiration of their term, it was found necessary to impose certain restrictions upon the individuals to whom these pardons were granted. It was about 1655 that the form of pardons was amended to include specific conditions and provide for the nullification of the pardon if the recipient failed to abide by the conditions imposed.

[1] Reprinted and edited from the *Parole Officer's Manual*, New York State Division of Parole, 1953.

Transportation to America

During the early days of transportation, the Government paid a fee to each contractor for each prisoner transported. Subsequently this was changed and the contractor was given "property in service" of the prisoner until the expiration of the full term. Once a prisoner was delivered to the contractor, the Government took no further interest in his welfare or behavior unless he violated the conditions of the pardon by returning to England prior to the expiration of his sentence.

Upon arrival of the pardoned felons in the Colonies, their services were sold to the highest bidder. The contractor then transferred the "property in service" agreement to the new master and the felon was no longer referred to as a criminal but became an indentured servant. This indenture bears a similarity to the procedure now followed by parole boards in this country. Like the indentured servant, a prisoner conditionally released on parole agrees in writing to accept certain conditions included on the release form that is signed by the members of the parole board and the prisoner. Even some of the conditions imposed today on conditionally released prisoners are similar to those included on the indenture agreement.

The termination of the Revolutionary War ended transportation to America, and England then sent her convicts to Australia until 1867.

ENGLAND'S EXPERIENCE WITH TICKET OF LEAVE

The English Penal Servitude Act of 1853, governing prisoners convicted in England and Ireland, substituted imprisonment for transportation. By this act, prisoners who received sentences of fourteen years or less were committed to prison, but the judge was granted permissive power to order the transportation of individuals who had received terms of more than fourteen years. This law also specified the length of time prisoners were required to serve before becoming eligible for conditional release on Ticket of Leave.

THE IRISH SYSTEM OF TICKET OF LEAVE

Sir William Crofton became head of the Irish prison system in 1854, one year after the enactment of the Servitude Act. The Irish convict system under Crofton's administration became famous for its three stages of penal servitude, with the final stage being conditional release on Ticket of Leave. Ticket of Leave men residing in rural districts were supervised by the police, but those residing in Dublin were supervised by a civilian employee who had the title of Inspector of Released Prisoners. He worked cooperatively with the police, but it was his responsibility to secure employment for Ticket of Leave men. He required them to report at stated intervals, visited their homes every two weeks and also verified their employment.

In England and Ireland after 1864, Prisoners Aid Societies were established, with the Government contributing a share of funds equal to the sum raised by the Society for its work. These Societies employed agents who devoted their full time to the supervision of released prisoners.

DEVELOPMENTS IN THE UNITED STATES

By 1865, the Crofton System had been widely publicized in America. Supporters of Crofton's System, however, did not believe that the adoption of the Ticket of Leave would ever be accepted in the United States. Their attitude was apparently based on the conception that it would be un-American to place any individual under the supervision of the police, and they did not believe that any other form of supervision would be effective. A letter written by Crofton in 1874, in reply to an inquiry sent to him by the Secretary of the New York Prison Association, stressed that the police of Ireland were permitted to delegate competent individuals in the community to act as custodians for Ticket of Leave men, and he suggested a similar system for the United States.

Modern Parole

Parole originated at the Elmira Reformatory, formally opened in 1876. Its first Superintendent, Z. E. Brockway, had been head of the House of Correction in Detroit and while there had drafted an indeterminate sentence law. His special features for the Elmira System included an indeterminate or indefinite sentence, the length of time served to be dependent upon the behavior and capacity of the prisoner, within statutory limitations. Under this system, provision was made for the release on parole of carefully selected prisoners. The vital principle of the indeterminate sentence was that no prisoner would be paroled until he was fit for freedom. The main opposition to the enactment of indeterminate sentence laws came from the judges, who were unwilling to relinquish their traditional role of fixing the time prisoners must serve. Despite their opposition these laws were enacted and provisions were made for the parole of prisoners. At the beginning of the twentieth century twenty-six states had adopted these measures.

Before being considered for parole, each inmate was required to maintain a good record of conduct for a period of twelve months. One of the conditions of his parole was that he must report on the first day of every month to his guardian and provide an account of his situation and conduct. The guardian's report was then transmitted to the superintendent of Elmira. Parolees were required to report for a minimum period of six months. It was the belief that a longer period under supervision would be discouraging to the average parolee.

No thought was given to the training of prisoners toward their future adjustment in the community, and both prison administrators and inmates soon accepted the idea that reformed or unreformed, allowance of time for good behavior was automatic and release at the earliest possible date was a right, rather than a privilege. After release, supervision was either non-existent or totally inadequate.

By 1930 all states had a parole law, and within the past four decades drastic action has been taken by a number of states to render parole an effective part of the criminal justice system. We shall review just how successful in the following chapters.

ADMINISTRATION OF PAROLE

The administration of parole is less complex than that of probation because parole services are administered centrally on a statewide basis.[2] There are two basic models for administering parole services. In one model, parole is placed under the administration of an independent parole board. In the other model, parole is placed within a larger department that also administers correctional institutions.

The President's Commission summarized the arguments for placing parole under an independent parole board:

1. The board is in the best position to promote parole and to generate public support and acceptance. Since the board is often held account-

[2] An exception to this is the New York City Parole Commission, which was merged with the New York State system in 1967.

able for parole failures, it should be responsible for supervising parolees.

2. The parole board in direct control of administering parole services can more effectively evaluate and adjust the system.

3. Supervision by the parole board and its officers properly divorces the parolees from the correctional institution.

4. An independent parole board in charge of its own services is in the best position to present its own budget request to the legislature.[3]

Critics in oppostion to this model contend that it is wont to be insensitive to correctional programs in the institution, and that this insensitivity can result in the wrong persons being paroled.[4]

The President's Commission also summarized the arguments for including both parole and institutions in a single department of correction:

1. The correctional process is a continuum. All staff, institution and parole, should be under a single administration rather than being divided, with resultant competition for public funds and friction in policies.

2. A consolidated correctional department has the advantage of consistent administration, including staff selection and supervision.

3. Parole boards are ineffective in performing administrative functions. Their major focus should be on case decisions, not on day-to-day field operations.

4. The growing number of programs part way between institutions and parole, such as work release, can best be handled by a single centralized administration.[5]

Critics of this model maintain that institutional operating considerations rather than the offender's or the community's needs too often determine parole decisions. Overcrowding, a desire to get rid of "troublemakers," or the need to enforce relatively petty rules, may be the basis for parole decision-making.[6]

The President's Commission believes that if the management of a state prison system is stagnant and the parole board is active and effective, parole services should be independent. However, if the

[3] *Task Force Report*, p. 71.

[4] Vincent O'Leary and Joan Nuffield, "A National Survey of Parole Decision-Making," *Crime and Delinquency* (July 1973), p. 380.

[5] *Task Force Report*, p. 71.

[6] O'Leary and Nuffield, p. 380.

THE INDEPENDENT MODEL
Florida Parole and Probation Commission*

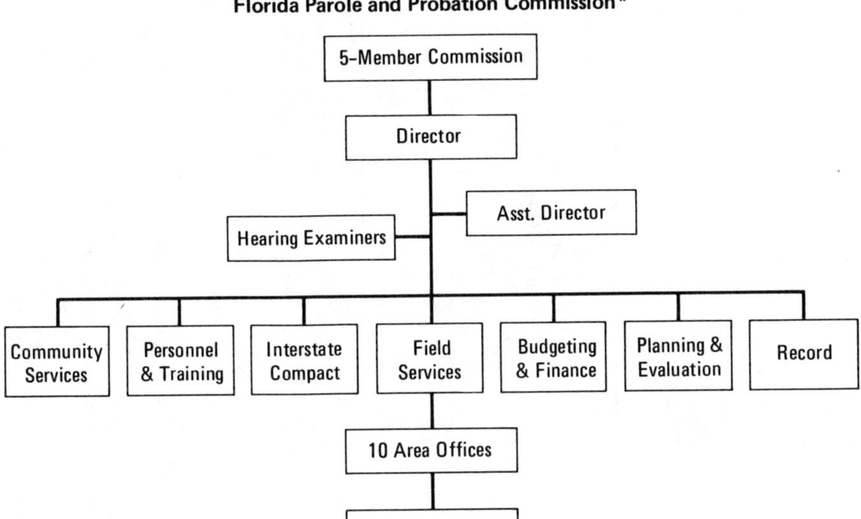

*Note that this agency provides probation and parole services

opposite is true, or if both are equal with respect to effectiveness, then parole services should be combined within the department of correction.[7]

Over the years there has been a growing trend toward the consolidated model. New York adopted this model in 1970, and in his annual report then-Governor Nelson Rockefeller stated why: "By merging responsibilities for institutional and field supervision of convicted offenders in one department with unified leadership and direction, a coordinated, consistent, and continuous system of rehabilitation can be insured." The governor emphasized that under this system "a strong and independent Board of Parole was continued, thereby guaranteeing that the critical decision to release inmates from correctional institutions will continue to be based upon the single goal of successful return to society."[8]

Currently 30 states have the consolidated model, while 20 states still have autonomous parole boards.[9] The President's Commission, back in 1967, had reported that no state gives the final power to grant or deny parole in adult cases to the staff directly involved in the operation of a correctional institution.[10]

[7] *Task Force Report*, p. 71.

[8] Department of Correctional Services, p. 1.

[9] Parker, p. 30.

[10] *Task Force Report*, p. 65.

THE CONSOLIDATED MODEL
Ohio Department of Rehabilitation & Correction
Table of Organization

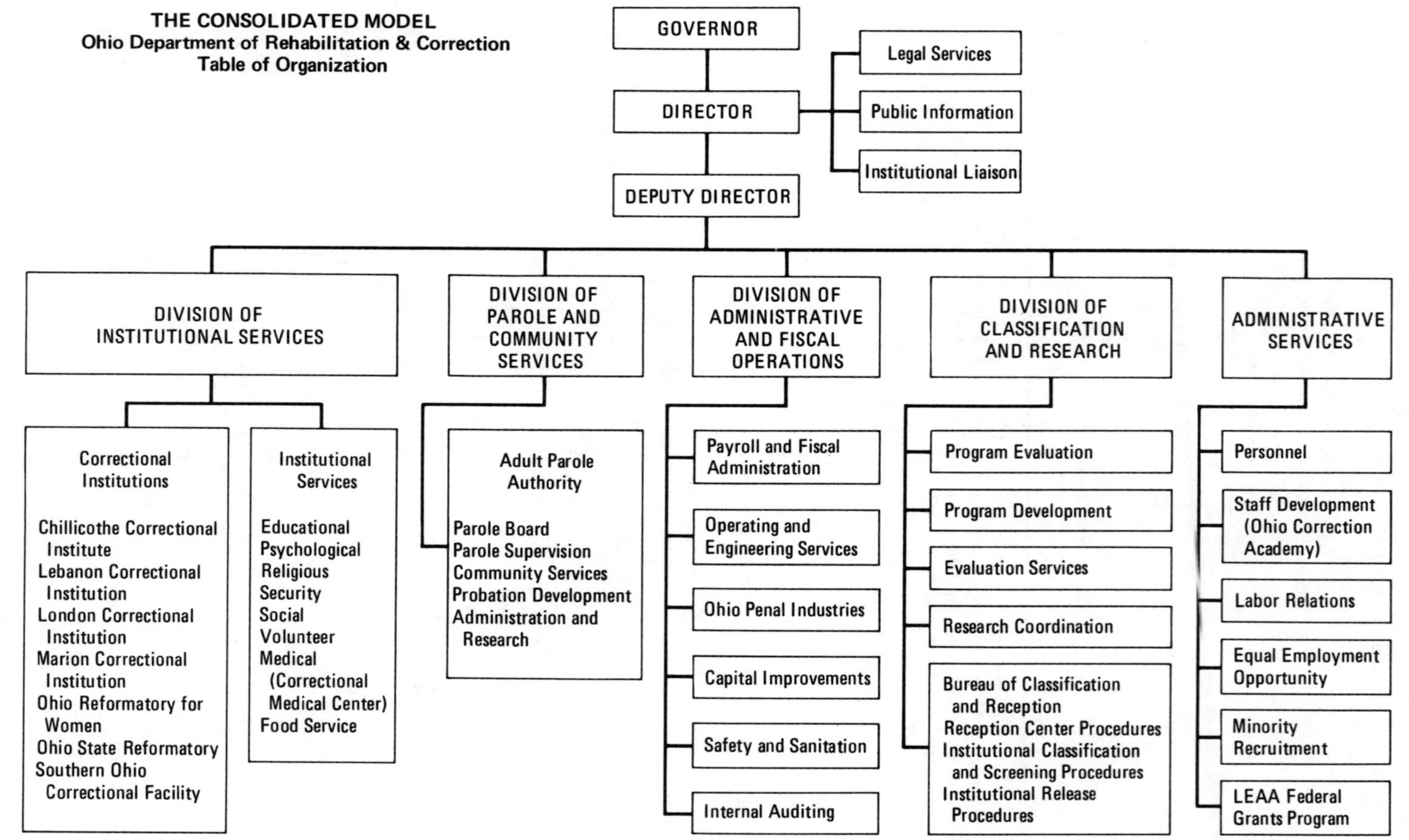

TENNESSEE DEPARTMENT OF CORRECTION*

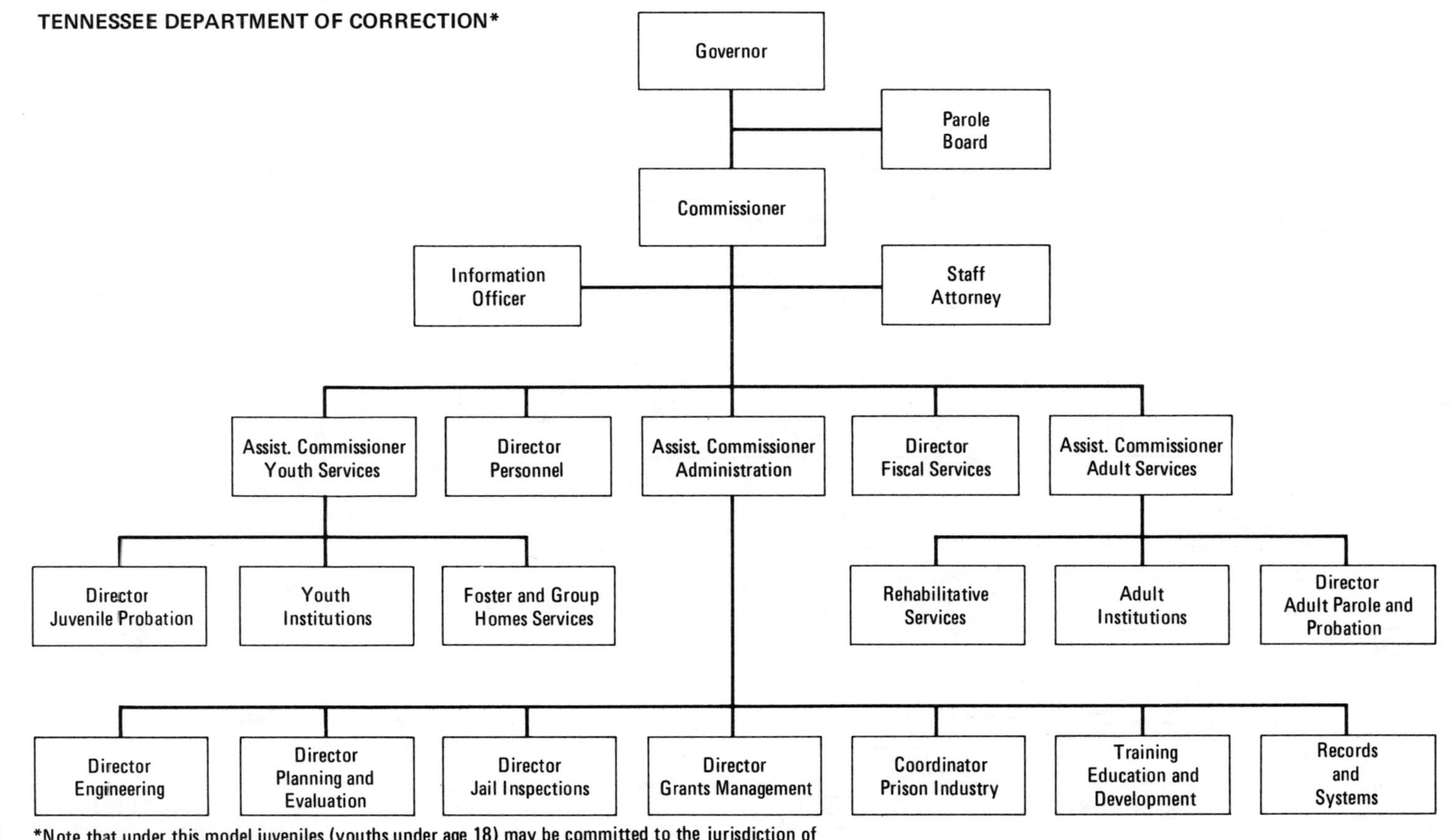

*Note that under this model juveniles (youths under age 18) may be committed to the jurisdiction of the Department of Correction whose juvenile probation officers provide after-care/parole services.

VIRGINIA DEPARTMENT OF WELFARE AND INSTITUTIONS*

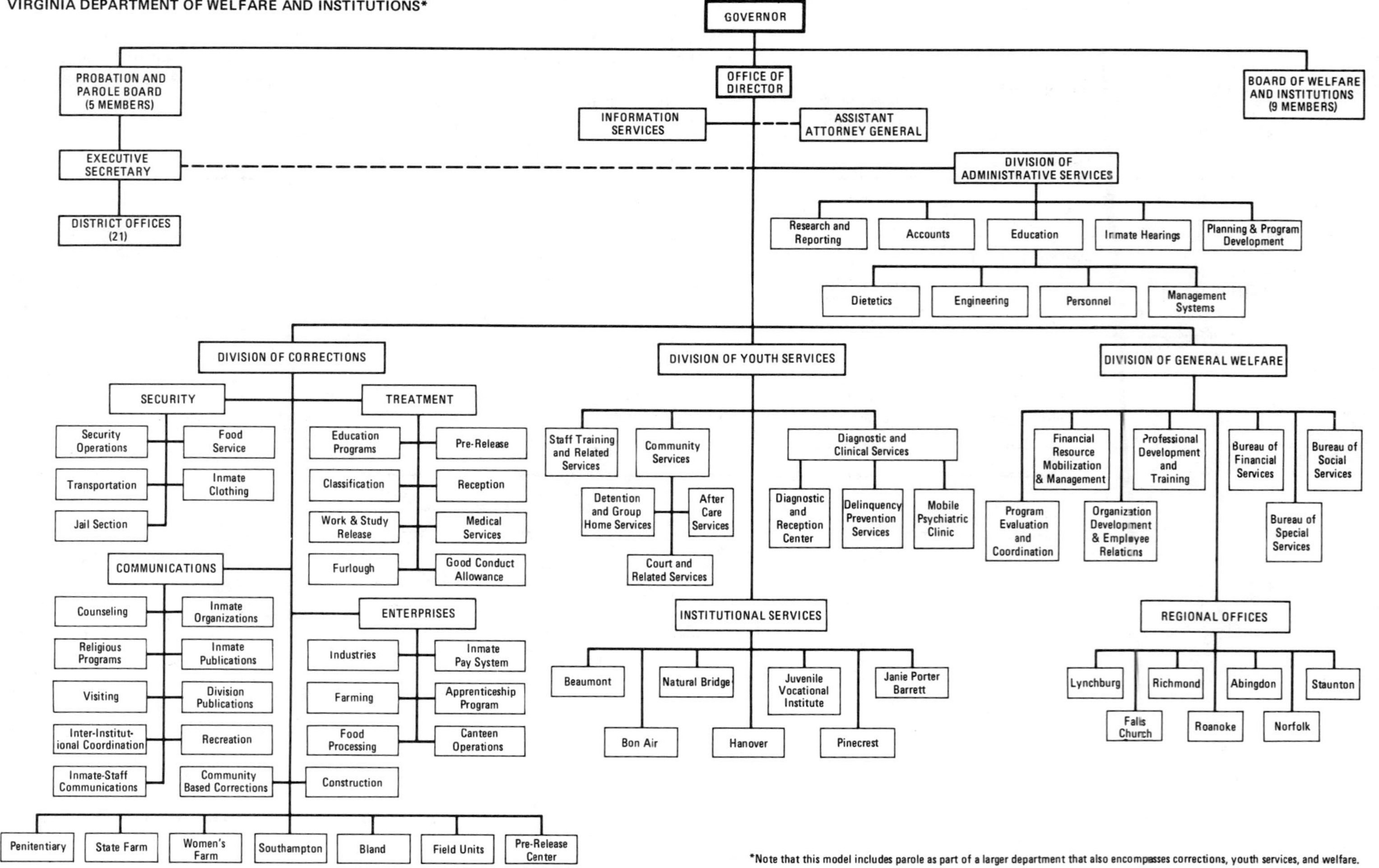

*Note that this model includes parole as part of a larger department that also encompasses corrections, youth services, and welfare.

Administrative Structure of Adult Parole Authorities
1972

Jurisdiction	*Agency within which authority is located*	*Administrator of parole field services*
Alabama	Autonomous	Parole Board
Alaska	Department of Health and Social Services	Division of Correction
Arizona	Department of Correction	Department of Correction
Arkansas	Autonomous	do
California	Department of Correction	do
California Women	do[a]	do
Colorado	Division of Correction	Department of Institutions
Connecticut	Department of Correction	Department of Correction
Delaware	Autonomous	Department of Adult Correction
District of Columbia	do	Department of Correction
Florida	do	Parole Board
Georgia	do	do
Hawaii	Department of Social Services and Housing	do
Idaho	Board of Correction	Board of Correction
Illinois	Department of Correction	Department of Correction
Indiana	do	Adult Authority
Indiana Women	do	Department of Correction
Iowa	Department of Social Services	Bureau of Adult Correction
Kansas	Autonomous	Parole Board
Kentucky	Department of Correction	Department of Correction

Administrative Structure of Adult Parole Authorities
1972

Jurisdiction	*Agency within which authority is located*	*Administrator of parole field services*
Louisiana	do	do
Maine	Department of Mental Health and Correction	Bureau of Correction
Maryland	Department of Public Safety and Correction	Department of Public Safety and Correction
Massachusetts	Department of Correction	Parole Board
Michigan	do[a]	Department of Correction
Minnesota	Department of Correction	Division of Adult Correction
Mississippi	Autonomous	Parole Board
Missouri	Department of Correction	do
Montana	Autonomous	do
Nebraska	Division of Correction	do
Nevada	Autonomous	do
New Hampshire	do	do
New Jersey	Department of Institutions and Agencies	Division of Correction and Parole
New Mexico	Autonomous	Department of Correction
New York	Department of Correctional Services	Department of Correctional Services
North Carolina	Department of Social Rehabilitation and Control	Parole Board
North Dakota	Autonomous	Board of Pardons
Ohio	Division of Correction	Division of Correction
Oklahoma	Department of Correction	Department of Correction

Administrative Structure of Adult Parole Authorities 1972

Jurisdiction	*Agency within which authority is located*	*Administrator of parole field services*
Oregon	Correction Division	Correction Division
Pennsylvania	Autonomous	Parole Board
Rhode Island	Department of Social and Rehabilitation Services	Department of Correction
South Carolina	Autonomous	Parole Board
South Dakota	do	do
Tenessee	Department of Correction	Department of Correction
Texas	Autonomous	Parole Board
U.S. Parole Board	Department of Justice	Federal District Courts
Utah	Division of Correction	Division of Correction
Vermont	Autonomous	Department of Correction
Virginia	Department of Welfare and Institutions	Parole Board
Washington	Autonomous	Department of Health and Social Service
West Virginia	do	Division of Correction
Wisconsin	Department of Health and Social Services	do
Wyoming	Autonomous	Department of Probation and Parole

Note: For felony offenders only.

[a] General policy matters, etc., are shared by the Board and the larger Department of Correction.

Source: U.S. Law Enforcement Assistance Administration, *Sourcebook of Criminal Justice Statistics–1974* (Washington, D.C.: U.S. Government Printing Office, 1975), p. 162.

Chapter 9

Conditional Release and Parole

There are several ways for an offender to be released from a correctional institution. Few receive pardons and most do not remain in prison until the expiration of the sentences. Conditional release and parole are the two processes by which most inmates are released.

CONDITIONAL (MANDATORY) RELEASE

Conditional release means that an inmate is released at the expiration of his sentence, less time he earned for good behavior (referred to as "good time"). In New York an inmate can earn good time at the rate of ten days for each thirty days of time served. If he is serving a nine-year sentence he can be conditionally released at the end of six years. Good time can be lost for infractions of institutional rules. In some states, such as New York and Florida, inmates who are conditionally released are subject to the same conditions as parolees and are placed under the supervision of a parole officer.

PAROLE

In practice, the parole board and not the sentencing judge determines how long an offender will serve in a correctional institution. Under the indeterminate sentencing procedure, a judge sets the maximum term (and perhaps a minimum term, depending on state law), but the parole board determines how long an offender actually serves. The basis for the indeterminate sentencing procedure is rehabilitation, and the parole board is considered to be in the best position to evaluate an offender's progress toward this goal.

Parole Boards

Parole boards have come under increasing scrutiny and criticism in recent years. One reason was the Attica riot and the subsequent public report that identified parole as a source of inmate discontent. Parole boards, as opposed to the courts, operate in relative secrecy. Their hearings are closed and their methods unknown to the general public.

Membership. The number of members on each board varies from three to twelve. Sixteen jurisdictions have three members, while twenty-four jurisdictions have five members. New York has the largest board with twelve members. The salary range of board members varies from just expenses in Hawaii, to $36,000 annually in New York. Board chairmen usually receive an additional compensation. In 45 states the Governor is responsible for parole board appointments, although in several states he may appoint committees to recommend qualified persons. Only two states (Wisconsin and Ohio) appoint members from a civil service list. In only a few states are there any specific professional qualifications for board members—in most states and the federal government, there are either no qualifications or they are stated in broad terms such as "good character" or "experience in corrections." [1]

The above data was compiled by William Parker for the American Correctional Association, and he concludes that "the only real qualification [for board members] may be the political responsiveness and reliability of the board members to the appointing power." [2] While the President's Commission recommended that parole board members

[1] Parker, pp. 67–191.

[2] *Ibid.*, p. 30.

"be appointed solely on the basis of competence," [3] Milton Rector, of the National Council on Crime and Delinquency (NCCD), states that the professionalism of parole boards continues to be impeded by political appointments.[4] The role of politics and patronage in the appointment of parole board members is quite similar to their role in the selection of judges.

Parole Release

Typically, from one to three members briefly interview an inmate who is eligible for parole. In a few jurisdictions this aspect of the parole release process is handled by hearing examiners. However, not all jurisdictions conduct parole hearings with inmates. The President's Commission noted that some states make decisions solely on the basis of written reports.[5] The percentage of inmates released by parole boards varies from a high of 90% in New Hampshire, Washington, and Kansas, to a low of 20% in South Carolina, Wyoming, and Oklahoma.[6]

As in probation, there are restrictions on granting parole for certain offenses in different states; for example, kidnapping, escape from prison, assault on a correction officer, incest, and first degree murder.[7] The amount of time that an inmate is required to serve before he is eligible for parole depends on the statutes in each state, and there are wide variations in minimum and maximum terms for the same crime in different states. These minimums and maximums can be set by law, by the sentencing judge, or by the parole board.

In sixteen states an inmate is eligible for parole after completing his minimum sentence; in ten of these states "good time" is deducted from the minimum. In ten states, the District of Columbia, and the federal system, an inmate is eligible for parole after serving one-third of his maximum sentence. Some states set eligibility according to the number of previous felony convictions or the length of the sentence, and there are almost as many variations in eligibility as there are parole boards.[8]

[3] *The Challenge of Crime in a Free Society*, Pres.'s Commission on Law Enforcement and Administration of Justice (New York: Avon Books, 1972), pp. 429–30.

[4] Rector cited from Harleigh B. Trecker, ed., *Goals for Social Welfare* (New York: Association Press, 1973), p. 116.

[5] *Task Force Report*, p. 64.

[6] Frank P. Prassel, *Introduction to American Criminal Justice* (New York: Harper and Row, 1975), p. 208.

[7] Parker, p. 9.

[8] *Ibid.*, pp. 60–66.

Decision-Making

Sol Rubin, former chief legal counsel of the NCCD, states that "Parole boards exercise some functions that are exactly the same as judicial sentencing—for example, fixing minimum and maximum terms." [9] What criteria does a parole board use when it sets minimum and maximum terms, or when it is considering the parole release of an inmate? New York reports the following: [10]

1. The inmate's previous criminal record; the nature and circumstances of the crime and his present attitude toward it; his attitude toward the police officer who arrested him, toward the district attorney who prosecuted him, toward the judge who sentenced him, and toward the complainant.
2. His conduct in the institution, his responses to efforts made to improve his mental and moral condition, together with his academic, vocational, and industrial records; his character, capacity, mentality, physical and mental condition, habits, attitudes; the kind of work he is best fitted to perform and at which he is most likely to succeed when he leaves the institution.
3. The environment to which he plans to return.
4. The kind of employment, educational or other specified program secured for him.

The Florida Parole and Probation Commission, while including much the same type of criteria as New York, also lists "the capability of the Commission's field staff to provide adequate parole supervision once the person is paroled." [11]

In a 1975 memorandum, the Chairman of the California Adult Authority presented some of the salient factors used by his board:

Typical or Aggravated Offense. A decision is made as to whether the inmate's offense falls within the typical or aggravated range according to the following criteria:[12]

[9] Sol Rubin, "The Impact of Court Decisions in the Correctional Process," *Crime and Delinquency* (Apr. 1974), p. 131.

[10] New York Secretary of State, *Board of Parole*, Chapter XII, Part 1910.15.

[11] *Annual Report* of the Florida Parole and Probation Commission, 1974, p. 16.

[12] The same factors apply in deciding whether a parole violation is more or less serious.

a. the seriousness of any personal injury to victims of the crime

b. the number of victims of the crime

c. the degree to which the individual was involved in inflicting personal injury

d. the extent of damage to or loss of property

e. the professionalism with which the crime was carried out

f. possession or use of weapons

g. quantities of contraband possessed or sold

h. prior felonies.

Personal Adjustment. Inmates must be free of serious or major disciplinary actions and indicate a willingness to perform regular institutional work or other assignments. Inmates with significant psychiatric problems, multiple termers whose criminal behavior has been persistent, and any other particularly complex cases need to demonstrate long-term evidence of a change before release can be considered. Other factors include:

a. the individual's age

b. the individual's pattern of criminality not otherwise considered

c. whether the individual is a professional, systematic criminal or an amateur, or occasional offender.

Parker notes that many parole boards do not have written criteria for parole selection, or have statutes that are very broadly written and merely state that the inmate should "have a lawful occupation," or "not be a threat to himself or the community." [13] The American Law Institute in its *Model Penal Code* recommends to parole boards four primary reasons for denying an inmate parole:[14]

1. There is a substantial risk that he will not conform to the conditions of parole; or

2. his release at that time would depreciate the seriousness of his crime or promote disrespect for law; or

3. his release would have a substantially adverse effect on institution discipline; or

[13] Parker, p. 33.

[14] Don M. Gottfredson, Peter B. Hoffman, Maurice H. Sigler, and Leslie T. Wilkins, "Making Paroling Policy Explicit," *Crime and Delinquency* (Jan. 1975), p. 36.

4. his continued correctional treatment, medical care, or vocational or other training in the institution would substantially enhance his capacity to lead a law-abiding life when released at a later date.

Parole boards usually consider the crime, the length of time served, the inmate's age, prior criminal history, use of drugs or alcohol, and institutional record. Some parole boards may request a recommendation from the prosecutor. All will certainly consider opposition to an inmate's parole from the police and the news media. A poll of parole board members revealed that their major consideration was whether or not they believed the inmate was likely to commit a serious crime if paroled.[15]

In order to make these decisions, in addition to interviewing the inmate, the board members review the presentence report and institutional reports relative to the inmate's adjustment. Daniel Glaser recommends that the boards also make use of "prediction tables," compilations of statistics on the post-release behavior of different types of offenders. Glaser believes that these tables will provide the basis for case prognostication.[16]

In some jurisdictions, should parole be denied, an inmate is not provided with the reasons. This lack of information has been criticized by many in the legal and correctional field as being unfair and arbitrary. Maurice H. Sigler, Chairman of the United States Board of Parole, states that all inmates should be given written reasons for being denied parole.[17] The following is a sample of a statement presented to an inmate by a state parole board whose policy is to provide written reasons whenever parole is denied:

> After consideration of the circumstances of your present offense, and in the absence of any statement by the sentencing court tending to indicate the contrary, the Board has concluded that there are certain punitive and deterrent aspects to your sentence. In the absence of any special or equitable circumstances or any affirmative evidence that you can avoid criminal behavior and since your minimum sentence has not yet expired, the Board feels that the punitive and deterrent aspects of your sentence have not been fulfilled and that, therefore your release would not be compatible with the community welfare.

[15] *Ibid.*, p. 34.

[16] Daniel Glaser, *The Effectiveness of a Prison and Parole System* (Indianapolis: Bobbs-Merrill, 1969), p. 207.

[17] Sigler cited from Orland and Tyler, p. 103.

After consideration of all records relevant to your confinement, treatment and efforts towards self-improvement while in the State Prison system, the Board is unable to conclude that there is reasonable probability that you will return to society without violation of law.

After consideration of all relevant records and your hearing, the Board notes that you still minimize your delinquent behavior and indicate the shooting of the victim was accidental although you entered a plea of guilty. Professional staff reports still persuade the Board that you are lacking in insight into your delinquent activities, and that your judgment is impaired. It is further indicated that you are still a potential assaultive risk. The Board notes that your work record in the institution continues to be good. The Board is unable to conclude that there are sufficient affirmative indications to persuade the Board that you would be able to control your assaultive behavior and delinquent activities in the community. Parole is therefore denied, and you will be reheard as scheduled in this Notice of Decision.

A PAROLE HEARING

The following is an actual hearing that was held on January 20, 1976, and the inmate being interviewed was granted parole.

Examination by Nelson Harris, Member of the Board of Parole:

RE: *Smith, Louis* #092340136

Q. Louis Smith?

A. Yes.

Q. Smith, I am wondering if you got a chance on parole, what do you think would happen? Do you think the time is right?

A. I would go and pick up my life where I left it before.

Q. Do you think there was anything about the way you were living when you came in that needs changing?

A. A little could be altered so I am quite sure I would change them around now.

Q. Can you pinpoint, tell us some of the areas where you think you will change?

A. There is quite a few areas I can see where I am making mistakes. I am making a mistake coming here, that is one right there.

Q. Anything that you could do to stay out of places like this would definitely be something that would be of good intentions.

A. Yes.

Q. Do you have any plans? How are you going to try and go about making it when you get out of here?

A. First of all, I am starting back to work, which I am doing now and take it on from there.

Q. Staying in the big city area?

A. Yes.

Q. Can you cope with it?

A. I don't understand.

Q. Can you cope with the city, the bigness and all that?

A. Yes, I can.

Q. What is this job that you have?

A. It's the closest thing that they can give me to the job I have in the joint, that was all I have.

Q. Anybody that can get a foothold in that field really has something going for him and can make good money.

A. Yes.

Q. What can you do? How are your skills? What is the most you ever earned from it?

A. Well, the most I earned, brought in in one week was close to $500.

Q. You made that kind of money?

A. Yes.

Q. You noticed I have not referred to the crime?

A. Yes.

Q. You probably talked about it time and again.

A. Not very much, but some.

Q. This is thoroughly reported here. You did not have anything in your past like it and from what I read, it was certainly something you did not intend.

A. You are right, it wasn't intended. It was done through an accident. Mostly I was drinking and that is one problem I think I can handle now.

Q. Do you think you need anything outside yourself with reference to any drinking you did before?

A. I wasn't a regular drinker, I just drank sometimes. Now one thing I learned that if I get a problem, stay away from a bottle, that's what I learned.

Q. As a result of this, you also know that even though you don't drink all the time, it can still be a problem?

A. I found that out.

Q. Okay, your recommendations here are reasonably good and folks that have worked with you say they believe that there is no reason why you can't make it.

A. I hope I can.

Q. In the event you get the opportunity—

A. I hope I can make it.

Q. You feel that way?

A. Yes.

Q. Maybe there is something that you want to call to our attention?

A. No.

Q. Thanks for coming in. We will make a decision and let you know what it is.

APPEALS

Some jurisdictions provide a procedure for inmates to appeal negative parole board decisions. In California, any person under the jurisdiction of the Adult Authority may appeal any decision of the Adult Authority which affects him on the basis that the decision is wrong and should be changed. In addition, any inmate may apply for reconsideration of any Adult Authority decision which has affected him on the basis that new facts or changed circumstances indicate that a new decision should be made. Offenders may appeal decisions to deny restoration of civil rights and parole revocation in addition to parole release decisions.

In California, an appeal must be made within 90 days of the decision, and a final denial of an appeal may not be reappealed.

The final level of appeals review (see flow chart) is the Appeals Committee, consisting of two members or a member and a representative, excluding any member or representative who reviewed the case at the second level of review. The Appeals Committee is assigned by the Chairman or by the Board coordinator, and will include at least one member of the board (Adult Authority). The Committee is authorized to take final action on all appeals and requests for reconsideration, including:

1. Sitting as a hearing panel and conducting a rehearing, if the inmate or parolee is available for an immediate hearing;
2. ordering the case placed on regular calendar for a rehearing; or
3. denying the appeal or request for reconsideration.

CALIFORNIA APPEALS PROCEDURE FLOW CHART

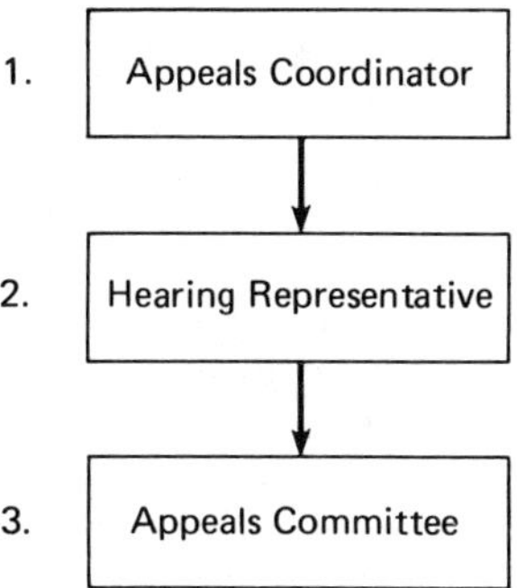

CRITICISM OF PAROLE DECISION-MAKING

Milton Rector states that parole developed as a response to unfair and inaccurate sentencing, but he decries the fact that parole boards are usually unwilling to submit their decision-making process to assessment and research, even though this might lead to better releasing criteria.[18] The same criticism leveled at the judiciary for "differential sentencing" is leveled at parole boards for their "differential releases." However, while judges announce their sentencing decisions in an open court and often provide reasons for the sentence, parole boards decide in private and frequently give no reasons for their decisions. There is often a feeling among inmates that board members respond according to their own personal biases and prejudices, rather than on the merits of the case. In view of the cloud of secrecy that surrounds board decisions, these feelings are not easily dispelled.

Gottfredson, Hoffman, Sigler and Wilkins believe that it is important for parole boards to avoid even the appearance of arbitrariness in their decision-making process. In addition, they question whether boards are using the right determinants for parole selection. They note that boards commonly use the crime, prior criminal record, etc., but that there are no predetermined guidelines for the importance to be accorded to each criterion considered. While they accept the notion

[18] Rector cited from Trecker, p. 117.

that each case is unique, they believe that there must be a reasonable basis for comparing parole decisions.[19]

In response to these criticisms the NCCD Research Center, in conjunction with the United States Board of Parole, and supported by a grant from the Law Enforcement Assistance Administration, developed a model program called the *Parole Decision-Making Project.*[20] The result of the project is a system which its advocates maintain promotes fairness and equity in the parole release process. Maurice Sigler describes the system:

> First, the examiner panel gives each case a salient factor score, ranging from zero to 11, with the higher the score, the better the prospects for successful completion of parole. The case gets points, or loses them, on the basis of such factors as prior convictions, prior commitments, education, employment history, marital status, etc. All of the factors were determined on the basis of research to have some predictability for success on parole.
>
> The case is then given an offense severity rating—low, low moderate, moderate, high, very high, and greatest. This rating does not depend simply on the subjective judgment of the examiners. They are provided with a chart that lists offense categories under each severity rating.
>
> Then, with the salient factor score, and the offense severity rating in hand, the examiners consult a second chart which indicates the amount of time an offender with a given background and salient factor score should serve for an offense of a given severity, assuming reasonably good institutional performance. For example, an offender with a salient factor score of 11 and an offense severity rating of low might be expected to serve 6 to 10 months before going out on parole. Or an offender with a salient factor score of 3 and a severity rating of very high may be expected to serve 55 to 65 months. For an offender with a severity rating of greatest, the most serious or heinous offenses, there is no maximum range stipulated.
>
> For most offenders, the mix of salient factor score and offense severity rating involves a certain amount of risk in parole, and the system is intended to bring about a reasonable degree of fairness by insuring that they serve about the same amount of time as others in their situation.
>
> But, for those cases where in the clinical judgment of the examiners the inmate has a much better prospect of success on parole than his score and rating suggests, the examiners can shorten the amount of time to be served below those specified by the guidelines. Or where the prospect of success on parole is much worse than that suggested by the score and

[19] Gottfredson, *et al.*, pp. 34–37.

[20] A complete report of this project is available from the National Technical Information Service, 5285 Port Royal Road, Springfield, Virginia 22151.

rating, the examiners can extend the amount of time to be served beyond that specified.[21]

REPRESENTATION AT PAROLE HEARINGS

As we will review in the *Menenchino v. Oswald* decision, an inmate is not legally entitled to be represented at a parole release hearing. In fact, he may not even be "entitled" to appear at a hearing. However, the National Advisory Commission believes that representation helps promote a feeling of fairness, and can enable an inmate to communicate better and thus participate more fully in the hearing. The Commission states that "Representation can also contribute to opening the correctional system, particularly the parole process, to public scrutiny.[22] The Commission suggests that "Lawyers are only one possible kind of representative; citizen volunteers also could serve as offender representatives." [23] The Commission makes note of the fact that representation at parole hearings may be considered "annoying to parole officials." (There is fear that the hearing may take on the form of an adversary proceeding.) However, the Commission states that "these inconveniences seem a small price for the prospective gains."[24]

In 1972, the United States Board of Parole initiated a pilot project that allowed inmates to have representatives at parole release hearings. These representatives included institutional staff, parents, peer group members, family, friends, and employers. Later in the program inmates were also able to be represented by attorneys. A study of the project indicated that adults with representatives were paroled an average of six weeks earlier than inmates without representatives.[25]

Employment for Parole Release

Most parole boards require an inmate to have an offer of employment before he can be released on parole. The American Correctional Association reports that only 12 states do not have this requirement. Some states provide for a waiver of the requirement in certain cases,

[21] Maurice H. Sigler, "Abolish Parole?", *Federal Probation* (June 1975), p. 44.

[22] Nat. Adv. Comm., *Corrections*, p. 403.

[23] Ibid.

[24] *Ibid.*

[25] James L. Beck, "The Effect of Representation at Parole Hearings," *Criminology* (May 1975), pp. 114–17.

while others provide for furloughs from the prison for the inmates to secure a job. In New York parole is granted based upon an offer of employment assistance from a recognized social agency or union. These cases are referred to as "reasonable assurance (that he or she will secure employment) cases."

Because of the importance of securing an offer of employment in order to secure parole release, various subterfuges are often used. These usually involve a fake offer of employment, commonly referred to as a "can opener." This type of activity is more prevalent in states where the release jobs are not closely investigated.

Hearing Examiners

Several jurisdictions utilize examiners to hold parole hearings. In these jurisdictions the parole board usually acts upon a report and recommendation from the examiner. The federal board has eight examiners who handle about 75% of the parole interviews, with the remainder handled by board members. The examiner holds a hearing at the institution and dictates a summary that is sent to the board with a

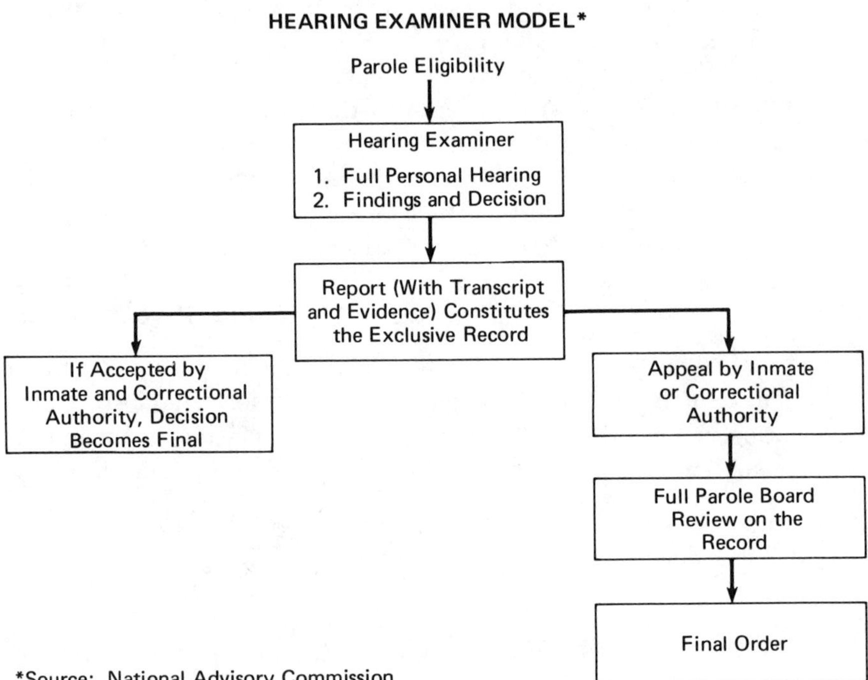

recommendation. The board then votes on whether to grant parole.[26] The Florida Parole and Probation Commission also uses hearing examiners. Inmates are interviewed on an annual basis, after which a report of the examiner's findings and recommendation is submitted to the Commission for parole consideration.[27]

Another hearing examiner model appears above. In this model the hearing officer makes a decision on whether or not to grant parole. As noted on the extreme right of the diagram, if the inmate is dissatisfied with the decision of the hearing officer, he can appeal to the full board of parole. It should be noted that the inmate is not interviewed by the parole board in this, or any other, hearing examiner model.

Hearing examiners are usually utilized in order to reduce the workload of the parole board. Since hearing examiners tend to be selected on the basis of professional competence, their use portends an improvement in the parole process.

[26] Orland and Tyler, p. 103.

[27] *Florida Annual Report*, 1974, pp. 16–17.

Chapter 10

Parole Services–Institutional and Field

INSTITUTIONAL SERVICES

Parole services are usually divided into institutional services and field services. The basic responsibility of the institutional parole staff is to prepare reports on inmates for the parole board. They also help inmates secure furloughs, work-release or halfway house programs, and they may assist with personal problems ranging from matters relating to a wife and children to questions of a technical or legal nature.

Under ideal conditions, when an offender is first received at the institution he is interviewed by the parole staff. The results of the interview, psychiatric and psychological tests, and the information in the presentence report are then used to plan an institutional program for the inmate. The parole staff periodically updates the material with additional information. They discusss tentative release plans with inmates, and request the field staff to visit and interview family members and prospective employers. When an inmate is ready to meet the parole board, they provide a report on the inmate that includes an evaluation of changes made since he was first interviewed at the prison. The report may also contain a recommendation, if this is requested by the board.

Unfortunately, ideal conditions do not usually exist in the parole system. Because of a lack of trained staff most parole boards receive institutional reports that are "thrown together" from the presentence report right before the hearing.[1]

Institutional parole staff may also hold group meetings with new inmates to orient them about parole. These group sessions are then followed up with individual interviews. There are also pre-parole group sessions at which the parole staff attempts to lower anxiety about meeting the board. When an inmate has been granted parole, or is eligible for conditional release, he or she will meet with a parole staff member for a final discussion of the release program and the rules of parole, prior to leaving the prison.

Institutional parole staff, in some jurisdictions, are responsible for notifying local law enforcement agencies of the impending release of certain offenders.[2] They also determine the probable disposition of any warrants that have been lodged against an inmate. When appropriate, they will arrange for an out-of-state program under the Interstate Compact.

In some states, non-parole institutional staff perform the same, or similar, functions as institutional parole officers. For example, New York and California utilize correctional counselors in their institutions. The counselors in both of these states do not have any direct parole responsibilities. California describes the correctional counselor position as follows:

> In a correctional institution, a Correctional Counselor's major responsibility is the study of the individual prisoner for purposes of understanding his needs and outlining a program for his rehabilitation. Following initial classification and assignment of the inmate to a rehabilitation program, the Counselor continues individual counseling and participates in the group counseling, study, and therapy programs aimed at preparing the inmate for eventual return to the community.[3]

FIELD SERVICES

The second basic service of a parole agency is the field service. Field service staff usually operate out of district offices located throughout

[1] Parker, p. 32.

[2] Some states require that when an offender is released, the police in the area where he is to reside, or where the crime occurred, must be notified. In some instances the parolee must register with the local enforcement agency. Some states require notification or registration for all sex offenders, while some, such as New York, require it for second (or more) felony offenders.

[3] California Personnel Board Announcement, March 26, 1975.

the state. They conduct field investigations requested by the institutional parole staff relative to release programs, and they supervise parolees.

CONDITIONS OF PAROLE

Every conditionally released or paroled prisoner is required to sign an agreement to abide by certain regulations. This aspect of parole has its origins in the Ticket of Leave, and modern conditions of parole resemble Ticket of Leave regulations. Parole conditions are markedly similar throughout most jurisdictions, and are also very similar to probation regulations.

Sixty percent of the jurisdictions either prohibit or require permission to associate with or correspond with "undesirables," usually defined as persons with criminal records; seventy-nine percent require periodic reports; eighty-seven percent require permission for or notification of any change in employment or residence; and seventy-two percent require an initial arrival report within a certain period after release from prison.[4]

The Attica Report noted that parole regulations are often petty and demeaning, "or of such broad sweep that they lend themselves to arbitrary and selective enforcement by parole officers."[5] The President's Commission states that "The strictness with which parole rules are enforced varies greatly from jurisdiction to jurisdiction, depending in part on the training of the parole officer, but chiefly on the formal and informal policies of the parole system." The Commission also points out that when rules are extremely detailed, they are often overlooked by the parole officer. The Commission states that when the conditions of parole are very broad, parole officers and parolees seem to understand that certain rules will operate even though they are not explicitly set out in the parole rules.[6]

The National Advisory Commission on Criminal Justice Standards and Goals recommends that parole rules be kept to an absolute minimum, with parole boards tailoring them to fit each individual parolee. Under their recommended system, parole officers would be given temporary authority to impose new conditions or amend old ones

[4] Parker, p. 36.

[5] N.Y.S. Spec. Comm. on Attica, p. xix.

[6] *Task Force Report*, p. 69.

in accordance with the needs of the case, subject to the approval of the board of parole.[7]

Conditions of parole can generally be grouped into two main categories: 1. Those that tend toward reform and urge the parolee toward a non-criminal and productive life, and 2. those that can be used by parole officers to control the parolee's actions. The parole regulations of California and Ohio will provide samples of these categories.

Conditions of Parole
State of California

1. RELEASE, REPORTING AND TRAVEL: I agree to report to my Parole Agent upon parole and to keep him continuously informed of my residence and employment locations. I will not leave the State of California without first having the written permission of my Parole Agent.

2. LAW: I shall obey all Federal and State laws, and municipal and county ordinances.

3. WEAPONS: I will not own, possess, use, sell, or have under my control any firearms or other deadly weapons as defined in Section 3024 of the Penal Code.

4. PERSONAL CONDUCT: I will not engage in assaultive activities, violence, or threats of violence of any sort. I shall behave in a manner justifying the opportunity granted by parole.

5. NARCOTICS OR DRUGS: I will not illegally possess, use or traffic in any narcotic drugs, as defined by Division 10 of the Health and Safety Code, or dangerous or hypnotic drugs as defined by Section 4211 of the Business and Professions Code. I further agree to participate in anti-narcotic programs in accordance with instructions from my Parole Agent.

6. PAROLE AGENT INSTRUCTIONS: I agree to comply with or respond to verbal and written instructions which may be imposed by my Parole Agent from time to time as may be governed by the special requirements of my individual situation.

7. SPECIAL CONDITIONS: I agree to abide by the following special conditions of parole as stipulated below.

[7] Nat. Adv. Comm., p. 413.

Conditions of Parole
State of Ohio

1. Upon release from the institution, report as instructed to your Parole Officer (or any other person designated) and thereafter report as directed.

2. Secure written permission of the Adult Parole Authority before leaving the State of Ohio.

3. Obey all municipal ordinances, state and federal laws, and at all times conduct yourself as a responsible law-abiding citizen.

4. Never purchase, own, possess, use or have under your control, a deadly weapon or firearm.

5. Follow all instructions given you by your Parole Officer or other officials of the Adult Parole Authority and abide by any special conditions imposed by the Adult Parole Authority.

6. If you feel any of the conditions, or instructions are causing problems, you may request a meeting with your parole officer's supervisor. The request stating your reasons for the conference should be in writing when possible.

Parole Field Services in California [8]

The Parole and Community Services Division is one of the four divisions within the Department of Corrections. Its primary function is to supervise the men and women released from the 13 state correctional institutions.

In 1975 there were nearly 20,000 men and women under the supervision of the Parole Division: 11,200 male felons, 800 female felons, 6,100 civil addicts (both male and female), and 200 work furloughees. These men and women are distributed geographically throughout the entire state, and for the most part live independently or with their families. Some parolees reside in community correctional centers or halfway houses in the community operated by either the state or private organizations. The parole Division presently operates community correctional centers in Sacramento, Los Angeles and Oakland. These semi-structured environments are particularly useful for men and women early in their parole who need gradual reintegration into the community.

[8] From the California Department of Corrections.

The Parole Division is divided into five geographical regions, with each region under the administrative direction of a Regional Parole Administrator. The Regional Parole Administrators report to the Deputy Director who is the chief administrative officer of the division. Each region consists of a number of parole units who are responsible for providing supervision and services to approximately 300 parolees/releasees in a specified geographical area. These units are supervised by a Unit Supervisor (Parole Agent III), and the units normally consist of seven parole agents and two clerical positions.

The Parole Division operates two outpatient clinics located in San Francisco and Los Angeles which provide a variety of psychiatric services for parolees. The division also operates a clinic in Los Angeles for approximately 350 parolees who participate in a methadone maintenance program which is one method of combating narcotic abuse.

A parole agent supervising felon parolees has a caseload of approximately 50 men or women. Caseloads in the non-felon or civil addict program average approximately 33. The parole agent provides public protection by staying knowledgeable about his parolees. Via field supervision of the parolee and collateral checks with his employer, family and friends, law enforcement and other public and private agencies, the parole agent remains abreast of the parolee's overall adjustment. An important part of this function is the timely intervention the parole agent applies to prevent or minimize any delinquent behavior by the parolee. This intervention may range from counseling or verbal instructions to placing the parolee in custody.

The best public protection results from the parole agent's ability to provide guidance and assistance in order that the parolee can live crime-free. Case assistance needs vary tremendously from parolee to parolee, and this function calls for ingenuity and initiative on the part of the parole agent. Case assistance ranges from helping the parolee to find lodging for the night, to developing a long-range program involving lasting commitment to a vocational or avocational pursuit.

The parole agent must know and utilize the various law enforcement agencies in his area for purposes of sharing information, additional surveillance in selected cases, and assistance in apprehension of parolees when indicated. The parole agent must have a thorough knowledge of resources in his community that can assist parolees with problems of housing, subsistence, employment, social, marital and mental problems, acceptable leisure-time activities, etc. Proper utilization of these resources can provide the information, structure and assistance that results in optimum public protection and parolee case assistance.

To achieve both the goals of public protection and case assistance, the parole agent constantly gathers and disseminates information. This includes sharing information about parolees with other criminal justice personnel when appropriate, furnishing parolees with information about available community resources, presentation of information about parolees to public and private agencies, potential employers, and to the public in order to gain support for a policy of parole rehabilitation.

In individual cases, parole agents are responsible to see that information is fully and accurately presented to law enforcement agencies, other public and private agencies, court personnel, including judges, district attorneys, public defenders and probation officers, and last and most important to California's parole boards.

The parole agent is responsible for keeping the paroling authorities (the Adult Authority, the Narcotic Addict Evaluation Authority, and the Women's Board of Terms and Parole) informed of negative behavior on the part of the parolee and for beginning the revocation process when the parolee's behavior has reached a point where his/her remaining in the community is no longer appropriate. The parole agent also informs the paroling authority of good adjustment on parole by recommending early discharge from parole supervision.

LENGTH OF SUPERVISION

The length of time an offender must spend on parole is governed by the length of his sentence and the laws of the state where he was convicted. However, parole usually lasts more than two years, with individual states averaging from one to seven years.[9] In New York a parolee is

[9] Frank P. Prassel, *Introduction to American Criminal Justice* (New York: Harper and Row, 1975), p. 202.

eligible for an unconditional discharge from parole after he has had an exemplary adjustment under supervision for at least five years. Other states permit an offender to be discharged from parole after a shorter period of supervision, as long as there have not been any indications of new criminality.

VIOLATION OF PAROLE

Parole violation procedures are in a state of flux as the result of court challenges. They may also vary from jurisdiction to jurisdiction. Accordingly, the procedures discussed in this section are general in nature and simplified for purposes of study. The flow chart at the end of this chapter presents an overview of the system and indicates the possibilities available at each stage of the process.

Probation violation remains part of the judicial (court) process, while parole violation is an agency administrative function divorced from the courts. The parole violation process begins with a request from the parole officer for a warrant based on alleged violations of parole. The warrant stage varies from agency to agency. For example, the United States Board of Parole is rather conservative about issuing parole violation warrants, and in the federal system this stage is a time-consuming procedure. However, in New York a parole violation warrant can be issued by a senior parole officer immediately.

After a warrant is issued, it can be enforced by a parole officer, warrant officer, or other law enforcement personnel. If the parolee is already in custody (as the result of a new arrest), the warrant will be filed against him as a detainer. If the parolee is not in custody, an attempt will be made to enforce the warrant by arresting him.

Preliminary Hearing

After the parolee is in custody, he is given a list of the charges of parole violation alleged against him. He is entitled to a preliminary hearing at this stage. (If he waives this right, he will be held in custody pending a revocation hearing.) At the preliminary hearing the parolee will have an opportunity to challenge the alleged violations and to confront adverse witnesses, including his parole officer. The hearing officer who presides at the preliminary hearing may be another parole officer or other employee of the agency. In New York members of the parole board served briefly as hearing officers, but currently senior parole officers are assigned to serve in that capacity. The hearing officer determines if there are reasonable grounds to believe that the parolee has violated one or more of the conditions of parole, referred to as "probable cause." If probable cause is found, the parolee will be held in custody pending a revocation hearing. If probable cause is not found, the parolee will be restored to supervision.

Revocation Hearing

A revocation hearing is similar to a preliminary hearing except that it is more comprehensive. The purpose of the revocation hearing is to determine if the violation of parole is serious enough to revoke parole and return the parolee to prison. If parole is not revoked, the parolee is restored to supervision.

Delinquent Time. If parole is revoked, the question arises as to just how much time the parolee must serve in prison. This can vary from jurisdiction to jurisdiction. In New York a parolee receives credit for the time he spends under parole supervision ("street time") prior to his violation. In the federal system parole violators do not receive credit for "street time."[10] Thus, in New York, an inmate who is paroled after serving two years of a four-year sentence is required to be on parole for two years, the remainder of his four-year sentence. If after one year he violates parole and is returned to prison, he will only have to serve the one year remaining on his sentence. However, in a jurisdiction that does not give credit for "street time," this same parolee will be required to serve two years in prison. The one year of satisfactory time on parole is not credited against his four year sentence in the event of a parole violation that results in his being returned to prison. The following section is provided by the American Bar Association and deals with this problem in much greater detail.

Street Time[11]

An overwhelming percentage of those who are convicted will, at one time or another, serve at least part of their sentence in a community correctional program as an alternative to, or an ad-

[10] 18 U.S.C. Section 4205.

[11] Richard C. Hand and Richard G. Singer, "Street Time," *Sentencing Computation Laws and Practice: A Preliminary Survey* (Washington, D.C.: American Bar Association Commission on Correctional Facilities and Services, Jan. 1974), Chapter 4.

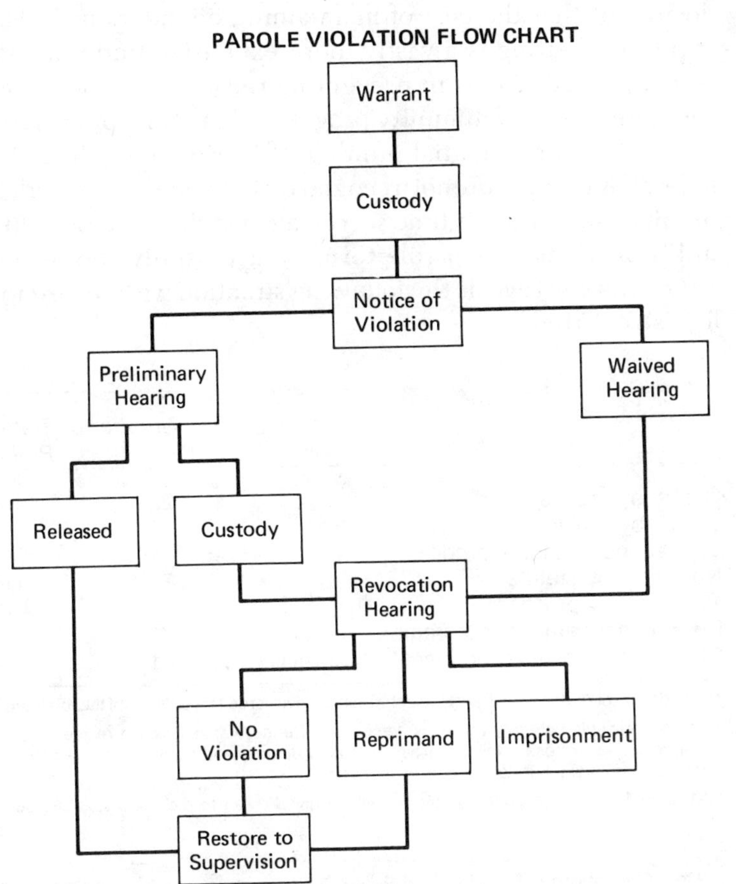

junct of, incarceration.[45] The expanding use of these community correctional programs—probation, suspended sentence, work and education release, and parole among them—takes on added significance as the reality of the failure of prisons to rehabilitate becomes manifest.[46] Further, studies are now beginning to

[45] It was estimated that 75% of all offenders in 1967–68 (or 836,000 individuals) were on probation or parole. By 1975, it is estimated that 81% of all offenders (or 1,320,000 individuals) will be on probation or parole. Final report of the Joint Commission on Correctional Manpower and Training, *A Time to Act* (1969). See also President's Commission on Law Enforcement and Administration of Justice, *Task Force Report: Corrections,* 3 (1967); Federal Bureau of Prisons, *National Statistics: Prisoners in State and Federal Institutions for Adult Felons* 22 (1972).

[46] See n. 15, *supra*. See also, Note, Jam in the Revolving Door: A Prisoner's Right to Rehabilitation, 60 *Geo. L. J.* 225 (1971); Note, Statutory Right to Treatment for Prisoners: Society's Right of Self Defense, 50 *Neb. L. Rev.* 543 (1971); Singer, Prison Conditions: An Unconstitutional Roadblock to Rehabilitation, 20 *Cath. U. L. Rev.* 365

document that the cost of maintaining offenders in a closed institutional setting is a vastly more expensive undertaking, with less apparent success in preventing recidivism, when compared with alternative community programs.[47] Yet, it appears from our survey that a substantial number of jurisdictions, including the federal system,[48] do not recognize that time spent under community supervision is time served against the sentence unless the full probationary or parole term is successfully completed.

Our survey reveals the following situation with regard to credit for "street time":

	Number of States	
	Parole	*Probation*
Credit, by statute	22*	4
Credit, by practice	1	2
Discretionary statute, credit	1	1
No credit, by statute	25**	14
No credit, by practice	1	10
Discretionary statute, no credit	1	17***
Discretionary statute, no identifiable practice	1	4

* Included in this category is New Hampshire which gives credit for only 1/3 of the total "street time".

** Included in this category are New Jersey and Pennsylvania which give credit to "technical" violators but not to those convicted of a new crime; Kentucky and North Carolina which give credit to conditional releases but not to regular parolees.

*** Included in this category is Louisiana which gives credit to technical violators but not those

(1971); Greenberg & Stender, The Prison as a Lawless Agency, 21 *Buff. L. Rev.* 799 (1972); Conrad, Corrections and Simple Justice, 18 *J. Cr. L. & Crim.* 208, 209 (1973). Further testimony of the total failure of prisons to rehabilitate may be found in the exhortations by a wide variety of groups concerned with criminal justice to declare a moratorium on new prison construction. Report of the Forty-Second American Assembly, *Prisoners in America* (1972); National Council on Crime and Delinquency, *Policies, Background and Information*—Institutional Construction (September, 1972); National Advisory Commission on Criminal Justice Standards and Goals, *Report on Corrections,* Standards 11.1 and 9.10 (1973); National Association of Social Workers, *Issues in Adult and Juvenile Justice* (May 1973). See also, Nagle, *The New Red Barn: A Critical Look at the American Prison* (1973).

[47] See e.g. Smith, *A Quiet Revolution* (1972); State of Maryland Criminal Justice Report, *Analysis of Comprehensive Plans to Develop a Statewide Community Corrections System* (July 1973); President's Commission on Law Enforcement and Administration of Justice *Task Force Report: Corrections* 28 (1967).

[48] 18 U.S.C. §4205. The constitutionality of this section has been attacked repeatedly without success. See e.g. *Hodge v. Markley,* 339 F.2d 973 (7th Cir. 1963); *Van Buskirk v. Wilkinson,* 216 F.2d 735 (9th Cir. 1954); *Hedrick v. Steele,* 187 F.2d 261 (8th Cir. 1951). See also, *Dolan v. Swope,* 138 F.2d 301 (7th Cir. 1943); *Bates v. Rivers,* 323 F.2d 311 (D.C. Cir. 1963) (upholding similar D.C. statute); *Woods v. Steiner,* 207 F. Supp. 945 (D. Md. 1962) (upholding similar Maryland statute).

With the practices of the various jurisdictions so dramatically divided, it is appropriate to briefly examine the legal defenses and justifications which underlie the posture of those states which continue to deny credit and likewise to advance emerging constitutional theories which argue for credit.[49]

The thrust of the constitutional argument for giving credit for time served to a revoked probationer or parolee is simply that if credit is not given, the prisoner, upon completion of sentence, will have served more time on parole (or probation) *and* in prison than that to which he was originally sentenced. Thus, in those jurisdictions which do not credit "street time" a prisoner might well serve without incident three-fourths or more of a parole term only to be revoked for a violation of condition of release and reincarcerated for the unserved portion of his sentence computed from the date of release from prison, undiminished by the months and perhaps years spent on parole.[50] This nonjudicial increase in sentence is accomplished without any of the constitutionally mandated due process protections which accompany conviction and sentence under normal circumstances. (Under modern standards, probation is increasingly deemed to be an independent sentence.)

McNeil v. Director of Patuxent Institution, 407 U.S. 245 (1972) established that a convicted person may not be held longer than the sentence imposed by the trial judge. There, a prisoner was sentenced to a term of five years (apparently *not* the maximum allowable), and complained that he had already spent six years at Maryland's Institution.[51] The Court found that the prisoner had indeed been confined in excess of his judicially imposed sentence despite the state's assertions that McNeil was being held for treatment. It is apparent from *McNeil*, and a substantial number of other cases as well, that *any* extra-judicial determinations which extend imprisonment beyond the term of the sentence set

[49] See, Note, A la Recherche du Temps Perdu: The Constitutionality of Denial of Credit on Revocation of Parole, 35 *U. Chi. L. Rev.* 762 (1968).

[50] *Gibbs v. Blackwell*, 354 F.2d 469 (5th Cir. 1965) represents the only case that might possibly be construed as a successful attack on the practice of denying "street time" credits. In Gibbs, supra, it appeared to the court that the petitioner had lost seven years parole time by virtue of technical violations of parole conditions. The court hinted that if such were the case application of the provision in question (18 U.S.C. §4205) might constitute cruel and unusual punishment.

[51] McNeil was held under provision of Maryland's Defective Delinquent Statutes. Md. Ann. Code art. 31B-5, et. seq. (1957).

by the sentencing court violate due process of law.[52] In *Bates v. Rivers*, 323 F.2d 311 (D.C. Cir. 1963), Judge J. Skelly Wright in dissent found that the practice of denying credit to parole violators for time spent on parole was indistinguishable, in legal effect, from other non-judicial extensions of sentence.

> When the period fixed by judgment for the prisoner's release from custody and control has arrived, he may no longer be held under the original sentence—no matter whether he has or has not had parole granted or revoked. To keep him in confinement longer than called for by his sentence would be to deprive him of liberty without due process of law. The statute (18 U.S.C. §4205) should not be read to require an unconstitutional confinement. *Id.* at 315.

The practice of denying credit for "street time" also raises a number of equal protection issues. For example, a parolee who served several weeks on parole and who is then revoked has only those several weeks added to his custody. On the other hand, a parolee who observes his parole conditions for several years and is then violated for an identical offense, faces a term of custody that is substantially longer. Further, none would argue that a prisoner serving a sentence inside an institution may be held beyond his judicially imposed term, irrespective of his institutional record during the period of confinement. Yet the paroled person, by violating a condition of parole through actions which are often noncriminal,[53] is subject to an increase in sentence simply because the form of custody at the time of the commission of the act was parole rather than imprisonment. Thus, the denial of "street time" credit results in vastly dissimilar treatment of convicted persons absent any compelling, or even legitimate, state purpose that would justify such differentiation.

[52] *Jackson v. Indiana,* 406 U.S. 715 (1972) (confinement of prisoner for over three years pending a determination of competency to stand trial held illegal); *Baxstrom v. Herold,* 383 U.S. 107 (1966) (confinement of prisoners, upon completion of their prison sentences, to mental institutions absent adequate judicial approval or procedure held illegal); *North Carolina v. Pearce,* 395 U.S. 711, 718 (1969) (discussing unconstitutionality of increased sentences upon retrial, the Court said ". . . the constitutional violation is flagrantly apparent in a case involving the imposition of a maximum sentence after reconviction"); *Williams v. Illinois,* 399 U.S. 235 (1970) (confining indigent persons beyond the maximum statutory sentence for the offense simply because they are unable to pay fines which were imposed is illegal). Cf. *Rouse v. Cameron,* 373 F.2d 451 (D.C. Cir. 1966); *Short v. United States,* 344 F.2d 550 (D.C. Cir. 1965).

[53] See e.g. Arluke, A Summary of Parole Rules, 15 *Crime and Delinquency* 267, 272–73 (1969); ABA Resource Center on Correctional Law and Legal Services, *Parole Conditions in the United States,* Table I and related text (1973).

Yet, these arguments notwithstanding, courts have consistently upheld the right of states to withhold "street time" credits. Many have done so on the theory that denial of "street time" does not result in an extension of sentence since the releasee was not physically confined (not "in custody") and therefore, during this period of time, was not "serving" a sentence.[54] Most others, conceding that while probation and parole may involve custody, insist that it is not the type of custody which, in the "contemplation" of the sentencing court, satisfies a prison sentence.[55]

Both arguments overlook fundamental realities concerning the nature of conditional release. In fact, as well as in theory, conditional release involves significant restraints on the liberty and freedom of movement of the releasee which are in legal effect, no less custodial than actual confinement.[56] For example, the conditions of release may require that a person live continuously at one specific residence or remain in a designated geographic area; they may require continuous employment at a specified job as a precondition to continuous release; they may make failure to present a timely report of activities or to give notification of a change of address grounds for revocation; they may prohibit the parolee or probationer from driving or owning a car, from possessing alcoholic beverages, from associating with known criminals or persons of "bad reputation," or even from marrying.[57]

Similarly, conditional releasees suffer from the loss of many rights taken for granted by the ordinary citizen. Thus, those placed on probation or parole may be subject to "surprise" visits by a parole or probation officer.[58] Arrest or violator warrants may

[54] *E. G. Hedrick v. Steele,* 187 F.2d 261, 262 (8th Cir. 1951).

[55] E.G. *Dolan v. Swope,* 138 F.2d 301 (7th Cir. 1943); *Howard v. United States,* 274 F.2d 100 (8th Cir. 1960); *Yates v. Looney,* 250 F.2d 956 (10th Cir. 1958). For a discussion of the different problems which are raised in denials of "street time" credit upon revocation of probation, see Note, A la Recherche du Temps Perdu: The Constitutionality of Denial of Credit on Revocation of Parole, 35 *U. Chi. L. Rev.* 762, 773–775 (1968).

[56] Indeed, the acceptance of parole as a valid form of custody is acknowledged in both the statutes, e.g. 18 U.S.C. §4203; D.C. Code Ann. §24–204 (1971), and the case law, e.g. *Jones v. Cunningham,* 371 U.S. 236, 242, 243 (1963); *Hyser v. Reed,* 318 F.2d 225 (D.C. Cir. 1963), *cert. den. sub. nom. Thompson v. U.S. Board of Parole,* 375 U.S. 957 (1963); *Taylor v. United States Marshall,* 352 F.2d 232 (10th Cir. 1965); *Sobell v. Reed,* 327 F. Supp. 1299 (SDNY 1971) The Supreme Court just recently extended the definition of "custody" to include a convicted defendant who has been released on his own recognizance while his appeal is pending. *Hensley v. Municipal Court,* __ U.S. __ (1973), No. 71–1428 (April 18, 1973), 13 Cr. L. 3041.

[57] See n. 52, *supra.*

[58] See n. 58, *infra.*

be issued under less stringent standards than would apply to the private citizen. Cases continue to hold that a different standard of "reasonableness" applies to searches and seizures of conditional releasees than that which applies to the unconvicted person.[59] Finally restrictions on the right to travel,[60] the right to live with a person of one's own choosing,[61] and others[62] have been upheld as proper by various state courts. These restraints are substantial, and influence the lives of conditional releasees just as surely as if they were physically confined.

Finally, those courts which have held that parole is not the kind of custody intended by sentencing courts have done so largely on the strength of the now discredited notion that the granting and withholding of parole is a matter of legislative grace. Because parole is a privilege, it is said, so also is it a matter of parole board discretion as to the granting or withholding of "street time" credit. However, the Supreme Court's recent holdings in *Morrissey v. Brewer*, 408 U.S. 471 (1972), and *Gagnon v. Scarpelli*, 411 U.S. 718 (1973), that parole revocation proceedings must comply with due process standards, represents a whole new approach to the area of conditional release. By reason of *Morrissey* and related cases, where governmental actions affect substantial interests of individual citizens, such actions are subject to constitutional scrutiny regardless of whether the interests are characterized as "rights" or "privileges." [63] Where, as here, a criminal sentence is materially affected by administrative action

[59] *United States ex. rel. Santos v. New York State Board of Parole,* 441 F.2d 1216 (2nd Cir. 1970); *United States ex. rel. Spearling v. Fitzpatrick,* 426 F.2d 1161 (2nd Cir. 1970); *Dimarco v. Greene,* 385 F.2d 556 (6th Cir. 1967); *Lombardino v. Heyd,* 318 F. Supp. 648 (E.D. La. 1970); *United States ex. rel. Randazzo v. Follette,* 282 F. Supp. 10 (S.D.N.Y. 1968); *People v. Hayko,* 7 Cal. App. 2d 606, 86 Cal. Rptr. 726 (1970); *People v. Mason,* 14 Cal. App. 3d 859, 92 Cal. Rptr. 628 (1971). See also, White, The Fourth Amendment Rights of Parolees and Probationers, 31 *U. Pitt. L. Rev.* 196 (1969), Note, Extending Search and Seizure Protection to Parolees in California, 22 *Stan L. Rev.* 429 (1969).

[60] *Berrigan v. Sigler,* __ F. Supp. __ (D.D.C. 1973) (parole boards' refusal to permit travel to North Vietnam by parolees does not violate First or Fifth Amendment freedoms).

[61] *In re Peeler,* 266 Cal. App. 2d 623, 64 Cal. Rptr. 290 (1967) (allowing condition which effectively barred defendant from living with her husband).

[62] E.g. *State v. Garner,* 54 Wis. 2d 100, 194 N.W. 2d 649 (1971) (condition requiring probationer to take his family off county welfare rolls upheld).

[63] See *Bell v. Burson,* 402 U.S. 433 (1971); *Goldberg v. Kelly,* 397 U.S. 254 (1970); *Wisconsin v. Constantineau,* 400 U.S. 433 (1971); *Greene v. McElroy,* 360 U.S. 474 (1959). See also Van Alstyne, The Demise of the Rights-Privilege Distinction in Constitutional Law, 81 *Harv. L. Rev.* 1430 (1968).

(revocation of parole without crediting time to the expiration of the prisoner's sentence), the Constitution *demands* such scrutiny. As one commentator has noted,

> The essential distinction between simple revocation and revocation accompanied by denial of credit is the difference between the mode of custody and the duration of custody: while revocation merely provides that a prisoner's sentence be spent in prison, denial of credit actually extends the period of custody beyond that originally imposed. Since the denial of credit is administratively imposed under procedures far less stringent than those required for incarceration, (Section 4205) is open to attack on the ground that it denies liberty without due process of law.[64]

Constitutional theories aside, for systems that owe much of the vitality they enjoy today to their trumpeted objectives of both rehabilitating offenders and easing their return to productive citizenship, it is curious that correctional authorities continue to deny "street time" solely on the basis of narrow, technical arguments. For it seems contrary to the purpose and theory of parole to permit the paroling authorities' control over the parolee to weigh more heavily as the parolee nears completion of his sentence. There is no mistaking that those who have forfeited time spent on the streets on conditional release view the practice as grossly unfair. Model legislation dealing with the issue of "street time" has found this unfairness to be dispositive. The American Law Institute's *Model Penal Code,*[65] N.C.C.D.'s *Standard Probation and Parole Act*[66] and the National Advisory Commission on Criminal Justice Standards and Goals[67] all provide for full credit for time served on parole. It is past due time for the jurisdictions which do not give "street time" credit to remedy an ill-conceived practice.

[64] Note, A la Recherche du Temps Perdu: The Constitutionality of Denial of Credit on Revocation of Parole, 35 *U. Chi. L. Rev.* 762, 763 (1968).

[65] ". . . A parolee whose parole is revoked for violation of the conditions of parole shall be recommitted for the remainder of his maximum parole term, after credit thereon for the period served on parole prior to the violation and for reductions for good behavior earned while on parole." *Model Penal Code,* §305.17(1).

[66] ". . . The period served on parole or conditional release shall be deemed service of the term of imprisonment . . . the total time served may not exceed the maximum term or sentence." *Standard Probation and Parole Act,* §27 (1955).

[67] ". . . Time spent under parole supervision until the date of violation for which parole is revoked should be credited against the sentence imposed by the court." *Report on Corrections,* §16.15(3).

Credit for "Street Time"—Parole*

Alabama	*Yes*
Alaska	*No*
Arizona	*No*
Arkansas	*Discretionary*
California	*In part*
Colorado	*No*
Connecticut	*Yes*
Delaware	*Yes*
District of Columbia	*No*
Florida	*No*
Georgia	*Yes*
Hawaii	*Yes*
Idaho	*No*
Illinois	*Yes*
Indiana	*No*
Iowa	*Yes*
Kansas	*Yes*
Kentucky	*No*
Louisiana	*No*
Maine	*No*
Maryland	*Discretionary*
Massachusetts	*Yes*
Michigan	*Yes*
Minnesota	*Yes*
Mississippi	*No*
Missouri	*Yes*
Montana	*Yes*
Nebraska	*Yes*
Nevada	*Yes*
New Hampshire	*Yes*
New Jersey	*No*
New Mexico	*Yes*
New York	*Yes*
North Carolina	*Some classes of offenders may receive credit*
North Dakota	*No*
Ohio	*Yes*
Oklahoma	*Yes*
Oregon	*No*
Pennsylvania	*Some classes of offenders may receive credit*
Rhode Island	*No*
South Carolina	*No*
South Dakota	*No*
Tennessee	*Yes*
Texas	*No*
Utah	*Yes*
Vermont	*No*
Virginia	*No*
Washington	*Yes*
West Virginia	*Some classes of offenders may receive credit*
Wisconsin	*Yes*
Wyoming	*No*
Federal	*No*

**Source:* Richard C. Hand and Richard G. Singer, *Sentencing Computation Laws and Practice: A Preliminary Survey* (Washington, D.C.: American Bar Association, 1974).

EXECUTIVE CLEMENCY

Some states use parole officers to transport parole violators back to prison. New York parole officers conduct personal investigations of correction officer applicants, and may apprehend inmates who escape from prison. However, the more routine additional services usually provided by a parole agency are those relative to executive clemency.

Executive clemency is an act of grace that provides a benefit to an individual who has been convicted of a crime. Governors and the President of the United States have the power to exercise some form of executive clemency. Executive clemency was vividly and uniquely demonstrated by President Ford when he pardoned Richard Nixon for crimes that had not even been prosecuted.

In most states, if not all, it is the responsibility of the parole agency to provide an investigation report prior to the granting of executive clemency. The report is similar to a presentence report that a probation agency provides to the court. There are three basic acts of executive clemency; reprieve, commutation, and pardon.

Reprieve

A reprieve, as we studied earlier in this text, is the temporary suspension of the execution of sentence. Its use today is extremely limited, and usually concerns cases in which capital punishment has been ordered. In such cases a governor or the President can grant a reprieve, a stay of execution, in order to provide more time for legal action or other deliberations.

Commutation

A commutation is a modification of sentence to the benefit of an offender. Commutation has been used when an inmate provided assistance to the prison staff, sometimes during prison riots. It may also be granted to inmates with a severe illness, such as cancer. The laws governing commutation differ from state to state. In New York an inmate sentenced to more than one year who has served at least one-half of his minimum period of imprisonment, and who is not otherwise eligible for release or parole, may have his sentence commuted by the governor. According to the Executive Clemency Bureau, New York had five commutation cases in 1974, while the

Tennessee Department of Correction reports that from April 1975 to June 1975 there were twenty-two commutations granted.

Pardon

The basis for a pardon may vary in different states, but it is not used extensively anywhere. For example, while Tennessee granted four pardons in the second half of 1974, New York has not granted a pardon since 1945. (In New York the only basis for a pardon is new evidence indicating that the defendant did not commit the offense of which he was accused and convicted.)

Chapter 11

Legal Decisions Affecting Parole

As noted in Part One, legal decisions that affect probation also affect parole. Thus, the decision rendered in *Gagnon v. Scarpelli*, relating to probation, used precedents established in the *Morrissey v. Brewer* decision, which relates to parole. The three theories of parole are also similar, if not identical, to the three theories of probation.

THREE THEORIES OF PAROLE

Traditionally an individual on parole has not been considered a free man, despite the fact that he has been released from imprisonment. The basis for imposing restrictions on a parolee's freedom is contained in three theories:

1. GRACE Theory—parole is a conditional privilege, a gift from the board of parole. If any of the conditions of this privilege are violated, it can be revoked.
2. CONTRACT Theory—every parolee is required to agree to certain terms and conditions in return for his conditional freedom. A violation

of the conditions is a breech of contract which can result in a revocation of parole.

3. CUSTODY Theory—the parolee is in the legal custody of the prison or parole authorities, and as a result of this quasi-prisoner status, his constitutional rights are automatically limited and abridged.

The legal decisions discussed in this chapter often challenge one or more of the above theories.[1]

The Parole Hearing—Menechino v. Oswald, *U.S. Ct. of Appeals, Second Circuit, 1970*

Menechino was serving a 20 years to life sentence in New York for murder in the second degree. He was paroled in 1963 and returned to prison as a parole violator sixteen months later. He subsequently appeared before the board of parole and admitted consorting with individuals having criminal records and giving misleading information to his parole officer.

Two years later Menechino appeared before the board for a release hearing and parole was denied. He brought a court action claiming that his rights were violated by the absence of legal counsel at both his revocation and parole release hearings. The case reached the United States Court of Appeals, which rendered a decision in 1970. The Court held that:

1. Parole proceeding is non-adversary in nature, since both parties, the board and the inmate, have the same concern, rehabilitation.
2. Parole release hearings are not fact-finding determinations since the board makes a determination based upon numerous tangible and intangible factors.
3. The inmate has no "present private interest" to be protected since he is already imprisoned, and this "interest" is required before due process is applicable.

The Court further stated that "it is questionable whether a board of parole is even required to hold a hearing on the question of whether a prisoner should be released on parole." Relative to the question of parole revocation, the court advised that a minimum of procedural due

[1] *See* H. Richmond Fisher, pp. 23–29. "Probation and Parole: The Anomaly of Divergent Procedures," *Federal Probation*, (September 1974).

process should be provided since at this stage of the parole process a parolee has a present private interest in the possible loss of his conditional freedom.

Although Menechino's case before the Federal Court was initiated with regard to parole release, it set forth important legal arguments relative to parole revocation. The opinions of the three judges who heard the case clearly indicate that if he had initiated an action concerning his parole revocation, he would have won his case on a two-to-one basis. This fact was duly noted by the New York State Court of Appeals in the next *Menechino Case*.

REASONS FOR DENYING PAROLE

As noted in Chapter 9, some states provide reasons for denying parole to an inmate and some do not. The 1975 session of the New York State Legislature, for example, reversed the parole board's long-standing policy against providing written reasons for denying parole. There are court decisions that have ordered parole boards to provide written reasons for denying parole (*Childs v. U. S. Board of Parole,* U.S. District Ct., Washington, D.C. October 15, 1973 and *Solari v. Regan,* N.Y. Appellate Division, January 20, 1975), but no decision had been rendered that would apply to all parole cases and all parole boards. The author believes that such a decision will be forthcoming.

Parole Revocation—Menechino v. Warden, *New York State Court of Appeals, January 12, 1971.*

Until recent times parole agencies operated without any interference from the judiciary. However, this all changed when the New York Court of Appeals handed down the *Menechino* decision that granted parolees, for the first time, the right to counsel and the right to call their own witnesses at parole revocation hearings. While the decision only applied to New York, it indicated the direction in which the courts would rule in future decisions.

This 4-3 decision caused the release of Joseph Menechino and required that an attorney be present at a parole revocation hearing. It also permitted a parolee to call upon witnesses who would speak in his behalf. The New York Court recognized that it was entering into an uncharted area of parole revocation. The issue they were called upon to resolve was stated succinctly at the very beginning of the majority opinion:

> . . . whether parolees are constitutionally entitled, under the Federal and State Constitutions, to the assistance of counsel in parole revocation hearings.

Menechino cited other legal decisions, such as *Mempa v. Rhay* and *In Re Gault*. While probationers, juveniles, and welfare recipients had already obtained limited due process protections at hearings that might cause the loss of freedom or financial distress, these protections had not yet been granted to parolees.

Parole Revocation—Morrissey v. Brewer, *408 U.S. 471, 92 S. Ct. (1972)*

This case marked the beginning of the Supreme Court's involvement with parole revocation procedures. Up until June, 1972, the United States Supreme Court had not ruled in this area. The issue before the United States Supreme Court in this case was whether the Due Process Clause of the Fourteenth Amendment required that a state afford an individual some opportunity to be heard prior to revoking his parole.

Morrissey was convicted of the false drawing of checks in 1967 in Iowa. After pleading guilty, he was sentenced to 7 years in prison. He was paroled from the Iowa State Penitentiary in June 1968. Seven months later, at the direction of his parole officer, he was arrested in his home town as a parole violator and held in a local jail. One week later, after review of the parole officer's written report, the Iowa Board of Parole revoked Morrissey's parole, and he was returned to prison. Morrissey received no hearing prior to the revocation of his parole.

Morrissey violated the conditions of his parole by buying a car under an assumed name and operating it without the permission of his parole officer. He also gave false information to the police and insurance company concerning his address after a minor traffic accident. Besides these violations, Morrissey also obtained credit under an assumed name and failed to report his residence to his parole officer. According to the parole officer's report, Morrissey could not explain any of these technical violations of parole regulations adequately.

Also considered in the *Morrissey* case was the petition of Booher, a convicted forger who had been returned to prison in Iowa by the Board of Parole without any hearing. Booher had admitted the technical violations of parole charges to his parole officer when taken into custody.

The Supreme Court considered all arguments that sought to keep the judiciary out of parole matters, and it rejected the "privilege" concept of parole as no longer viable. The court pointed out that parole is an established variation of imprisonment of convicted criminals.

The Court noted that parole revocation does not occur in just a few isolated cases—it has been estimated that 35–40 percent of all parolees are subjected to revocation and return to prison. The Court went on to state that with the numbers involved, protection of parolees' rights was necessary. The court did note, however, limitations on a parolee's rights:

> We begin with the proposition that the revocation of parole is not part of a criminal persecution and thus the full panoply of rights due to the defendant in such a proceeding does not apply to parole revocation. Supervision is not directly by the court but by an administrative agency which is sometimes an arm of the court and sometimes of the executive. Revocation deprives an individual not of absolute liberty to which every citizen is entitled but only the conditional liberty properly dependent on observance of special parole restrictions.

The Court noted that the traditional arguments against judicial intervention were no longer viable:

> It is hardly useful any longer to try to deal with this problem in terms of whether the parolee's liberty is a "right" or a "privilege." By whatever name the liberty is valuable and must be seen within the protection of the Fourteenth Amendment. Its termination calls for some orderly process however informal.

Also found in the decision is the New York State Court of Appeals response to the problem in the *Menechino Case*. The United States Supreme Court held as follows:

> Society thus has an interest in not having parole revoked because of erroneous information or because of an erroneous evaluation of the need to revoke parole, given the breach of parole conditions. See Parole ex rel *Menechino v. Warden*.

The Supreme Court in *Morrissey v. Brewer* considered parole revocation as a two-stage process (a) arrest of the parolee and preliminary hearing, and (b) the revocation hearing. Because there was usually a significant time lapse between the arrest and revocation hearing, the Supreme Court established the preliminary hearing for all parole violators. The Court set up the preliminary hearing in this fashion:

> Such an inquiry should be seen in the nature of a preliminary hearing to determine whether there is probable cause or reasonable grounds to believe that the arrested parolee had committed acts which would constitute a violation of parole condition.

The court specified that the hearing officer at this preliminary hearing be someone who is not involved in the case, that the parolee should be given the notice of the hearing, and that its purpose be to determine whether there is probable cause to believe that the parolee has violated a condition of his parole. On the request of the parolee, persons who have given adverse information on which parole violation is based, are to be made available for questioning in the parolee's presence. Based upon this information presented before the hearing officer, there should be a determination if there is reason to warrant the parolee's continued detention. The court stated that "no interest would be served by formalism in this process; informality will not lessen the utility of this inquiry in redressing the risk of error."

In reference to the revocation hearing, the Court stated:

> The parolee must have an opportunity to be heard and to show if he can that he did not violate the conditions or if he did, that circumstances in mitigation suggest the violation does not warrant revocation. The revocation hearing must be tendered within a reasonable time after the parolee is taken into custody. A lapse of two months as the state suggests occurs in some cases would not appear to be unreasonable.

The Court also suggested minimum requirements of due process for the revocation hearing:

> Our task is limited to deciding the minimum requirements of due process. They include (a) written notice of the claimed violation of parole; (b) disclosure to the parolee of evidence against him; (c) opportunity to be heard in person and to present witnesses and documentary evidence; (d) the right to confront and cross-examine adverse witnesses (unless the hearing officer specifically finds good cause for not allowing confrontation); (e) a "neutral and detached" hearing body such as a traditional parole board, members of which need not be judicial officers or lawyers; and (f) a written statement by the fact finders as to the evidence relied on and reasons for revoking parole.

The United States Supreme Court left open the question of counsel when it stated: "We do not reach or decide the question whether the parolee is entitled to the assistance of retained or to appointed counsel if he is indigent."

For further discussion of the right to be represented by counsel, refer back to the *Gagnon Decision*, Chapter 6.

DISCUSSION TOPICS

1. Compare early prisons to modern correctional institutions.
2. Compare the different options available for the administration of parole.
3. Examine the various criticisms of parole boards and provide suggestions for their improvement.
4. Discuss the criteria that should be used in considering the granting of parole.
5. Compare probation granting criteria with that used for granting parole.
6. Compare probation violation procedures with parole violation procedures.
7. Compare "street time" practices in probation and parole.
8. Compare the *Morrissey Decision* with the *Gagnon Decision*.

PART THREE

Supervision and Treatment

Chapter 12

Classification

Systems for classifying criminals (or typologies[1]) have been devised by such notables as Cesare Lombroso, Enrico Ferri, and Raffaele Garofalo who, like their more contemporary colleagues, often disagreed with each other's systems.[2] Schafer suggests that the "legion" of systems can be arranged as follows:[3]

Legal: criminals are placed into existing statutory categories.

Multiple-cause: criminals are grouped according to biological and social factors.

Sociological: criminals are classified according to societal factors.

Psychological: criminals are divided along psychiatric lines.

Constitutional: criminals are classified according to biopsychological functions.

Normative: criminals are placed according to their proclivity for commiting certain crimes.

[1] There is a technical difference between *classification* and *typology*. A typology is a form of categorization, while classification implies some form of action, e.g., treatment.

[2] Stephen Schafer, *Theories in Criminology* (New York: Random House, 1969), pp. 140, 142.

[3] *Ibid.*, p. 143.

Life-trend: criminals are referred to according to their overall life-styles.

In corrections, classification is a process for determining the needs and requirements of offenders and thereby assigning them to programs according to their needs and existing resources.[4] The classification schemes used in corrections are ostensibly for treatment purposes, but the National Advisory Commission notes that "even a cursory analysis of these schemes and the ways in which they are used reveals that they would more properly be called classification systems for management purposes."[5] In this respect, probation and parole agencies often use classification to determine the level of surveillance that should be employed in each case.[6]

The Commission reflects on its being "one of the ironies of progress that just as the development of 'treatment-relevant typologies' at last appears likely, there is growing disenchantment with the entire concept of the treatment model."[7]

Classification procedures are usually carried out through one of four organizational arrangements:[8]

1. classification within an existing institution
2. classification committees
3. reception-diagnosis centers
4. community classification teams.

The first system, when used within a state prison, usually involves a reception unit whose primary responsibility is to act as a diagnostic section. The professional personnel assigned to the unit make diagnostic studies and treatment recommendations. Treatment is based on a careful study of offenders by competent staff. This type of system suffers from several shortcomings. Reception unit reports are submitted to administrative authorities, and the concern of the latter may be with such problems as security rather than with treatment. As a result, recommendations may not be followed. Oftentimes the diagnosis is not linked directly to any operationally available programs. With the cur-

[4] Nat. Adv. Comm., p. 197.

[5] *Ibid.*

[6] *Ibid.*, p. 202.

[7] *Ibid.*, p. 197.

[8] *Ibid.*, pp. 205–16.

rent stress on research in criminal justice, this type of system has the additional handicap of usually not having a research component.

The classification committee is an arrangement whereby a professional committee studies case records and collectively makes judgments as to the disposition of inmates in the institution. In addition to making a diagnostic evaluation, the committee has the direct responsibility for converting inmate information into recommendations for inmate programs. The committee determines inmate security ratings, assigns individuals to educational and vocational training programs, and decides where they will work in the institution. In practice, the workload and the demands on time result in very little effective programming. Interviews with inmates tend to be brief and "ritualized." The staff on the committee usually have other pressing institutional responsibilities. In the end, the decisions of the committee tend to be based on administrative and not treatment needs.

The reception-diagnostic center is a manifestation of the late 1940's and early 1950's and the development of reception centers. Under this system, all offenders are sent to a central receiving institution for study, classification, and recommendations for training and treatment programs. A primary function of the reception center is to determine to which institution an offender is to be sent. The reception center system has several drawbacks. It places the major responsibility for collecting diagnostic information on one facility, thereby requiring a high degree of specialization. In addition, inmates tend to be held too long, and there is a great deal of anonymity. The National Advisory Commission considers the system obsolete, especially with the current emphasis on developing and programming correctional efforts at the community level.

A more recent development in correctional classification is the community classification team. This model can include probation and parole officers who are responsible for collecting the social history, and local practitioners who provide the necessary medical and psychiatric information. Institutional personnel, on a state and local basis, in cooperation with the other members of the team, review the records and match the offender's needs to the appropriate programs available.

Reception Centers in California and Georgia

In California, an extensive evaluation is provided each person received at a Reception Center. Staff members compile a complete personal history on each inmate, incorporating information from many sources including law enforcement agencies, courts, other correctional programs, military authorities probation offices, family members, friends, and employers.

Selected combinations of personality, educational achievement and intelligence tests along with personal interviews and observations provide clues to past and present behavior patterns, problem areas, and treatment needs. This mass of information is put together in the form of a case summary which serves as a basis for institutional assignment, treatment plans, custody status, and parole programming.

Following the initial reception-diagnostic process, individuals are assigned to institutions judged best suited to their treatment, training and security needs after review and approval by central office classification staff representatives.

In Georgia, there are two diagnostic and classification systems. All offenders 19-years-old and under are initially sent to the Georgia Industrial Institute in Alto, Georgia. Offenders 20-years-old and older are sent to the Georgia Diagnostic and Classification Center in Jackson, Georgia.

The diagnostic process begins the day an inmate arrives from sentencing. He is fingerprinted, photographed and assigned to a cell according to age, crime and previous record.

The inmate is then examined by a medical doctor and a dentist. Any problems are treated immediately or referred to the institution where the inmate is to be assigned.

The next step is an interview conducted on a one-to-one basis with a member of the evaluation team. A complete social history is obtained and letters are sent out to verify information.

The inmate is then given a series of tests. These include personality, intelligence and achievement tests along with manual dexterity tests.

After four or five weeks of gathering psychometrics and background materials from the family and the FBI, the inmate is scheduled for a final interview and evaluation. During the final interview, the inmate's desires are made known and are evaluated in light of test scores and replies from past schools and jobs. Plans for correctional education, vocational training, work assignments, treatment programs and institutional assignments are discussed.

The Classification Committee reviews each case for recommendations. The case is then sent to the assignment officer who then assigns the inmate to the correctional institution that best meets his individual needs.

The simplest way to classify criminals is by their arrest records. Roebuck presents a system that he derived from reviewing the records of 1,155 prison inmates in a District of Columbia reformatory. On the basis of an analysis of their pattern of arrests he proposes four types of criminal careers:[9]

1. *Single Pattern:* Three or more arrests for one type of crime.
2. *Multiple Pattern:* Two or more single patterns.
3. *Mixed Pattern:* Arrests for three or more offenses, but indicating no clear pattern.
4. *No Pattern:* Less than three arrests.

This system has many obvious shortcomings. An arrest record tells us little about the actual offense except the legal classification. An assault, for example, may have been part of a barroom fight or it may have been part of the collection procedure of a loan shark. Police officers often "overcharge" after making an arrest, thus inflating the seriousness of the crime, while prosecutors often permit plea bargaining that usually deflates the seriousness of the act.

Roebuck also proposes using "ten dimensions of study encompassing pertinent sociological and psychological variables": [10]

1. *Demographic:* age, educational level, and marital status.
2. *Offense Behavior and Interactional:* number and nature of criminal acts, their onset, and skill used.
3. *Group Support of Delinquent and/or Criminal Behavior:* association with criminal or delinquent groups, the intensity of the association, and the status in the group.
4. *Correctional Processing:* arrests and dispositions; probation, institutional, and parole adjustment.

[9] Roebuck cited from Marshal B. Clinard and Richard Quinney, *Criminal Behavior Systems* (New York: Holt, Rinehart, and Winston, 1967), pp. 5–6.

[10] Roebuck cited from John G. Cull and Richard E. Hardy, eds. *Fundamentals of Criminal Behavior and Correctional Systems* (Springfield, Ill.: Charles C. Thomas, 1973), pp. 156–58.

5. *Orientation and Reference Groups:* family background, social class, ethnic group, occupational group, delinquent or criminal subculture.

6. *Self-Concept:* subject's self-image; guilt or pride.

7. *Attitudes:* toward basic social institutions such as family, law, school, and government.

8. *Organic Variables:* physical health.

9. *Personality Structure:* psychiatric and psychological findings.

10. *Delinquent or Criminal Role Career:* pattern of criminality; progression, status level, or seriously mentally maladjusted criminal.

Clinard and Quinney suggest eight types of criminal systems (followed here by some legal categories of crimes for each): [11]

1. Violent Personal Crime: murder and assault.
2. Occasional Property Crime: auto theft and check forgery.
3. Occupational Crime: embezzlement and anti-trust violations.
4. Political Crime: treason and draft violations.
5. Public Order Crime: prostitution and drug usage (possession).
6. Conventional Crime: robbery and burglary.
7. Organized Crime: racketeering and organized gambling.
8. Professional Crime: confidence games and counterfeiting.

Clinard and Quinney present five classification characteristics, each with three possibilities, for the eight criminal behavior systems listed above. The possibilities are *low, medium,* and *high.* The classification characteristics are:

a. Criminal career of the offender

b. Group support of criminal behavior

c. Correspondence between criminal behavior and legitimate behavior patterns

d. Societal reaction

e. Legal categories of crime.

Within this scheme, for example, a criminal who is part of organized crime (Behavior System #7) would under classification characteristic b., Group support of criminal behavior, have the notation *high.* A

[11] *See* Clinard and Quinney.

criminal who commits 1, Violent Personal Crime, would under classification characteristic d, Societal reaction, have the notation *high*.

Abrahamsen, a psychiatrist, notes that "Classification is always forced on nature, and hence is artificial, which is one reason why people disagree on classification." [12] Abrahamsen divides his offender-types into classes: a. *Momentary Offenders*, and b. *Chronic Offenders*. Within class a. he lists three categories: [13]

1. *Situational Offender*. This person may commit a crime because an overwhelming opportunity arises, or because of a compelling situation, such as a strong feeling of injustice or a need for self-defense, or in the course of a temporary mental condition, such as a reactive depression. While a transgression is being perpetrated, the offender's impulse to act antisocially is overpowering, but as soon as this impelling force vanishes, his ego rejects the crime.
2. *Accidental Offender*. A person who unexpectedly runs into difficulties with the law through mistake or chance. For example, careless driving.
3. *Associational Offender*. This person is influenced by his own criminalistic tendencies, however weak, and also by his surroundings when certain situations arise, especially with respect to others who may exert influence on him.

Within class b., Abrahamsen lists five categories:

1. *Offenders With Organic or Functional Disorders*. The personality structure of this group is impaired by some destructive agent, toxic, degenerative, or infectious, or by some functional agent which damages the personality ego. In this category are psychotics, mental defectives, epileptics, and all those individuals whom the law does not regard as criminally responsible.
2. *Chronic Situational, Accidental, and Associational Offenders*. This type is an acute version of the types in class a.
3. *Compulsory-Obsessional Neurotic Types*. This group consists of offenders such as kleptomaniacs, pyromaniacs, and child molesters.
4. *Neurotic Sociopaths:* This type includes persons with faulty

[12] David Abrahamsen, *Crime and the Human Mind* (Montclair, N.J.: Patterson Smith, 1969), p. 93.

[13] *Ibid.*, pp. 93–126.

superego development who act out their aggressions in an anti-social manner.

5. *Environmental Sociopaths.* These people are brought up in a criminal environment that adversely affects the superego, resulting in acts directed against society. Their only regret is getting caught and punished.

In 1968, the (New York State) Governor's Special Committee on Criminal Offenders, headed by Paul McGinnis, then Corrections Commissioner, and Russell G. Oswald, then Chairman of the Board of Parole, presented its *Preliminary Report.* Although the report did not result in any concrete action, it does present an interesting classification methodology. Like the systems that follow, this system is tied to treatment.

It is suggested, on the basis of the causal theories and on the basis of experience obtained through working with offenders, that fourteen fundamental characteristics can be postulated as being both social impedimenta and crime related. These characteristics are as follows:

1. Inadequacy
2. Immaturity
3. Dependency
4. Ill-Equipped in Social Skills
5. Ill-Equipped in Education
6. Vocational Maladjustment
7. Cognitive Deficiency
8. Compulsive Pathology
9. Organic Pathology
10. Anti-Social Attitudes
11. Career Commitment
12. Catalytic Impulsivity
13. Habitual Impulsivity
14. Asocial Attitudes

Inadequacy is a characteristic that can be associated with psychogenic theory and with the social identity category of bridging theory. Inadequacy is characterized by (a) a pervasive feeling of inability to cope with needs, (b) a generalized feeling of helplessness, (c) the inability to plan ahead, (d) frequent feelings of despair, negativism and cynicism, (e) diffuse anxiety—*i.e.*, not seen as related to a specific cause, (f) the perception of tasks as likely to lead to failure rather than success, and (g) a disproportionate fear of rejection.

Immaturity is a characteristic that can be associated with psychogenic theory and with the adolescent problem and family relationship categories of bridging theory. Immaturity is characterized by (a) inability to postpone gratification, (b) general attitude of irresponsibility, (c) preoccupation with concrete and immediate objects, wishes and needs, (d) an orientation of the individual as receiver and a tendency to view others as givers, (e) manipulativeness, (f) self-centeredness, and (g) petulance.

Dependency is a characteristic that can be associated with psychogenic theory and with the adolescent problem and the family relationship categories of bridging theory. Dependency is characterized by (a) difficulty in coping with an unstructured or complex environment, (b) anxiety in situations requiring independent action, (c) a feeling of guilt with respect to elements (a) and (b), and (d) feelings of resentment toward what is believed to be the source of dependency.

Ill-equipped in social skills is a characteristic that can be associated with all of the theories but is most generally thought to be related to the socio-cultural theories. This factor is characterized by (a) lack of ability to articulate feelings and ideas and a resulting inability to communicate meaningfully with others except at superficial levels, (b) lack of ability to function in subordinate-superordinate roles, *e.g.*, inability to take orders from a superior in a work situation, (c) inability to "take the role of the other," *i.e.*, to empathize with others, and (d) inadvertent, socially disapproved behavior, *e.g.*, use of language inappropriate to various social situations, dress inappropriate for job interviews, failure to conform to norms of personal hygiene.

Ill-equipped in education is a characteristic primarily related with socio-cultural theories, but it may also play a significant role in the social identity category of bridging theory. This characteristic simply implies that an individual is functionally illiterate in English or demonstrates a disproportion between his present level of education and his potential level, or both.

Vocational maladjustment is a characteristic that has the same theoretical relationships as ill-equipped in education. This characteristic implies a lack of appropriate technical skills for employment that would be meaningful to the individual, or a disproportion between the aptitudes of the individual and realistic opportunities, or both.

Cognitive deficiency is a characteristic related to constitutional and psychogenic theories. This characteristic refers to a state of mental retardation, restricted mental potentiality or incomplete development existing from birth or early infancy as a result of which the individual is (a) confused and bewildered by any complexity of life, (b) overly suggestible and easily exploited, and (c) able to achieve a mental age within a range of 8–12 years.

Compulsive pathology is a characteristic derived from psychoanalytic theory. This factor is characterized by (a) a sense that criminal behavior is forced upon the individual against his will (he is aware of the peculiarity of his behavior, but is unable to control himself), (b) inability to obtain any lasting satisfaction from the act committed, *e.g.*, no apparent gain to individual from act nor any reason for injury to another, (c) repetition of such acts, and (d) usually accompanied by other obsessive-compulsive symptoms.

Organic pathology is a characteristic related to constitutional theory. This factor involves such things as glandular and neurological anomalies, *e.g.*, brain damage, organic brain disease, etc. Conduct stemming from organic pathology is not usually typified by any single behavioral pattern.

Anti-social attitudes is a characteristic that can be associated with all of the theories. This characteristic consists of a configuration of attitudes which are defined by society as delinquent, criminal and anti-social. An individual who possesses anti-social attitudes demonstrates positive affective responses toward trouble, toughness, smartness, excitement, fate, autonomy, and short-run hedonism.

Career commitment is a characteristic that can be associated with socio-cultural theory and with the identity process category of bridging theory. Basically, career commitment is a way of describing a professional criminal and this would include many of the persons involved in organized crime. This factor refers to an offender's commitment to anti-social behavior as his chief occupation and major source of income for his adult life. Such commitment involves (a) a life-orientation pervasively concerned with criminal pursuits, (b) extensive knowledge of techniques applicable to one's criminal activities, (c) the maintenance of a strong identification with criminals of similar pattern with whom he may from time to time share common criminal acts, (d) the use of the argot of one's profession, (e) an insistence upon carefully planned criminal activities, (f) the derogation of the "amateur" criminal, (g) the perception of the possibility of apprehension and imprisonment as an occupational risk, and (h) the manipulation of the law enforcement system through bribery.

Catalytic impulsivity is a characteristic that can be associated with psychogenic theory (*i.e.*, psychoanalytic and personality trait theory) and with the family relationship category of bridging theory. This form of impulsivity requires the presence of a catalyst for it to appear, *i.e.*, criminal acts *only occur while the normally over-controlled person is affected by the catalyst. The catalyst may take the form of alcohol or of an overwhelming need stemming from psychic or physical dependence (e.g.,* narcotics), or a specific emotional stimulus (*e.g.*, cursing one's mother). The central concept of catalytic impulsivity is the impulsive, spontaneous, unplanned nature of the criminal act while the offender is under the influence of, or is affected by, the catalyst. Under normal circumstances, *i.e.*, in the absence of the catalyst, the catalytic impulsive individual is not anti-social and possesses adequate and even excessive self-control. Under the influence of the catalyst, however, the criminal act almost invariably precipitates and there is total disregard for the consequences of such acts.

Habitual impulsivity is a characteristic that can be associated primarily with all of the psychogenic and most of the constitutional theories. This form of impulsivity differs from catalytic impulsivity by the absence of the need for a catalyst as a trigger. An habitually impulsive individual may use alcohol or drugs, but the crucial aspect is that these substances are neither necessary nor sufficient for causation of the criminal act. The act itself is always spontaneous and unplanned, and the individual who possesses this characteristic is temperamental, exhibits a low frustration tolerance and high reactivity. His volatile temperament typically demonstrates rapid mood swings. The triggering source for impulsive criminal acts cannot be definitively indicated. Such a characteristic may be seen in individuals who react variously to situations of temptation, slight provocation, and frustration. Rages may be a typical reaction for one offender, while another may react by petty thievery.

Asocial attitudes is a characteristic associated with socio-cultural theory and with the family relationship category of bridging theory. Such attitudes give rise to cheating, bribe giving or taking, shoplifting, insurance fraud and like matters, by persons who otherwise seem to be law-abiding members of the community. Asocial attitudes are commonly found in offenders who have respectable positions in the community and who articulate support for the general value system. Such attitudes are characterized by (a) selfishness, (b) disregard of responsibility to others or to certain other persons, (c) feelings that society is dishonest and that the individual is foolish if he does not "get his," (d) feelings that the test of whether conduct is improper is whether one can "get away with it," (e) feelings that most people are "suckers," and (f) feelings that it is all right to steal from certain businesses or from certain categories of people because they have "too much money," or because they have "exploited the public anyway" (*i.e.,* social rationalization).

The aforementioned fourteen characteristics may appear singly, or in combinations of two, three, or four in one individual offender at one time. Thus, more than one of these characteristics may operate to impede the functioning of an individual simultaneously. An offender may, it is true, be described as an inadequate offender, or another one as an ill-equipped offender, if that is the only characteristic which operates to impede normal functioning; but for the most part, offenders can be described as possessing more than one of the fourteen characteristics—each with a different relative impact upon the individual's behavior.

It must be emphasized that crime can arise without attribution to the aforesaid characteristics, and this should be recognized in treatment of offenders. Sometimes a fairly extraordinary configuration of events coupled with lowered individual tolerance may cause a person to commit a crime. For example, a person who is extremely agitated because of trouble at home or on the job may get into an automobile accident, and upon being yelled at by the driver of the other car may just lash out and assault him. Sometimes ignorance of the law or of fact may cause a person to commit a crime—*e.g.,* statutory rape of a girl who appears to be of age, or where the offender is unaware of the age of consent and the girl seems mature. Sometimes the conduct is technically criminal, but it is part of the custom of a group to which the individual belongs and the group does not view the conduct as anti-social, *e.g.,* use of peyote by certain Indian tribes, and production of untaxed alcohol by members of certain ethnic groups. Finally, there is the offender who believes that his act is in the better interest of society and who violates the law in order to focus attention upon what he believes to be a harmful or unjust practice—*e.g.,* distribution of birth control information where such is prohibited by law, violation of overseas travel restrictions, draft card burning, etc. All of such conduct may justifiably result in the use of sanctions, but may not be such as to indicate the need for rehabilitation.

Application of Treatment to Individual Characteristics

The next step in prevention of recidivism is to attempt to align appropriate treatment methods with the characteristics that seem to be relevant in each individual case. As previously noted, this requires an examination of each individual and the profiling of characteristics in order of saliency for the individual (on the theory that the most salient characteristic should receive the greatest degree of treatment emphasis).

Putting aside for the moment the difficulty involved in administering the appropriate treatment to those offenders who must be kept in high security institutions and to those offenders who must be incarcerated for a minimum term for public oriented purposes, and assuming complete flexibility, one can set forth all of the currently used treatment methods and select from among them the method or methods that seem most promising in the treatment of the particular characteristics. To illustrate, we can set forth fifteen basic treatment options, as follows (the order of listing does not, of course, imply any general priority of one over the other):

A. Academic Education

B. Social Education (training in dress, public speaking, personal hygiene, behavior in common social situations, civics, etc.)

C. Vocational Training, Guidance and Counseling (training in skills, behavior on the job, how to find employment, good work habits, job placement, reconciling skills to vocational potential)

D. Individual Psychotherapy (psychoanalysis, reality therapy, etc.)

E. Group Counseling, Group Therapy, Group Psychotherapy, Sociodrama; etc.

F. Medical Methods (chemotherapy, conditioning therapy, plastic surgery, etc.)

G. Milieu Therapy (therapeutic community)

H. Team Sports and Recreation

I. Casework and Individual Counseling

J. Occupational Therapy

K. Family/Marital Counseling (counseling parents or spouses of offenders to educate them to problems and experiences of the offender, or counseling offender with the family to foster favorable family relations, etc.)

L. Religious Counseling

M. Incarceration*

N. Intermittent Jail

O. Fine

Assume that an offender is found to be vocationally maladjusted, inadequate and possesses anti-social attitudes in that order of saliency. One might then utilize a program involving milieu therapy heavily oriented toward vocational guidance and training. The milieu therapy (*i.e.*, community meetings and group sessions) would be to cope with inadequacy and anti-social attitudes; and, of course, the heavy orientation toward vocational guidance and training would be to cope with vocational maladjustment. To systematize this, one would use the numbers assigned to the characteristics and the letters assigned to the treatment methods so as to show the specific characteristics diagnosed in order of saliency and the treatment prescribed for each.

Thus, applying the numbers on pp. 218–22 and the letters on page 223 to the above example, the profile and the prescription would be summed up as follows:

Characteristics:	6	1	10
Treatment:	C/G	G/C	G/C

The characteristic line shows the diagnosis in order of saliency (the number 6 representing vocational maladjustment, the number 1 representing inadequacy and the number 10 representing anti-social attitudes). The treatment line shows the type of treatment best suited for each characteristic—not separately but taken in conjunction with the others (C/G representing vocational training in a milieu therapy setting, G/C representing milieu therapy with emphasis upon vocational training). In this example, the same type of treatment is indicated as beneficial for all of the characteristics; however, in some cases the treatment

*Item M is included as a treatment method rather than as a custodial instrumentality. The purpose of item M as a treatment method is individual deterrence. This must be separated from the concept of selecting the appropriate custodial instrumentality for minimizing risk to the public. Items N and O are also for individual deterrence. Field supervision is not included because without a specific form of treatment (*e.g.*, casework) it is essentially a custodial instrumentality.

methods may be different. Suppose, for example, that the diagnosis revealed catalytic impulsivity (number 12), inadequacy (number 1), vocational maladjustment (number 6) and ill-equipped in social skills (number 4). One might select a group psychotherapy program to get at the factors that underly the outbursts and to cope with the inadequacy. This would be coupled with vocational training and social education. Hence, the diagnosis and treatment instructions would be as follows:

Characteristics:	12	1	6	4
Treatment:	E	E	C	B

The coding system, as presented here, is, of course, quite gross and merely used to illustrate the form in which basic information can be conveyed for the purpose of giving treatment instructions. The characteristic line would have to be refined by the addition of symbols to indicate the relationship between the characteristic and the individual's criminality; and the treatment line would have to be refined by the addition of symbols to indicate the precise nature of treatment prescribed. The point is, however, that such a coding system facilitates focusing upon individual characteristics and the alignment of treatment methods to the characteristics. It also gives a shorthand picture of the case. Additionally, it helps to show—in a broad sense—the rationale for selection of treatment in a particular case; and permits rapid detection of obvious errors. Further, it can be used as a method for organization of data for research.

Before examining the problems in utilizing any such approach and, in fact, the problems in determining the appropriate treatment to be applied, two other dimensions of the approach should be discussed. These dimensions are: (a) the selection of the custodial instrumentality; and (b) the sequence of treatment phases.

Selection of the appropriate custodial instrumentality means determination as to whether treatment is to be administered while the offender is under field supervision, or under incarceration, or is under both at the same time. Additional symbols can be added to the coding system to specify the custodial instrumentality to be used.

The sequence of treatment phases will depend upon the time the post adjudicatory system has to deal with the offender, the programs available, and the results of periodic evaluations. Additionally, treatment can be scheduled for phasing-in as part of an overall treatment design.

Perhaps the most difficult aspect of determining the type of treatment to be administered inheres in the fact that any rational system must relate the treatment to the dynamics through which the characteristic operates to impede the offender's functioning. It does little good to know, for example, that the offender is vocationally maladjusted, inadequate and possesses anti-social attitudes unless one has a theory as to why this might be so. Such combination of characteristics could have resulted from a set of events typical of the "adolescent problem" category of bridging theory, or from a set of events typical of the socio-cultural Differential Opportunity Theory (or from other events). If they resulted from the former the treatment might be different than if they resulted from the latter. A middle class youth whose problems stem from family dynamics and who has opportunities available, if only he had the skills and the attitudes to grasp them, is a different treatment problem from a youth who feels society is discriminating against him. In the latter case, if treatment of the characteristics is not focused upon the discrimination problem and is not followed up to the extent of seeing to it that the youth is afforded an opportunity which is realistic in terms of his potential, the treatment may merely heighten expectations which, if not fulfilled, will confirm his sense of discrimination and inadequacy. This, in turn, may solidify the delinquent attitudes and propel him into a life of crime.

Further, in administering group treatment methods, one must have some conception as to the underlying causal processes that brought the participants to crime before deciding upon the proper composition of the group. If the group is to contain a mixture of offenders—rather than a number of persons who all share the same basic problems—this should be based upon a deliberate treatment strategy.

Another example might be seen in the three characteristics: cognitive deficiency, ill-equipped in education and dependency. In one case the cause might be psychogenic and in another case the cause might be socio-cultural. It would obviously be essential to identify the cause before planning treatment.

In addition to the need for a theory as to the process of causation in each case, there is also the fact that very little is known with respect to the effectiveness of various treatment methods in general, or when applied to specific characteristics. Thus, it is difficult to tell, for example, whether in dealing with anti-social attitudes it is more appropriate to use group methods, individual methods, education, milieu therapy, religious counseling or all of these. We do know that certain types of problems must be assigned to certain disciplines (*e.g.*, organic pathology to the physician, compulsive pathology to the psychiatrist, and ill-equipped in education most often to the educator); but there is little concrete evidence as to whether the treatment applied is effective in removing the impediment.

If the State were to establish the panel and board system referred to in Part Two of the Report, the method—suggested here—of approaching diagnosis and aligning treatment methods with characteristics would fit well. The diagnostic panel would be responsible for administering, or overseeing the administration of, the various psychological tests and interviews, the psychiatric and medical examinations, the gathering of social histories, and like matters. The unified file would contain all of the data and the background material for the development of the diagnostic and treatment profile. This would then be summed up by use of a coding system on the order of the one described above.

The advantages of this method are as follows. First and foremost, this approach forces a focus upon factors related to causation in individual cases. Second, and almost equally important, this approach facilitates rational application of treatment methods. Third, this approach lays the foundation for systematic acquisition of treatment effectiveness data. Fourth, the approach points the way toward development of treatment programs (where certain groupings of characteristics appear in a sufficient number of cases, programs can be designed around the cluster of characteristics, and perhaps specific institutions would deal with specific clusters). Fifth, the approach facilitates transmission of information, uniformity of diagnostic and treatment language, an understanding of the basic rationale for ordering the use of particular treatment methods, and a method for rapid detection of gross errors.

The method suggested here has no value in and of itself unless it is used in conjunction with a continuing program of evaluative research; and, indeed, no other method would have any value without such research. Research would supply an ongoing source of data for diagnostic refinement and for more precise alignment of treatment methods with characteristics.

The rudiments of another system are provided by Howard Gill, who believes that roughly 90% of all offenders can be classified as: [14]

1. offenders who are overwhelmed with situational difficulties and are in need of casework and economic assistance;
2. offenders with personal psychological problems in need of psychological and psychiatric help; and
3. offenders who are essentially immature individuals and who express their anti-social tendencies in an illegal manner; they are in need of guidance and education.

The Kennedy Youth Center, as described by Roy Gerard,[15] uses a classification system that matches staff to residents, and treatment is based on the classification. This differs from most correctional institutions, where classification is usually based on security, not treatment, needs.

First, each resident is diagnosed on the basis of staff observations, a questionnaire completed by the youth, and an evaluation of his presentence report data.

Second, the youth is placed in one of four classification categories:

BC-1: Inadequate—immàture delinquency

[14] Howard Gill cited in Karl Menninger, *The Crime of Punishment* (New York: Viking Press, 1968), pp. 262–63.

[15] Roy Gerard, "Classification By Behavioral Categories and Its Implications For Differential Treatment." In Leonard J. Hippchen, ed., *Correctional Classification and Treatment* (Cincinnati: Anderson Publishing Co., 1975), pp. 94–103.

BC-2: Neurotic—disturbed delinquency
BC-3: Unsocialized—psychopathic delinquency
BC-4: Socialized—subcultural delinquency

Third, residents are matched to staff according to their classification and the particular attributes of the worker, including his or her interests and abilities to work with a particular type of youth.

Fourth, the type of treatment that would be beneficial for each category is built into and tied to the classification process. For example, youths in BC-1 tend to be dependent, and show a general lack of interest in things. They have a low frustration tolerance, and they require structure and support. For this category, rewards are given for mature behavior, for example, self control, while punishments are avoided. Group and individual counseling are directive in their approach, and there are opportunities that are made available whereby the youngster can do something for others, and thus gain the "reward" of warm approval.

Another system for classifying probationers and parolees was developed by the Oklahoma Department of Corrections, based on an in-depth examination of 170 randomly selected offenders. As the result of probing their past criminal history, reasons for crime involvement, familial, peer and work parameters, and attitudes toward the future, the researchers decided on four typologies: [16]

1. *early offender*—any subject involved in a single criminal act for which he was adjudicated prior to his 21st birthday
2. *late offender*—any subject involved in a single criminal act for which he was adjudicated after his 21st birthday
3. *intermittent offender*—any subject who had been involved in a series of criminal acts, for which he had been adjudicated with at least a one (1) year interim period between adjudications
4. *persistent offender*—any subject who had been involved in a series of criminal acts, for which he had been adjudicated with no lapse of non-criminal involvement

Early Offender. This group, though average in intelligence, was more intelligent than the intermittent and persistent offenders. They were also more independent minded, unconventional, hostile, rebellious, and headstrong than the other two groups. They are bohemian in outlook, imaginative, careless of practical matters, and somewhat frustrated and overwrought as compared to late offenders. The mean age of this cate-

[16] Law Enforcement Assistance Administration, *Reintegration of the Offender into the Community* (Washington, D.C.: Government Printing Office, 1973), pp. 31–40.

gory was 18.80 years of age, the youngest of the four groups, and 95 percent of these offenders were single in marital status. Two noteworthy findings were the greater use of marijuana and their indifference to their family. This alienation from the family, bohemian outlook on life, use of drugs, and detachment with practical matters reflects on the social disintegration and atomization of the present younger group of offenders. Efforts to reintegrate them in the family and in the community were indicated. Group therapy with some family involvement could be helpful. Their prognosis was good as these offenders had not developed the self-image of a criminal as yet.

Late Offender. Their first criminal involvement was reported late in life at the age of 28.07 years, and their present age was 30.94 years. This group was comprised of 28.8 percent females and 34 percent Negroid members. Maritally, this group had more married persons (53.8%) and a large number of divorcees (25%). They perceived their relationship with their parents as unsatisfactory. Psychologically, this group was the most normal of all the groups. This group was the least criminal in its attitudes and tendencies and was expected to do very well with minimal supervision.

Intermittent Offender. These offenders committed offences intermittently and were the oldest of the four groups with a mean age of 30.11 years and with their onset of criminality of age 16.68 years. These offenders were artless and sentimental on the one hand and apprehensive, worrying, depressive, moody and brooding on the other hand. They had weaker superego strengths and were apt to disregard rules. When they were not employed, they felt greatly bothered, fearful, and worried. Showing neurotic tendencies, they needed psychiatric help. They appeared to have an equal chance of success or failure under probation or parole. Using Merton's typology, these offenders tended to make ritualistic adaptation. There was a good time lapse (4–5 years) between offenses, and it appeared that their offenses were periodic and episodic. They were law-abiding in most instances and only occasionally disregarded laws.

Persistent Offender. These offenders moved in and out of prison. They were involved in burglary, auto theft, juvenile offenses, and probation or parole revocation. They were easily upset, low in frustration tolerance, forceful, highly anti-social, deficient in superego strength with few obligations, suspicious, mistrusting, unconcerned about other people, wrapped up in inner urgencies, dissatisfied, and maladjusted. All these characteristics put together indicate a psychopathic or sociopathic personality. They, however, did show some apprehension which does not fit in with the psychopathic characteristic. A majority of them (57 percent) perceived themselves as criminal. This self-concept and the psychopathic tendencies render them difficult cases for treatment and rehabilitation. They need intensive supervision, and every type of therapy should be tested, hoping for a positive response to one of them.

Another rather interesting, if not somewhat oversimplified, classification system that is linked directly to various treatment approaches is presented by Don Gibbons in the following tables.[17]

TABLE 1. Defining Characteristics of Offender Types

Type	*Offense Pattern*	*Self-Definition and Attitude*
Semiprofessional property offender (Antisocial)	Robbery, burglary, larceny, and allied offenses; unskilled repetitive crime with small profit	Self-definition as a criminal, but as a victim of society; hostile toward police and correctional authorities
Auto thief—joyrider (Antisocial)	Repetitive auto theft for pleasure; "car clouting" and other auto offenses for profit not included	Self-definition as a criminal, and as tough, manly; concerned with others' perception of him as a "tough guy"
Naïve check forger (Prosocial)	Passing bad checks, usually without skill; often passes checks while drinking	Self-definition as a non-criminal, and as a person burdened with personal problems
Embezzler (Prosocial)	Illegal conversion of property from a position of financial trust	Self-definition as a non-criminal, as different from "real criminals"; rationalizes acts as not really criminal
Personal offender ("one-time loser") (Prosocial)	Crimes of violence under situational stress — murder, manslaughter, assault	Self-definition as a non-criminal, but as deserving of punishment; no pronounced antisocial attitudes
Psychopathic assaultist (Asocial)	Offenses against persons or property or both, characterized by violence in "inappropriate" situations	Self-definition as a criminal, but as a victim of the treachery of others; views others as generally untrustworthy
Violent sex offender (Prosocial)	Sexual assaults upon physically mature females, characterized by extreme violence, mutilation, etc.	Self-definition as a non-criminal
Non-violent sex offender (Prosocial)	Sex offenses—such as child-molesting—usually with immature victims; statutory rape and similar offenses not included	Self-definition as a non-criminal; frequently rationalizes himself as Christian and his offense as not sexual but "educational"
Heroin addict (Antisocial)	Use of heroin or other opiate; property offenses as source of income for purchase of drugs	Self-definition as a criminal, but sees criminal status as unjust; holds that drug usage is a relatively harmless personal vice

[17] Don C. Gibbons, *Changing the Lawbreaker: The Treatment of Delinquents and Criminals* (Englewood Cliffs, N.J.: Prentice-Hall, 1965), pp. 146–47.

TABLE 2. Treatment Dimensions and Diagnostic Types

Semiprofessional property offender	
Formal treatment program	Guided-group-interaction form of therapy in group composed of other "antisocial," "right guy" offenders
Adjunct program	Vocational training or educational program
Goal	Modification of attitudes toward police, work, crime, and society; development of "prosocial" attitudes
Periods	Institutional group therapy carried on most intensively during last few months of incarceration and continued during parole
Frequency	Intensive in the pre-release period, with group meeting at least several times a week
Auto thief—joyrider	
Formal treatment program	Guided-group-interaction form of therapy in group composed of other "antisocial," "right guy" offenders, but with some members who have been non-joyriders
Adjunct program	Recreational program with active participation in athletics
Goal	Demonstration of inappropriateness of "tough guy" criminal activity, aid to offender in developing a self-image which is tough and masculine but consistent with socially acceptable behavior
Periods	Same as for semiprofessional property offender
Frequency	Same as for semiprofessional property offender
Naïve check forger	
Formal treatment program	Client-centered individual therapy, group therapy in groups composed of other forgers, or both
Adjunct program	Alcoholics Anonymous
Goal	Breaking down the offender's rationalizations for forgery, discouraging dependent behavior, building up a fund of acceptable solutions to problems
Periods	Intensive treatment if on probation or institutionalized, continued during parole, including group treatment, at least in part, and involvement in Alcoholics Anonymous during parole
Frequency	Several times a week
Embezzler	
Formal treatment program	Intensive treatment not usually required; superficial assistance from time to time

TABLE 2 (continued)

	from treatment workers; isolation from more criminalistic types of prisoners
Adjunct program	Assignment to clerical or other service position in the institution
Goal	Preservation of the offender's prosocial self-image and attitudes
Periods	During parole some help in adjusting to altered social and economic status
Frequency	Infrequent—once a week or less
Personal offender ("one-time loser")	
Formal treatment program	Similar to that for embezzler
Adjunct program	Assignment to institutional position
Goal	Similar to that for embezzler
Periods	Intensive treatment during parole
Frequency	Infrequent—once a week or less
Psychopathic assaultist	
Formal treatment program	Some form of group treatment combined with intensive psychiatric counseling
Adjunct program	None specific
Goal	Development of "normal" personality structure; resocialization of essentially undersocialized person, including development of loyalty attachments, role-taking abilities
Periods	Intensive treatment during entire period of incarceration and parole
Frequency	Relatively intense—several times a week
Violent sex offender	
Formal treatment program	Psychiatric therapy conducted by psychiatrist or clinical psychologist
Adjunct program	None specific
Goal	Modification of bizarre sexual orientations
Periods	Intensive treatment during entire period of incarceration and parole
Frequency	Relatively intense—several times a week
Non-violent sex offender	
Formal treatment program	Intensive psychiatric therapy, particularly at initial stage of incarceration; possibly supplemented with group treatment in group of other non-violent sex offenders at later stage of prison term
Adjunct program	None specific
Goal	Modification of offender's self-image of inadequacy and sexual impotency; breaking down rationalizations regarding deviant sex acts; directing offender toward more aggressive and dominant relations with adults, particularly with his spouse
Frequency	Relatively intense—several times a week

TABLE 2 (continued)

Heroin addict	
Formal treatment program	Individual therapy designed to deal with personality problems, along with guided group interaction designed to modify group-supported norms and attitudes regarding drug use and criminality
Adjunct program	Vocational or educational program
Goal	Modification of "antisocial" attitudes, particularly attitudes toward drug use, law enforcement agencies, and drug addiction treatment programs; reduction of severe personality problems
Periods	Individual treatment and withdrawal from use of narcotics during early period of incarceration; group treatment toward end of prison term and in parole period
Frequency	Relatively intense—several times a week

Harlow, Weber and Wilkins stress the importance of finding a classification system for workable probation/parole supervision. It is a fact that "some offenders will succeed under supervision regardless of the type of service; while others will violate no matter how much treatment they receive; and that with identification of these offenders (probation/parole) officer time could be allocated to give the most attention to those whose success depends on the presence of certain types of supervision." [18]

Classification, if adequate, allows for better individualization of cases. Treatment activities are concentrated on those who could benefit most from it, while surveillance and law enforcement activities are stressed in appropriate cases.

[18] Harlow, et. al., cited from Edward Edelfonso, *Issues In Corrections* (Beverly Hills: Glencoe Press, 1974), p. 343.

Chapter 13

Treatment

A Comprehensive Dictionary of Psychological and Psychoanalytic Terms defines *treatment* as "any measure to ameliorate an undesirable condition." In this book *treatment* will refer to all the efforts of a probation/parole officer to help his clients. These efforts may be tangible or intangible. The former include help with vocational training, education, employment, financial support and medical treatment. Intangible efforts are more abstruse; they include a variety of treatment modes.

Some modes of treatment are more easily applied to probation/parole practice than others. Some require more training than most probation/parole officers have received, and their use may require an expenditure of time that is not realistic in most probation/parole agencies. In practice, probation/parole officers use a variety of techniques, tailoring them to different clients. They often use techniques without recognizing them as part of a particular mode of treatment. Gibbons states that "As for treatment techniques, the use of unshared and largely intuitive procedures by different workers is predominant. These tactics are frequently vague and ambiguous, even to the worker, and they are not based upon the available empirical evidence regarding the nature of offenders. Instead, they are compounded out of gross behavioral theories and speculative hunches arrived at by trial and error in the work setting." [1]

Three methods of treatment are used extensively in probation/parole practice, although not necessarily in the same proportion:

1. social casework
2. reality therapy
3. behavior modification.

In order to better understand these methods, it is necessary to review a method of treatment that is not used extensively, if at all, in probation/parole. The above methods of treatment can be delineated according to the degree to which they accept, use, or reject psychoanalytic theory and methods.

PSYCHOANALYSIS AND PSYCHOANALYTIC THEORY

Psychoanalysis is a method of treatment based on a body of theory fathered by Sigmund Freud. Over the years, both theory and method have undergone change, although Freud's basic contribution, his exposition of the importance of unconscious phenomena in human behavior, remains.

Psychoanalytic theory divides unconscious mental phenomena into two groups:

1. *Preconscious:* thoughts and memories that can easily be called into conscious awareness.
2. *Unconscious:* repressed feelings and experiences that can be made conscious only with a great deal of difficulty.

The unconscious feelings and experiences that are normally repressed relate to the stages of psychosexual development through which each person passes on the way to adulthood. In brief, they appear as follows:

1. ORAL: birth to 1½ years; the mouth, lips and tongue are the predominant sexual organs of the infant. The infant's desires and

[1] Gibbons quoted from David M. Peterson and Charles W. Thomas, eds., *Corrections: Problems and Prospects* (Englewood Cliffs, N.J.: Prentice-Hall, 1975), pp. 178–79.

gratifications are mainly oral. For example, sucking, mouthing, and biting are all sources of pleasure.

2. ANAL: 1½ to 3 years; the anus becomes the most important site of sexual gratification. Pleasure is closely connected to the retention and expulsion of feces, as well as the bodily processes involved and the feces themselves.

3. *PHALLIC:* 3 years to 5 years; the main sexual interest begins to be assumed by the genitals, and in normal persons is maintained by them thereafter. During this period of life the child experiences *Oedipus* (in boys) and *Electra* (in girls) *wishes* in the form of fantasies of incest with the parent of the opposite sex.

4. *LATENT:* 5 years to adolescence; there is a lessening of interest in sexual organs during this period and an expanded relationship with playmates of the same sex and age.

5. *ADOLESCENCE-ADULTHOOD:* 13 years to death; there is a reawakening of genital interest and awareness, and the incestuous wish is now expressed in terms of mature (adult) sexuality.

These normal stages of psychosexual development are unconscious and serve as a source of anxiety and guilt, the basis for psychoneurosis and psychosis. The stages overlap, and transition from one to the other is gradual, the time spans being approximate. In certain abnormal cases, the infantile sexual interests become the chief source of adult sexual gratification.

Each stage is left behind, but never completely abandoned. Some amount of psychic energy *(cathexis)* remains attached to earlier objects of psychosexual development. When the strength of the cathexis is particularly strong, it is expressed as a *fixation*. For example, instead of transferring his affections to another woman in the adolescent-adult stage, the person may remain fixated on his mother (or a girl on her father). When a person reverts to a previous mode of gratification, it is referred to as *regression*. This type of behavior can be seen in young children who revert to thumb-sucking or have elimination "accidents" when a sibling is born.

While a person is passing through the stages of psychosexual development, concomitantly, the mind undergoes the development of three psychic phenomena:

1. *Id:* This mass of powerful drives seeks discharge or gratification. Comprised of wishes, urges, and psychic tensions, it seeks pleasure

and avoids pain. The id is the driving force of the personality, and from birth until about seven months of age, it is the total psychic apparatus.

2. *Ego:* Through contact with the reality around him and the influence of training, the infant modifies his expressions of id drives. This ego development permits the person to obtain maximum gratification with a minimum of difficulty in the form of restrictions that his environment places on him. For example, an id drive (desire) to kill a sibling rival is controlled by the ego.

3. *Superego:* The superego is often viewed as a "conscience-type" mechanism, a counter-force to the id. It exercises a criticizing power, a sense of morality. The superego is tied to the incestuous feelings of the phallic stage, at which time the development of controls becomes an internal matter, and no longer exclusively dependant on external forces (parents, for example).

The id drives impel a person to activity leading to a cessation of the tension or excitement caused by the drives. The person seeks discharge or gratification. For example, the hunger drive will result in activity that eventually satisfies (gratification) the person experiencing hunger. These drives are divided into two categories, but elements of each appear whenever either drive is activated:

1. Sexual drives
2. Aggressive drives

In this case the aggressive drive does not refer to the behavior we normally attach to that label. The drives are exhibited through one of two processes:

1. *Primary Process:* that which tends toward immediate gratification of the id impulses.

2. *Secondary Process:* the tendency to shift from the original object or method of discharge, when something blocks it or it is inaccessible, to another object or method. For example, a desire to play with feces arising out of an anal cathexis, will be transferred to playing with mud as a result of toilet training. This transfer is called *displacement,* and it is one of the many *defense mechanisms* that the human mind employs to adapt to its environment. Other defense mechanisms include:

Repression: activity of the ego that prevents unwanted id impulses, memories, emotions, desires, or wish fulfilling fantasies, from entering conscious thought. Repression of charged material (for example, incestuous fantasies) requires the expenditure of psychic energy and sets up a permanent opposition between the id and the ego. The delicate balance (equilibrium) between the charged material and its opposing expenditure of energy can shift at any time, usually as a result of some stress. When repression is inadequate in dealing with charged material, psychoneurotic symptoms develop.

Reaction Formation: a mechanism whereby an individual gives up some form of socially unacceptable behavior in favor of behavior that is socially acceptable. This more acceptable behavior usually takes the form of being opposite to the real desire (drive). For example, a child who desires to kill a sibling will become very loving and devoted. In adult behavior, a sadistic impulse toward animals can result in a person becoming a veterinarian.

Projection: a person attributes his own wish or impulse to some other person. This is pathological in cases of paranoia.

Sublimation: a drive that cannot be experienced in its primary form, such as a desire to play with feces, is accommodated by modeling clay or, perhaps, becoming a proctologist.

Another important concept that is part of psychoanalytic theory is *anxiety*. While the concept has been the subject of considerable debate and change, anxiety can be divided into two types:

1. *Internal anxiety:* emanating from unconscious id drives that are in danger of overwhelming the ego. This state of mind is compounded by the strength of opposing psychic energy from the superego, causing a state of consternation.
2. *External anxiety:* emanating from an influx of outside stimuli that overwhelms the psyche. This can be seen in cases of patients who are informed that they are suffering from a fatal illness.

There is a delicate balance maintained by unconscious forces as a person experiences the various socio-cultural and biological aspects of existence. When the balance is upset, the psyche passes from the normal to the psychoneurotic and/or the psychotic (mental illness). It is basic to psychoanalytic theory that there is a "very thin line" between the normal and the neurotic, and between the neurotic and the psychotic. In fact, there is only a difference of degree between the normal and the abnormal. The degree to which there is a malfunctioning in the psychic apparatus is the degree to which a person is abnormal or "sick."

Psychic disorders are treated by psychoanalysis or one of its various offshoots such as psychotherapy. Freud stated that psychoanalysis "aims at inducing the patient to give up the repressions belonging to his early life and to replace them by reactions of a sort that would correspond better to a psychically mature condition." [2] In order to do this, a psychoanalyst attempts to get the patient "to recollect certain experiences and the emotions called up by them which he has at the moment forgotten." [3] To the psychoanalyst, present symptoms are tied to repressed material of early life. The symptoms will disappear when the repressed material is exposed under psychoanalytic treatment.

In order to enable the patient to "re-live" the past, the analyst uses dream interpretation and "free-association," whereby a patient gives up ideas as they come to mind. In addition, psychoanalysis takes advantage of the phenomena of *transference*. This is the development of an emotional attitude, positive or negative, by the patient towards the therapist. It is a reflection or imitation of emotional attitudes that were experienced in relationships that had an impact on psychosexual development. Thus, the therapist may be viewed as a "father-figure" or a "mother-figure" by the patient. Through the use of transference the therapist recreates the emotions tied to very early psychic development, unlocking repressed material and "freeing" the patient from his or her burden. As Freud noted, transference "is particularly calculated to favor the reproduction of these (early) emotional conditions." [4]

If we review some of the classifications in the last chapter, we can see their psychoanalytical basis. Many of the 14 fundamental characteristics of offenders suggested by the Governor's Special Committee are based on psychoanalytic theory. For example, category #2, *Immaturity*, is the result of a poorly developed ego that is unable to control id drives. Likewise, category #1, *Inadequacy*, is the result of poor ego functioning, and the "diffuse anxiety" referred to in the definition of inadequacy is clearly that which we have discussed in terms of *internal anxiety*, emanating from id drives. Category #10, *Anti-Social Attitudes*, is the same as Abrahamsen's category of a *Neurotic Sociopath*, a phenomenon that results from a defective

[2] Philip Reiff, ed., *Freud, Therapy and Techniques* (New York: Crowell-Collier, 1963), p. 274.

[3] *Ibid.*

[4] *Ibid.*

superego. Category #14, *Asocial Attitudes,* is the same as Abrahamsen's *Environmental Sociopath,* also caused by a defective superego.

Alexander and Staub, in a psychoanalytically-based interpretation of crime and criminals, state that "the majority of ['normal'] people resist some of their own tendencies toward anti-social behavior, not because of moral qualms, but because of fear of real consequences." [5] They note that "There is no fundamental difference between the neurotic criminal and all those socially harmless representatives of the group of neurotic characters; the difference lies merely in the external fact that the neurotic lawbreaker chooses a form of acting out of his impulses which is socially harmful." [6] Feldman presents the criminal as "a person suffering from a neurotic illness which, in no fundamental way, differs from any of the other forms of neurotic phenomena." [7] Feldman is also critical of what he sees as a tendency of psychoanalysis to minimize or overlook the learning process that leads to crime. He notes that this learning process has an effect on the personality.[8]

Fitzpatrick is also critical of the psychoanalytical approach to criminal behavior: "While unconscious conflicts exert an obvious impact on behavior, behavior is subject to multiple determinants, and it remains an unproven assumption that what is unconscious exerts a more basic motivational influence than conscious or social determinants" such as the environment.[9]

According to psychoanalytic theory, criminals may suffer from an overwhelming superego with a compulsive need to be punished. This punishment alleviates powerful feelings of guilt resulting from unresolved conflicts in the unconscious. Persons employed in the criminal justice system often see cases in which the crime committed was so poorly planned and executed that it would appear that the perpetrator wished to be caught.

At the other extreme are criminals who have such a poorly developed superego that they feel no guilt and engage in anti-social actions without any remorse. Between these extremes are various

[5] Franz Alexander and Hugo Staub, *The Criminal, The Judge, and the Public* (Glencoe, Ill.: The Free Press, 1956), p. 122.

[6] *Ibid.*, p. 106.

[7] Feldman cited from Donald R. Cressey and David A. Ward, eds., *Delinquency, Crime and Social Process* (New York: Harper and Row, 1969), p. 437.

[8] *Ibid.*, p. 441.

[9] John J. Fitzpatrick, "Psychoanalysis and Crime: A Critical Survey of Salient Trends in the Literature," *The Annals* (Jan. 1976), p. 71.

neurotic disorders and ego problems that cause an individual to come into conflict with criminal laws. This type of neurotic disorder may be seen in *Kleptomania,* which is considered to have its roots in an *oral fixation.* Tensions, which are sexual in nature, give rise to compulsive stealing. Otto Fenichel describes the unconscious mechanism of Kleptomania as being represented by the statement "If you don't give me love, I'll take it (or at least the representative of love in the form of a stolen object)." [10]

SOCIAL CASEWORK

Social casework is one of the three basic specialties of social work, the others being group work and community organization. There have been many definitions of social casework. Swithun Bowers offers the following:

> Social casework is an art in which knowledge of the science of human relations and skill in relationship are used to mobilize capacities in the individual and resources in the community appropriate for better adjustment between the client and all or any part of his total environment.[11]

Social work has its roots in charity work and the supplying of concrete services to persons in need. Mary Richmond, whose colleagues included many physicians, presented the practice of social casework as including (non-psychoanalytical) psychological and sociological aspects of a person's behavior. She also set the groundwork for what is sometimes referred to as the *medical-model* of treatment which deals with non-physiological problems through the method of *study, diagnosis, and treatment.*

Following World War 1, Freudian thought "impacted" on social casework. Caseworkers began examining a client's feelings and attitudes in order to understand and "cope with some of the unreasonable forces that held him in their grip." [12] Casework was thus expanded to include work with psychological as well as social or environmental stress.

[10] Otto Fenichel, *The Psychoanalytic Theory of Neuroses* (New York: W. W. Norton and Co., 1945), pp. 370–71.

[11] Swithun Bowers quoted from Cora Kasius, ed., *Principles and Techniques in Social Casework* (New York: Family Service Assoc. of America, 1950), p. 127.

[12] Helen Harris Perlman, *Perspectives on Social Casework* (Philadelphia: Temple Univ. Press, 1971), p. 76.

While social casework borrowed much of its theory from psychoanalysis, it avoided the psychoanalytical goal of trying to effect personality changes. Instead it worked to help clients maintain constructive reality-based relationships, solve problems, and achieve adequate and satisfying independent social functioning within the client's existing personality structure.[13] To do this, social caseworkers use encouragement and moral support, persuasion and suggestion, training and advice, comfort and reassurance, along with reeducation and some sort of guidance.[14]

The importance of social casework in probation/parole practice goes beyond theory and into the skills and training that schools of social work provide. These include "an extension and refinement of information on how to interview, how to obtain facts about the client's background, how to identify and distinguish surface from underlying problems, what community resources exist, and how to refer." [15] Wilensky and Lebeaux note that such practice is pragmatic, based on rule-of-thumb experience rather than on theory.[16]

There are three basic operations practiced in social casework methodology:[17]

1. *Study:* fact-finding.
2. *Diagnosis:* thinking about and organizing facts into a meaningful goal-oriented explanation.
3. *Treatment:* implementation of conclusions as to the what and how of action upon the problem.

While we shall review these three operations separately, it should be noted that "study-diagnosis-treatment" have "a close mutual relationship and form one theme." Ostrower also notes that, while for teaching purposes these steps are referred to separately, they "are not actually performed in sequence, but are interwoven and in reality comprise a unity." [18]

[13] Fernando G. Torgerson, "Differentiating and Defining Casework and Psychotherapy," *Social Casework* (Apr. 1962), p. 41.

[14] Kasius, p. 25.

[15] Harold L. Wilensky and Charles N. Lebeaux, *Industrial Society and Social Welfare* (New York: Russell Sage Foundation, 1958), pp. 288–89.

[16] *Ibid.*

[17] Helen Harris Perlman, *Social Casework: A Problem-Solving Process* (Chicago: The Univ. of Chicago Press, 1957), p. 61.

[18] Roland Ostrower, "Study, Diagnosis, and Treatment: A Conceptual Structure," *Social Work* (Oct. 1962), p. 86.

Study

During the initial phase the worker must establish a relationship with his client. In order to be able to do this, the worker must be what Hamilton calls "a person of genuine warmth."[19] Using face-to-face interviews the worker conveys acceptance and understanding. Friedlander notes the "Caseworkers communicate their respect for and acceptance of the client as a person whose decisions about his own living situations are almost always his own to make." [20] The worker knows that the way he communicates will have an effect on the client's perception of him and their relationship. Therefore, he must be cognizant of the way he greets his client, the tone of his voice, facial expressions, posture, and the way he verbally expresses himself. In probation/parole practice the worker who exudes authority, who is curt, and who emphasizes the enforcement aspect of his position will encounter difficulties in establishing a sound casework relationship.

The worker engages the client in the helping process. He makes certain judgments about the client's motivation, how much he wants to change, and how willing he is to contribute to bringing about change. The worker recognizes that the client brings attitudes and preconceptions about being on probation or parole. The probation/parole client is fearful, or at least realistically on guard, since he recognizes the power of the p/p worker.

An anxious client will be resistant to the worker's efforts, and in the non-voluntary p/p setting, the worker can easily raise the client's anxiety level, thus increasing resistance. P/p clients often have negative impressions of all authority figures. This is usually based on experiences with parents, school officials, police, courts, training schools or prisons. In addition, the client may have a low self-image, a severe superego, or chronically high anxiety level. The result will be resistance.

There are ways of lessening resistance. The worker can discuss the client's feelings about being on p/p, allowing him to ventilate some of his feelings and anxiety. This will also enable the worker to clear up any misconceptions that his client has about p/p supervision.

The client's motivation can also be influenced by *transference*. He

[19] Gordon Hamilton, *Theory and Practice of Social Casework* (New York: Columbia University Press, 1967), p. 28.

[20] Walter A. Friedlander, *Concepts and Methods of Social Work* (Englewood Cliffs, N.J.: Prentice-Hall, 1958), p. 22.

may view the worker as a friendly parent, or authoritative and demanding mother or father. The worker can be influenced by *countertransference*, since he may view the client as a child-like figure, or when there is a great age difference between worker and client, the former may view the latter as a father or older brother.

The worker prepares a psychosocial study of his client. In non-probation/parole agencies workers often stress the importance of early childhood development and experiences with a view toward applying psychoanalytic explanations to the client's behavior.[21] This is not the usual practice in p/p settings, where it is more appropriate to analyze "the unique constellation of social, psychological, and biological determinants of the client's current stressful situation." [22] In p/p practice, the main focus is on the present or immediate past.

The p/p worker seeks information that will provide an indication of the client's view of his present situation. He concerns himself with his client's plans for improving his situation and weighs the sincerity and intensity of the latter's commitment to change. He reviews the client's relationship with his family and evaluates the impact of his current situation. While engaged in his study, the worker must also be aware of the cultural, racial and ethnic factors that influence his client.

In p/p, material from the unconscious is not sought. However, with clients who are mentally ill, material which in the better-functioning person is normally repressed, may be brought into the fore. In such situations, the worker must direct his efforts toward keeping the client in touch with reality, and he usually avoids exploring the normally repressed material.

Diagnosis

A diagnosis is a "summation of the symptoms of some underlying causation." [23] It determines the nature of the client's difficulty and provides a realistic assessment for individualized treatment. Some of the questions that a diagnosis seeks to answer are:[24]

1. What are the client's social-role problems?
2. What are his dominant and alternate modes of adaption?

[21] *Ibid.*, p. 134.
[22] *Ibid.*, p. 47.
[23] *Ibid.*, p. 146.
[24] *Ibid.*, pp. 84–85.

3. What are the etiological factors that can be traced to his present situation?
4. What are his ego strengths and weaknesses?

The diagnosis focuses particular attention on ego-functioning. The client's capacity to deal consciously with difficult inner forces is dependent on his ego-functioning, a facet of personality that develops its strength through interaction with other persons.[25] Ego adequacy will have a direct impact on the client's efforts to deal with his difficulties.

Perlman suggests that the diagnosis in casework consists of:[26]

1. the nature of the problem and the goals sought by the client, in their relationship to
2. the nature of the person who bears the problem, his social and psychological situation and functioning, and who needs help with his problem, in relation to
3. the nature and purpose of the agency and the kind of help it can offer and/or make available.

In order for a diagnosis to be complete, psychological testing and/or a psychiatric evaluation is necessary. The results of a clinical examination will indicate if the client is in need of any special treatment—for example, if he is psychotic.

Perlman, in discussing the etiology of the client's malfunctioning calls this a "history of his development as a problem-encountering, problem-solving human being," and she notes that this can provide the worker with an understanding of the client's present difficulties and the likely extent of his ability to cope with them.[27]

Friedlander notes that "In an on-going relationship, diagnoses are continually reformulated, as the caseworker and the client engage in appropriate corrective action or treatment." [28]

Treatment

It is a basic concept in social work that the worker has no right to impose his goals upon the client. The client has a right to *self-determination*. Obviously, the authority inherent in the p/p

[25] *Ibid.*, pp. 134–35.

[26] Perlman, pp. 168–69.

[27] *Ibid.*, p. 176.

[28] Friedlander, p. 22.

worker limits self-determination. How is this reconciled when social casework is the mode of treatment in p/p?

Hardman notes that a review of some of the literature on the subject reveals that in treatment, authority is

1. impossible
2. possible only in mild cases of delinquency
3. both detrimental and beneficial, or
4. essential but not necessarily harmful.

Hardman states that "authority conflict is a major causative factor in delinquency," a proposition that is widely accepted in correctional treatment.[29] Therefore, assisting the offender in coming to grips with the reality of authority is a basic goal in p/p treatment. The client's relationship with a p/p worker is often the only positive experience he has ever had in dealing with an authority figure.

However, social caseworkers in other than correctional settings must also deal with the reality of their authority. They require clients to keep appointments, provide personal information, and pay fees, usually under the threat, implied or expressed, of denying the client the service for which he is asking. Workers at child welfare agencies may even be required to remove children from their parents or guardians in neglect or child abuse cases. In addition, because of the impact of an agency setting, or the phenomena of transference, the social caseworker is always an authority figure. The concept and the use of authority and the limits placed on self-determination by reality, are not alien to the practice of social casework.

However, we should consider the admonition of Smith and Berlin, who state that "No matter how evident the need for counseling . . . appears to the probation and/or the parole officer, it cannot be forced upon the offender unless it is directly related to his crime." [30] For example, a client who has a history of drug usage that has resulted in the need to steal could be required to accept counseling because it is "directly related to his crime." However, the author questions the usefulness of "counseling" that has to be "forced upon the offender." The author would recommend instead that no form of treatment be

[29] Dale G. Hardman, "Constructive Use of Authority," *Crime and Delinquency* (July 1960), p. 250.

[30] Alexander B. Smith and Louis Berlin, "Self-Determination in Welfare and Corrections: Is There a Limit?", *Federal Probation* (Dec. 1974), p. 3.

forced upon any offender. This will preserve the client's right not to be treated, while allowing the worker to better use his treatment time and skills with clients who wish help.

Ross and Shireman note that the illusion "that all, or almost all, offenders need and will respond to rehabilitative efforts if such efforts are sufficiently massive and persistent" has led us "to assign most offenders to programs of active intervention in their lives. The result is the choking of programs with large numbers of individuals who do not need, do not want, and cannot use the sort of relationship-and-communication-based treatment that is the basis for most probation or parole services." [31]

The plan for treatment, based on the diagnosis, will hopefully use procedures that will move the client toward the goal of enhancing his ability to function within the realities placed upon him by society in general, and his present probation/parole status in particular. There are three basic techniques involved:

Changing the Environment. This may involve obtaining needed resources if these are available from the agency, or locating other agencies that can provide them. In using this technique the worker may assume a *mediator* or *advocate* role when the client is unable to secure a service which he needs and to which he is entitled. In p/p practice this is a common role for the worker. The technique is used by the juvenile worker when he is seeking placement for a youngster in a foster home, group home, or residential treatment center. The after-care worker who is trying to place a juvenile back into public school after a stay at a juvenile institution is often a *mediator-advocate*. The p/p worker is often required to intervene on behalf of clients who require financial assistance from the welfare department. P/p workers may help a client to secure a civil service position or a necessary license/certificate to enter a particular trade or profession.

The p/p worker may help his client by talking to an employer or school official, while at the same time helping the client to modify his behavior relative to problems encountered at work or school. Many p/p clients have had few positive work or school experiences, and their difficulty with authority extends to employers and teachers. By using role playing, reflection, and suggestion the worker tries to modify the client's behavior, at least to the degree required for continued schooling or employment.

[31] Bernard Ross and Charles Shireman, *Social Work and Social Justice* (Wash., D.C.: National Assoc. of Social Workers, 1972), p. 24.

The worker, while being of direct assistance when necessary, should promote independence on the part of his client. The worker realizes that he is not continually available, and treatment is rarely indefinite. *The worker should not do anything for his client that the client is capable of doing for himself.*

Ego Support. The use of this technique entails attempts by the worker to sustain his client through expressions of interest, sympathy and confidence. The worker, through the use of his relationship with his client, promotes or discourages behavior according to whether or not the behavior is consistent with the goals of treatment. He encourages the client to ventilate, and he deals with any anxiety that may inhibit functioning.

The worker imparts a feeling of confidence in his client's ability to deal with problems. He makes suggestions about the client's contemplated actions. He indicates approval or suggests alternatives relative to steps that the client has already taken. He may, at the very least, provide a willing and sympathetic ear to a troubled or lonely client. It is not unusual for the p/p worker to be the only person that an offender has available to whom he can relate and talk. When the relationship is a good one, the client cannot help but view his worker as a friend.

The worker is also supportive of the client's family, parents or spouse. In p/p practice, home visits are a usual part of the worker's responsibilities. During the home visit, the worker has an opportunity to observe his client's environment directly. This adds another dimension to the worker's knowledge of his client.

The knowledge that a client lives in substandard housing or in a high delinquency area is easy for a worker to incorporate into his working methodology. But the concept is an intellectual one. A home visit will provide the smell of urine in the hall, the roaches, the broken fixtures and bathroom facilities; it will enable the worker to experience the presence of drug addicts huddling in a hallway, waiting for their "connection." The worker will be able to see, hear, and smell the environment in which his client is forced to live. He will be able to understand the hostility and frustration that fills the life of many p/p clients almost from the time they are born.

By working directly with parents or a spouse, in addition to working with the client, the worker broadens his delivery of help to his client. The worker can make referrals for the client's children when special aid is necessary—indeed, he can intervene on behalf of his client in the role of *mediator-advocate* to get services for any family member. He can assist with marital problems. Marital discord is an acute problem in many parole cases where a client has been incarcerated for many years. The worker may try to deal with the problem directly, or he may provide a referral to a specialized agency for the client and spouse. It is not unusual for a distraught wife to call the p/p worker in order to complain about her husband. Sometimes she is merely seeking some way of ventilating her feelings, while at other times the situation may be more serious—for example, she may have been beaten.

When a client is living with parents, the worker strives to involve them in the rehabilitation effort. This is often difficult. The client may come from a large family where he is the perennial "black sheep". He may come from a family that has other members of the unit on probation, in prison, or on parole. This may dissipate the family's energy and resources, and directly affect their ability to help the client.

Clarification. Hollis states that clarification is sometimes called counseling because it usually accompanies other forms of treatment in casework practice. Clarification includes providing information that will help a client to see what steps he should take in various situations. The worker, for example, may help the client weigh the issues and alternatives in order to provide a better picture on which to base a decision. Hollis notes that the client "may also be helped to become more aware of his own feelings, desires and attitudes." [32]

The client is encouraged to explain what is bothering him. If the problem is external, this may be relatively easy. However, if the difficulty is internally-caused, it may go deep and provoke anxiety. This will cause resistance and the worker will require great skill to secure enough information about the problem to be able to be of assistance. In response to the information, the worker may provide a direct interpretation to the client; more often he will ask questions and make suggestions designed to help the client to think out his problem more clearly and to deal with it in a realistic manner.

REALITY THERAPY

Reality therapy was developed as a mode of treatment by William Glasser, a psychiatrist. It is probably the easiest of the three modes of treatment to describe, and its simplicity is one of its advantages in

[32] Hollis cited from Kasius, pp. 418–19.

practice. Glasser's book, *Reality Therapy,* contains only 166 pages. Glasser describes reality therapy as a method "that leads all patients toward reality, toward grappling successfully with the tangible and intangible aspects of the real world. . . ." [33]

While Glasser accepts the developmental theories of psychoanalysis, he rejects it as a useful method of treatment. "It is wishful thinking to believe that a man will give up a phobia once he understands either its origin or the current representation of its origin in the transference relationship." [34] Glasser believes that conventional treatment "depends far too much on the ability of the patient to change his attitude and ultimately his behavior through gaining insight into his unconscious conflicts and inadequacies." [35]

In a recent work, Glasser reiterates some of his previous positions and elaborates on others.[36] Various mental problems, Glasser argues, are merely symptomatic illnesses that have no presently known medical cause. They act as companions for the lonely people who *choose* them. Glasser states that in cases of so-called mental illness, the behaviors or symptoms are actually chosen by the person from his lifetime of experiences residing in the subconscious. Alluding to the fact that reality therapy does not always work, Glasser states that the fault is with the therapist who is unable to become involved in a meaningful way with the client.

In his latest work, Glasser expresses a great deal of support for the work of probation and parole officers, although he cautions persons in corrections, as well as other fields, against the use of punishment:

> For many delinquents punishment serves as a source of involvement. They receive attention through delinquent behavior, if only that of the police, court, probation counselor, and prison. . . . A failing person rationalizes the punishment as a reason for the anger that caused him to be hostile.[37]

Instead of punishment, Glasser recommends that praise and positive motivations be applied through the medium of reality therapy.

Schmidelberg, another reality-oriented psychiatrist, states that "Dwelling on the past encourages the patient to forget his present

[33] William Glasser, *Reality Therapy* (New York: Harper and Row, 1975), p. 6.

[34] *Ibid.*, p. 53.

[35] *Ibid.*, p. 51.

[36] *See* William Glasser, *The Identity Society* (New York: Harper and Row, 1976).

[37] *Ibid.*, p. 95.

problems, which is a relief at times, but often—undesirably—the patient feels that after having produced so many interesting memories he is now entitled to rest on his laurels and make no effort to change his attitude or plans for the future.[38] This diverts attention from the client's current problem, which is a reality that should be dealt with directly. Glasser states that conventional treatment does not deal with whether a client's behavior is right or wrong, in terms of morality or law, but "Rather, it contends that once the patient is able to resolve his conflicts and get over his mental illness, he will be able to behave correctly." [39] Glasser maintains that societal realities require direct intervention with a client, with the therapist not accepting "wrong" behavior.

The reality therapist denies the claims of psychoanalysis that cure depends on the recovery of traumatic early memories that have been repressed. Schmidelberg states that the ability of psychoanalysis to cure persons has never been substantiated clinically.[40] In place of conventional treatment, the reality therapist proposes first substituting mental health labels (neurotic, personality disorder, psychotic) with the term *irresponsible.* A "healthy" person is called *responsible,* and the task of the therapist is to help an irresponsible person to become responsible.

According to Glasser, people with serious behavior problems lack the proper involvement with someone—and lacking that involvement, they are unable to satisfy their needs. Therefore, in order to help, the worker must enable the client to gain involvement, first with the worker and then with others. Whereas the traditional therapist maintains a "professional" objectivity or distance, the reality therapist strives for strong feelings between worker and client. This type of relationship is necessary in order for the worker to be able to have an impact on his client's behavior. The worker, while always accepting of his client, firmly rejects irresponsible behavior. He then teaches his client better ways of behaving.

To accomplish this "re-educating," the worker must know about the client's reality, the way he lives, his environment, his aspirations, his total reality. Reality is always influenced by the client's culture, ethnic and racial group, economic class, and intelligence. The worker must be

[38] Melitta Schmidelberg, "Some Basic Principles of Offender Therapy: Two," *International Journal of Offender Therapy and Comparative Criminology* (No. 1, 1975), p. 29.

[39] Glasser, p. 56.

[40] Schmidelberg, p. 28.

willing to listen openmindedly and learn about his client.[41] While doing this he develops a relationship with his client, a relationship that can effect an influence leading to responsible behavior.

Like behavior modification, reality therapy is symptom-oriented. The probation/parole client is in treatment because he has caused society to take action as a result of his behavior. If the worker can remove the symptoms and make the client responsible, he will satisfy society and relieve the client of anxiety caused by a fear of being incarcerated. Schmidelberg states that for a delinquent symptom to disappear it is usually necessary for the person to:[42]

1. face it fully with all its implications and consequences,
2. decide to stop it and consider the factors that precipitate it, and
3. make a definite effort to stop it.

She maintains that a general and non-directive method is not likely to change symptoms that the client may find quite satisfying (for example, drugs to the addict, forced sex to the rapist, or money and excitement to the robber).

Rachin outlines 14 steps that the reality therapist follows to attain responsible behavior in his client:[43]

1. *Personalizes.* The reality therapist becomes emotionally involved. He is a warm, tough, interested, and sensitive human being who genuinely gives a damn—and demonstrates it.

2. *Reveals Self.* He has frailties as well as strengths and does not need to project an image of omniscience or omnipotence. If he is asked personal questions he sees nothing wrong with responding.

3. *Concentrates on the "Here and Now."* He is concerned only with behavior that can be tried and tested on a reality basis. He is interested only with the problems of the present, and he does not allow a client to waste time and avoid confronting reality by dwelling on the past. He does not permit a person the luxury of blaming irresponsible behavior on past difficulties.

4. *Emphasizes Behavior.* The reality therapist is not interested in

[41] *Ibid.*, p. 24.

[42] *Ibid.*, p. 26.

[43] Richard Rachin, "Reality Therapy: Helping People Help Themselves," *Crime and Delinquency* (Jan. 1974), pp. 51–53, reprinted with permission of the publisher.

uncovering underlying motivations or drives; rather, he concentrates on helping the person act in a manner that will help him meet his needs responsibly.

5. *Rarely Asks Why.* He is concerned with helping a client understand what he is doing, what he has accomplished, what he is learning from his behavior, and whether he could do better than he is doing now. Asking a person the reasons for his actions implies that they make a difference. To the reality therapist irresponsible behavior is just that—he is not interested in explanations for self-defeating behavior. He conveys to the client that more responsible behavior will be expected.

6. *Helps the Person Evaluate His Behavior.* He is persistent in guiding the client to explore his actions for signs of irresponsible, unrealistic behavior. He does not permit the client to deny the importance of difficult things he would like to do. He repeatedly asks the person what his current behavior is accomplishing and whether it is meeting his needs.

7. *Helps Him Develop a Better Plan for Future Behavior.* By questioning *what* the person is doing now and *what* he can do differently, he conveys his belief in the client's ability to behave responsibly. If the client cannot develop his own plan for future action, the reality therapist will help him develop one. Once the plan is worked out, a contract is drawn up and signed by the person and the reality therapist. It is a minimum plan for behaving differently in matters where the person admits he has acted irresponsibly. If the contract is broken, a new one is designed and agreed upon. If a contract is honored, a new one with tasks more closely attuned to the person's ability is designed.

8. *Rejects Excuses.* He does not encourage searching for reasons to justify irresponsible behavior, thus avoiding the implication that the client has acceptable reasons for violating his agreement. Excuses are not accepted—only an honest scrutinizing examination of his behavior.

9. *Offers No Tears of Sympathy.* Sympathy can indicate that the worker lacks confidence in the client's ability to act responsibly. Sad tales, past and present, are avoided. Sympathizing with a person's misery and self-pity will not lead to more responsible behavior. The worker must convey to his client that he cares enough about him that, if need be, he will try to force him to act more responsibly.

10. *Praises and Approves Responsible Behavior.* The worker makes appropriate indications of recognition for positive accomplishments.

However, he does not become unduly excited about the client's success in handling problems that he previously avoided or handled poorly.

11. *Believes People Are Capable of Changing Their Behavior.* The worker's positive expectations enhance the client's chances of adopting a more productive lifestyle, regardless of what has occurred in the past. The worker is encouraging and optimistic.

12. *Tries to Work in Groups.* The use of a peer group allows for more influence or pressure on the members. It enables the members to express themselves before people with similar problems. It enables the member to test out "reality" in a controlled environment.

13. *Does Not Give Up.* The worker rejects the idea that anyone is unable to learn how to live a more productive and responsible life. Historical information contained in long case records is not allowed to interfere with the worker's involvement with his client, and his belief that all persons can begin again.

14. *Does Not Label People.* Avoids the diagnostic rituals, and does not classify people as sick, disturbed, or emotionally disabled—they are either responsible or irresponsible.

Reality therapy was developed by Glasser while he was a psychiatrist at the Ventura School, an institution for the treatment of older adolescent girls who had been unsuccessful on probation. Because the technique evolved within the field of corrections and the realities of dealing with delinquent behavior, it has been widely accepted and applied to p/p treatment.

BEHAVIOR MODIFICATION

If we view the various modes of treatment as if they were on a continuum represented by a straight horizontal line, with total acceptance of psychoanalytic theory/treatment on the extreme left, and total rejection on the extreme right, reality therapy would tend toward the right of center, while social casework would tend toward the left of center. Behavior modification would be firmly on the right of our imaginary line.

Behavior therapy, which emanated from the science laboratory and experimental psychology, rejects psychoanalytic theory as an unscientific basis for an even more unscientific mode of treatment. Ian Stevenson, a psychiatrist, is extremely critical of the paucity of evidence indicating that the therapeutic procedures that are based on psychoanalytic theory are effective.[44]

Behavior therapists, on the other hand, take pride in displaying and subjecting to scientific analysis their methods and results. Indeed, the use of behavior modification requires the maintenance of extensive objective treatment data, including outcomes, in quantifiable terms.[45] *A Dictionary of Psychology* defines *behaviorism* as an approach to psychology which emphasizes the importance of an objective study of actual responses.

Behavior modification proceeds on the theory that all forms of behavior are the result of learning responses to certain stimuli. Disturbed behavior, for example, is a matter of learning responses that are inappropriate.[46] The behaviorist contends, and has been able to prove, that animal behavior, human and otherwise, can be modified through the proper application of behavior therapy. Indeed, such techniques as *conditioned reflex therapy* are "based completely on the work of Pavlov and Bechterev,"[47] who demonstrated that such observable and measurable activity as the flow of a dog's saliva, could be controlled by the use of laboratory conditioning. (Pavlov's dogs were conditioned to salivate at the sound of a bell.) When behavior modification moved out of the laboratory, its use was "confined to specific problems such as children's fears and bedwetting, and alcoholism."[48]

There is considerable opposition to behaviorism in theory and practice. To many conventional therapists the theory lessened the dignity of a human being, reducing him to the level of an animal, with the techniques used reminiscent of animal training. Ogden Lindsley, for example, humorously reminisces about his early days with behaviorism, stating "that if the bottom fell out of the whole thing, I would drop out of graduate school and try to get a job with Ringling Brothers' circus training gorillas to dance and play the piano."[49]

[44] Stevenson cited from Joseph Wolpe, Andrew Salter, and L. J. Reyna, eds., *The Conditioning Therapies* (New York: Holt, Rinehart, and Winston, 1964), p. 7.

[45] Task Force Report, *Behavior Therapy in Psychiatry* (Washington, D.C.: American Psychiatric Assoc., 1973), p. 3.

[46] Perry London, *The Modes and Morals of Psychotherapy* (New York: Holt, Rinehart, and Winston, 1964), p. 83.

[47] Wolpe, et al., p. 21.

[45] *Ibid.*, p. 170.

[49] Philip J. Hilts, *Behavior Mod* (New York: Harpers Magazine Press, 1974), p. 7.

A pioneer in behavior modification, B. F. Skinner, observed that when some aspect of behavior is followed by a certain type of consequence—a reward—it is more likely to occur again. The reward is called a *positive reinforcer.* When punishment is used to prevent a repetition of some aspect of behavior, it is called a *negative reinforcer.*[50] Reinforcement is the basis of a technique called *operant conditioning.* This technique uses pleasant and unpleasant stimuli to influence a particular piece of behavior. In order for it to be effective, the stimuli (reinforcement) must follow rather closely the behavior that is to be influenced. Timing thus plays a crucial role in this form of treatment. The need for timely reinforcement also makes this technique difficult to apply to probation/parole practice.

Token Economies

Operant conditioning is used extensively in the form of a *token economy.* This technique originated in the closed wards of psychiatric institutions, one of the few places where early behaviorists were permitted to use their techniques. Its use has been extended to other institutional settings, including training schools, prisons, and public schools.[51] The token economy was used at Draper prison in Alabama, where correction officers were taught to be behavior modifiers. Each inmate was given a punch card with numbers every morning, and as he moved through various prison activities during the day he earned points that were punched out on the card. Point-earning activities ranged from bed-making to academic performance.

With the points (tokens), the inmate was able to earn access to the TV room, snacks, cigarettes, movies, etc. The results of the program included dramatic improvements in inmate behavior. It virtually eliminated the need for correction officers to use punishment in the 'normal" prison sense.[52]

A widely heralded token economy was used by Harold Cohen at the National Training School for Boys (NTS) in Washington, D.C.[53] The project involved 41 adjudicated juvenile delinquents whose crimes ranged from auto theft to homicide. A point system was tied to educational work and academic achievement. The points that were earned

[50] B. F. Skinner, *Beyond Freedom and Dignity* (New York: Alfred A. Knopf, 1972), p. 27.

[51] APA Task Force Report, p. 25.

[53] Hilts, pp. 124–27.

[53] *See* Harold L. Cohen and James Filipczak, *A New Learning Environment* (San Francisco: Jessey-Bass, 1971), pp. 1–192.

allowed a boy to purchase refreshments, clothing and even items selected from a mail-order catalog. Cohen reports that by establishing this incentive plan, the program enabled youngsters to increase their academic growth "two to four times the average for American public school students."

Cohen notes that the conventional method used in the public school system and correctional institutions is to assign students on the basis of their I.Q. score and reading level. Those who score low are assumed to be basically incompetent to perform in such areas as algebra and physics. They are assigned to tasks considered appropriate to their level of ability, and these usually do not require reading and other academic skills. Before Cohen arrived at the NTS, this was the method used there.

Cohen began by considering every inmate a potential student capable of upgrading. His goal was to prepare them to return to public school or to pass the high school equivalency test. "The environment was planned to include choices and perquisites normally available to the average wage-earning American but not available to these youths in a prison. The students earned points for academic performance and paid for their rooms, clothing, amusement and gifts," with them. Even showers had to be rented with points. Points could not be gained in any other way except "work." They could not be loaned, given away, or stolen.

Another aspect of the system was that the students "were able to earn some powerful nonmonetary rewards. Respect, approval by one's peers . . ." etc. Families were permitted to visit, but all transactions within the project were made with points, and visitors were not permitted to purchase items for residents.

The principal objective of the program was the development of appropriate academic behavior. No assumptions were made by the program originators relative to the resident's adjustment when he returned to the community. However, a follow-up on recidivism indicated that during the first year the recidivist rate was two-thirds less than the norm, although by the third year the rate was near the norm. Cohen reports that the program evidently delayed a return to delinquent activity, but did not necessarily prevent it. He states that to do this would require additional services outside the institutional setting.

Other Systems

Operant conditioning can also use punishment, *negative reinforcement*. When punishment is used, it is called *Aversion Therapy*. This involves the avoidance of punishment in a controlled situation in which the therapist specifies an unpleasant event that will occur if the subject performs an undesirable behavior. The American Psychiatric Association Task Force noted that "The most effective way to eliminate inappropriate behavior appears to be to punish it while at the same time reinforcing the desired behavior." [54] This method of treatment is obviously controversial, and among many behaviorists, Aversion Therapy is not considered "ethical."

Another one of the many behavior modification techniques is *Systematic Desensitization,* which is designed to treat anxiety or phobic reactions by substituting muscular relaxation responses for the tension response of anxiety. A program is devised in which the anxiety or phobic-producing stimuli is introduced gradually and progressively. The technique may also be used by asking a subject to imagine anxiety-producing situations that cannot be readily reproduced in the clinical setting; for example, picturing oneself on top of a mountain for a person who has a fear of high places.

Behavior modification has had some dramatic successes. The American Psychiatric Association has reported on them,[55] and Hilts, in quite an interesting fashion, relates the varieties of success in using behavior modification. (He also relates "horror stories" in which the use of behavior modification has become the subject of public concern. For example, in California prisoners were given a drug that induced such symptoms as loss of muscle control and inability to breath, all approximating death. At the same time the therapist would tell the subject in a highly authoritarian manner that he must change specific behavior.[56]) In one of many cases, behaviorists worked with a young retarded girl who could not speak or walk. Her tested I.Q. was zero, and she was destined to vegetate in an institution for the rest of her life. The end of the story: "she was released from the institution (walking) with an I.Q. score that allowed her to attend public school." [57]

Criticism

Therapists who are psychoanalytically oriented have been critical of behavior modification over the issue of *symptom substitution.* These therapists do not question the ability of behavior modification to re-

[54] APA Task Force Report, p. 36.

[55] *Ibid.*, pp. 1–131.

[56] Hilts, pp. 128–31.

[57] *Ibid.*, p. 9.

move or diminish certain undesirable behavior. However, according to traditional psychoanalytic theory, this symptom reduction will merely lead to new symptoms that will replace the old ones with each new emotional difficulty experienced by the subject.[58] The APA Task Force stated that this is not necessarily so. Furthermore, they indicated that reduction of unwanted behavior provides an opportunity to teach a person more desirable behavior.[59]

Behavior modification analyzes symptoms in terms of their observable behavior components. The therapist keeps a record of "frequency counts" on a particular behavior. For example, a parent will be asked to record the number of outbursts exhibited by a child within a given period of time. The therapist then makes a functional analysis designed to determine the circumstances under which the undesirable behavior seems to occur, and the elements within the environment that may be supporting the behavior. In this case, the parent is told to ignore the child's outbursts, no matter what the intensity, while at the same time to provide rewards (reinforcement) for more positive behavior. These rewards can be praise and attention, or sweets and toys.

The use of positive reinforcement has been criticized as being a form of "bribery." The use of tokens has been criticized as being "artificial." Positive reinforcement, the timely application of rewards, is more easily accomplished in the institutional setting, where the environment can be controlled, than in the community where most probation/parole treatment occurs. All of these reasons may account for the paucity of articles on the use of behavior modification in p/p in professional journals. However, Thorne, Tharp, and Wetzel reported on the successful use of behavior modification, *operant conditioning*, in work with young juveniles on probation.[60]

Behavior Modification in Probation/Parole

The probation officers first gained the cooperation of the child's parents—not an easy task. The officers then explained the behavioral techniques to be used and taught the parents how to apply them. Behavior was monitored by the parents, and charts were used to record frequency counts. Positive reinforcers were given for desired be-

[58] Kate Friedlander, *The Psychoanalytical Approach to Juvenile Delinquency* (New York: International Universities Press, 1947), p. 199.

[59] APA Task Force Report, p. 53.

[60] Gaylord L. Thorne, Roland G. Tharp, and Ralph J. Wetzel, "Behavior Modification Techniques: New Tools for Probation Officers," *Federal Probation* (June 1967), pp. 21–27.

havior, such as attendance at school, scholastic work, and satisfactory behavior, and were withheld when the child misbehaved. The rewards were specific and related directly to particular positive behavior. For example, a girl on probation was given telephone privileges and permitted weekend dates, contingent on her attendance at school all day. In this case the attendance officer would give a note to the child at the end of each day indicating her attendance. When the child gave her mother the note she earned the privilege of receiving and making calls that day. If she received four notes, she earned a weekend date, and five notes earned two weekend dates.

In another case, rewards included both tangible and intangible items. For example, for studying 30 minutes a day, the youngster was both praised and given permission to ride his bicycle. The authors[61] call the praise a *back-up reward.* Money, access to TV, etc., were all used as reinforcers for specific behavior on a specified and scheduled basis. The authors point out that uncooperative parents can defeat any type of productive change.

Polakow and Doctor report that "experimental literature on behavioral approaches to probation work with adults is almost nonexistent." [62] They report the use of *contingency management* in working with adult drug offenders on probation. While contingency management is supposedly a behaviorist approach, it actually comes closer to reality therapy than behavior modification. This is because it lacks the crucial element of timeliness—the reinforcement does not closely follow the desired action. In the cases cited by Polakow and Doctor, the probation officers used reduction in probation time as a reinforcer.

Actually, most probation/parole agencies use some form of contingency management, without labeling it as such. For example, an offender who is employed will be placed on a reduced reporting schedule, e.g., once monthly, while an unemployed offender will be required to report in person once a week. In addition, discharge from probation and parole is often conditioned on satisfactory behavior under supervision, and this is explained to offenders at the beginning of their probation or parole.

Shah states that for behavior modification to be effective, it is essential that there be "a variety of facilities for carefully graduating the

[61] *Ibid.*

[62] Robert L. Polakow and Ronald M. Doctor, "A Behavioral Modification Program for Adult Drug Offenders," *Journal of Research in Crime and Delinquency* (Jan. 1974), pp. 63–69.

release process, and also for providing a wide range of follow-up and other services in the community." [63] Braukmann, Fixsen, Phillips, and Wolf indicate a "need for increased emphasis on community-based behavioral approaches." They report that a 1973 probation program used behavior modification for 26 adult probationers who advanced through program levels by attending and participating in probation meetings. In the final stage, in order to be discharged from probation, the offenders negotiated behavioral contracts in which the goals were the development of new and positive modes of behavior—for example, gainful employment. When the goals were reached an offender would be discharged from supervision. Although there were no control groups, the probationers in the program were said to have made significant progress under this system.[64]

Perhaps the most important criticism of behavior modification is contained in its apparent success. As a "learning tool," behaviorism is amoral and politically neutral—like a gun—and thus easily lends itself to misuse. Some critics, the so-called radical school for example, maintain that behaviorism is a tool for keeping persons with legitimate grievances from expressing or acting on them. Behavior modification, as has been noted, is successful in maintaining prison discipline and order. Where order and legitimate dissent begin and end is a matter of obvious subjectivity. Unlike other forms of treatment, behavior modification does not need the acquiescence of its subjects in order to be effective. In fact, it may be more successful at times when used without the knowledge of those who are being subjected to it. Since behavior modification serves to modify undesirable behavior or attitudes, who is to determine what is undesirable. What one observer considers education, another may consider brainwashing.

SOCIAL GROUP WORK

Treatment of clients in groups is used in social work, reality therapy, and behavior modification. The use of a group has certain advantages over conventional one-to-one methods. Northern notes that "One of the advantages of the use of groups in social work is that stimulation toward improvement arises from a network of interpersonal influences

[63] Shah quoted from Hippechen, p. 132.

[64] Braukmann, et al., cited in Polakow and Doctor.

in which all members participate." [65] The basic theory underlying the use of the group is that the impact provided by peer interaction is more powerful than worker-client reactions within the one-to-one situation.

In probation/parole, groups are comprised of members who share a common status, in this case legally determined. Groups in p/p may also be organized on the basis of age, or around a common problem such as drug addiction. The group is a "mutual aid society" in which members are given an opportunity to share experiences and assist each other with problems in a safe, controlled environment. The group helps to confirm for each member the fact that others share similar problems, thus reducing the sense of isolation.

The group can reduce the anxiety of having to report alone to a p/p officer; it tends to offset the more direct authority of the one-to-one situation; and it tends to lower the impact of socio-cultural differences between client and worker.

The summary and analysis that follows is based on the author's experience with a group of young offenders in a parole setting. The method used reflects an approach suggested by William Schwartz, who stresses several key concepts in working with groups: the *contract* is made verbally between the client group and the worker and it provides the framework for the tasks that the group will work on; the *contract* is mutually agreed upon and it is based on the common ground and needs of the group members; *work* is the means by which the group comes to grips with mutual needs and problems, and it is a part of the worker's role to *demand* that the group *work* as mutually agreed upon in the *contract.* [66]

In 1971, the New York State Department of Correctional Services formed a specialized parole supervision unit called the Young Offender Bureau. The YOB supervised offenders released to the New York City Area Office who were under 21 years of age at the time of their parole. A most significant feature of the YOB was an expectation that each parole officer in the unit would utilize group methods in the supervision process. No particular method of group work was specified since an attempt was being made to see what kind, if any, of group techniques would be useful in the parole setting. Thus, each parole

[65] Helen Northern, *Social Work With Groups* (New York: Columbia Univ. Press, 1969), p. 52.

[66] William Schwartz, *Some Notes On The Use of Groups In Social Work Practice* (Address delivered to the Annual Workshop for Field Instructors and Faculty of the Columbia Univ. School of Social Work, mimeo, 1966).

officer was free to use whatever method he or she wished, within the requirements of sound parole supervision. Caseload size was kept at about 32 to enable each p.o. in the YOB to devote more attention to each case, both individually and on a group basis.

The author decided to see if a voluntary approach to forming a group would be successful. Consideration in the selection process included a parolee's reporting schedule. He could not be reporting on a monthly basis to be selected, since traditionally this is a reduced reporting schedule and is considered a "reward" for good performance on parole. The group would meet once per week, and to ask a man reporting on a monthly basis to report on a weekly basis could be considered as punitive. A parolee who worked or attended school in the evening would also not be available for the group, which would meet at night. In addition, parolees who were believed to be in violation of parole were omitted during the group formation stage.

Each parolee who was considered for the group was informed individually about the general purpose and meeting schedule of the group. Specifically, it would meet once per week for one hour to discuss topics or problems raised by group members. Attendance and participation would be voluntary, although those who did not attend were expected to report on an individual basis. The initital reaction was good, and ten parolees volunteered out of the twelve that were asked. However, after five sessions, attendance began to fall off to a point where we no longer constituted a viable group.

Upon reflection, it appeared that most of the parolees who volunteered did so out of fear that refusal to volunteer would somehow result in some form of punishment. When they began to realize that the group was indeed voluntary, they stopped attending. The author believed that a parole group could work and be beneficial to its participants if only they would attend the sessions consistently enough to gain something from them. A second group was organized. This time it was decided to make the group as normal a part of the parole process as possible. Attendance was made mandatory. This was readily understood by the members, so there was no need to test out the voluntary aspect as had the first group. Each parolee was required to attend ten sessions. After the ten sessions, the continuance of the group would be a decision made by the group members, and no member would be required to attend any further sessions if he chose not to.

Initially, ten parolees were selected for the group. One was arrested by the police after attending two sessions; one was arrested as a parole violator by the author before the sessions began, and one was arrested as a parole violator after attending two sessions (no special consideration was given for participation in the group). Of the remaining seven members, one was a persistent attendance problem, with a rate of 30%, and his individual reporting was almost as bad. The other six had an attendance rate of 80%. Four members were added to the group after the first five sessions and they showed an attendance rate of 90%. At the end of the ten sessions, only two members stated that they did not want to continue with further group sessions, and they were excused. Of the two, one was the parolee with a 30% attendance rate, and the other explained that traveling difficulties made it impossible for him to leave work and arrive at the sessions on time. The rest of the group requested that the sessions be continued.

When the group sessions began the members started calling upon late arrivers to explain their tardiness. Those who missed sessions were also called upon to explain why by the group members. They were a "demanding jury," quick to point out what they believed to be falsehoods in any explanation. The author told the members that each session was being limited to exactly one hour, explaining that this was being done because of the tendency in all types of groups to leave important matters until the end, often wasting time at the beginning. The purpose of the group was stated in terms of mutual concerns. The author pointed out that the group members had much in common; their parole status, age, ethnicity (all were black or Puerto Rican; the author's area of supervision was the South Bronx), and difficulties with school or employment. It was suggested that in the group setting each member could help the other because of a similar background and common problems.

During the first session, the discussion turned to the rules of parole. The author explained that although he was now a participant in the group, he was still a parole officer with all of the obligations that that engendered. It was made clear that the rules of parole were still to be observed by all group participants. The opening sessions were filled with testing of roles, and conversation tended to dwell on the problem of employment which, although a real problem among the group, was also a "safe" topic. Discussions were lively from the beginning, and as the sessions progressed, personal problems were discussed openly and candidly. These included problems with parents, drugs, police, and the attitude of the community toward parolees. Support was freely given by the group to those who needed it, but those who tended to boast were restored firmly but gently to their proper perspective by the group. With at least one parolee, who had an extensive history of drug usage, the group was successful in getting him to stop the use of drugs, and this parolee remained drug-free and gainfully employed months after the sessions ended.

Leaders quickly emerged in the group, and they often competed for leadership by attempting to outdo each other in confronting and supporting other members. When conversation moved into *non-work* areas—baseball or boxing for example—most often group members, and not the author, would *demand* a return to *work* on areas of importance. Group members described their experiences on parole, and compared feelings about their parole status. A common recognition that others seemed to be experiencing the same feelings was something that all members received from the group experience.

During one session, Robert, a former gang member with a serious organic speech defect, who was not a member of the group, came into the session. However, he sat through the beginning of the session in silence and looked quite sullen. The other group members did not refer to Robert, so I asked what was bothering him. He began telling the group of the murder of his best friend, Dennis, who had been on parole to the author. (Dennis was killed by some adults when he shouted at them for almost running him over while he was crossing the street—he was shot several times after a furious street fight.) Another member described what he had heard about the incident. The other group members listened intently to both boys, and expressed their support for Robert's feelings over the loss of his best friend. I confronted the group with the fact that they had seemingly ignored Robert, despite the fact that he seemed troubled. Members became defensive, and said that they recognized that Robert had something on his mind, but felt he did not want to talk about it. Why then would he come to the session, I asked. They responded that it was better to let Robert bring up the matter himself.

In other sessions, the group dwelled on the question of drugs, with the non-drug users defending the use of Methadone for helping addicts, and those with drug histories calling Methadone a "cop-out" to the problem. During one session, a non-drug using parolee asked for help in dealing with his 17-year-old sister who had been using heroin. Members shared similar problems they had with older and younger brothers or friends. The discussion, and expressions of support for member's efforts with this problem, provided some excellent approaches and insights into dealing with their immediate concerns.

When a new member joined the group, the older members would describe the workings of the group. In particular, two things were stressed. First, that one can say whatever he wants in the group; and second, that whatever is said is confidential. The members understood that this confidentiality did not extend to the author, who took notes during the sessions, and who had explained that these notes were reviewed by his supervisor. Confidentiality was for group members who, according to their own *contract*, were not to discuss what happened in the group outside of the group. The sessions that followed the first ten sessions were voluntary. They included a review of one of the author's group recordings, a copy of which was given to each member. It proved to be a lively session with members agreeing or challenging the author's observations and interpretations. This exercise enabled the group to gain some insight into how they are viewed by others, either the author or members of the group. The group expressed a great deal of pride in their ability to work together.

The use of the group approach provides an atmosphere where problems can be worked upon by others who share similar problems, and who are sympathetic. It reduces the tensions created by the conventional one-to-one relationship between p.o. and parolee, and it allows for changes in behavior and attitudes that are stronger and more meaningful.

Chapter 14

The Supervision Process

The supervision process in both probation and parole is similar, if not identical. In fact, probation and parole are handled by the same agency in some areas. However, parolees by definition have been imprisoned, and imprisonment generally reflects the severity of the offense and the criminal history of the offender. Therefore, parolees are generally considered a greater danger to the community than probationers. Sutherland and Cressey believe that this difference is reflected in the supervision process since they state that "parole is less 'purely' treatment than is probation." [1] They also question the use of the term *treatment* in probation and parole supervision, since they view the efforts of probation/parole officers as mostly educational.[2]

Parolees may differ from probationers as a result of their prison experiences. Studt reports that based on his research there are certain highlights of the reintegration process that stand out in most parole cases. He notes that the changeover from prison life to community living requires a major readjustment. In prison the offender's life is rigidly controlled; he is told when to sleep, when to eat, when to work,

[1] Edwin Sutherland and Donald R. Cressey, *Principles of Criminology* (New York: Lippincott Co., 1966), p. 639.

[2] *Ibid.*, p. 492.

and when to have recreation. When he is released to the community he must adjust to managing his own life.[3] This is compounded in some cases by police harassment, especially in smaller communities. Social agencies often do not recognize the parolee's needs and somehow believe that he should be receiving assistance from the parole agency. Unfortunately, most parole (and probation) agencies are extremely limited in their ability to deliver tangible services. This fact, coupled with the usual lack of employable skills, often makes the parolee a burden on his family, worsening what may be an already difficult family situation.[4] (Milton Burdman, Deputy Director of the California Department of Corrections, believes that the reintegration of probationers presents similar problems. He notes that there may be a long period of pre-trial confinement in addition to the disabling effects of arrest and prosecution.)

Parolees have told the author that even so minor an experience as taking a bus ride can be traumatic to a newly released offender. Several stated that they were not aware of the fare and the need for exact change. They had the feeling that everyone on the bus, especially the driver, recognized that they had just been released from prison. Being in prison also isolated them from normal social contacts with members of the opposite sex. Several parolees expressed their reactions to the new dress styles to which they were exposed for the first time after release from prison, especially the "mini-skirts." They were very self-conscious, and they often felt that because of the way they looked at women everyone would realize that they had been in prison.

Studt points out that the parolee must "unlearn" prison habits and acquire new patterns of behavior if readjustment is to be accomplished quickly. Parolees are often subjected to social rejection because of their status, and they usually lack the necessary connections and economic resources that are effective in dealing with crisis situations.[5]

The similarities in probation supervision and parole supervision are greater than any differences. Administrative problems encountered by both services are also similar. For example, the problem of large caseloads is inherent to both services. While most observers in the field recommend caseloads of no more than 50 (with each completed presentence report counting as from three to five cases), the

[3] Elliot Studt cited from Law Enforcement Assistance Administration, *Reintegration of the Offender into the Community* (Washington, D.C.: Government Printing Office, 1973), p. 43.

[4] Sutherland and Cressey, p. 492.

[5] *Reintegration of the Offender into the Community*, pp. 43–45.

President's Commission noted that probation agencies are "badly undermanned in general by staff who are often undertrained and almost always poorly paid." [6] The Commission also noted that "there are simply not enough parole officers available to carry out the tasks assigned to them." [7] These observations are confirmed by reports of caseload size from three agencies that supervise both probationers and parolees: Georgia reports caseloads of more than 80;[8] Florida reports the same;[9] the U.S. Division of Probation reports that its officers are just about able to cover emergencies in many federal court districts.[10] However, caseload size is not a problem with every agency. The parole caseloads in New York, for example, have rarely gone beyond 50 in the last several years. (Probation officers in New York City, however, still report that their caseloads are not manageable.) Ohio reports a reduction in caseloads, and as of June 1975 the average caseload size was 40.

THE INITIAL INTERVIEW

The client first comes to the probation/parole office as the result of being placed on probation in lieu of imprisonment, or after being released from imprisonment. In either event, the first meeting with the p/p officer is a time of apprehension and anxiety. Arcaya states that the officer "represents a power that can, and does, limit his freedom." The offender is in the office involuntarily in a situation "where two individuals are joined by legal force in a counseling . . . relationship." The offender encounters the p/p officer for the first time with a mixture of fear, wariness, and defiance.[11]

The "sizing up" process works both ways. The p/p officer is meeting a stranger he knows only through the information in the case record and/or the presentence report. While the record says much about the offender's background, it may not reflect his current attitude toward p/p supervision. How will the offender deal with his current problems? Will he follow p/p regulations? Will he abscond from supervision if

[6] President's Commission on Law Enforcement and Administration of Justice, *Task Force Report: Corrections* (Washington, D.C.: Government Printing Office, 1966), p. 29.

[7] *Ibid.*, p. 70.

[8] Annual Report of the Georgia Dept. of Corrections and Offender Rehabilitation, 1975.

[9] Annual Report of the Florida Parole and Probation Commission, 1975.

[10] Personal interviews with federal probation officials.

[11] Jose Arcaya, "The Multiple Realities Inherent in Probation Counseling," *Federal Probation* (Dec. 1973), pp. 58–59.

pressured or frustrated? Will the officer be responsible for having a warrant issued and sending the offender to prison? Will this be, instead, an easy case with a minimum of problems?

The client is asking similar questions. Will this p/p officer give me a hard time? Will he be rigid about every minor p/p rule? Is he quick to seek delinquency action? Does he have the knowledge and ability to help me secure employment, training, education, a place to live?

What role will the p/p officer assume? Will he be *the law enforcement officer-type* who concentrates on surveillance and compliance, or the *social worker-type* who concentrates on treatment? Klockars calls the latter the *Therapeutic Agent,* and he notes that this type of officer usually belongs to professional organizations and displays professional degrees and certificates. He calls the former type the *Law Enforcer,* and notes that this type usually acts on the basis of "the public safety." In the middle is the *Synthetic Agent* who recognizes both the treatment and law enforcement components of the p/p officer's job.[12]

P/p officers must integrate their law enforcement and treatment roles, while maintaining the flexibility to stress one over the other in an individualized response to each case. For example, a young offender under supervision for "joy-riding" in a stolen car will receive a different response than an experienced offender who is associated with organized crime. In p/p treatment the officer adapts those methods that are useful to his practice, while sacrificing the rest, sometimes cynically, on the altar of reality.

During the initial interview the officer will explain the p/p rules, answering questions while attempting to set realistic standards for his client. (For many years the author struggled with a parole regulation that prohibited single parolees from engaging in sexual relations.) Several items are usually emphasized:

1. the need to make in-person, telephone, or mail reports
2. the need to keep the p/p officer informed of his residence
3. the need to seek and maintain lawful employment
4. the need to report any contacts with law enforcement officers.

When there is a special problem, the officer may set special conditions, and 89% of the parole jurisdictions have a provision in their

[12] Carl B. Klockars, Jr., "A Theory of Probation Supervision," *Journal of Criminal Law and Police Science* (1972), pp. 550–52.

regulations that permits the imposition of special conditions of parole.[13] An offender with a history of child molestations may be required to keep out of areas where children normally congregate, such as playgrounds. An offender with a history of alcoholism may be directed to refrain from using any intoxicating beverages. A young offender may be required to keep a curfew. Offenders with substance abuse (drugs and alcohol) problems may be required to attend treatment programs such as Alcoholics Annonymous.

The p/p officer explains that he will be visiting the offender's residence periodically. He offers his client assistance with employment or other problems. Some clients may need financial assistance. One of the immediate problems encountered by a newly-released parolee is a financial one. The amount of money that an inmate receives upon release, "gate money," is usually between $20 and $30, although seven states provide $60 or more. There is usually a nominal clothing and transportation allowance, and the parolee may have some wages as the result of prison work. However, only nine states pay more than $1 a day, and only two states provide loans in any substantial amounts to new releasees.[14] The p/p officer may refer the client to the department of welfare, or to private agencies such as the Salvation Army or a halfway house.

The initial interview in p/p practice is considered a crucial time in the supervision process. The New York State parole officer is provided with the following guidelines relative to the initial interview.

Initial Interview

As the name implies, this is the first major interview between the parole officer responsible for the supervision of the case and the newly released parolee. If the Arrival Report is taken by the parole officer who will supervise the case, it may be combined with the Initial Interview. It is at this time that the parole officer initiates his counselling or casework relationship with the parolee.

Since the parole officer is endeavoring to establish this relationship with individuals whose knowledge of and acceptance of

[13] Wm. Parker, *Parole* (College Park, Md.: American Correctional Association, 1975), p. 38.

[14] Kenneth J. Lenihan, "The Financial Condition of Released Prisoners," *Crime and Delinquency* (July 1975), p. 266.

parole varies to a great degree, the interview must be planned and handled with the best casework skills. There are those whose attitudes toward parole are based upon prejudices, doubt and fears brought about by rumors. With this group, only patience and skill will overcome the hostility and resistance to a working relationship.

This is the interview upon which the planning for future supervision of the parolee will be based. Therefore, it is important that the parole officer prepare for it by studying all the pertinent information contained in the case folder. It is also important that this interview be well planned, unhurried and without interference, if possible. It is the key to the future of the case.

The parole officer undertakes the Initial Interview with four major objectives in mind:

1. Establish a casework relationship with the parolee.
2. Secure the parolee's participation in an analysis of his problems.
3. Make constructive suggestions that will give the parolee "something to do" toward beginning his over-all parole program.
4. Leave the parolee with some positive assurance of what he has to look forward to as his parole progresses.

Suggested Content of Initial Interview

Realizing that the content of the interview will vary with the needs and problems of the individual case, the following items are presented for the parole officer's general guidance:

1. Description of the parolee. This should include a brief physical description of the parolee, pointing out any special defects such as tics, acne, blindness, lameness, noticeable scars or other physical disability, his reaction to these physical conditions or defects if they are apparent to the parole officer, a brief description of his dress and habit of dress, any unusual personal attitude or habits that are obvious to the parole officer.

2. His attitude toward the parole officer and the interview. Information with regard to the parolee's attitude should include, in addition to a description of his attitudes, the parole officer's interpretation of the attitudes and a basis for such interpretation.

3. Analysis of problems and initiating casework processes. In

conducting an Initial Interview, the parole officer is expected to secure the parolee's participation in a discussion of his problems. This discussion should be based upon information contained in the classification or parole investigation and in the service unit chronological recording.

Since this information is contained in these various reports, it is not necessary to repeat it in the case history. It is sufficient to point up briefly problems that are discussed, the parolee's reaction to them, what suggestions are made by the parole officer toward their immediate or eventual solution.

There should be a discussion of the parole program; both the residence and employment should be gone over carefully for the purpose of answering any questions which the parolee may have regarding his program.

During the initial interview, the parole officer directs the parolee to report promptly to his prospective employer. The parole officer should verify the parolee's actual employment as soon as possible.

Before concluding the interview, it is imperative that the parole officer determine whether there are questions, reservations, misconceptions concerning the parolee's relationship to the Division of Parole and the conditions of parole and to assure him that we are ready and willing to assist him with any problems which may arise from time to time.

4. Reporting instructions. Before concluding the Initial Interview, the parolee should be clearly told why office reports are necessary and helpful. He should also be clearly told when, where and with what frequency he is to report to the parole officer. If the parolee is to report to the parole officer at a different location, he should be clearly given the address of the location. It might be well to give the parolee one of the parole officer's business cards, on the back of which the parole officer might write the address of the reporting station.

The parolee is to be clearly informed that he must obtain permission in advance if, for good and sufficient reason, he will be unable to make a scheduled report.

The following description of an interview with an offender in jail indicates how the probation officer approached a hostile and uncooperative offender. It is important to note that the officer guides the interview to avoid futile and repetitious rationalizations but explores to find some area in which he and the offender can work constructively together.

> Peter, aged eighteen, has been on probation for two months. He was accorded youthful offender treatment following indictment for an assault during which he threatened, but did not use, a knife. During the course of our contact, he has been on a weekly reporting schedule. I have concentrated on trying to help him get work. He has conformed in rather surly fashion, and never has volunteered to discuss any of his problems. He lives at home with his mother, a divorcee, and an older brother, who is a conforming person, who did well in school, has regular employment and generally does everything he should, thereby winning the mother's approval.
>
> Recently Peter was arrested for drunk and disorderly conduct. He pleaded guilty and received a 30 day jail sentence, which he is just beginning to serve. Arresting officer's report indicated that he was assaultive and it required three policemen to get him to the station. I visited him at the jail in order to obtain information for a violation report to be submitted to the court for action regarding his probation status. When I explained this, Peter went into what threatened to be a long harangue against the police and everyone connected with the current offense. He was in jail, he said, only because his girl friend's father objected to him and was trying to keep him from dating her. I stated briefly and flatly what I knew about his present situation and noted that his own conduct was the reason for his being here. I asked him to tell me something about his girl, but he cut this off by saying that she and her family had moved to get the girl away from him, and he would not be seeing her any more. I asked what he had been assigned to do in jail. He was just washing dishes and it was a bore and everyone here was a jerk. Had his family visited him? His mother had, but not his brother. I wondered how he got along with his brother. As if I had turned on a faucet, the story of his resentment toward his brother gushed out. He recalled things that had happened when he was only about six years old, and revealed that he is conscious of his jealousy over the mother's favoritism.

ONGOING SUPERVISION

The offender is usually somewhat relieved to be out of the office after his first visit. He generally leaves with mixed feelings. If the officer has been warm, concerned, and helpful, then positive feelings will predominate. If the officer was not sensitive to the attitude he conveyed, and if he did not evince a feeling of acceptance, negative feelings will predominate. Mangrum notes that "There is nothing necessarily incompatible between warmth and acceptance and firm enforcement of the laws of the land. We must take whatever corrective measures are necessary; but these must not permit us to demean the dignity of the individual." [15]

During the periodic visits to the client's residence, the p/p officer should try to spend enough time to be able to relate to his client and/or the client's family. The home visit provides an opportunity to meet family members and interpret the role of the p/p agency to them. The worker should leave his business card and invite inquiries for information or help. When the officer visits the home, it is incumbent upon him to try to protect the confidentiality that is inherent in each case. The officer does not advertise his business, nor draw unnecessary attention to himself and his visit to a client's home. In many cases the client's p/p status will be known to neighbors, and the officer himself may be a familiar figure in the neighborhood. It is not too unusual for a client, or client's family, to escort the officer back to his automobile, as a gesture of concern, in high delinquency areas.

The following excerpt from a case record shows how increased understanding of an offender caused a change in the direction of treatment. It also reveals the value of home visiting as a means of gaining new insights into an offender's situation.

QUARTERLY SUMMARY, March through May, 1975.

3/9 Office report

3/23 Failed to report.

3/30 Home visit. Mother and aunt seen.

4/6 Failed to report. Notice, giving 48 hours to report sent.

[15] Claude T. Mangrum, "The Humanity of Probation Officers," *Federal Probation* (June 1972), p. 48.

4/8 Reported.
4/13 Failed to report.
4/20 Home visit. Offender and aunt seen.
4/27 Reported.
5/1 Contact made with Community Settlement.
5/11 Reported.
5/25 Reported.

During March and April attempts were made to get the offender to look for work. Early in March, he reported that he had a temporary job as a truck driver, and thought that because of this he did not have to report. I corrected this idea and emphasized the importance of keeping his appointments. He had little to say, but seemed amenable to conforming. The failure to report in April was excused because of illness.

During the home visits, the mother reported that offender is keeping reasonable hours. She informed me that he spends most of his spare time at the Community Settlement and recently won a trophy for basketball. The aunt, a single woman who lives in the home takes an active interest in him. She said that offender is really very shy and needs special attention, which she tries to give him because the mother has little time to spare from the younger children. She has accompanied him to State Employment Office where he has been trying to obtain work, but as he is unskilled, he has few opportunities. Such protectiveness seems inappropriate for a 19 year old youth.

I called at the Community Settlement and talked with the Director, Mr. Apt. He is very much interested in the offender, but told me confidentially that he is afraid he might be getting into a neighborhood gang that is beginning to form. He has noticed that when offender leaves the settlement, he often joins other young men, some of whom have been in trouble. The settlement has an employment service for members, and will try to help offender obtain employment. When offender reported, I suggested that he apply at the settlement employment service. The next day, Mr. Apt telephoned. Offender had been referred to a job in a downtown warehouse. He returned to the settlement in tears. He was so frightened that he had been unable to apply. He doesn't think he could do such work, though it is simple unskilled labor. Mr. Apt thinks that offender needs psychiatric attention, but this may be the first time the offender has tried to seek work by himself.

At the time of the last report, offender discussed some of his fears about work. He speaks warmly of the personnel at the settlement, but somewhat resentfully of his mother and aunt who "keep nagging" him about work.

It is planned to try to encourage this offender by building up his self esteem, giving recognition to his success in settlement activities and by planning visits when he is at home, dealing with him directly rather than with relatives. The possibility of psychiatric referral will be explored.

Employment for Offenders

The securing and maintaining of employment or training for employment, are crucial aspects of supervision. It is generally believed that there is a direct relationship between successful employment and avoidance of further legal difficulties. Basically, in addition to providing economic rewards, employment also enhances the self-worth and image of the offender. When the economy is poor, when unemployment is unusually high, this has a direct effect on p/p supervision.

In assisting his client with employment the officer may make a direct referral to a particular employer, if he has the necessary contacts, or he may refer his client to another agency, such as the state employment services, for help. The officer may also have to provide guidance and counseling concerning some of the basic aspects of securing employment. For example, the officer will emphasize the need to be on time for interviews. He will help with filling out applications, and he may use role playing in order to accustom his client to job interview situations. It is often important to discuss various aspects of good grooming and what type of clothes to wear on an interview. The following checklist is an example of interview instructions that might be given a client.

CHECKLIST FOR OFFENDER EMPLOYMENT*

A. Greet Receptionist

1. Give your name and reason for visit. Example—"Good morning, my name is John Smith and I have a 10:00 a.m. employment interview with Mr. Jones."

*From Phyllis Groom McCreary and John M. McCreary, *Job Training and Placement for Offenders and Ex-Offenders* (Washington, D.C.: Government Printing Office, 1975), pp. 79–80.

2. Be punctual. Example—For a 10:00 a.m. interview, try being there by 9:30 or 9:45 a.m.

3. Be prepared to fill out an application. Example—(Refer to #2)—By arriving at 9:30 a.m. or 9:45 a.m., you can fill out an application and go in at 10:00 a.m. to see Mr. Jones.

4. Have a copy of your social security number, names of past jobs with addresses and dates, names of references with addresses, etc., written on a card to aid you in filling out the application.

5. Be prepared to take a test for the job you are applying for if required. Example—Electronic, clerical or industrial machines, etc.

6. Have a list of questions you wish to ask prepared. Example:

   a. How old is the company?
   b. How many employees are with the company?
   c. What is the potential for promotion and growth?
   d. What are the duties that the job entails?
   e. What is the starting salary?
   f. What is the top salary potential?
   g. What are the working hours?
   h. Is there paid overtime?
   i. What benefits are offered by the company?
   j. Does the company offer tuition for night school?
   k. Does the company promote from within?

B. Procedure for the Interviewer

1. Walk slowly and quietly, stand right, hold your head up.
2. Greet the interviewer.

   a. Shake hands firmly if interviewer offers his hand.
   b. Look interviewer in the eye and say, "How do you do Mr. Jones."
   c. Stand until the interviewer asks you to be seated.
   d. Wait for the interviewer to start the interview and lead it.
   e. You may smoke if the interviewer states so.
   f. Be prepared to answer questions. Examples:

Why do you want to work for this company?
Where do you see yourself in five years?

Are you planning to further your education?

What do you know about this company?

Do you have any particular skills or interests that you feel qualifies you for a position with this company?

What makes you feel you are qualified for this particular job?

Do you have any plans for marriage in the immediate future?

Now is when you present your questions.

C. Attitudes and Behavior During the Interview

1. Sit up straight, feet on floor, hands in lap.
2. Sit quietly (do not keep moving around or fidget).
3. Use your best manners.
    a. Be attentive and polite.
    b. Speak slowly and clearly.
    c. Look interviewer in the eye (do not wear sunglasses).
    d. Use correct English, avoid slang.
    e. Emphasize your good points.
4. Speak of yourself in a positive manner.
5. Talk about what you can do.
6. Do not apologize for your shortcomings.
7. Do not talk to an excess about your personal problems.

D. What an Interviewer Sees Immediately During an Interview

1. Hygiene.
    a. Bathe just before an interview.
    b. Clean and clip nails if necessary.
    c. Brush teeth.
    d. Use a good deodorant.
    e. Wear an outfit that is clean and conservative regardless of the fashion trend or style.

E. Interviewer Closes the Interview

1. Do not linger when he indicates it is time to stop.
2. Be sure to thank the interviewer as you leave.

F. Staying on the Job

1. With the great shortage of available jobs, employers can afford to be highly selective in choosing an employee.
2. Accepting positions in related fields so when positions are re-opened, you will have first choice at these positions.

IN CONCLUSION

Remember the four (4) A's.

1. Attendance.
2. Attitude.
3. Appearance.
4. Ability.

One critical aspect of employment for ex-offenders is the question of revealing their record. The author allowed his clients to decide for themselves. However, he did provide guidance by discussing the experiences of other clients relative to this issue. Many clients reported that they believed that their candor resulted in not securing employment. Others reported that some employers were interested in providing them with an opportunity to make good. Unfortunately, many employers will not hire ex-offenders.

Some offenders are required by law or policy to reveal their records when applying for certain jobs. For example, most civil service jobs require individuals having a criminal conviction to reveal this fact. Banks, hospitals, and other sensitive areas of employment may also require disclosure. Certainly, allowing an offender with a history of drug abuse to work in a hospital, or any other similar situation, would not be advisable, especially if the employer did not know the person's record.

Sol Tropp, an expert in the field of ex-offender employment, recommends that "The employer should be made aware of an offender's status only when the pattern of the offender's behavior may result in anti-social behavior," such as a drug addict working in a hospital.[16] Robert Hannum, Vocational Director of the Osborne Association,

[16] *Vocational Counseling With the Offender* (mimeo produced by the N.Y. State Employment Services Correctional Vocational Rehabilitation Service, 1965), p. 8.

states that "We do not lie about the individual's record but, because of the prejudice that employers may have, we try to postpone complete revelation until the employer has had a chance to try out the offender on the job." [17]

The officer may also visit his client's place of employment. He will do this to verify the employment—as a New York State parole pamphlet notes: "The parole officer does not naively accept the information that a parolee provides; he goes out into the community to verify it."

A study by John Berman deserves mention at this point.[18] Eighty-seven parolees in Illinois were interviewed in an attempt to measure the parolees' attitudes toward the parole system, parole agents, and parole rules: "Contrary to expectations, those interviewed indicated a relatively positive attitude toward the parole system." Most agreed that if it were not for parole supervision, many more offenders would be back in prison shortly after their release. Berman noted that the parolees also showed a very positive attitude toward their parole agents by agreeing with the statement "Your parole agent does everything he can to help parolees."

Berman considered the real possibility of the answers being less than candid, but states his confidence in their being a reliable indicator of the parolees' true feelings. Another interesting finding of this study was the fact that "there were no black-white differences in respondents' attitudes toward the parole system, parole agents, or parole rules."

THE STIGMA OF CONVICTION: THEORETICAL AND PRACTICAL CONSIDERATIONS

Reed and Nance have stated what is all too often obvious in probation/parole practice: "A record of conviction produces a loss of status which has lasting consequences." [19] They note that while probation and parole are rehabilitatively thought of as more desirable than prison, "both visibly display the offender in the community under a disability—his conditions of probation of parole. In some jurisdictions, he must register as a criminal, supposedly for the protection of the

[17] *Ibid.*, p. 5.

[18] John J. Berman, "Parolees' Perception of the Justice System: Black-White Differences," *Criminology* (February 1976), pp. 507–520.

[19] John P. Reed and Dale Nance, "Society Perpetuates the Stigma of a Conviction," *Federal Probation* (June 1972), p. 27.

community. The unintended effects of registration are to broadcast his conviction and preserve his criminal stigma." [20] The authors call this a form of value conflict, whereby the protective concerns of society run counter to the rehabilitative philosophy that is espoused.[21]

One of the more important studies on the impact of a criminal conviction was conducted by Schwartz and Skolnick.[22] They studied the effects of a criminal record on the employment opportunities of unskilled workers. They prepared four employment folders which were the same in all respects except for the criminal record of the applicant, as follows:

1. the first folder indicated that the applicant had been convicted and sentenced for assault;
2. the second, that he had been tried for assault and acquitted;
3. the third, also tried for assault and acquitted, and with a letter from the judge certifying the finding of not guilty; and
4. the fourth made no mention of any criminal record.

The study involved one hundred employers who were divided into units of twenty-five, with each group being shown one of the four folders on the mistaken belief that they were actually considering a real job applicant. The results are as follows:

1. Of the 25 employers shown the "no record" folder, 9 (36%) gave positive responses.
2. Of the 25 employers shown the "convict" folder, only one (4%) expressed interest in the applicant.
3. Of the 25 employers shown the "accused but acquitted" folder, 3 (12%) expressed interest in the applicant.
4. Of the 25 employers shown the "accused but acquitted" folder, which also contained the judge's letter, 6 (24%) expressed an interest in the applicant.

Since a significant majority of persons on probation and parole are unskilled, the ramifications of these findings are obvious.

An interesting contrast to this study is one conducted by Charles

[20] *Ibid.*

[21] *Ibid.*, p. 30.

[22] *See* Richard Schwartz and Jerome Skolnick, "Two Studies of Legal Stigma," in R. Henshel and R. Silverman, eds., *Perception in Criminology* (New York: Columbia University Press, 1975), pp. 401–15.

Winick.[23] He notes that narcotic addicts in the United States are routinely subjected to severe sanctions in addition to the stigma that results from being identified with this form of deviance. Winick found, however, that medical doctors addicted to narcotics were not similarly treated and stigmatized. Indeed, he found that sanctions were minimal, and "Where the physician had to leave his practice, he generally turned the practice over to a colleague and resumed it upon his return."

Earlier we looked briefly at the problem of stigma in conjunction with the juvenile court. We will now take another look at the theoretical perspective that makes stigma the focus of the study of crime and deviance. The three best known of the *societal reaction* or *labeling theorists* are Kitsuse, Becker, and Erikson.

Erikson states that "Deviance is not a property *inherent* in any particular kind of behavior; it is a property *conferred upon* that behavior by the people who come into direct or indirect contact with it." [24] Becker states that "social groups create deviance by making rules, whose infraction constitutes deviance, and by applying those rules to particular people and labeling them outsiders." [25] Kitsuse states that "it is not the fact that individuals engage in behaviors which diverge from some theoretically posited 'institutionalized expectations' or even that such behaviors are defined as deviant by the conventional and conforming members of the society which is of primary significance for the study of deviance." He concludes that it is the societal reaction to such deviance, the application of sanctions, for example, that must be the focus of study.[26] The labeling approach focuses on society's reaction to an individual actor, rather than the more traditional causal approach to the study of crime (and other forms of deviant behavior).

A person on probation/parole is labeled by virtue of this status, and often "sub-labeled" as a robber, rapist, addict, etc. The label locks in the offender by limiting his employment opportunities. Besides the real and direct damage done by the label, there is the more subtle, but nevertheless harmful, effect on the offender's self-image. Embellish-

[23] *See* Charles Winick, "Physician Narcotic Addicts," in Howard S. Becker, ed., *The Other Side: Perspectives on Deviance* (New York: The Free Press, 1964), pp. 261–79.

[24] Kai T. Erikson, *Wayward Puritans* (New York: John Wiley and Sons, 1966), p. 6.

[25] Howard S. Becker, *Outsiders: Studies in the Sociology of Deviance* (New York: The Free Press, 1963), p. 9.

[26] John I. Kitsuse, "Societal Reaction to Deviant Behavior," *Social Problems* (Winter 1962), p. 256.

ing this negative self-image is what Garfinkel refers to as "degradation ceremonies." [27] Forms of degradation abound: news media coverage, court procedures, the queing and waiting to see a probation/parole officer, prison clothes, parole board hearings, etc.

The label results in a negative self-image whereby the offender's view of himself is that of an inferior and unworthy person. In such a condition, the offender may seek the companionship of others similarly labeled; he may engage in further antisocial activities in an effort at striking back at the society that has labeled him.

The criminal label creates certain expectations that may result in what Merton refers to as the "self-fulfilling prophecy." [28] The public, for example, does not express much surprise when an offender is arrested for another crime. Indeed, it is usually the first question raised when a person has been arrested: "Has he been arrested before?" There is a saying among the "sages" that call the street their home: "If you have the *name,* might as well play the *game.*" This fatalistic mode of thinking and acting presents a challenge to every probation/parole officer in the practice of his profession.

The labeling perspective is also concerned with the phenomenon of *secondary deviation,* a concept developed by Edwin Lemert.[29] Perhaps the best example of this concept concerns narcotic addiction. The use of heroin is a *primary deviance.* However, the societal reaction to heroin—it is unlawful to possess—creates *secondary deviance* by forcing the addict to violate the law in order to use heroin, and of course to support his expensive habit. In England, where the use of heroin is not unlawful and is under medical control, an addict may be a deviant, but not necessarily a criminal.

SURVEILLANCE AND LAW ENFORCEMENT

Basic to any p/p system that strives for public acceptance and support is the need to protect the community. The most effective way to accomplish this is through the rehabilitation of offenders. However, rehabilitation is obviously not possible in all cases. In recognition of this fact,

[27] *See* Harold Garfinkel, "Conditions of Successful Degradation Ceremonies," *American Journal of Sociology* (March 1956), pp. 420–24.

[28] *See* Robert K. Merton, *Social Theory and Social Structure* (New York: The Free Press, 1957), pp. 421–36.

[29] *See* Edwin M. Lemert, *Social Pathology* (New York: McGraw-Hill, 1951).

and in response to public concern, most p/p agencies have the authority to investigate and arrest probationers/parolees who present an immediate danger to themselves or the community, or who are unable or unwilling to abide by the conditions of their p/p status. The use of this authority is not without controversy.

The *Attica Report* is critical of the surveillance or "watchdog" role of parole officers: "The parole officer's supervision and surveillance functions prevent the development of any beneficial relationship with parolees." [30] The Citizen's Inquiry on Parole and Criminal Justice is in agreement with this view. Their report states that the conflict between the surveillance and treatment roles of the parole officer "precludes the development of a relationship of mutual trust." [31] Newman states that surveillance is essentially a police activity that should not be handled by p/p officers.[32] On the other side of the question is Dressler, a former official in the N.Y. State parole system, who states that p/p agencies are responsible for community protection and "are expected to eliminate from their caseloads individuals who are obvious and immediate hazards." [33] Ed Tromanhauser, a convict with a history of armed robberies, writes that when an "unreformed" offender is closely checked on parole, he is far less dangerous to society than if he was not subject to surveillance.[34] Some observers (Conrad[35] and Newman, for example) maintain that surveillance and investigation are the role of the police, who they consider more capable of performing these functions than p/p officers. The author who, along with other colleagues from parole, teaches criminal investigation to college students, some of whom are policemen, believes that this may not necessarily be so. He finds it interesting that most police agencies are stressing the need for a college education, something that virtually all p/p officers have when they enter the field. The skills and discipline necessary for a college

[30] N.Y.S. Spec. Comm. on Attica, p. 100.

[31] *Survey Report on New York State Parole* (New York: Citizen's Inquiry on Parole and Criminal Justice, Inc., 1973), p. 13.

[32] Charles L. Newman, "Concepts of Treatment in Probation and Parole," *Federal Probation* (Mar. 1961), p. 14.

[33] David Dressler, *Practice and Theory of Probation and Parole* (New York: Columbia Univ. Press, 1969), p. 29.

[34] H. Jack Griswold, et. al., *An Eye For An Eye* (N.Y.: Holt, Rinehart and Winston, 1972) p. 248.

[35] Surveillance: "What the parole officer can do . . . can be better done by the police." John P. Conrad, "Who Needs a Door-Bell Pusher?" (paper presented at the American Society of Criminology Annual Meeting, Nov. 1, 1975).

education provide a background that can easily be adapted to the requirements of surveillance and investigative activities.

In many areas of our country, especially in large cities, the police are not able to keep pace with the plethora of activities that require surveillance and investigation. It is irrational to assume that they would be willing or able to assume the additional burden of surveillance or investigation of probationers and parolees. In New York, it has been the author's experience that many criminal cases are solved by the police on the basis of surveillance and investigative activity conducted by parole officers.

The way in which "hazards" are removed from caseloads is perhaps even more controversial than the p/p officer's surveillance functions. Should p/p officers carry firearms, and should they arrest p/p violators? In general, parole agencies tend to be more law enforcement oriented than probation agencies. However, because of the number of probation agencies it is difficult to collect comprehensive statistics concerning law enforcement questions as they relate to probation officers. A recent survey by this author of 53 adult parole agencies, representing all 50 states, plus the District of Columbia, Puerto Rico, and the United States Division of Probation, indicates that parole agencies differ greatly with respect to officers[36] carrying firearms and arresting violators. For example, Texas parole officers are prohibited from carrying firearms and never personally arrest parole violators, while Massachusetts parole officers are required to carry firearms and frequently arrest parole violators. The survey revealed that:

> sixteen provide firearms training for parole officers;
> six permit parole officers to carry firearms in special situations, such as when arresting or transporting dangerous offenders, or when the officer's life has been threatened; and
> eight encourage or mandate their parole officers to carry firearms.
>
> Only four report that parole officers never personally arrest parole violators. The others report that their officers frequently (14), occasionally (16), or infrequently (19) personally arrest parole violators.

A survey of parole board members indicated that 27% believed that parole officers should arrest parole violators, and 13% believed that

[36] Title varies with the agency. Several states use "probation/parole agent;" Illinois uses "parole counselor;" Arizona uses "correctional program officer;" Georgia uses "probation/parole supervisor;" the federal government uses "probation officer."

parole officers should be allowed to carry firearms.[37] The President's Commission stated that "The predominant opinion in the parole field is that supervision staff should not assume the role of police officers." [38] The National Advisory Commission on Criminal Justice Standards and Goals stated that guns are antithetical to the character of a probation/parole officer's job.[39] Schoonmaker and Brooks state that "if treatment is to be the focal point of probation and parole, then arrest by the supervisory officer is harmful or, at least, inappropriate." [40] Clegg, however, notes that "it is usually considered the duty of the probation or parole officer to make the arrest" when the conditions of probation or parole are violated. He states that the carrying of firearms is more controversial, but since there is danger in dealing with offenders, the carrying of firearms can be justified. Clegg also advises that the police should be used to make arrests whenever possible.[41]

The author believes that the dual responsibility of p/p officers, treatment and control, permits them to provide the strength and to reinforce the conscience or superego of offenders who often lack self-discipline and control. The sound use of the p/p officer's authority enables the offender to internalize controls and incorporate them into his own personality and behavior pattern.

The author believes that, based on his more than ten years in the field, arrest powers and the carrying of a firearm increases public confidence in the p/p officer's ability to protect the community. It provides a degree of confidence to p/p officers who visit their clients in high delinquency neighborhoods and crime-ridden buildings. It is the home visit that provides a basis for both sound casework and surveillance. In the office setting, the use of casework is difficult because of the minimal amount of time usually allotted to office interviews, and given the lack of privacy found in many p/p offices. It is in the residence, where the client interacts with his family and where he is

[37] National Parole Institutes, *Description of Backgrounds and Some Attitudes of Parole Authority Members in the United States* (New York: NCCD Mimeo, 1963).

[38] *Task Force Report: Corrections*, p. 69.

[39] National Advisory Commission on Criminal Justice Standards and Goals, *Corrections* (Washington, D.C.: Government Printing Office, 1973), p. 434.

[40] Myressa H. Schoonmaker and Jennifer S. Brooks, "Women in Probation and Parole," *Crime and Delinquency* (Jan. 1974), p. 113.

[41] Reed K. Clegg, *Probation and Parole, Principles and Practices* (Springfield, Ill.: Charles C. Thomas, 1974), pp. 93–94.

comfortable, that casework can be effective. However, in order to visit the offender in relative safety, the p/p officer may need to carry a firearm.

The adult p/p client is a law violator who has proved to be a potential danger to the community. Many have been involved in crimes of violence, and the public and its lawmakers expect that probationers and parolees will be under the scrutiny of p/p authorities. This is why the law of most jurisdictions empowers p/p agencies with law enforcement responsibilities. However, the question is often raised as to whether or not the p/p officer should be the law enforcer or merely the treatment agent. Many p/p agencies employ warrant officers or use other law enforcement agencies to enforce their violation warrants. Do arrest powers and the carrying of a firearm interfere with the p/p officer's ability to form a relationship with which to provide treatment? The author is of the opinion that they do not. Indeed, because of the p/p officer's relationship with his client, in delinquency situations, he is able to effect an arrest without the tension and hostility that often accompanies arrests made by other law enforcement officers. However, whether or not the p/p officer actually makes the arrest, his client knows that his p/p officer initiated the warrant action. As noted, p/p clients are potentially dangerous, reason enough to be armed.

On the basis of the author's experience, he recommends that all p/p agencies should review their approach to law enforcement and reevaluate their methods with a view toward effective casework and community protection. Items that should be reviewed include:

1. police disinterest in enforcing warrants
2. the attitude of probation/parole officers toward the carrying of firearms and making arrests
3. incidents and/or complaints arising out of enforcement of warrants by non-probation/parole officers
4. probation/parole officers being threatened or assaulted
5. the inability of an agency to expeditiously arrest and detain serious probation/parole violators
6. probation/parole officers reluctant to make field visits
7. indications that probation/parole warrants are being used to extort money or force violators into becoming informants.

National Law Enforcement Survey of Adult Parole Agencies

State or Agency	*Authorized to Carry Firearms*	*Attitude Toward Carrying Fire-arms*	*Firearms Training*	*Personally Arrest Parole Violators*
Alabama	Yes	Discouragod	Nu	Infrequently
Alaska	No	Discouraged	Yes	Occasionally
Arizona	No	Prohibited	No	Infrequently
Arkansas	Yes	Discouraged	Yes	Occasionally
California	Yes	Prohibited	No	Frequently
Colorado	Yes	Encouraged	Yes	Frequently
Connecticut	Yes	Encouraged	Yes	Occasionally
Delaware	Yes	Prohibited	No	Occasionally
District of Columbia	No	Prohibited	No	Never
Florida	Yes	Discouraged	No	Occasionally
Georgia	Yes	Discouraged	No	Infrequently
Hawaii	No	Prohibited	No	Occasionally
Idaho	Yes	Prohibited[1]	Yes	Frequently
Illinois	Yes	Prohibited	No	Never
Indiana	Yes	Prohibited	No	Infrequently
Iowa	Yes	Prohibited	No	Frequently
Kansas	No	Prohibited	No	Never
Kentucky	Yes	Discouraged[2]	Yes	Occasionally
Louisiana	Yes	Encouraged[3]	Yes	Infrequently
Maine	No	Prohibited	No	Frequently
Maryland	No[4]	Prohibited	No	Infrequently
Massachusetts	Yes	Mandated	Yes	Frequently
Michigan	Yes	Prohibited[5]	Yes	Infrequently
Minnesota	No	Discouraged	No	Infrequently
Mississippi	Yes	Discouraged	No	Infrequently
Missouri	Yes	Prohibited[6]	No	Infrequently
Montana	No	Prohibited	No	Occasionally
Nebraska	No	Prohibited	No	Frequently
Nevada	Yes	Encouraged	Yes	Frequently
New Hampshire	No	Prohibited	No	Infrequently
New Jersey	No	Prohibited	No	Infrequently
New Mexico	No	Prohibited	No	Infrequently
New York	Yes	Encouraged	Yes	Frequently
North Carolina	No	Discouraged	No	Infrequently
North Dakota	Yes	Discouraged	No	Frequently
Ohio	Yes	Discouraged	Yes	Occasionally
Oklahoma	Yes	Discouraged	Yes	Occasionally
Oregon	Yes	Prohibited[7]	No	Frequently
Pennsylvania	Yes	Encouraged	Yes	Frequently
Puerto Rico	No	Discouraged	No	Infrequently
Rhode Island	No	Prohibited	No	Infrequently
South Carolina	Yes	Prohibited[8]	No	Frequently
South Dakota	No	Discouraged	No	Frequently
Tennessee	No	Prohibited	No	Infrequently
Texas	No	Prohibited	No	Never
U.S. Probation	No	Discouraged	No	Occasionally

National Law Enforcement Survey of Adult Parole Agencies

State or Agency	*Authorized to Carry Firearms*	*Attitude Toward Carrying Fire-arms*	*Firearms Training*	*Personally Arrest Parole Violators*
Utah	Yes	Encouraged	Yes	Occasionally
Vermont	No	Prohibited	No	Infrequently
Virginia	No	Prohibited	No	Infrequently
Washington	No	Prohibited	No	Occasionally
West Virginia	No	Prohibited	No	Occasionally
Wisconsin	No	Prohibited	No	Occasionally
Wyoming	Yes	Discouraged	Yes	Occasionally

[1] Idaho: except if transporting or apprehending dangerous individuals.

[2] Kentucky: only in the case of an arrest or transporting a prisoner.

[3] Louisiana: encouraged only when arrest is anticipated or when working in high crime areas.

[4] Maryland: warrant agents carry firearms.

[5] Michigan: except when life is threatened or on specific and limited transfer assignment.

[6] Missouri: except in very rare circumstances.

[7] Oregon: except if a parole officer or his family comes under immediate threat; permission is granted during the emergency.

[8] South Carolina: except when making an arrest.

A Composite Day in the Life of a Parole and Probation Officer*

5:15 a.m. The officer is awakened by a phone call. A deputy at the local Sheriff's Office advises him that they have one of his probationers in jail charged with Breaking and Entering with Intent to Commit a Felony. The officer writes down the pertinent information supplied by the deputy which includes the report that the probationer is intoxicated. The officer then requests the deputy to place a Parole and Probation Officer "Hold" on the individual so that no bond can be made until the officer has thoroughly investigated the situation. He then closes his eyes in hopes of getting a little more sleep before his actual work day begins. He is on duty 24 hours a day, 7 days per week.

7:56 a.m. Upon arriving in the parole and probation office he finds two notes on his desk telling him that the

* *Source:* Florida Parole and Probation Commission.

individual the deputy called about had been arrested . . . both of the officers who wrote the notes had a person on their caseload who had allegedly been a co-defendant with this officer's case in the breaking and entering.

The officer then turns to the stack of paperwork which includes both unfinished business from yesterday and mail which he has received this morning. First, he sifts through the mail pulling out the monthly reports submitted by "his" parolees and probationers. Each person under supervision is required to send in a written monthly report on a standardized form. The officer carefully reviews this report making certain that the person still is residing at his approved address and is still employed. He also carefully checks the reported earnings and financial status, and looks to see if there are any special problems noted.

Most of the remaining correspondence and paperwork is related directly to his caseload and he dictates the appropriate responses as well as recording important entries in his field book. The officer shares a secretary with two other officers. The time she has to file is limited and often the officer must do his own.

9:15 a.m. An integral part of every Parole and Probation Officer's duty is that of reporting statistical information to the Central Office in Tallahassee. These statistics are detailed and time consuming. Being constantly interrupted by telephone calls as well as persons coming to his office the officer begins his statistical reports realizing it will be five days before they're due.

Without these statistical reports it would be practically impossible to monitor what type of progress or impact the Florida Parole and Probation Commission is having upon the parolees and probationers in Florida. The statistical data is time consuming but must be done!

9:31 a.m. Florida Bureau of Law Enforcement calls to advise that a probationer is being investigated for drug trafficking.

9:48 a.m. A parolee calls to say he has been fired because he came in late. An appointment is set for tomorrow. Officer makes note to call employer before appointment.

10:05 a.m. The wife of one of the officer's probationers calls. She reports her husband, John, got drunk and beat her up last night. She wants the officer to do something about it but doesn't want her husband to know she called.

10:27 a.m. The mother of the fellow arrested that morning calls informing the officer that her son did not come in all night and she is concerned as to his whereabouts and welfare. The officer explains the circumstances surrounding her son's arrest and questions her as to why she feels he may have become involved in the armed robbery. He queries her regarding her son's drinking habits. The information is recorded in the field book and the Parole and Probation Officer then returns to filling out his statistical reports.

10:45 a.m. The officer collects his necessary files and goes to the local felony court. He has recommended revocation of probation on a felony probationer. As the case is called, the officer stands before the court along with the probationer, the State Attorney, the defendant's attorney, and members of his family.

The charges are read and a plea of not guilty entered. The Parole and Probation Officer is then asked to explain the reasons for recommending revocation of probation. The officer points out that this individual has failed to pay support payments to his wife as required by court; has failed to submit his monthly reports, and he absconded from supervision. The officer spent several hours compiling and filling out the appropriate revocation reports, affidavits, and warrants for this case.

After a plea by the defense attorney of *nolo contendere* the judge agrees to allow the individual's probation to be re-instated with the understanding that he would bring his payments of support to his wife and child up to date within two weeks; that he would never again be late with his monthly report; and that he would not leave the county again without getting approval from his Parole and Probation Officer.

11:34 a.m. The officer leaves court and proceeds to the local elementary school where he is checking the school records on a person who has been referred to the Parole and Probation Commission by the court for a presentence investigation. The officer is usually given between two to four weeks to complete this investigation. The presentence report includes the individual's prior arrest record and the circumstances as well as the offense for which the individual has been charged. School records and employment histories are checked. Community attitudes regarding the defendant and his reputation therein are ascertained and other information obtained which will provide the court with a comprehensive diagnostic report which will assist in determining the appropriate treatment methodology, whether it be probation or prison.

The presentence investigation is the most important investigation that the officer prepares, and they consume about 60% of his time.

Other investigations performed by the officer include postsentence investigation, preparole, mandatory conditional release, pardon board, work release, security, and release on recognizance investigations as well as other specialty type investigations.

12:10 p.m. The officer stops by John's place of employment. Being a roofer he is out on a job site. The employer reports John is very dependable and doubts that he has a drinking problem. He feels the wife is a trouble maker who he suspects has a boyfriend. The employer assures the officer that if he detects any problems he will call the officer.

12:33 p.m. The officer meets with the Assistant Director of the local drug counseling center to have lunch at the cafeteria. The conversation mainly centers around more effective ways to refer probationers and parolees to the drug center and to receive information regarding their progress from the center.

Historically the Parole and Probation Officer has been an individual required to "wear many hats." If a person needed drug counseling it was provided by the officer, if he needed marital counseling it was provided by the officer, if he needed employment counseling it was provided by the officer or any other service for the most part was provided by the Parole and Probation Officer.

As community resources in areas of mental health, employment counseling, drug abuse prevention, alcohol treatment and others have been established, the officer is learning to depend more and more on these resources. His job is slowly evolving into that of a diagnostician and case manager. This is consistent with the National Advisory Commission on Criminal Justice Standards and Goals which has been modified and proposed to be adopted by the Governor's Task Force on Corrections in Florida. As set forth in standard 10.2 "Each probation system should develop by 1975 a goal oriented service delivery system that seeks to remove or reduce barriers confronting probationers. The needs of the probationer should be identified, priorities established, and resources allocated based on the established goals of the probation system. The primary function of the Parole and Probation Officer should be that of community manager of probationers."

The individual officer spends a good portion of his time concentrating on the utilization of community resources and establishing effective cooperative work relationships with those resources. The more positive impact the officer can have on his cases the greater the probability of improvement. His time is limited and he must rely heavily on referrals to other agencies to increase the quality and quantity of time effecting the case.

1:31 p.m. The officer goes to the County Jail to talk with the probationer who was arrested in the early morning hours. He admits the offense and having been intoxicated. He also admits it is not the first time he has become intoxicated and that he and his mother have not been getting along well at all over the last three months. The officer queries further and finally, in frustration, asks him one simple question, "Why did you do it?" He receives the classic answer, "I don't know, I just did it because the other guys were doing it." In the day to day life of Parole and Probation Officers successes are subtle and often go unnoticed, failures are blatant and result in an individual wasting part of his life behind bars.

This individual will probably be convicted of the new offense and be sentenced to prison for five years. In addition he may be found guilty of violation of probation and receive an additive sentence. Now, the officer will have to go through the lengthy process of violation reports, warrants, affidavits, court hearings, and conversations with both the defense attorney and state attorney. That will take time, precious time which will detract from his rehabilitative efforts.

2:00 p.m. The Parole and Probation Officer attends a meeting of the local Alcohol Treatment Center Halfway House in order to provide input from the Florida Parole and Probation Commission on how to deal with alcoholics. He constantly seeks ways to increase his impact and expand his range of effectiveness.

Again the officer's main concern is that of a more rapid referral with a minimum of red tape and more meaningful feedback with regard to the progress that an individual is making at the halfway house.

2:30 p.m. The officer now begins to make contacts with people under his supervision. Some of these contacts are with the individual on his job site and include conversations with the employer to make certain that the individual is on the job and to make certain that the individual is remaining dependable on the job and is doing well. The officer will also contact family members especially in the home and will talk to neighbors or other interested citizens with whom the officer associates. In most cases the officer is expected to make at least one contact in the home, with the individual, with the employer, and with other persons in the community each month. These contacts are recorded in the officer's case field book. Naturally those cases that the officer considers "unstable" are visited much more frequently.

The average caseload in Florida is 89.3 cases. This is almost three times the size recommended by National Professional Standards of 35 cases. Because of this vast overloading of the officer there is a serious discrepancy between the number of and quality of contacts the officer is expected to make with his clients and what he in reality is able to make.

3:46 p.m. The Officer returns to his office to dictate information on one of the eight presentence investigations he is working on.

He calls the mother of the probationer who is in jail, to explain that her son has admitted guilt and that he will have to recommend revocation of probation. The mother becomes extremely emotional and pleads on behalf of the son. The officer explains as best he can that this is in the best interests of both her son and for the protection of society. "He needs closer supervision than I can provide."

4:03 p.m. The officer talks to John's wife. He explains that without proof or testimony on an assault no charges can be made. She tells him it's his job to do something, but she will not admit that she talked to the officer if he took it to court.

4:30 p.m. The officer instructs four new probationers on the conditions of probation trying to hurriedly explain reasons for each. Two of them do not have jobs and he sets appointments to see both again tomorrow.

5:49 p.m. The officer leaves the stack of paperwork, yet to be completed on one side of his desk, the statistical reports which remain to be done, and a pile of casefiles which need studying and goes home.

7:00 p.m. After finishing supper the officer telephones four parolees with whom he was unable to make contact during the day to assure they are still in town. Many of the contacts must be made after regular work hours.

7:30 p.m. The officer hurries off to a meeting of volunteers who are working on a one-to-one basis with some of the people that he has under supervision. During this meeting he elaborates on some of the specific conditions of probation and discusses ways in which the volunteer can work more effectively as role models.

"Government programs for the control of crime are unlikely to succeed alone. Informal private citizens, playing a variety of roles, can make a decisive difference in the restoration of offenders to the community." The National Commission on the Causes and Prevention of Violence.

"Criminal justice professionals readily and repeatedly admit that, in the absence of citizen assistance, neither more manpower, nor improved technology, nor additional money will enable law enforcement to shoulder the monumental burden of combating crime in America!" National Advisory Commission on Criminal Justice Standards and Goals.

9:00 p.m. The officer finally returns home to his wife and children and settles down for the evening.

11:47 p.m. A city Police Detective calls from the local hospital. He advises that John's wife is in intensive care. She had a serious cut across her face and possible internal head injuries as well as a broken wrist. Her husband was being held for Assault With Intent to Commit Murder. Arrested with John was his employer. They were both found intoxicated at a local bar. The bartender told the Police Officer that the two frequented the bar often. And this ends the day of a typical Parole and Probation Officer.

As noted earlier the officer spends approximately 60% of his time doing investigations for the court and the Parole and Probation Commission. If that officer only worked 40 hours during the week he would spend 24 hours working on investigations, leaving 16 hours for casework. The average officer has a caseload of 89 individuals which would allow 11 minutes per week to work with each person under his supervision or a total of 44 minutes per month.

That 44 minutes must be used for personal counseling, contacts at home and on the job, contacts with employer, family members, friends, volunteers, or any other person or agency providing assistance. That 44 minutes includes the time it takes to travel to and from these various individuals involved. If the parolee or probationer in any way disrupts the status quo it will take the officer additional time to deal with the disruption. Some will have to wait to see him next month.

The average beginning officer is young, has a college degree, is married and usually just beginning a family. He took the job because he wanted to help people. He knew he would never become rich because the starting pay is relatively low and increases are not likely to keep up with the cost of living.

It's little wonder that there is a 20% turnover in Parole and Probation Officers staff in this state each year. People usually stay on a job because of one or two factors or the combination of both. Obviously, a Parole and Probation Officer is not entering this profession for his pay. He or she is coming in for one reason and that is the desire to help other people.

The second factor which keeps a person on the job is job satisfaction; the feeling that he is achieving goals which are meaningful. In the case of Parole and Probation Officers this is helping other people. The Officer has 44 minutes per month to help a person who may have spent a lifetime developing to the point where he has broken the law.

As mentioned before the Parole and Probation Officer's successes are subtle and go unnoticed, his failures are blatant and result in individuals wasting parts of their lives behind bars. There can be little job satisfaction in that environment.

It has been said that whenever you talk to a Parole and Probation Officer he says he is overlooked, overworked, over-extended and underpaid. It just might be that he has a point!

Chapter 15

The Case of John Fenton

This is a six-month excerpt from a fictional case that was used to train probation officers in New York State. It illustrates the officer's use of casework skills to help an extremely dependent youth who is on probation for striking his mother with a hatchet. Although it is a probation case, the techniques used and the method of recording case contacts would be the same for a parole case.

At the time of the attack on this mother Fenton was 16 years of age, and although the assault was not fatal, it caused severe lacerations of the face and scalp. The presentence report indicates that Fenton is an out-of-wedlock child whose father died when he was an infant. Fenton's mother neglected him, and at age 8 he was removed from his mother's care by the juvenile court, and placed in a children's home.

For the first two years his mother did not visit him at the home. At age 16 he was discharged to live with her. Shortly thereafter, Fenton argued with his mother about her drinking and her boyfriend, with the resulting offense of assault. Following his arrest, Fenton was remanded to the state hospital for a psychiatric evaluation. (While in the hospital his mother died in an automobile accident.) Fenton was diagnosed as without psychosis, a "sociopathic personality." He was described as being of dull-normal intelligence.

On January 30th, John Fenton was placed on probation for a term not to exceed five years, after pleading guilty to a charge of assault.

The Fenton Case indicates the various steps used to help an extremely dependent client. Fenton is not, as are many offenders, "street-wise," but, on the contrary, is a young man suffering from the "social shock" of returning to the community after a life spent in institutions.

The case is written by the probation officer in the usual probation/parole agency chronological summary manner. It reviews some of the routine work of the probation/parole officer, such as assisting the offender with a residence and employment. However, in this case the officer provides more assistance than is usual in most p/p cases. Of course, Fenton requires more help than a "typical" offender. In reality, because of the considerable amount of time spent on this case by the officer, Fenton could be considered a "caseload" by himself. In most, if not all, p/p agencies a "John Fenton" would not be able to receive the service reflected in this fictionalized case.

Another routine task performed by the officer concerned his handling of Fenton's new arrest. As indicated in the case record, it is standard p/p practice to interview the client and the arresting officer, in addition to reviewing the police or court record.

As a condition of his probation, Fenton is required to go for psychiatric treatment. However, as the officer notes, Fenton is resistant to psychiatric treatment. In this case, the officer wisely decides not to coerce the offender into treatment. Unfortunately, some p/p agencies will coerce an offender into psychiatric treatment.

This case indicates a concerned officer who not only shows an interest in the tangible needs of his client, but also deals with his social needs—the client is viewed as a total person.

Office Reports: Feb. 4, 14, 19, 21, Mar. 18, 19, 26, Apr. 2, 9, 16, 23, 30
Home Visits: Feb. 4, 8, 29, Apr. 26, 29
Other Contacts: Feb. 4 (3), 5, 6, 7, 19, 25 (2), 27, 28, Mar. 28, Apr. 25
Telephone Reports: Feb. 5, 7, 9, 13, 19, 25, Mar. 7, 18, 19, 21, 22
Employment Verification: Mar. 27, Apr. 16

The Probation Officer had been directed to make arrangements for Fenton, who had no relatives, friends or resources prior to his release from jail.

When Fenton obtained his possessions in two cardboard boxes from the jail, he was taken by the Probation Officer to the Salvation Army office where he was given a loan of $40. He was placed in a room reserved for him several days earlier by the Probation Officer at the Y.M.C.A. at a weekly rental of $32.50. The Probation Officer then accompanied him to the Department of Social Services, where at the Intake Unit, he applied for Public Assistance which was granted the following day. He was also escorted by the Probation Officer to the Social Security Administration, where he obtained a registration card necessary for application for employment to private firms.

Fenton seemed very careful and almost child-like as he traveled about the city with the Probation Officer. He mentioned that everything appeared strange to him, and it will take a long time to adjust. He declined food, saying that he was very excited and had no appetite. The Probation Officer offered him suggestions as to how to look for employment and he thanked the Probation Officer for his assistance when we separated at 4:15 P.M. Shortly thereafter, while riding on a bus, the Probation Officer observed him walking in the vicinity of the Y.M.C.A. looking in every direction at buildings and people. He seemed a lost, pathetic figure.

Although Fenton made a few friends at the Y.M.C.A., he spoke several times—during both office reports and home visits—about telephoning or visiting Mr. Johnson, the Director and others at the Thomasville Home. We voiced no disapproval, but suggested that he defer visiting until employment was found and he had proper clothing.

On February 9, the probationer telephoned that he had received an allowance of $35.25 from the Department of Social Services. He mentioned that he had attended the movies and had made a few friends at the Y.M.C.A. He no longer felt quite so lonesome as he had during the first few days at which time he had difficulty sleeping. A few days later, he reported that he had received an allowance of $125.25 from the Department of Social Services for clothing. We saw the itemized account by Caseworker P. Wolfe, but Fenton, before coming to our office or asking anyone for advice, had cashed the check in a cashing agency, which charged him $.73. We pointed out that he could have saved this amount by cashing the check at any bank or department store where he might purchase clothing.

When the probationer came to the office on February 19, he had a blue gabardine top coat which he had purchased for $40.10.

In addition, he had about $150 in his pockets, adding that he had saved the balance of the clothing money and some food money, as he had eaten sparingly. He mentioned happily that he had met a friend, James Westrup, whom he knew at the Williams State Hospital. Westrup, he stated, has one arm, is married and employed as a bookkeeper. Fenton spent the preceding Sunday with the Westrup family and had a good chicken dinner. He mentioned that it was the most enjoyable day he had experienced in recent years.

The Probation Officer then took Fenton to Blastons Employment Agency and explained his situation as discretely as possible to one of the interviewers to whom the P.O. had been introduced. After filing an application, Fenton was asked to return the following day for a possible job referral. As it turned out, he was unsuccessful that day, but on February 21 he gave the agency a $25 deposit and was referred to a job as helper at the Cotton Converting Company, East River Street. The prospective employer, who had offered a salary of $92.00 per week, told Fenton that he wanted a machine operator. Fenton was rejected for the position. We suspect that the employer realized there was something amiss, as this 22 year old man had no employment history or references.

New Arrest: On February 24, the Probation Officer received a telephone call at his home from a guard at the jail relaying a message from probationer who requested an interview before going to Criminal Court on a new charge. The following day, Fenton was seen at the jail; he had been arrested on a larceny charge for snatching a woman's handbag, and tearfully protested his innocence. We noted, however, that despite signs of agitation, Fenton spoke in a flat, almost toneless voice in a manner denoting apathy and resignation. He related further, that he had met the woman in a bar and grill at Main Street and Monroe Avenue and that his friend had offered to take the woman home in a taxicab. Fenton went along as he had been unable to gain entrance to the Y.M.C.A. after midnight, and while waiting downstairs for Westrup who had escorted the woman to her apartment, he had remained some 15 minutes when Westrup came toward him hurriedly and said, "Let's get out of here." As they ran a Police Officer commanded them to halt, fired shots and both stopped. At that time, Fenton had $45.00 of his savings and $95.00 more in the Y.M.C.A. He had drunk no intoxicants, he claimed, and had no idea that his friend planned to commit a crime.

After reading the complaint in Criminal Court and talking with the arresting officer, Patrolman Lahey of the 2nd Precinct, the Probation Officer was of the opinion that Fenton had given a true account of the offense. The arresting officer acknowledged that Fenton and Westrup were both sober, but that the complainant was under the influence of intoxicants. The latter admitted she had accepted Westrup's offer to take her home, where he snatched her pocketbook. According to the arresting officer, Westrup stated upon his arrest, that Fenton was not involved in the offense. In the meantime, the Probation Officer communicated with the Department of Social Services and the Y.M.C.A. At the latter, on February 25, the night manager was asked to vacate Fenton's room so that he would not owe more rent. The Probationer's effects and funds will be placed in safe keeping at the Y.M.C.A. office the night manager promised.

The case was heard in Criminal Court on February 28, before Judge Rober at which time Fenton was discharged while Westrup was held on a reduced charge of petit larceny. The Probation Officer found, on reading the court papers, that Westrup is 26 years old and resides at 1933 Eastern Drive. He had previously been arrested in Lincoln County for homicide (knife), but no disposition was recorded. Apparently at that time, Westrup was found to be psychotic and committed to the Williams State Hospital, where he met Fenton.

After discharge in court, Fenton immediately appeared at this office and arrangements were made by the Probation Officer for him to revisit the Department of Social Services, reapply for assistance and regain his former lodgings at the Y.M.C.A. We discussed the probationer's involvement with Westrup, causing his recent arrest and attempted to impress upon him how important it will be in the future for him to choose his associates carefully and to confine his activities to wholesome interests.

The following day probationer reported, stating he had obtained his same room at the Y. and that his clothing had been returned to him. The probationer told us that he had been unable to sleep that night and had smoked a large quantity of cigarettes.

Noting that probationer appeared bewildered, the Probation Officer painstakingly explained to him the procedure necessary to obtain Public Assistance again. He was urged to tell his case worker what had happened and under what circumstances. At this time, Fenton was reaccepted for Public Assistance and for the first time, showed initiative by reporting that he had visited the Employment Agency and applied for a job. He was told to return there within a few days.

On March 20 and 22, we talked with the Welfare Caseworker, Mr. Carson and his supervisor, Miss Louks. Both are interested in the probationer and plan to refer him to their Employment Division and possibly, to a Mental Hygiene Clinic.

An effort will be made to interest the Y.M.C.A. staff further in encouraging Fenton to make wider social contacts and to partake of the supervised group activities of the Y.

Through the employment agency, Fenton was given a job as helper at the Downs Brass Company, 67 Wooster Street, on March 27 at a salary of $2.30 per hour for 40 hours plus over-time. The Probation Officer notified the Department of Social Services, which after giving Fenton $46.00, closed their case as of April 3. Upon learning this, we discussed it with probationer during his office report on April 2, advising him of the amount he would receive and suggesting ways he might budget his remaining funds so as to provide for carfares, lunches and work clothing until his first pay. At this time he showed us his hands which were scarred and bruised from putting threads on piping at his work. He declared he would keep this employment until he could find something better, but that he really wants a job as presser. While employed, he regularly showed this Probation Officer his paycheck stubs indicating amounts earned, time off and deductions. Because he was ill for four hours during the week of April 9th, his gross earnings were $82.80. He mentioned he had no complaints about the job at this time, and this Probation Officer gains the impression that Fenton is becoming more stable.

On his next reporting date, he asked if he could have permission to spend the week end at Lake Nomo. He had been invited there by a friend, Jim Colin, who lives in the Y.M.C.A. He is certain that Colin, who has resided there for several years, is a decent person and it has been arranged that they will stay with this man's grandmother.

We mentioned at this time that probationer should be receiving psychiatric treatment as indicated by the court. He said that he did not feel the need of such treatment now, but would go to a psychiatrist if we insist. He added, with a show of apparently genuine frankness, that he would tell the Probation Officer first, if he felt the need for such help. (The matter was later discussed with Case Supervisor Dawson, who said that no useful purpose would be accomplished at this time by sending Fenton to a psychiatrist if he is resistive.)

On his report the following week, probationer mentioned that he had enjoyed the week end at Lake Nomo at a cost of $15. In a game of chance he had won a large ham, coffee and other items which he gave to his friend's grandmother in exchange for her hospitality. Aside from being often tired and having little energy, Fenton made no complaints to the Probation Officer, but did write a letter to his former Welfare Caseworker, Mr. Carson, asking if he were eligible for supplementary assistance, as his gross salary is only $92.00 per week. Mr. Carson telephoned the Probation Officer advising of the letter, and agreed to explain his agency's policy and allowance to the probationer by return mail.

Summary: May-July,
Dictated: August 7
Office Reports: May 7, 14, 21, 28, June 4, 11, 18, 25, July 2, 9, 16, 18, 19, 22
Home Visits: May 22, 31, June 7, 14, 18, 21, July 24, 29
Other Contacts: July 24, 25, 29
Employment References: May 7, 21, 28, June 4, 11, 18, 21, 25, July 2, 16, 19

The probationer continued to live at the Y.M.C.A., preferring to pay weekly rental of $32.50 for an adequate room, hot water, showers and recreational activity, rather than seek a low-cost furnished room at a private home where he might be unhappy. The P.O. agreed with his thinking in this regard and suggested he might seek extra work, particularly as his weekly income is so small. His pay stubs verify that his salary at the Downs Brass Company is usually $92.00 per week, but on May 28, he received a .10 an hour raise making his gross weekly income $96.

During each of his office reports, probationer is friendly and talkative. He mentions frequently that his goal is to work in a dry cleaning shop, as a presser, because this is the type of work he did at Williams State Hospital. The P.O. has noticed that his hands were often cut, bruised or blistered from his present type of work. Another development during the month was the probationer's report that he finds it difficult to get along with his employer's son, whom he describes as uncouth and domineering. The P.O. provided as much support to probationer as possible in this situation, pointing out the value of tolerating this difficulty, temporarily, while saving some part of his small weekly salary so that he can return to the employment agency for a better job. He indicated willingness to try both, but doubted whether he could save any sum whatever since his small income is totally consumed by rent, carfare, clothing, laundry and food. Somehow, probationer had managed to visit friends at Lake Nomo frequently. On one occasion he mentioned that he had taken several children to the rides, but that his friend's grandmother had paid the expenses.

Numerous visits have been made to the Y.M.C.A., but on these occasions even as late as 9:00 P.M., probationer has either been out or failed to answer the buzzer. The desk clerk confirmed in each instance, that Fenton lives in room 607. In office visits Fenton advised that he continues to work for the same employer; his gross salary being $96. On June 18, the P.O. noted an advertisement in the *Daily Star* for a presser of pants to work for a large clothing chain. Carfare was given to probationer to apply for this job, and he later reported that he had done so, but the job had been filled. He is making efforts to find other employment through friends met at the Y.M.C.A. He believes he will be able to obtain a summer job shortly at Lake Nomo, but such would be of little assistance after September when he would again have to look for regular work.

Since he reiterated that he desires employment as a presser, P.O. arranged for him to visit a friend who has a small dry cleaning shop. It was explained to probationer that the owner was doing us a favor and that if he found Fenton as a qualified presser, he would make a sincere effort to give him employment. Fenton visited this establishment on two Saturdays and was permitted to do some pressing and observe the owner work. When next seen, he told the P.O. that the owner had found him good on men's clothing, but inadequate on women's. He will ask the owner for further instruction. Several weeks later, the P.O. saw the owner, who stated that Fenton is a very poor presser and noted, without knowing probationer's background, that he was a "little odd." One Saturday morning when the owner appeared in the shop rather late, Fenton was standing in front of the door and said in stern tones, "I've been here since 10 A.M. and you did not show up." He explained to probationer tactfully that he is sole owner and his own boss. Probationer mentioned during this period, that he is growing more discontented with his employment at the Brass Company where the work is growing heavier. He is now interested in seeking work in a large steam laundry and will apply to several toward the end of the month. He reported that he wished to resign from the Brass Company because he had a serious quarrel with his employer's son, who had used profane language to him. He felt like assaulting this young man who is 22 years old, but realized the serious consequences, and restrained himself.

On July 28, he notified the P.O., during an office report, that he had resigned his employment at the Downs Brass Company, after the employer's son had remarked that "he was going to fire him that night." At this time the probationer thought he could move to the home of his friends in Lake Nomo and find employment there. He promised to report immediately any new address or employment. However, two days later he telephoned stating that he had not moved and had found no new job.

On July 31, he applied for Public Assistance and was accepted. He was notified by letter that he would receive $46 plus rent on the 3rd and 18th of each month. Welfare Caseworker checked with Downs Brass. Fenton was regarded as a good worker and had had no trouble on the job. As the employer did not know Fenton was on probation, the P.O. refrained from contacting the employer, but obtained the necessary information through the Welfare Caseworker, who had similarly maintained probationer's confidence and did not disclose his probation status.

Evaluation: During the five months Fenton has been under our supervision, he has been cooperative and responsive. He does not want psychiatric treatment which has been recommended by the court's psychiatric clinic as necessary. In most instances, so far, he has shown good judgment. His one difficulty, the arrest, was the type of situation in which anyone might become innocently involved. He apparently maintained his employment under most trying physical conditions for approximately four months. Almost weekly his hands were cut, bruised or blistered, and the net pay barely maintained his material needs. He sought work as a presser, but from a test given him by a friend of the P.O., he is not qualified at this time.

The probationer enjoys spending week ends at Lake Nomo with a Y.M.C.A. friend, the latter's grandmother and numerous children. This appears to provide him with some semblance of a family. He has wanted to move to that locale and may do so when he finds steady employment. At all times, the probationer has appeared rational and in contact with reality. Undoubtedly he is odd in some ways, but these seem to be minor deviations from the normal. We attribute some of his lacks to having spent virtually all his life in institutions. It will take time for him to learn finesse in interpersonal realtionships and the ordinary demands of everyday living. His faults do not seem serious at this time. They are to be expected of one who has had little training for living in an open community.

THE CRIMINAL OFFENDER: SOME THEORETICAL CONSIDERATIONS

In previous sections we discussed the classical and positive approaches to crime and the criminal. In this part of the book we have explored the methods of treatment which are an outgrowth of positivist thought. The "radical" views of such observers as Quinney, who was quoted earlier, and the societal reaction or labeling approach were also discussed. In this section we will review some of the more "traditional" views of sociology in order to provide a more rounded theoretical understanding of the offender who represents the population with which probation and parole is directly concerned. The three approaches that will be reviewed here, although they can be seen as emanating from a positivist framework, are to be contrasted with the psychoanalytical or medical model approach discussed earlier. The sociologists being discussed here, and sociologists in general, do not stress the importance of individual pathology as a basis for crime. Instead, they tend to stress societal causes, as will be seen in the theories of *anomie, differential association*, and *delinquency and opportunity*.

Anomie

Anomie, as developed by Emile Durkheim, results from unstable societal conditions fostered by a high rate of change—through industrialization, for example. Durkheim studied rates of suicide and determined that the rate of suicide increased when masses of people were unable to keep *synchronized* with rapid social changes. This theory conjures up an image of a helpless army recruit who is unable to keep in step with his veteran colleagues.

Anomie was further developed by Robert Merton in an influential article written in 1938.[1] Merton viewed crime as a "normal" response to given social situations that foster this type of behavioral response. Thus, crime is not based on individual pathology, but is seen as part of an expected reaction to certain circumstances in a given environment.

In the United States there is a great deal of stress on achieving material success, highlighted by what Veblin referred to as "conspicuous consumption." The rather inordinate emphasis on wealth is often not accompanied by the means to achieve it. This situation sets the stage for anomie, which results when a person accepts the goals of society, but rejects the approved means for securing them. More importantly, insofar as probation/parole practice is concerned, is the fact that legitimate means of financial success are often blocked by such realities as discrimination, lack of educational opportunities, etc. When the goals are accepted, but the means are not readily available, a person may resort to *innovation*. An urban ghetto youngster, for example, may take advantage of the illegitimate opportunities available "on the street." Anomie, to be sure, provides one theoretical explanation of why most persons on probation/parole are poor, lack education, and are disproportionately from minority groups that have been subjected to discrimination.

The theory of anomie has its limitations as an explanation for crime. It fails to adequately account for a great deal of criminal activity that is non-utilitarian. As we noted in the section on treatment and psychoanalytical theory, some illegal acts appear to be quite irrational. As was noted, some offenders seem to desire punishment as a way of satisfying an overbearing superego. A great deal of criminal behavior appears impulsive, and it cannot easily be reconciled or accounted for by allusions to anomie.

[1] Robert Merton, "Social Structure and Anomie," *American Sociological Review* (Oct. 1938), pp. 672–82.

What does the theory of anomie offer to the probation/parole officer, and the very real problems of his practice? One consideration has to do with aspirations. Offenders often have quite unrealistic goals; their aspirations surpass their ability. In such cases, the role of the officer is to help the client to make a realistic assessment of the situation, and then to assist him with achieving goals that are reality-based. Each client should be encouraged and assisted to achieve to the limits of his ability. The officer has a responsibility to see to it that his client's goals are not blocked by such barriers as discrimination. In such instances he must make use of the various agancies that are responsible for enforcing equal opportunity laws.

Differential Association

Edwin Sutherland (1883-1950) is a giant among American criminologists. His most widely-known theories concern "white-collar crime" and differential association. Because of its applicability to the client population on probation/parole, we shall review only differential association in this book.

Differential association "conceives of criminality as participation in a cultural tradition and as the result of association with representatives of that culture." [2] The basis for this theory is a set of beliefs that:

1. criminal behavior is learned
2. criminal behavior is learned in interaction with other persons in a process with other persons
3. the learning of criminal behavior occurs primarily within intimate personal groups
4. the learning of criminal behavior includes techniques, motives, and attitudes.

Sutherland states that crime results when there is "an excess of definitions favorable to violation of law over definitions unfavorable to violation of law." [3]

Crime results from the strength or intensity of criminal associations and is the result of an accumulative learning process. A pictorial portrayal of differential association can easily be conceived of in terms of a balanced scale that starts out level. On each side is accumulated the

[2] Edwin Sutherland, "Differential Association," in Karl Schuessler, ed., *Edwin Sutherland: On Analyzing Crime* (Chicago: University of Chicago Press, 1973), p. 5.

[3] *Ibid.*, pp. 8–9.

varying weights of criminal and non-criminal associations. At some theoretical point criminal activity will result if there is an excess of criminal associations over non-criminal associations.

What import does this theory have for probation/parole practice? As noted earlier in the discussions of probation/parole regulations, they invariably contain prohibitions against certain associations. A person on probation/parole is usually cautioned against associating with others similarly situated. This can easily be seen as a practical attempt to respond to the theory of differential association. In addition, the probation/parole officer can provide exposure to a non-criminal association; an exposure and influence that conceivably can help to balance our theoretical scale. The officer can assist his client with securing other non-criminal associations through charitable, community, church, fraternal, and other such organizations.

Delinquency and Opportunity

Richard Cloward and Lloyd Ohlin "attempt to integrate these two streams of thought as they apply to the problem of delinquency." [4] They unite the theories of anomie and differential association in a discussion and analysis of delinquent gangs and subcultures. In focusing on the different types of criminal activities that result from anomie and differential association, they distinguish several categories:

1. rackets—organized crime subculture
2. fighting gang subculture
3. retreatist drug oriented subculture

Each of these types of subcultures arises out of a different set of social circumstances or *opportunity.* Crime is viewed not as an individual endeavor, but as part of a collective adaptation or manifestation within a given set of social circumstances. Cloward and Ohlin recognize that in some instances, not only are legitimate means of achieving success blocked, but certain illegitimate ones as well. This phenomenon is discussed by Nicholas Gage in a book appropriately entitled *The Mafia Is Not An Equal Opportunity Employer:*[5] "no door is more firmly

[4] Richard A. Cloward and Lloyd E. Ohlin, *Delinquency and Opportunity* (New York: The Free Press, 1960), p. x.

[5] Nicholas Gage, *The Mafia Is Not an Equal Opportunity Employer* (New York: McGraw-Hill, 1971), p. 113.

locked to blacks than the one that leads to the halls of power in organized crime."

When access to legitimate and important illegitimate means of attaining goals is not readily available, urban ghetto youngsters may resort to less utilitarian forms of deviant behavior, such as gang fighting activities or drug addiction.

The application of this hybrid theory to probation/parole practice is similar to the two strains on which it is based. However, it also provides an insight into adolescent gang behavior, which appears to be on the rise in many urban areas. In addition, it offers an explanation of why many probation/parole clients have a history of drug addiction.

Chapter 16

Probation and Parole Officers

The selection of probation and parole officers is by a process similar to that used to select most other civil servants. Two systems are generally employed, the merit system and the appointment system. In both systems minimum qualifications are established; for probation and parole officers they are usually a bachelor's degree, and sometimes a master's degree or experience in social work or counseling.

MERIT SYSTEM

Under the (so-called) merit system an applicant who meets the minimum qualifications is required to pass a written examination in order to be eligible for the position. If he passes, his name is placed on a list according to the grade he received, and it is from this list that staff are selected. This system has been criticized by those who maintain that a written test cannot determine who will be a good probation or parole officer.

APPOINTMENT SYSTEM

Under the appointment system an applicant who meets the minimum requirements is hired on the basis of an evaluation by the agency. The applicant does not take a written examination, although he is usually interviewed by agency representatives. This system has been criticized because of its potential for abuse. There is a history of the appointment system being used for political purposes.

COMBINED SYSTEM

While not necessarily a distinct system, some jurisdictions use elements of the merit system and the appointment system. For example, applicants are first required to pass a qualifying examination, then those who pass the examination are interviewed, and the agency selects those they consider best suited for the position.

GRADUATE EDUCATION

The minimum qualification for probation/parole officers is usually a bachelor's degree. Some agencies require graduate degrees and some provide scholarships for staff members to pursue graduate education. In order to ascertain what graduate degrees are favored by parole agencies, the writer surveyed 53 parole agencies, representing all 50 states, plus Puerto Rico, the District of Columbia, and the United States Division of Probation. While the survey was limited to parole agencies because of the difficulty imposed by the number of probation agencies, there is good reason to believe that probation agencies generally favor the same graduate education. The results of the survey indicate that the two most preferred degrees on a master's level are in social work and criminal justice. Other master's degrees favored were in criminology, sociology, psychology, law, and educational counseling, in that order.

PERSONAL QUALITIES

The characteristics generally considered desirable for probation and parole officers are:

1. Basic Knowledge—a probation/parole officer should have a working understanding of psychology and sociology, the criminal statutes, police operations, and the court and correctional systems.

2. Individual Characteristics—a probation/parole officer needs the ability to relate to all offenders and to deal with their sometimes subtle or open hostility; to exercise authority in an appropriate manner; to work well with other staff members, and to be able to organize work properly and prepare written reports in a coherent and timely manner.

3. The Agency—the probation/parole officer must be willing to accept the responsibilities engendered by working for a public agency that handles offenders, and to enforce rules and adhere to regulations.

4. Other Agencies—the probation/parole officer has to be able to deal with many kinds of agencies, usually divided into law enforcement (police, district attorneys, judges, etc.) and social service (welfare, employment, educational, etc.). These agencies often have varying attitudes toward offenders that must be handled appropriately.

WOMEN PROBATION AND PAROLE OFFICERS

The 1964 Civil Rights Act, which prohibited discrimination against women (and minority groups), and the strength of the feminist movement have had an important impact on the criminal justice system. In the area of police personnel practices, police agencies are now hiring women on an equal basis with men. Women police officers are no longer only assigned to "female duties," but now go on uniformed street patrol.

Traditionally, probation and parole have also been a man's field; approximately 90% of probationers and parolees are men, and prior to 1970 most probation and parole agencies did not permit officers to supervise clients of the opposite sex. This limited the number of positions available to women probation/parole officers. Currently, most probation and parole agencies routinely mix caseloads, thereby increasing the number of women who can be hired for this work.[1]

Some agencies assign male offenders to women because they believe that women can do as effective a job as men, while others do so to better equalize the size of their caseloads. A few agencies will make an assignment on the basis of what is believed to be the needs of the particular case. Ellis Stout, probation chief in the State of Washington,

[1] Schoonmaker and Brooks, p. 109.

notes, for example, that some agencies will have women supervise youthful male offenders who are believed to be in need of a mother surrogate. He states that some agencies do not assign "assaultive" or "aggressive" male offenders to female officers out of concern for the officer's safety. Field work assignments may be adjusted for women officers to keep them out of high delinquency areas or from having to make night visits.[2]

NON-PROFESSIONALS

Probation and parole have historical roots in the work of such non-professionals as John Augustus and the agents of prisoner aid societies. The non-professional is very much a part of probation and parole practice. Indeed, the requirement of a college degree, and the use of salaried, full-time probation/parole officers is a relatively recent phenomenon in corrections.

PARAPROFESSIONALS

A paraprofessional is an employee who does not possess the credentials traditionally viewed as necessary for work as a p/p officer in a modern p/p agency. Frequently, the paraprofessional will be further identified as being *indigenous,* which usually means that he possesses a similar background, social, economic, racial, etc., to the p/p clients serviced by the agency. He is often viewed as "an extension of the client . . . who can bridge the gap between the professional and the client." [3] The extensive use of paraprofessionals is an outgrowth of the "War on Poverty" of the 1960's. The basic motives for using paraprofessionals are:[4]

1. the desire to compensate for the shortage of skilled manpower, particularly workers trained at the graduate level;

2. the desire to increase employment opportunities for disadvantaged workers and the unemployed poor;

[2] Ellis Stout, "Should Female Officers Supervise Male Offenders," *Crime and Delinquency* (Jan. 1973), p. 68.

[3] Research Report No. 3, *Overview Study of Employment of Paraprofessionals* (Washington, D.C.: Government Printing Office, 1974), p. 15.

[4] *Ibid.*, p. 44.

3. the desire to develop an efficient division of labor so that manpower with different levels of skill could be assigned appropriate duties;

4. the desire to modify organizations so that the resulting service delivery system would be more directly related to the problem of clients and more efficient in meeting their needs; and

5. the desire to provide work experience in which workers, by helping clients with problems similar to their own, improve their social functioning and become better prepared for work.

Since the paraprofessional is likely to come from the same environment as a large segment of the p/p population, he can relate to clients without the inhibiting factors engendered by the socioeconomic gap that often exists between client and professional. Cressey states that the criminals who are to be rehabilitated and the people expected to effect the change, must have a strong sense of belonging to one group.[5]

The tasks assigned to paraprofessionals are varied. The (N.Y.) Governor's Special Committee on Criminal Offenders recommended that paraprofessionals be used to make all field visits and conduct all surveillances, thus freeing professional staff to concentrate on therapy. The committee also noted that paraprofessionals would be excellent sources for community job vacancy information.[6] While the recommendations have not been put into effect in New York, paraprofessionals are performing the recommended tasks in other states.

In 1968, the *Probation Officer Case Aide Project* in Chicago began using paraprofessionals to work with federal probation and parole clients. The Probation Officer Aides (POA) were employed on a part-time basis, although four were subsequently employed full-time as part of an experimental program. Some of the POA's were ex-offenders—they worked as assistants to the probation officers. Some provided direct counseling. Most helped provide concrete services such as assistance with housing, securing medical and psychiatric services, and finding employment or a vocational training program. Some POA's were used primarily for surveillance activity.[7]

Scott notes that ex-offenders are employed as paraprofessionals in 16

[5] Cressey cited from Paul Lerman, ed., *Delinquency and Social Policy* (New York: Praeger Publishers, 1970), p. 346.

[6] *Preliminary Report of the Governor's Special Committee on Criminal Offenders*, 1968, p. 249.

[7] Donald W. Beless, William S. Pilcher and Ellen Jo Ryan, "Use of Indigenous Non-Professionals in Probation and Parole," *Federal Probation* (Mar. 1972), p. 10.

states (Alaska, California, Florida, Idaho, Illinois, Iowa, Kentucky, Michigan, New Jersey, Ohio, Pennsylvania, Utah, Vermont, Virginia, Washington, and Wisconsin). He also provides an in-depth review, a brief summary of which follows, of the program in Ohio, which utilizes ex-offenders as Parole Officer Aides.[8]

The POA Program, which began in 1972, uses ex-offenders to bridge the gap between the agency and its clients, and to facilitate communication between the agency and the community, with a view toward increasing confidence and trust in the agency while decreasing parole violations. By 1974, there were 29 POA's employed by the Ohio Adult Authority. Originally they supervised caseloads of 30 parolees, although this has now been increased to 50. The cases were drawn from existing caseloads of other parole officers, and, although they were supposed to be "typical," the author states that they tended to have more extensive criminal records and to be those parolees who had been "given up on."

The POA's are over 22 years of age; they have completed parole successfully and possessed good interpersonal skills; and they are free of psychopathological tendencies. The ex-offenders used in the program are described as the "winners" within the "offender-class." They receive intensive training and do the same work as regular Ohio parole officers, with some exceptions. They cannot arrest parolees, nor carry firearms. In addition, a regular parole officer is supposed to visit each of the aide's clients every month in order to check on the progress of the case and to provide extra assistance, if necessary.

Scott reports that there are very few problems with the program. The most serious would seem to be the lack of cooperation with the aides on the part of policemen. The author reports that 30.6% of the cases handled by the aides spent time in jail while under supervision, while 23.9% of the cases handled by parole officers spent time in jail while under supervision. Scott states that the difference can be explained by the fact that the aides supervise more difficult cases.

A career ladder has been built into the program so that POA's can become full fledged parole officers. Since the program began, two POA's have been promoted to other positions, one as a parole officer and the other as a correctional counselor.

The Ohio Adult Authority reported on the "outstanding features" and the "weaknesses" of the POA Program:

[8] Joseph E. Scott, *Ex-Offenders as Parole Officers* (Lexington, Mass.: D.C. Heath and Co., 1975), pp. 1–200.

> The most significant feature of utilizing ex-offenders as Parole Officer Aides is their obvious ability to bridge the communication gap with hard-core offenders. The 2.8 percent recidivism rate is extremely low and this reduction has resulted in savings to taxpayers in terms of costs of incarcerations. Further input from the ex-offender in developing treatment strategies has been very significant in modifying behavior. Moreover, the "reformed delinquents" have spoken to 5000 high school students regarding the fallacy of criminal careers. The students were given an opportunity to discuss their personal problems with the ex-offender—a person who has been there and tells it like it is. Further, we have demonstrated that a female ex-offender can be successful in supervising male offenders.
>
> Two areas which are significant should be discussed. First, Aides were not employed using academic accomplishments as a criterion but were screened more on their knowledge of the criminal subculture and their ability to effectively relate this information to bring about change in the behavior of offenders they were counseling. The lack of comprehensive writing skills has created problems; however we have instituted a remedial program at the onset of training.
>
> Second, law enforcement agencies have not fully accepted the use of ex-offenders in some areas. As a group they are opposed to the program, but individually they are receptive. In 95% of the law enforcement agencies throughout Ohio, the Aides are accepted and have full access to records of the police and courts. Some departments have put out broad general policies concerning ex-offenders visiting their agencies but do not adhere to the policies. It is interesting that Aides working in the same office have differential communication patterns with law enforcement agencies. It appears that policies are instituted to ban a certain Aide. It is probably more correct to say that 95% of our Aides have no difficulty in communicating with law enforcement and court personnel.[9]

Paraprofessionals receive a lower salary than professionals employed by the same agency. Some professionals in p/p agencies believe that the presence of lower paid paraprofessionals on staff may undermine their efforts at securing salary increases and other benefits. Some contend that the willingness of paraprofessionals to accept lower rates of pay than professionals is often the *real* reason that they are employed.

Some probation and parole officers maintain that paraprofessionals over-identify with the client, sometimes in opposition to the agency and its policies. However, others maintain the opposite; that paraprofessionals tend to over-identify with the agency (and middle-class

[9] Personal Communication with Mr. Nick J. Sanborn, Regional Supervisor, Ohio Adult Authority, March 26, 1976.

values) and are often less flexible than their professional colleagues. Scott, and other observers, have not found either criticism to be valid.

Some probation and parole agencies provide an opportunity for paraprofessionals to attend college, and/or they have set up a career ladder whereby paraprofessionals can eventually enter the professional ranks.

Criteria and Rating Scale for Hiring Offenders*

1. The criteria used by the Boston Court Resource Project for hiring ex offenders for advocate positions in a pretrial intervention project was

   (a) A man who had served time in prison and who had been out of prison for at least a year.

   (b) One who had demonstrated responsibility in previous job(s).

   (c) An above-average intelligence.

   (d) An ability to establish rapport with varying types of people easily. (This would include a flexibility of approach, warmth, and sensitivity.)

   (e) A strong commitment to human services, with some related work experience.

   (f) No recent (two years) drug history.

   (g) Demonstrated responsibility in financial obligations and stable personal life.

   (h) Ability to articulate, and sufficient education (or equivalent) to do narrative reporting.

   (i) History of personal counseling and a positive attitude toward treatment methods and toward professionals.

   (j) Freedom from prejudices and judgmental attitudes.

   (k) Maturity, good judgment, and self-awareness.

2. Based upon the criteria shown above a rating scale was devised with adjectival and numerical values. The applicant was rated in each area and points given were summed. The minimum acceptable level was +15 points. The "gut reaction" of the interviewers to the applicant also carried some weight that was not qualified but could overrule the scale results. The rating scale was as follows

* *From* Richard Ku, *The Volunteer Probation Counselor Program, Lincoln, Nebraska* (Washington, D.C.: Government Printing Office, 1975), pp. 57–62.

Age	24–32	+½ pt.			Over	0 pt.
Health	Good	+1			Poor	−1
Education (Reporting)	Good	+½	Fair	+½	Poor	−1
Family life	Good	+2	Fair	+1	Poor	−1
Finances (Mgr. Responsibility)	Good	+1			Poor	−1
Has Auto	Yes	+1			No	0
Drug History	Over 2 yrs.	+0	Only 1 yr.	−1	Under 1 yr.	−3
Personal Habits	Good	+1	Fair	+½	Poor	−1
Work History	Good	+1½	Fair	+½	Poor	−0
Prejudices (Race, Judicial)	Yes	−2	Fair	−1½	Poor	−½
Flexibility	Good	+1½	Fair	+½	Poor	−1½
Attitude regarding system	Healthy	+½	Fair	+½	Poor	−1½
"Warmth"	Good	+2	Fair	+1	Poor	−2
Ability to articulate	Good	+2	Fair	+1	Poor	−2
Commitment	Good	+3	Fair	+1½	Poor	−1

VOLUNTEERS

The American Bar Association reports that all states are using volunteers in corrections, with many working in p/p agencies.[10] The largest group of volunteers work in court settings, and the National Advisory Commission on Criminal Justice Standards and Goals (NACCJSG) reports that there are about 100,000 volunteers in such court-affiliated agencies as probation.[11]

One of the first such programs was initiated by Judge Keith J. Leenhouts of Royal Oak, Michigan, who remains a leading figure in the volunteer movement. Through his efforts, a national organization called Volunteers in Probation (VIP) was formed in affiliation with the National Council on Crime and Delinquency.[12] VIP publishes a quarterly newspaper, the *VIP Examiner,* that reports on the activities of volunteers in the entire criminal justice system (*VIP Examiner,* P.O. Box 31, Flint, Michigan 48501).

[10] Trisha Streff, *Volunteer Program in Corrections,* a 1975 survey report by the American Bar Association's National Parole Aide Program.

[11] Community Crime Prevention Task Force, *A Call For Citizen Action: Crime Prevention and the Citizen* (Washington, D.C.: Government Printing Office, 1975), p. 9.

[12] Marie Buckley, *Breaking Into Prison* (Boston: Beacon Press, 1974), pp. 125–26.

Judge Leenhouts began using volunteers to staff a probation service in his court. Studies of the *Royal Oak Program* indicate that "volunteers and professionals working together can provide intensive probation services that cannot be supplied in any other way."[13] Studies revealed that the recidivism rate from Royal Oak was lower than that in similar nonvolunteer probation agencies.[14]

The NACCJSG reports that court volunteers have been used in the following capacities:[15]

advisory council member
arts and crafts teacher
home skills teacher
recreation leader
coordinator or administrator of programs
employment counselor
foster parent (group or individual)
group guidance counselor
information officer
neighborhood worker
office worker
volunteer for one-to-one assignment with probationers
professional skills volunteer
public relations worker
community education counselor
recordkeeping volunteer
religious guidance counselor
tutor

There has been an increase in the use of volunteers in parole, with the American Bar Association, theJaycees, and other professional and civic groups initiating volunteer programs. The ABA's National Parole Aide Program (VPA) began in 1971; since that time over 3200 volunteer lawyers and 2500 parolees have participated in the program in more than 20 states. The VPA pairs volunteer attorneys with parolees to provide one-to-one assistance in all service areas excluding legal help. It was believed that the attorney/client relationship would interfere

[13] CCP Task Force, p. 9.

[14] *Ibid.*

[15] *Ibid.*

with the development of an interpersonal relationship between the parolee and the volunteer.

The volunteer attorneys helped inmates to secure parole release residences and employment, and provided job counseling, tutoring and help with personal problems. They were particularly successful in helping to secure services for parolees from public agencies. The ABA notes that lawyers who enter parole as volunteers bring with them a knowledge of the criminal justice system, and prestige that makes their acceptance by parole agency management an easier task.

However, a study by John Berman of the VPA Program indicates that it "had no effect on arrest rates and no effect on employment rates, salaries, or job satisfaction." Berman notes that the average subject studied had been out six months before he became involved in the VPA Program. He states that the most critical period for parolees is generally the first month out of prison, and this could account for some of his findings.[16]

The Volunteer Probation Counselor Program in Lincoln, Nebraska has been hailed as "an excellent example of community involvement in the corrections process" by Gerald Caplan, Director of the National Institute of Law Enforcement and Criminal Justice.[17] With the increase in dispositions of probation, especially for young offenders, professional probation resources are often unable to keep pace with the growing caseloads. To meet this problem, the Lincoln program assigns high risk misdemeanants[18] between the ages of 16 and 25 to a volunteer for supervision and assistance. The youth and the volunteer are matched on the basis of mutual interests and the probationer's interpersonal needs. The volunteers are carefully screened and trained in counseling. Each volunteer works with only one probationer, and after the assignment is complete he can agree to be reassigned to another offender.

Volunteers are recruited through the news media and by probation officers who appear as speakers before community and University of Nebraska groups. The screening process includes psychological testing, and examines the applicant's motives for wanting to become a

[16] John Berman, "The Volunteer in Parole Program," *Criminology* (May 1975), pp. 111–12.

[17] *The Volunteer Probation Counselor Program* (Washington, D.C.: Government Printing Office, 1975), p. 3.

[18] A high risk offender was described as likely to commit additional offenses because of the presence of some or all of the following conditions: significant mental or emotional problems, antisocial attitudes, a relatively unstable family or living situation, anti-authority attitudes, and relatively limited personal assets.

counselor. Training involves three sessions totaling eight hours, during which applicants are given a description of the program, a review of relevant community resources, and instruction in counseling techniques. Volunteers are sworn in by a judge at a formal ceremony at which they receive identification cards.

The program is coordinated by a member of the probation staff, and the volunteers also receive ongoing supervision and guidance from probation staff members. There are regular monthly seminars and the performance of each volunteer is evaluated with a view toward his success in reducing recidivism. The clients are also asked for their opinion of the volunteer's availability and effectiveness. A study of the program revealed that there has been a considerable reduction in recidivism because of the program, while there were no expenses beyond the time requirements of recruiting, training, and supervising the volunteers, about 12% of the total probation staff time.[19]

The Florida Parole and Probation Commission has an extensive volunteer program. Applicants are screened and trained, and they work on a one-to-one basis with a probationer or parolee. The volunteer is required to make at least one weekly contact with the client, and a monthly contact with the Parole and Probation Officer in person or by telephone. In addition, the volunteer submits a monthly report summarizing his or her contacts and activities. (A copy of the report form appears at the end of this chapter.) The Commission cautions volunteers against exercising or using authority with offenders, since the Commission believes that the volunteer must provide influence by example. The Commission states that this is more difficult if the volunteer is stigmatized as an authority figure.[20]

The *Volunteers in Probation* (VIP) Program in San Diego County, California, also uses volunteers who work on a one-to-one basis with probationers, providing a "role model" and an "individualized service" function. Other volunteers in the program provide specialized assistance such as employment counseling and tutoring, or they meet other needs outlined by the probation officers.[21]

Volunteer programs in Boulder, Colorado, *Attention Homes* and *Foster Homes*, provide a supervised environment for boys and girls ages 10 to 18 who are referred by the juvenile court. Using 450 volunteers and donations from the community, the program provides

[19] *The Volunteer Probation Counselor Program*, pp. 1–10.

[20] *The Volunteer Handbook*, a publication of the Florida Parole and Probation Commission.

[21] CCP Task Force, pp. 45–46.

group home care for youngsters who would ordinarily be placed in a custodial facility. Volunteer couples are screened and trained by the court staff to serve as houseparents.[22]

The Tarrant County (Fort Worth, Texas) Juvenile Probation Department has been using a novel volunteer program since 1971 called *Recreation and Rap.* It provides for group activities such as arts and crafts, sports, and role-playing for probationers, using volunteers and professional staff. The program has the following purposes:

1. to provide the probationer with an opportunity to experience success in activities of a creative nature and to broaden the opportunity for constructive experiences;
2. to provide the youth with relationships with adults not employed by school, police or the probation department, based on a concern and a desire to give of one's self. It is believed that the awareness that volunteers give of themselves without pay, can lead to a positive experience with adults for the child in the program;
3. to afford a positive peer group experience in settings other than delinquent, that will fill some of the needs that precipitated the child's delinquent behavior;
4. to provide increased exposure, quantitative and qualitative, to probation officers, volunteers and programs in an effort to bring about new experiences and change, not only in behavior but in attitudes and values; and
5. to more closely involve the community in constructive relationships with delinquents.[23]

Probably the most extensive use of volunteers in probation and parole is in Japan. When that country reorganized its non-institutional treatment system after the war, there was a debate over whether or not p/p services should be thoroughly professionalized. Because of a shortage of funds and a large potential for volunteers, a new organization combining professional and volunteer workers were created. The 1950 Volunteer Probation Officer Law resulted in nearly 50,000 persons being nominated as Volunteer Probation Officers (VPO).

The VPO performs all of the supervisory functions normally assigned to a p/p officer in the United States. The VPO is considered a

[22] *Ibid.*, p. 46.

[23] "Recreation and Rap," *VIP Examiner* (Fall 1975), p. 5.

public official of the National Government and is entitled to the benefit of compensation if injured while performing his or her duties. The VPO receives no salary, but is paid a minimal amount for expenses related to training and travel. As in the United States, the VPO program depends on a sense of mission and purpose to provide motivation for volunteer workers. In addition to the gratification that each VPO feels, there is a great deal of prestige and public recognition. Candidates for the VPO position are screened by an advisory committee of criminal justice specialists, and those who pass the screening are appointed by the Minister of Justice. A national federation links VPO associations throughout the country.

The actual supervision process in p/p in Japan is carried out through the collaborative efforts of the VPO and a professional probation officer. However, field work is handled by the volunteer and the probation officer rarely involves himself in field work after he has assigned the case to the volunteer. The VPO submits regular reports to the probation officer and only when an unusual situation arises does the probation officer make a field visit.[24]

Criticism. Some probation/parole agencies and staff members are critical of the use of volunteers. They may view the efforts of volunteers as interference with their prerogatives, and they may be concerned about sharing information with volunteers because of the confidential aspect of probation/parole practice. Some of the criticisms leveled at paraprofessionals are also used against volunteers in p/p.

Since volunteers are not paid, they need to derive some satisfaction from their work. Satisfaction results when there is a level of success, and in order to be successful volunteers require adequate training and supervision.

In the following case study a psychosocial diagnosis provides the basis for a plan of treatment that integrates professional and volunteer help for a disturbed seventeen year-old probationer.

Case History*

Person and Offense. M.M. was a 17 year old male who was charged with drunkenness while engaging in a typical behavior

[24] Rehabilitation Bureau, *Non-Institutional Treatment of Offenders in Japan* (Japan: Ministry of Justice, 1970), pp. 1–59.

**From* Richard Ku, *The Volunteer Probation Counselor Program, Lincoln Nebraska* (Washington, D.C.: Government Printing Office, 1975), pp. 57–62.

pattern: drinking, fighting, and goofing around. The youth's problems with authority figures were long-standing; i.e., he had been referred for psychiatric treatment while in the fourth grade. The previous year he committed seven criminal offenses which involved destructive acting out or thefts.

Family. M.M. was the oldest of seven children. The father was an alcoholic who maintained full time employment. The mother was a kind, understanding person, overburdened with a large family and the father's drinking problem. The youth moved out of the family home because of recurring fights with his father. M.M. lived with his grandparents when arrested.

Education. The youth did not complete 10th grade because of low grades and lack of interest. He had average intellectual ability.

Employment. The youth worked about 30 hours each week for his grandfather on a garbage route. He earned enough spending money to get by and did not worry about losing his job if he missed work.

Self and Interpersonal Relationships. Because of the potential for serious antisocial behavior, M.M. was referred for additional psychological evaluation. At the time of the psychological assessment, M.M. had been on a 30-day drinking binge. The youth was pale, emaciated, distraught, and had teeth marks on his left hand. He could not recall much of what had happened to him during previous weeks, though he did acknowledge some blackouts from the excessive alcohol use. The youth was moderately depressed, felt hurt, rejected, lonely, and very insecure. He did appear to realize that drinking did not solve problems but only increased them.

The short-term goals were to stabilize the life situation of this individual by encouraging support from the family. He moved back into the family home where family members made an honest effort to be supportive and sympathetic. Frequent contact with the professional staff also occurred. The basic approach was to be sensitive, warm, accepting, and concerned.

The psychological evaluation indicated that the personality structure was immature and ill suited for coping with adult responsibilities. Dependency needs were prominent, though often denied. This youth would often express his needs for independence and for handling situations on his own. He often resented people trying to tell him what to do, especially authority figures. However, unconsciously the young man greatly feared independence. Consequently, it was likely that gestures toward independence would be short lived. The joys of irresponsibility and pleasure-seeking had great appeal to him. His self concept resembled an irresponsible, playful little boy who enjoyed having fun but who could not control what happened to him. He felt almost totally at the mercy of his surroundings. Self esteem was very low. Feelings of deprivation, inferiority, loneliness, and resentment were present. Although the youth often talked big, he was very insecure and genuinely doubted his own ability to be successful. He was aloof from others so that he was not attracted to or influenced by his friends, who were antisocial persons. He appeared to share with them an interest in drinking and expressing anger at authorities.

Resentment appeared to stem from his subconscious feeling of inferiority and the realization that he was often a failure. Much of his acting-out behavior had the quality of self-punishment. This kind of a youth could very easily give up on himself and insure ultimate failure by breaking the law and getting himself put in prison.

Fear of his own impulses was great. Heterosexual relationships were very threatening to him and likely to produce feelings of inadequacy and inferiority. Aggressiveness, self-assertive behavior, and competing with others were likely to be inconsistently exhibited.

Dependent relationships appeared to be the only kind which would make him feel more secure. The youth appeared to get along well with older people, such as grandparents. He also had very positive feelings toward his mother whom he perceived as an understanding, affectionate, and caring person. Some mixed feelings about the father were present. The prediction was that he would be able to readjust to the family situation, though problems with authority and getting along with his own father were likely to recur.

The youth appeared to be very vulnerable to situational pressure. When situational stress occurred, his coping skills were likely to include drinking, running away, or fighting.

The youth appeared to have virtually no insight into himself as a person. He was remarkably insensitive to his own feelings. He was also remarkably insensitive to needs and wishes of other persons.

Summary of Indepth Psychological Evaluation

1. The potential for more serious criminal offenses was very great.

2. Self defeating behavior was a serious problem which could take the form of acting out which would lead to prison. Punishment through incarceration would confirm his continuing feelings of inferiority and inadequacy.

3. The youth appeared to be unable to benefit from professional treatment. He had virtually no insight into himself or the kinds of verbal skills needed to participate successfully in professional counseling. Furthermore, he was very threatened by any suggestion that he might be mentally disturbed.

4. The youth required external structure to make a stable adjustment. The exaggerated dependency needs indicated that he would feel secure with structure but if he began to perceive the structure as authoritarian, he would resent the situation and begin to act out against the authority.

5. This was a very fragile individual whose overall adjustment was tenuous.

6. The change process was likely to be time consuming with setbacks expected.

Relationships Needed. Primary counseling; professional staff.

Volunteer Probation Counselor. A 53-year-old airport executive was selected. The volunteer was a personable, likeable, self assured individual who appeared to have good common sense. The man was a grandfatherly type of person who would not threaten M.M. in a relationship. Both M.M. and the volunteer counselor held conventional values. There was therefore little danger of a generation gap between them.

Counseling. The youth responded well to the security of the family situation and the attention he received from the professional staff and the volunteer probation counselor. He re-enrolled in high school and continued to work part time. He resolved to turn his life around and, for a while, was able to devote his energy to achieving his goal. However, despite the diminishing of emotional pressure from the arrest, the familiar patterns of irresponsibility, acting out, and drinking behavior emerged.

Counseling was focused to deal with attitudes toward authority figures, especially the police. M.M. was implicated in a theft again but no legal charges were filed. The theft was retaliation against former friends, also high-risk offenders, who had stolen from him. He was tempted to get back with his old crowd of antisocial friends but did not. His attendance at school became irregular. Indeed, the only way to guarantee that he would attend school was for his mother to drive him. Despite occasional setbacks, he began to feel some rewards from his new life style. He received praise at school for some of his accomplishments. Parents and staff praised him for breaking off with his antisocial acquaintances who were often in jail. Gradually, the appeal of the new style became greater for him. As he became more successful, however, a new period of conflict and emotional stress occurred.

The basic problem was the long-term feeling of low self esteem and fear of success. Because the youth perceived himself to be a failure, he greatly feared success and began to engage in self-defeating behavior. A crisis occurred when the youth was selected to be a spokesman for his school. He was to speak before educators about the special education program he was in. He panicked, became very insecure, became very anxious, and began drinking. He was being pushed too far too fast. He handled the problem by running away. He left the state; his trip included more drinking, some fighting, and several scrapes which could have led to criminal charges being filed. Eventually he ran out of money and returned home. A period of depression, emotional insecurity, feelings of guilt, and the need for support from others followed. Gradually, he was able to put himself back together. Although progress continued to be steady, occasional periods of running away followed by feelings of guilt and embarrassment occurred.

Although the youth eventually began to feel comfortable with his external situation, he feared the loss of security he had achieved on probation. He asked that his probation period be extended for another year. In order to be certain this would occur, he committed an additional minor traffic offense shortly before the end of probation. A tense court room scene occurred where he kept pleading guilty to the offense despite cries from his own attorney that he was not guilty and they could beat the ticket. The youth had strong needs to be found guilty which he believed would guarantee additional probation for him.

Progress. During the entire two year period he received only one minor traffic ticket which he deliberately caused himself. Otherwise, he was not charged with any additional offenses. Furthermore, during the second year, he usually avoided any kind of antisocial behavior.

The youth was able to complete his high school education. He maintained steady employment on a part time basis. He was able to obtain a full time job with a reputable firm and had good prospects for a career. He was very satisfied with the position. He paid off all debts and established an excellent credit rating for himself. Because of his excellent credit rating he was able to obtain a loan to purchase a new automobile which he used to reward himself for his past two years of accomplishments. The youth took great pride in himself and his accomplishments. He was better able to perceive himself as a successful person.

Post-Probation. Shortly after the probation period, he got married and tried to establish a home for himself. Unfortunately, the marriage did not go well and problems began to occur. The youth had invested much of himself with the fantasy of a good marital life and a comfortable family situation. He was very frustrated and unable to cope with his new life and domestic strife. He also felt too embarrassed to ask for more help through probation but instead began to experience some minor problems on the job and with social relationships. He incurred two additional alcohol-related offenses which finally forced him to his senses. He sought additional help on an informal basis. Another crisis in his life situation existed, but he could now deal directly with feelings about himself and self esteem, which he had been unable to do before.

Because he had been able to gain some successes for himself, he was better able to look at himself objectively and see some personal weaknesses. He met with a professional staff member for informal counseling, during which time the opportunity for development of greater understanding and insight occurred. He could only tolerate so much counseling, and the change was slow.

Following the short-term professional counseling, he entered yet another period of relative stability. For two years he led a generally healthy and productive life where he was very successful with his career. He has not had additional problems with the law. The question remains as to how long the young man will be able to lead a stable and productive life. He will probably always be vulnerable to some situational stress.

Volunteers—Twelve Ways to Help*

1. JOBS. Help generate interest and motivate the parolee or probationer to participate in vocational training. Identify vocational interests and aptitude through discussions and testing by local community resources such as State Employment, Vocational Rehabilitation, Adult Technical Education, Vocational Schools, and other means.

Assist in the actual enrollment and follow up with the youthful offender. Make contacts with training school, offender, family and others to encourage course completion. Assist in upgrading the underemployed who are not working up to employment potential.

Encourage job stability, punctuality, regular attendance, productiveness, proper notice for employment changes, regular employment and other job connected responsibilities.

2. EDUCATION. Encourage and motivate toward completion of high school. Suggest regular academic pursuits or completion of necessary requirement for General Equivalency (GED) Diploma. Enrollment in college programs and other educational programs is important when potential and interests are present.

3. LISTEN. One of the foremost qualifications of a good one-to-one volunteer is the ability to be a good listener. Much constructive therapy is administered through the art of merely allowing a person to "talk out" his or her problems. The venting of feelings offers great promise in therapeutic changes.

4. RELIGION. Religious and spiritual growth can provide the ingredients for a balanced and secure future. Character guidance

*Florida Parole and Probation Commission.

and moral values which are grounded in religious beliefs, can help strengthen the youthful offender's internal resources. Volunteers may encourage church attendance and provide counseling in areas within the offenders own denominational preferences. *(Volunteers should not propound their own denominational beliefs but leave this to the offenders' own choosing.)*

5. INSPIRE. Pointing out strengths and enthusiastic encouragement with an occasional "slap on the back" motivates many people to do their very best. The offender is no exception to the rule and he needs to experience some successes to bolster his ego, instill pride, and inspire greater achievement. Good influences change attitudes, appearance, mannerism, dress and other factors conducive to good adjustment.

6. FRIEND. "In poverty and other misfortunes of life, true friends are a sure refuge.—The young, they keep out of mischief; to the old they are a comfort and an aid in their weakness; and, to those in the prime of life they are an insight to noble deeds." *Aristotle*

Meaningful friendships and associations can provide the necessary influences which will permeate the lifestyle of the offender and leave indelible impressions and ideals toward successful living.

7. RESOURCES. Parolees, probationers, and mandatory conditional releases very seldom have developed hobbies and healthy recreational pursuits or cultural interests. Citizen volunteers can help broaden the offender's perspective and interests through exposure to cultural events, sports programs and other community activities which assist in self-improvement and enjoyment.

8. ALCOHOL. Excessive use of alcohol contributes to the plight of many law violators. Encouragement toward attendance at Alcoholics Anonymous meetings, counseling with family and fostering self-control provide services to offenders.

9. NARCOTICS. The abuse of drugs is a growing menace to the viability of our society especially in regard to the youth. Many youthful offenders placed on probation were convicted of a narcotic offense. Thousands of others have admitted the illegal use of drugs. Counseling in prevention, control, and the dangers of drug abuse are important areas of concentration. New interests

and associates can assist in overcoming problems of drug addiction and alcoholism.

10. VISIT. Personal contacts are important in rehabilitating criminal offenders. They need to know that someone cares and is interested in their future. Often they have not had the advantage of parental encouragement, direction, interest, or concern. Frequent and regular contacts by the volunteer helps solidify their relationship, gain confidence, and depict genuine interest.

11. STRUCTURED TREATMENT PROGRAMMING. The volunteer can serve as a catalyst for implementation of Structured Treatment Programming. This program employs principles of Management By Objectives whereby specific treatment goals are agreed upon, recruited, implemented and evaluated.

12. ADVISORY COMMITTEES. Serves as community members to identify problems and an accompanying solution in the parole and probation system with part emphasis on helping to improve rehabilitative effectiveness.

The above suggestions are not all inclusive and are intended to point out only a few areas of concentration. One-to-one volunteers may be involved in any combination of the above and in a host of other areas. By identifying the problems and assisting the offender in arriving at constructive solutions, the volunteer can make significant contributions in stabilizing the offender.

PART THREE - DISCUSSION TOPICS

1. Compare the various systems for classifying offenders.
2. Discuss social casework and how it is applied in probation/parole.
3. Discuss reality therapy and the easy acceptance that this method of treatment found in probation/parole.
4. Explain why behavior modification is a controversial method of treatment.
5. What is the importance of psychoanalytic theory to probation/parole practice?
6. Discuss the concept of *self-determination* in social casework, and how it is reconciled in probation/parole.

7. Explain why group work is considered a useful method of treatment in probation/parole.

8. Compare the supervision of probationers with the supervision of parolees.

9. Discuss the different types of probation/parole officer.

10. Analyze the importance of the "home visit" as a tool in probation/parole supervision.

11. Explore the problem of offender employment.

12. Contrast the different views of the law enforcement role of the probation/parole officer.

13. Analyze the John Fenton Case, applying the concepts and practices of sound probation and parole supervision.

14. Compare the different methods of appointing probation/parole officers.

15. Analyze the use of paraprofessionals and volunteers in probation/parole.

16. Discuss the use of ex-offenders as probation/parole officer aides.

PART FOUR

Programs and Research

Chapter 17

Interstate Compact

In 1937, a group of states signed the Interstate Compact for the Supervision of Probationers and Parolees. By 1951, all fifty states, Puerto Rico, and the Virgin Islands were signatories of the compact. The compact provides a method for a person under supervision to leave the state of conviction and proceed to another state for employment, family, or health reasons and, at the same time, guarantees that the receiving state will provide supervision of the offender. The state of original jurisdiction where the crime was committed retains authority over the offender and is kept advised of his whereabouts and activities.

Prior to the establishment of the compact, thousands of convicted felons were permitted to leave the state of conviction with no verified or approved plan in the receiving state. On occasion, dangerous criminals were released by states and permitted to enter other states without the knowledge of any official body of the receiving state. The compact provides a systematic method for supervision purposes for the receiving state to verify and approve a plan of residence and employment or education before the probationer or parolee is permitted to enter the state. The compact also regulates interstate travel by probationers and parolees. Each state issues a travel pass, a copy of which is sent to the Interstate Administrator, who notifies the receiving state of the impending visit.

The Association of Administrators of the Interstate Compact, which meets at least once per year, prepares uniform reports and procedures, and attempts to reconcile any difficulties that have arisen with respect to the compact. The Council of State Governments acts as a secretariat for the Association, and publishes the *Interstate Movement of Probationers and Parolees Under the Probation and Parole Compact.*

Some problems still remain. One problem exists because of the differences in probation and parole administration. In all states parole is an executive function with state-wide procedures; interstate activities are centralized through a compact administrator in each state. However, probation is often administered on a county basis, and it may lack state-wide coordination. The local autonomy that often exists in the court system can cause difficulties in utilizing and administering the pact in probation cases.

Another problem is the result of different approaches to supervision between states. One state may exercise close control and require strict enforcement of the conditions of probation or parole. Another state may be more flexible, or it may be incapable of close supervision and control because of the size of caseloads. When a "strict" state notifies a "liberal" sending state that one of its probationers or parolees is in violation, the sending state may not consider it serious, and leave the offender in the receiving state with a request that they continue supervision. In some cases, the sending state may not wish to incur the expense of transporting a violator back to one of its state prisons. The receiving state has two options: continue to supervise an offender it considers in violation, or discontinue supervision and leave the offender with no controls at all. P/p officers, faced with this dilemma, generally continue supervision, since it is preferable to leaving an offender without any controls.

States sometimes allow probationers and parolees to go to a receiving state under the guise of a visit, when the offender's intentions are to stay permanently. The receiving state is then contacted by the sending state to investigate "with a view towards accepting supervision." The receiving state is faced with a *fait accompli.*

Interstate Compact for the Supervision of Parolees and Probationers

Consented to by the Congress of the United States of America

1934

THE UNIFORM ENABLING ACT

(Contains the exact wording of the Interstate Compact for the Supervision of Parolees and Probationers)

AN ACT PROVIDING THAT THE STATE OF . . . MAY ENTER INTO A COMPACT WITH ANY OF THE UNITED STATES FOR MUTUAL HELPFULNESS IN RELATION TO PERSONS CONVICTED OF CRIME OR OFFENSES WHO MAY BE ON PROBATION OR PAROLE

Be it enacted, etc.:

SECTION 1. The governor of this state is hereby authorized and directed to execute a compact on behalf of the state of . . . . with any of the United States legally joining therein in the form substantially as follows:

A COMPACT

Entered into by and among the contracting states, signatories hereto, with the consent of the Congress of the United States of America, granted by an act entitled "An act granting the consent of Congress to any two or more states to enter into agreements or compacts for cooperative effort and mutual assistance in the prevention of crime and for other purposes."

The contracting states solemnly agree:

(1) That it shall be competent for the duly constituted judicial and administrative authorities of a state party to this compact (herein called "sending state"), to permit any person convicted of an offense within such state and placed on probation or released on parole to reside in any other state party to this compact (herein called "receiving state"), while on probation or parole, if

(a) Such person is in fact a resident of or has his family residing within the receiving state and can obtain employment there:

(b) Though not a resident of the receiving state and not having his family residing there, the receiving state consents to such person being sent there.

Before granting such permission, opportunity shall be granted to the receiving state to investigate the home and prospective employment of such person.

A resident of the receiving state, within the meaning of this section, is one who has been an actual inhabitant of such state continuously for more than one year prior to his coming to the sending state and has not resided within the sending state more than six continuous months immediately preceding the commission of the offense for which he has been convicted.

(2) That each receiving state will assume the duties of visitation of and supervision over probationers or parolees of any sending state and in the exercise of those duties will be governed by the same standards that prevail for its own probationers and parolees.

(3) That duly accredited officers of a sending state may at all times enter a receiving state and there apprehend and retake any person on probation or parole. For that purpose no formalities will be required other than establishing the authority of the officer and the identity of the person to be retaken. All legal requirements to obtain extradition of fugitives from justice are hereby expressly waived on the part of states party hereto, as to such persons. The decision of the sending state to retake a person on probation or parole shall be conclusive upon and not reviewable within the receiving state, *Provided, however,* That if at the time when a state seeks to retake a probationer or parolee there should be pending against him within the receiving state any criminal charge, or he should be suspected of having committed within such state a criminal offense, he shall not be retaken without the consent of the receiving state until discharged from prosecution or from imprisonment for such offense.

(4) That the duly accredited officers of the sending state will be permitted to transport prisoners being retaken through any and all states parties to this compact, without interference.

(5) That the governor of each state may designate an officer who, acting jointly with like officers of other contracting states, if and when appointed, shall promulgate such rules and regulations as may be deemed necessary to more effectively carry out the terms of this compact.

(6) That this compact shall become operative immediately upon its execution by any state as between it and any other state or states so executing. When executed it shall have the full force and effect of law within such state, the form of execution to be in accordance with the laws of the executing state.

(7) That this compact shall continue in force and remain binding upon each executing state until renounced by it. The duties and obligations hereunder of a renouncing state shall continue as to parolees or probationers residing therein at the time of withdrawal until retaken or finally discharged by the sending state. Renunciation of this compact shall be by the same authority which executed it, by sending six months' notice in writing of its intention to withdraw from the compact to the other state party hereto.

SEC. 2. If any section, sentence, subdivision or clause of this act is for any reason held invalid or to be unconstitutional, such decision shall not affect the validity of the remaining portions of this act.

SEC. 3. Whereas an emergency exists for the immediate taking effect of this act, the same shall become effective immediately upon its passage.

Application for Compact Services

Parole and Probation Interstate Compact

Form

TO: INTERSTATE BUREAU

I, ______________________, hereby apply to supervision as a parolee pursuant to the Interstate Compact for the Supervision of Parolees and Probationers. I understand that the very fact that supervision will be in another state makes it likely that there will be certain differences between the supervision I would receive in this state and the supervision which I will receive in any state to which I am asking to go. However, I urge the authorities to whom this application is made, and all other judicial and administrative authorities, to recognize that supervision in another state, if granted as requested in this application, will be a benefit to me and will improve my opportunities to make a good adjustment. In order to get the advantages of supervision under the Interstate

Compact for the Supervision of Parolees and Probationers, I do hereby accept such differences in the course and character of supervision as may be provided, and I do state that I consider the benefits of supervision under the Compact to be worth any adjustments in my situation which may be occasioned.

In view of the above, I do hereby apply for permission to be supervised on parole in ______________ (state), for the following reasons:

I (have read the above) (have had the above read and explained to me), and I understand its meaning and agree thereto.

Signature______________

Witnessed by ______________

Date: ______________

Parole and Probation Form III
Agreement to Return

SENDING STATE ______________
RECEIVING STATE ______________

RE: ______________

I, ______________, in consideration of being granted parole by the ______________ and especially being granted the privilege to leave the state of ______________ to go to ______________, hereby agree:

1. That I will make my home with ______________, until a change of residence is duly authorized by the proper authorities of ______________.
2. That I will comply with the conditions of parole/probation as fixed by both the states of ______________ and ______________.

3. That I will, when duly instructed by the ____ return at any time to the state of ______________________.

4. That I hereby do waive extradition to the state of ______________________ from any jurisdiction in or outside the United States where I may be found and also agree that I will not contest any effort by any jurisdiction to return me to the state of ______________________.

5. Failure to comply with the above will be deemed to be a violation of the terms and conditions of parole for which I may be returned to the state of ______________________.

DATED ________________

SIGNED ______________________

Witnesses:

____

____

On the ________ day of ________________ 19____, permission was granted to the above person to reside in the state of ______________________ and to be supervised by ______________________.

Signed: ______________________

Chapter 18

Offender Disabilities

The ABA reports that in all but five states and the federal system, offenders convicted of certain crimes are deprived of such civil rights as the right to vote, to hold office, or to serve on a jury.[1] Even more serious, because of its direct effect on rehabilitation, are civil disabilities that hinder an offender's efforts to gain certain types of employment. Daniel Glasser states that unemployment may be a major factor in causing recidivism,[2] and so any bar to offender employment can have adverse effects in probation and parole practice.

A special study by the ABA disclosed that there are 1,948 separate statutory provisions in the United States that affect the licensing of persons with conviction records. Connecticut was the highest with 80, while New Hampshire was among the lowest with 22.[3] For example, in order to qualify for a barber's license 45 jurisdictions have a requirement of "good moral character," which usually translates into not

[1] ABA, p. 54.

[2] James W. Hunt, James E. Bowers, and Neal Miller, *Laws Licenses and the Offender's Right to Work* (Washington, D.C.: American Bar Association, 1974), p. 1.

[3] *Ibid.*, p. 8.

having a criminal record, while 24 deny the license to an applicant convicted of a felony. Only four states—Alabama, Massachusetts, New Hampshire, and South Carolina—have no statutory restrictions for licensing ex-offenders as barbers.[4]

Ten states—Arkansas, California, Connecticut, Indiana, Iowa, Louisiana, Missouri, New Jersey, New York, and Pennsylvania—have laws that place restrictions on ex-offenders involved in the manufacturing, retailing, wholesaling, or distribution of alcoholic beverages. Occupations that are affected by these laws include waiters, bartenders, dishwashers, deliverymen, and all other occupations related to business establishments where alcoholic beverages are sold or consumed.[5]

Other restricted occupations include manicurist (16 jurisdictions), chauffeur (12 jurisdictions), and masseur (12 jurisdictions). Professional occupations such as doctor, dentist, accountant, teacher, and lawyer are also barred to ex-offenders in various jurisdictions.[6]

In the probation and parole field it is the prevailing belief that if there is to be any bar to employment for ex-offenders, it should be directly related to the occupation or profession. For example, a state might restrict the issuance of a pharmacy license to persons with a record of narcotic law violations. The ABA states that "We expect our corrections system to correct, but we hinder that process by allowing the former offender to be subjected to continued penalties through restrictions that deny him fair consideration for a job or license even after he has supposedly paid his debt to society."[7]

In an effort to correct these restrictions and make employment easier for the ex-offender, some states, such as Florida and Illinois, have removed statutory restrictions for employment of ex-offenders. Maine has done the same by executive order, and Connecticut and Hawaii have enacted fair employment laws that benefit ex-offenders.[8] In 1966 the City of New York ended its 50-year-old policy of automatically rejecting ex-offenders, and probationers and parolees are now employed by the City of New York.[9]

[4] *Ibid.*, p. 9.

[5] *Ibid.*, p. 10.

[6] *Ibid.*, pp. 11–12.

[7] *Ibid.*, p. 17.

[8] Committee on Youth and Corrections, *Civil Disabilities* (New York: Community Service Society, 1973), p. 14.

[9] *Task Force Report*, p. 34.

RELIEF FROM DISABILITIES

States vary in the method and extent to which they provide relief from the civil disabilities incurred by probationers and parolees. The pardon, which is available in all states, is one method, but it is rarely used. At least 13 states have adopted automatic restoration procedures upon completion of probation or parole.[10] About a quarter of the states have statutes designed to restore forfeited rights, although they may be subjected to restrictive interpretation in licensing and occupational areas.[11] In certain states, such as New York, the judiciary and the parole board have the power to restore certain rights.

BONDING

Employment that requires bonding has presented a problem in probation and parole practice. Bonding companies are usually reluctant, if not unwilling, to bond certain ex-offenders. In order to alleviate this problem, the federal government has provided for the issuance of bonds of from $500 to $10,000 for ex-offenders. However, the limit of the bond is 18 months, and within that time an employer must assimilate the person into his regular bonding program or drop the bonding requirement.[12]

Washington Statute Removing Offender Employment Restrictions

House Bill No. 337

AN ACT Relating to removing the disqualification of felons from certain employment; adding a new chapter to Title 9 RCW; and declaring an effective date.

BE IT ENACTED BY THE LEGISLATURE OF THE STATE OF WASHINGTON:

[10] Merril A. Smith, *As A Matter of Fact* . . . (Washington, D.C.: The Federal Judicial Center, 1973), p. R-6.

[11] *Ibid.*

[12] Personal correspondence from the New York State Bonding Coordinator.

New Section. Section 1. The legislature declares that it is the policy of the state of Washington to encourage and contribute to the rehabilitation of felons and to assist them in the assumption of the responsibilities of citizenship, and the opportunity to secure employment or to pursue, practice or engage in a meaningful and profitable trade, occupation, vocation, profession or business is an essential ingredient to rehabilitation and the assumption of the responsibilities of citizenship.

New Section. Sec. 2. Notwithstanding any other provisions of law to the contrary, a person shall not be disqualified from employment by the state of Washington or any of its agencies or political subdivisions, nor shall a person be disqualified to practice, pursue or engage in any occupation, trade, vocation, or business for which a license, permit, certificate or registration is required to be issued by the state of Washington or any of its agencies or political subdivisions, or a person may be denied a license, permit, certificate or registration to pursue, practice or engage in an occupation, trade, vocation, or business by reason of the prior conviction of a felony if the felony for which he was convicted directly relates to the position of employment sought or to the specific occupation, trade, vocation, or business for which the license, permit, certificate or registration is sought, and the time elapsed since the conviction is less than ten years.

New Section. Sec. 3. This chapter shall not be applicable to any law enforcement agency; however, nothing herein shall be construed to preclude a law enforcement agency in its discretion from adopting the policy set forth in this chapter.

New Section. Sec. 4. Any complaints or grievances concerning the violation of this chapter shall be processed and adjudicated in accordance with the procedures set forth in chapter 34.04 RCW, the administrative procedure act.

New Section. Sec. 5. The provisions of this chapter shall prevail over any other provisions of law which purport to govern the denial of licenses, permits, certificates, registrations, or other means to engage in a business, on the grounds of a lack of good moral character, or which purport to govern the suspension or revocation of such a license, permit, certificate, or registration on the grounds of conviction of a crime.

New Section. Sec. 6. Sections 1 through 5 of this act shall constitute a new chapter in Title 9 RCW.

New Section. Sec. 7. This act shall take effect on July 1, 1973.

New York State Relief from Civil Disabilities

LAWS GOVERNING THE ISSUANCE OF CERTIFICATES OF RELIEF FROM DISABILITIES

(The laws governing the issuance of certificates of relief from disabilities are set forth in Article 23 of the New York State Correction Law. The excerpts below summarize certain portions of those laws and are set forth merely for convenience. They are not intended as administrative interpretations and they do not relieve any party of full knowledge of and compliance with the applicable provisions of law.)

This certificate is issued to relieve the holder, an "eligible offender" as defined in § 700 of the Correction Law, of all or of enumerated forfeitures, disabilities, or bars to employment automatically imposed by law by reason of his conviction of the crime or offense specified on the face of this certificate.

This certificate shall be considered a "temporary certificate" where (1) issued by a court to a holder who is under a "revocable sentence" as defined in § 700 of the Correction Law and the court's authority to revoke such sentence has not expired, or (2) issued by the State Board of Parole and the holder is still under the supervision of the Board. Where the holder is under a revocable sentence, this certificate may be revoked by the court for violation of the conditions of such sentence and shall be revoked by the court if it revokes the sentence and commits the holder to an institution under the jurisdiction of the State Department of Correctional Services. Where the holder is subject to the supervision of the State Board of Parole, this certificate may be revoked by the Board for violation of the conditions of parole or release. Any such revocation shall be upon notice and after an opportunity to be heard. If this certificate is not so revoked, it shall become a permanent certificate upon expiration or termination of the court's authority to revoke the sentence or upon termination of the jurisdiction of the Board of Parole over the holder.

RIGHTS OF RELIEF FROM DISABILITIES

A. Where the certificate is issued by a court at the time sentence is pronounced, it covers forfeitures as well as disabilities. In any other case the certificate applies only to disabilities.

B. A conviction of the crime or the offense specified on the face of this certificate shall NOT cause automatic forfeiture of any license, permit, employment or franchise, including the right to register for or vote at an election, or automatic forfeiture of any other right or privilege, held by the eligible offender and *covered* by the certificate. Nor shall such conviction be deemed to be a conviction within the meaning of any provision of law that imposes, by reason of a conviction, a bar to any employment, a disability to exercise any right or a disability to apply for or to receive any license, permit or other authority or privilege, covered by the certificate. Provided, however, that no such certificate shall apply, or be construed so as to apply, to the right of such person to retain or to be eligible for public office.

C. A conviction of the crime or the offense specified on the face of this certificate shall NOT prevent any judicial, administrative, licensing or other body, board or authority from relying upon the conviction specified on the reverse side of this certificate as the basis for the exercise of its discretionary power to suspend, revoke, refuse to issue or renew any license, permit or other authority or privilege.

Chapter 19

Special Programs and Research

This chapter will provide a review of some of the more widely discussed programs and research projects in the probation and parole field.

PRE-TRIAL PROBATION

The President's Commission noted that prosecutors often deal with offenders who need treatment or supervision, but for whom criminal sanctions would be excessive.[1] Programs implementing this theory are referred to by many names, including *pre-trial diversion* and *deferred prosecution.* These programs use the fact that an arrest has occurred as a means of identifying defendants in need of treatment, or, at least, not in need of criminal prosecution. They generally incorporate specific eligibility criteria, a treatment program, and the opportunity to monitor and control the decision not to prosecute. In eligible cases, the prosecutor agrees not to prosecute for periods ranging from three to twelve months, contingent upon satisfactory performance during the

[1] *The Challenge of Crime in a Free Society,* p. 331.

pre-trial supervision period. At the end of a successful pre-trial supervision period, the charges are dismissed. Diversion helps to remove minimal risk cases from crowded court calendars, while providing treatment to those who are in need of this service.[2]

In New York City, the five district attorneys had the resources of the Youth Counsel Bureau which provided counseling for young offenders aged sixteen to twenty. (This Bureau has been discontinued because of the New York City budget crisis, as of June 1976.) These are youngsters that have been arrested and charged with a crime, but had prosecution deferred or the charges dismissed and the case turned over to the bureau for supervision. The YCB stresses getting youngsters into military service, in addition to employment and other types of counseling.

A much publicized program is the Genessee County (Michigan) Citizen's Probation Authority, which began operations in 1965. The program began using volunteers with social work and other related professional backgrounds, but has been expanded to include paid staff. Most of the CPA cases are adults who agree to submit to supervision in return for not being prosecuted. At the end of the supervision period, charges are dropped and police records are expunged.[3] In order to qualify for the CPA program, a defendant must not have committed a crime of violence or possess an extensive criminal history.[4]

The Des Moines Pre-Trial Release Project is patterned after the well-known Vera Project in New York City, and it permits defendants who are not able to make bail to be released on their own recognizance under the supervision of a counselor. Each defendant is interviewed after arraignment by a program interviewer who is a part-time court employee recruited from the Drake University Law School. If the defendant is unable to provide for his own bond, and is considered a safe risk, he is released on recognizance pending trial. The program is aimed at persons who, though without sufficient financial assets, have significant family and community ties to guarantee their appearance in court. The program is directed primarily at lesser offenders, although persons accused of serious crimes will be considered under more stringent procedures.

[2] Joan Mullen, *The Dilemma of Diversion* (Washington, D.C.: Government Printing Office, 1974), pp. 5–6.

[3] As a practical reality, this may be difficult, if not impossible, to accomplish.

[4] National District Attorney's Association, *Screening of Criminal Cases* (Chicago: NDAA Publications Department, 1973), p. 26.

The program proceeds on the basis of the following observation: A defendant who is incarcerated while awaiting trial has the probability of his obtaining probation reduced "because of his inability to obtain or maintain those positive personal and environmental circumstances that courts look to in evaluating an individual's potential for community rehabilitation." [5] Emanating from this is the use of pre-trial supervision that is geared to helping defendants to "cope with problems, aiding the development of a more stable behavior pattern for the defendant and thereby obtaining a more favorable disposition of his case." [6] The program does not concern itself with the guilt or innocence of the defendant.

Deferred prosecution is not without its critics. Gaylin cites an unnamed judge: "Deferred prosecution is what it is called, and in effect it means no prosecution. You postpone a criminal case indefinitely, you lose your witnesses—that's the end of it." [7] From a different perspective, deferred prosecution is criticized by Balch as the "juvenilization" of the adult criminal process, with all of the inherent defects in due process of the "pre-Gault" juvenile court. Balch notes that while a defendant must volunteer for these programs, his alternatives may be quite limited. For the innocent defendant, accepting the program means that he is admitting guilt, even if he is not doing so in the legal sense of the term.[8]

Mullen notes that while the overwhelming majority of programs do not require an admission of guilt, there is a presumption of guilt inherent in the system. She notes that if defendants fail on pre-trial supervision, they are returned for prosecution that may be more vigorous than the original prosecution without any intervention would have been. Mullen states that in attempting to circumvent basic deficiencies in the administration of criminal justice (such as crowded court calendars) "a new system with its own attractions and deficiencies has begun to mature without furnishing convincing evidence that it has seriously affected the basic problems that attend the pre-trial criminal process." She suggests that greater efforts should be made to deal with the problem of delay in disposing of court cases or moving release or diversion back to an earlier stage, perhaps "pre-arrest." She concludes

[5] Mullen, p. 17.

[6] *Ibid.*, p. 19.

[7] Gaylin, p. 110.

[8] Robert W. Balch, "Deferred Prosecution: The Juvenilization of the Criminal Justice System," *Federal Probation* (June 1974), pp. 46–50.

that "the generous resources many diversion programs have enjoyed might play an important part in the ability of probation to function as a viable sentencing alternative."[9]

As a result of the concern expressed over the waiver of rights attendant to these programs, some have begun to provide legal counsel before a defendant is asked to agree to diversion. Nancy Goldberg states that "In order to ensure that any decision by a prospective divertee is truly voluntary, counsel must become involved from the very outset." [10] The National Advisory Commission states that "Emphasis should be placed on the offender's right to be represented by counsel during negotiations for diversion and entry and approval of the agreement."[11]

An example of a pre-arrest diversion program is the Columbus, Ohio, Night Prosecutor's Program which handles cases involving interpersonal disputes. The program, which began in 1971, uses law students as hearing officers for cases that are referred by the police or prosecutor's office. Arrests are avoided and no record of the case is entered on any official documents, although records are kept by the program in order to provide background if any of the parties return. The hearings are informal, allowing each party to tell his side of the story without interuption. When sanctions are necessary to insure compliance with a decision, the program uses *prosecutor's probation*, whereby a person is on probation for 60 days. If the conditions of probation are violated, the filing of a criminal affidavit is authorized.[12]

Discharge Order: Deferred Sentence

In the District Court of the State of Iowa in and for Polk County

Name______________ Crime______________

Address______________ Judge______________

Date of Sentence________ Length of Sentence________

STATE OF IOWA,

[9] Mullen, pp. 29–34.

[10] Nancy Goldberg, "Pre-Trial Diversion: Bilk or Bargain," a reprint from the World Correctional Center, Chicago, p. 500.

[11] *Ibid.*

[12] John W. Palmer, "Pre-Arrest Diversion: Victim Confrontation," *Federal Probation* (Sept. 1974), pp. 12–18.

Plaintiff, CRIMINAL NO.____________

vs.

Defendant

ORDER
DISCHARGE

NOW, on this ____ day of ________, 19____, it appearing to the Court that the above named defendant entered a plea of guilty to the indictment in the above entitled cause: and,

WHEREAS the Court, after investigation, placed the defendant on Probation under the supervision of the Department of Court Services; until the ____ day of ________, 19____, and,

WHEREAS the said defendant has fully complied with the conditions of said probation, and has earned and received the recommendation from the Probation Officer and the County Attorney of Polk County, Iowa; and

WHEREAS the said defendant now be permitted to withdraw the plea of guilty and that the motion to dismiss this case be sustained.

IT IS THEREFORE ORDERED that the defendant be, and is hereby authorized to withdraw a plea of guilty; that the withdrawal of the plea of guilty is accepted by this Court; and the motion to dismiss this case with prejudice be and the same is hereby sustained.

Dated at Des Moines, Iowa this ____ day of ________, 19____.

____
JUDGE

APPROVED:

________________ ________________
PROBATION OFFICER COUNTY ATTORNEY

PROBATION SUBSIDY

Kobartz and Bosarge define the probation subsidy as "a plan to encourage counties to reduce their rates of commitment to state correctional institutions in return for a reward that is commensurate with the degree of reduction they achieve."[13] Smith labels the program as "a form of behavioral modification applied to a social institution—probation."[14] Like numerous other programs, the subsidy is a California innovation. Probation in California is operated and financed on a county basis, and prior to the 1965 subsidy law, probation standards for the 58 counties were voluntary. The probation subsidy is based on three assumptions:[15]

1. Probation is as effective, if not more effective, than most institutional forms of correctional care;
2. probation is the least costly correctional service available; and
3. probation grants can be increased without substantially increasing the number of crimes committed by probationers. On the basis of several studies it was concluded that probation use by county courts could be expanded safely, thus diverting a substantial number of juvenile and adults away from state correctional institutions. These studies concluded that in order to expand the use of probation, the state must offer financial incentives: "Excessive probation caseloads and rising tax rates at the county level encouraged the probation officer to dispose of probation cases by recommending commitment to the Youth Authority or Department of Corrections."[16]

The subsidy program provides state funds to counties for not committing defendants to state institutions. The more cases not sent to prison, the greater the subsidy. Counties are reimbursed in proportion to the number of cases that are placed on probation in lieu of prison. The level of funding is determined by taking a county's commitment rate for a representative period, thereby providing a yardstick (base experience rate) for measurement. Reductions in commitments are measured against the yardstick and used to determine the level of the subsidy for the county. Thus, if on the basis of a county's population and base experience rate the state could reasonably expect the county to commit 100 persons, but in fact the county only sent 90, then a ten percent reduction was realized. These ten cases represent a savings to the state, and the county is then reimbursed a portion of the money saved. Actual reimbursement varies from county to county based on

[13] Kobartz and Bosarge, p. 339.

[14] Robert L. Smith, *A Quiet Revolution* (Washington, D.C.: Government Printing Office, 1971), pp. 2–3.

[15] *Ibid.*, p. 5.

[16] *Ibid.*, pp. 8–10.

the differences between them and the amount of effort that is required for a county to make a reduction.[17]

The program, which began in 1966, had 45 counties participating by 1971, and there have been substantial reductions in commitments with a corresponding percentage increase in the proportion of persons placed in probation. Other states without probation subsidies have also experienced a reduction in commitments, although Smith states that the reduction in California was roughly twice as great for those counties in the subsidy program as for those not participating in the program. Smith also cites some shortcomings of the program:

payment tables have not been adjusted as was originally intended;

inflation has eaten into the earnings of the probation departments, forcing a reduction in the level of special effort, in spite of their increased earnings;

in the area of training, probation departments have not made as effective use of the training resources as was expected;

many probation departments have not come to grips with the principle of classification which matches offender's needs with available staff resources;

there has been too little research, too little use of volunteers and case aides (paraprofessionals), and too much copying of someone else's ideas regardless of their appropriateness;

there has been a lack of development of halfway houses for adults, or day service centers that were originally expected; and

there has not been an enrichment of county jail services by probation departments working in concert with county sheriffs, except in a few counties.[18]

Other criticisms have been leveled:

a substantial amount of funds have been unused and thus lost to the counties;

many of the participants have been disappointed about the state's failure to keep pace with rising costs;

because the subsidy is funded on an annual basis, treatment is forced

[17] *Ibid.*, p. 28.

[18] *Ibid.*, pp. 85–86.

into an artificial time schedule, and the constantly changing commitment rate is a confusing factor;

judges' philosophies differ widely and affect the commitment rate; and

there is concern over the rate of arrests of subsidized probationers as compared to non-subsidy cases.[19]

Barkdull notes that although the subsidy in California was able to reduce the percentage of convicted adult felony defendants sentenced to prison, this trend has been reversed by the passage of laws restricting the granting of probation and mandating prison commitments.[20]

COMMUNITY TREATMENT PROJECT (CTP)

This two-part research project was designed "to find out if certain kinds of juvenile offenders could be allowed to remain right in their home communities, if given rather intensive supervision and treatment within a small-sized parole caseload." [21] The first phase took place during 1961–1969, during which the CTP used California Youth Authority parole agents to supervise caseloads of 12 youths aged 13 to 19. Excluded from the experiment were youths who had committed such serious crimes as armed robbery, assault with a deadly weapon, or forcible rape. For purposes of research two groups were randomly selected:

1. *Experimentals:* youths placed directly into the intensive CTP program without prior institutionalization; and
2. *Controls:* youths sent to an institution for several months prior to being returned home and given routine supervision within standard CYA caseloads.

The *experimentals* were classified into the following categories, based on an evaluation of personality characteristics:

a. Passive Conformist. This type of youth usually fears, and responds with strong compliance to, peers and adults who he thinks have the

[19] Carney, p. 310.

[20] Walter L. Barkdull, "Letter to the Editor," *Crime and Delinquency* (Apr. 1976), p. 230.

[21] Ted Palmer, "The Youth Authority's Community Treatment Project," *Federal Probation* (Mar. 1974), p. 3.

"upper hand" at the moment, or who seem more adequate and assertive than himself. He considers himself to be lacking in social "know-how," and usually expects to be rejected by others in spite of his efforts to please them.

b. Power Oriented. This group is actually made up of two somewhat different kinds of individuals, who, nevertheless, share several important features with one another. The first likes to think of himself as delinquent and tough. He is often more than willing to "go along" with others, or with a gang, in order to earn a certain degree of status and acceptance, and to later maintain his "reputation." The second type, or "subtype," often attempts to undermine or circumvent the efforts and directions of authority figures. Typically, he does not wish to conform to peers or adults; and not infrequently, he will attempt to assume a leading "power role" for himself.

Passive Conformist and Power Oriented youths are usually thought of as having reached a "middle maturity" level of interpersonal development. The group which is described next is said to have reached a "higher maturity" level.

c. Neurotic. Here again, we find two separate personality types which share certain important characteristics with one another. The first type often attempts to deny—to himself and others—his conscious feelings of inadequacy, rejection, or self-condemnation. Not infrequently, he does this by verbally attacking *others* and/or by the use of boisterous distractions plus a variety of "games." The second type often shows various symptoms of emotional disturbance—e.g., chronic or intense depression, or psychosomatic complaints. His tensions and conscious fears usually result from conflicts produced by feelings of failure, inadequacy, or underlying guilt.[22]

Each *experimental* was matched with a parole agent on the basis of the youth's personality or distinguishing behavior pattern in order to make the best use of the agent's particular skills and interests. The intensive supervision included a ready access to the agent by the youth and extensive surveillance by the agent, extending into evening and weekend hours. There was a ready availability of such support services as group homes and cultural or recreational activities.

Palmer reports that the results of Phase I indicate that boys who participated in the CTP program did substantially better than those in the control group during the typical two- to four-year duration of their CYA supervision. Those in category *a* seemed to perform somewhat better in CTP than in the traditional CYA program. Category *b* showed no difference, and category *c* youths performed somewhat better.

[22] *Ibid.*

Experimental girls in the program performed as well as in the regular CYA program—there was no significant difference between *experimentals* and *controls*. Palmer reports that there did not appear to be any significant financial differences in expenditures for the experimental program or the conventional CYA program.[23]

The second phase, 1969–74, was geared to correcting the deficiencies in the project relative to the 25–35% of the experimentals who were in trouble despite the intensive supervision. Phase II included the use of institutional treatment for the experimentals, who were randomly selected from males 13 to 21. (The higher age group in Phase II meant the inclusion of non-juvenile court commitments.) The experimentals were placed into one of two treatment possibilities on the basis of an evaluation of each case:

1. initial assignment to an intensive, CTP staffed and operated residential program—later to be followed by release to the intensive supervision program as operated in Phase I; or
2. direct release to intensive supervision as in Phase I.

The CTP residential program consisted of a small facility for about 25 youths, who were treated by carefully selected staff. Their program was considered superior to the routine CYA treatment facility. Eligibility for the experiment was expanded to include some categories ineligible in Phase I. These youngsters constituted a separate group for research purposes.

The results of Phase II indicated that for category *a* response to the CTP's residential facility has been unfavorable: for category *b* the use of the residence did not significantly change the outcome of the case; and category *c* youths were helped significantly by first being placed in the CTP residence. Palmer concludes that "CTP's originally stated ideal—that of changing delinquents into lifelong nondelinquents—is not being achieved in the large majority of cases. Nevertheless, the 'differential treatments' and 'differential settings' which have been utilized in this program do seem capable of *reducing* the total volume of delinquent behavior on the part of many, but by no means all, eligible males."[24]

There has been considerable criticism of the CTP research. Robinson and Smith suggest that the *experimentals* were no less delinquent

[23] *Ibid.*, pp. 3–7.

[24] *Ibid.*, p. 12.

than the *controls* but that the administrative treatment received affected case outcomes: they were less likely to have their parole revoked.[25] Martinson states that the *experimentals* were actually committing more offenses than the *controls*, but they were being treated more leniently while the *controls* were being revoked for lesser violations. He concludes that the study indicated "not so much a change in the behavior of the experimental youths as a change in the behavior of the experimental *probation officers*, who knew the 'special status' of their charges and who had evidently decided to revoke probation status at a lower than normal rate." [26]

Ohio's Shock Parole*

An Ohio law makes it possible for offenders to be released from prison six months after sentencing. The "shock parole" statute specifies that shock parole may be granted to a prisoner any time after he has served six months provided that:

> The offense for which he was sentenced is not aggravated murder or murder.
>
> The prisoner is not a second offender.
>
> The prisoner is not a dangerous offender.
>
> The prisoner does not appear to need future confinement as part of his correction or rehabilitation.
>
> The prisoner gives evidence that he is not likely to commit another offense and that he will respond affirmatively to early release on parole.

Of 600 persons studied since the law went into effect, only one person has had to be returned to prison. The average offender released was "spared" 2½ years incarceration. Under normal procedure, a person sentenced to ten years is not eligible for parole for six years, four months; three-year sentence, for two years, two months; one-year sentence, for ten months.

[25] Edelfonso, p. 345.

[26] Martinson, p. 44.

*Information from Ohio Adult Authority.

Before the end of the year it is expected that some 900 offenders may be released. With capital costs of new construction increasing rapidly and with imprisonment costs skyrocketing, shock parole is economically attractive. Some 25% of the offenders released were persons convicted of narcotic offenses. Many of these persons received "draconian" sentences of 10 to 20 years for "victimless" type offenses.

Since Ohio is the first state to enact such a law, an extensive research effort to assess the effect is being conducted by Prof. Joseph Scott of the Ohio State University through the university's Center for the Study of Crime and Delinquency. The study will measure the effects of the law on law enforcement, time saved, inmate population, etc.

Enactment of the shock parole law was prompted by the success of the state shock probation law, operating since October 1965. Under this law, judges are authorized to release convicted felons after 130 days or less. (Shock parole is administered by the Division of Parole and Community Services, whose parole board has the sole authority for selecting and releasing qualified prisoners.)

In Ohio, under the shock probation law, an offender is sentenced to a correctional institution and must file a petition to the court to suspend further execution of the sentence no earlier than 30, nor later than 60, days after the original sentence date. The court must act upon the petition within 90 days. In addition, the judge has the option of granting early release on his own initiative. Several states have a similar system whereby an offender is sentenced to incarceration for a specific, relatively short, period, followed by probation.[27] This is sometimes referred to as the *split sentence.*

According to the Ohio Adult Authority, of the "shock parole" hearings conducted in 1975, final decisions were made in 2,762 cases, with the remaining 1,708 cases being continued. Of those in which decisions were made, early parole releases were granted to 717 offenders or 16 percent of the total considered. In the other 2,045 cases, paroles were denied.

Departmental regulations governing operation of the "shock parole" program were revised during fiscal year 1975 to exclude

[27] Information from Ohio Adult Authority.

from early release consideration offenders convicted of a number of more serious and assaultive crimes.

While the original "shock parole" law ruled out only those convicted of murder and aggravated murder, the revised regulations, which became effective March 1, 1975, also excluded offenders convicted of first degree felonies, such as forcible rape, armed robbery, kidnapping and some burglaries.

Also denied "shock parole" consideration by the revised regulations were offenders convicted of major narcotic law violations, such as the sale of drugs and possession of drugs for sale.

The split sentence and shock probation/parole have been criticized by the National Advisory Commission: "This type of sentence defeats the purpose of probation, which is the earliest possible reintegration of the offender into the community. Short-term commitment subjects the probationer to the destructive effects of institutionalization, disrupts his life in the community, and stigmatizes him for having been in jail." [28]

CONTRACT PAROLE—MUTUAL AGREEMENT PROGRAMS (MAP)

Several states (Maryland, Florida, Georgia, Maine, Massachusetts, Michigan, Minnesota, North Carolina, Wisconsin, and the District of Columbia) are using a form of release from prison called a *mutual agreement*. At the end of 1975 there were about 4000 inmates involved in such programs.[29] Under the MAP concept, parole, and institutional authorities and the participating inmates agree to a three-way contractual agreement: [30]

1. Prisoners must assume responsibility for planning (with prison staff) and successfully completing an individually tailored rehabilitative program to obtain parole release at a mutually agreed upon date;
2. Parole board members must establish a firm parole date and honor it if the inmate fulfills the explicit, objective, and mutually agreed upon criteria for release;

[28] Nat. Adv. Comm., p. 321.

[29] Steve Gettinger, "Parole Contracts: A New Way Out," *Corrections Magazine* (Sept. 1975), pp. 3–4.

[30] Anne H. Rosenfeld, *An Evaluative Summary of Research: MAP Program Outcomes in the Initial Demonstration States* (College Park, Md.: American Correctional Association, 1975), p. 1.

Annual Institutional Commitment Rate, "Shock" Probation Rate and Commitment of "Shock" Probation Cases in Number and Percents

Calendar Year	*Shock Cases by Number*	*Shock Cases Recommitted by Number**	*Shock Cases Recommitted by Percent**
1966	85	5	5.8
1967	183	26	14.2
1968	294	18	6.1
1969	480	48	10.0
1970	632	68	10.7
1971	907	83	9.2
1972	1,292	115	8.9
1973	1,132	137	12.1
1974	1,079	118	10.9
1975	1,454	171	11.8
TOTALS	7,538	789	10.4

* Does not show probationers who absconded supervision.

Source: Ohio Adult Authority, 1975.

3. Institution staff must provide the services and training resources required by prisoners and must fairly assess their performance in the program.

Rosenfeld reports that MAP was developed in response to criticism that parole authorities were not considering participation in training programs in making release decisions. She states that "Underlying these problems was the frequent arbitrariness of Parole Boards in deciding release readiness." [31]

Different states have adapted the basic model to fit their own circumstances. Maryland, for example, has a contract parole voucher system for all women inmates. They are eligible for up to $3000 in vouchers in order to buy services, usually educational and vocational, largely from outside the institution, that are needed to fulfill their contracts. Massachusetts includes restitution for victims in an inmate's contract. While some states negotiate a date with the inmate, in other states the parole board sets the date without negotiations.

Supporters of MAP, such as the American Correctional Association, state that it forces correctional officials to review their programs and account for the availability and effectiveness of prison programs. They

[31] *Ibid.*, p. 3.

indicate that it is effective in holding down prison tension and for maintaining prison discipline. MAP is also viewed as a "screening device" that helps to identify "good risks" for parole. The American Correctional Association, through its Parole-Corrections Project, is a major force behind MAP.

The ACA is candid in reporting that on the basis of two early MAP projects, "it appears that prisoner rehabilitation is not MAP's major area of benefit." In addition, despite the certainty of the release date and the objective criteria utilized, "the program has not yet provided demonstrable time savings in prison terms." [32]

Critics maintain that many states are unable to provide for meaningful programs, the cost of which may be prohibitive; other states are concerned about the possibility of inmate lawsuits over the contracts. Some critics maintain that the contract is used to impose arbitrary and senseless requirements on inmates. Some observers point out the obvious: completion of contract terms does not necessarily mean that an inmate is rehabilitated or that he should be released. Ennis Olgiati, the late Chairman of the New York State Board of Parole, refers to the need to build a "just desserts" model into the parole release process.

States that are experimenting with the program have been receiving federal grants. Without this assistance states may not be willing to continue the plethora of training, educational, and therapeutic programs that must be provided if MAP is to be meaningful. Jacobs and Steele express concern about providing enriched services to offenders: "We should not be blackmailed. That prisoners can wreak more damage on the society if they are not appeased should not move us to treat them better. Their needs should be weighed against and in relation to the needs of other disadvantaged persons." [33]

Sample Contracts

Health and Social Services
Division of Corrections
Form C-205

1. MUTUAL AGREEMENT PROGRAMMING CONTRACT
WISCONSIN

Preamble

This Indenture made this day between John Doe, party of the first part, and Wisconsin Correctional Institution, the Wisconsin Parole Board, and the Wisconsin Department of Health and Social Services, by the Secretary thereof, parties of the second part:

Witnesseth that for and in consideration of the mutual covenants and promises hereinafter set forth, upon all parties hereto being fully and completely informed in the particulars, and upon merging and incorporating herein all prior offers, covenants, and agreements, the parties do hereby contract, covenant and agree as follows:

Part I Inmate

I, John Doe, understand and agree to successfully complete* the objectives

[32] *Ibid.*, p. 57.

[33] James B. Jacobs and Eric H. Steele, "Prisons: Instruments of Law Enforcement or Social Welfare," *Crime and Delinquency* (Oct. 1975), p. 353.

as they are specifically outlined in Part IV below in consideration for a specific date of parole. I understand that, at any time, I may petition for a renegotiation of this contract. I will to the best of my ability carry out the objectives of this contract, and realize that failure to do so will cancel and negate the contract.

*Successfully Complete—For the purposes of this contract "successfully complete" shall mean completed with a passing grade or evaluation of satisfactory, within the reasonable capabilities of the inmate, for the specific program or service objective being evaluated by the responsible staff member assigned to the individual program or service objective.

Part II Institution

I, David A. Johnson, representing the Wisconsin Correctional Institution, agree to provide the necessary program and services specified in Part IV below to enable John Doe to timely and successfully complete the objectives of and perform this contract.

Part III Parole Board

I Donald L. Quatsoe, of the Wisconsin Parole Board, representing the Secretary of the Department of Health and Social Services, agree that the above named inmate will be paroled on or before August 10, 1976, CONTINGENT UPON HIS SUCCESSFUL COMPLETION of the objectives mentioned below as certified to me by the State MAP Project Coordinator.

Part IV Objectives

1. Skill Training
Complete Basic Welding and complete present phase of Blueprint Reading.

2. Work Assignment
Continue work assignment when not in school.

3. Education
Complete preparation for and take HED. If not passed re-study and again take the HED.

4. Treatment
Continue Indian group participation. Become involved in a minimum of eight (8) counseling sessions. The sessions must be with a professional WCI staff member; areas to be covered in the counseling will include former problems associated with the use of alcohol and successful problem solving methods for the future. Other areas may be included by mutual agreement.

5. Discipline

6. Other
The negotiating team endorses, encourages and promotes a change of program to a minimum security setting after completing the objectives under No. 1, 3 and 4. If the HED diploma is received after taking the test in November, this contract can be renegotiated for an earlier parole date.

Prisoner's Name John Doe Number 99999-A

Target Release Date August 10, 1976 Date This Sheet Prepared November 9, 1975.

Part V Interpretation Provisions

Contract cancellation, negation or renegotiation shall take place in accordance with the terms and provisions of the approved Wisconsin Model, August, 1972, for Mutual Agreement Programming as amended and in effect on the date hereof. All questions, issues or disputes respecting determination of successful completion of any contract program or service objective shall be decided by the MAP Project Coordinator. Prior to his decision the Project Coordinator shall consult with both the inmate and the program staff member who made the evaluation respecting successful completion, and, in the Coordinator's discretion, he may mediate and consult jointly with the inmate and staff member respecting such question or dispute, or with any other person having material factual information regarding such question or dispute. The decision of the Project Coordinator shall be in writing and shall set forth the facts on which it is based and shall state the reasons for the decision. The project Coordinator's decision shall be final and binding on all parties hereto.

IN WITNESS WHEREOF the parties undersigned have hereunto set their hands and seals this 9th Day of November, 1975.

(Signed) John Doe (SEAL)
Inmate

(Signed) Donald L. Quatsoe (SEAL)
Member—Board of Parole

(Signed) David A. Johnson (SEAL)
Institution Representative

(Signed) Wilbur J. Schmidt (SEAL)
Secretary, Department of
Health and Social Services

Approved:

(Signed) Gerald L. Mills
Project Coordinator
Mutual Agreement Programming

2. PAROLE—CORRECTIONS PROJECT

MUTUAL AGREEMENT PROGRAM
ARIZONA

Introduction

This agreement made this day between John Doe ASP 99999, the Arizona Department of Corrections, and the Arizona Parole Board defines mutual responsibilities and utilizes an individualized program to prepare John Doe for a successful community adjustment following release on parole. All parties agree as follows:

Part 1 Inmate:

I, John Doe, understand and agree to successfully complete with a passing grade or an evaluation of satisfactory within my reasonable capabilities the objectives outlined in this document in consideration for a specific date of parole.

I understand that, at any time, I may petition for a renegotiation of this agreement. I will to the best of my ability carry out its objectives and realize that failure to do so will cancel it.

Part II Department of Corrections:

I, Ruie Green, representing the Department of Corrections, agree to provide the necessary programs and services specified in PART IV below to enable John Doe to successfully complete the objectives of this agreement.

Part III Parole Board

We, Keith E. Edwards, and Walter G. Jacobs, members of the Arizona Board of Pardons and Paroles, agree that the above named inmate will be paroled on or before July 1, 1976, CONTINGENT UPON HIS SUCCESSFUL COMPLETION of the objectives mentioned below as certified to us by the State MAP Project Coordinator but subject to minimal delay to allow administrative processing not to exceed ten working days beyond the specified date.

Inmate's Name John Doe No. 99999

Date November 21, 1975 Release Date July 1, 1976

Part IV Objectives

1. Education

2. Skill Training (Mr. Charles Ripley)
Will successfully complete Vocational Upholstery June 1976.

3. Treatment
(Mr. Ray Kimbrough)
Will participate in Alcoholics Anonymous regularly.
(Mr. N. Monohan)
Will meet for a minimum of 10 hours of counseling.

4. Discipline (Mr. Dale Brandfas)
Will comply with the institution rules and regulations outlined in the Inmate Rule Book and receive no referrals for serious disciplinary infractions.

5. Work Assignment

6. Other
Post-release program will include assistance in securing employment in trained area.

Part V Interpretation Provisions

Cancellation, negation or renegotiation of this agreement shall take place in accordance with the terms and provisions of the approved Arizona Model, August, 1972, for Mutual Agreement Programming as amended and in effect on the date hereof. All questions, issues or disputes respecting determination of successful completion of any program or service objective shall be decided by the Board of Pardons and Paroles. Prior to his decision the Project Coordinator shall consult with both the inmate and the program staff member who made the evaluation respecting successful completion, and, in the Coordinator's discretion, he may mediate and consult jointly with the inmate and staff member respecting such question or dispute, or with any other person having material factual information regarding such question or dispute. The decision of the Project Coordinator shall be in writing and shall set forth the facts on which it is based and shall state the reasons for the decision. The Project Coordinator's decision shall be final and binding on all parties hereto except the Board of Pardons and Paroles.

IN WITNESS WHEREOF the parties undersigned have hereunto set their hands and seals this 18th day of December 1975.

(Signed) John Doe (SEAL)
Inmate

(Signed) Keith C. Edwards (SEAL)
Member Board of Pardons and Paroles

(Signed) Walter G. Jacobs (SEAL)
Member Board of Pardons and Paroles

(Signed) Ruie R. Green (SEAL)
Institution Representative

Approved:

(Signed) Victor M. Reyes
Project Coordinator
Mutual Agreement Programming

PAROLE—CORRECTIONS—PROJECT
MUTUAL AGREEMENT PROGRAMMING

California
Educational Furlough and Parole Agreement

WHEREAS, the California Department of Corrections, the California Adult Authority, and the American Correctional Association's Parole Corrections Project have established an educational furlough and parole program in the State of California denominated the California Model, A Proposal for Mutual Agreement Programming and Individual Voucher Referral (hereinafter "the Program"); and

WHEREAS, John Doe has agreed to participate in the Program:

NOW, THEREFORE, the parties agree as follows:

I. I, John Doe, (hereinafter "the Participant") hereby agree that I shall conform my conduct to the Rules and Regulations established for this Program by the California Department of Corrections and incorporated into this Agreement by Paragraph V herein and that I shall successfully complete the requirements of my Individual Educational Furlough Plan set forth in paragraph IV herein. I understand that I may petition for either termination or renegotiation of this Agreement at any time before my release on parole. I agree to complete my Individual Educational Furlough Plan to the best of my abilities and further agree that failure either to successfully complete my Plan or to conform my conduct to said Rules and Regulations shall constitute sufficient grounds for any other Party to this Agreement to terminate or renegotiate this Agreement and my participation in the Program. I further agree that termination or renegotiation of this Agreement shall constitute sufficient grounds for the California Adult Authority to reconsider and redetermine my parole date.

II. I, Charles Wilcots, representing the California Department of Corrections, Division of Paroles and Community Services, and I, Donald McDonald, representing the American Correctional Association agree to provide the program and services specified in the Individual Educational Furlough Plan set forth in Paragraph IV herein to enable John Doe to timely and successfully complete said plan.

III. We, Curtis Lynum and Henry Kerr, representing the California Adult Authority agree that John Doe shall be paroled on or before December 21, 1976, contingent upon his successful completion of the Individual Educational Furlough Plan set forth in Paragraph IV herein and his successfully conforming his conduct to the Rules and Regulations established for this Program by the Department of Corrections and incorporated into this Agreement by Paragraph V herein.

Participant's Name John Doe No. B 09999

Agreement Date July 18, 1976 Parole Release Date 12/21/76

MAP Project Coordinator Donald McDonald

Individual Educational Furlough Plan

1. Education
July 23, to August 31, 1976: Central City Occupational Center
Remedial Education (Math, Reading, English)
9:00 a.m. to 12:00 noon
September 17, to December 18, 1976: Same as above (if necessary)

2. Skill Training
July 23, to August 31, 1976: Central City Occupational Center
Maintenance Mechanic
3:00 p.m. to 6:00 p.m.
September 17, to December 18, 1976: full time day student at L.A. Trade Tech.

3. Treatment
Counseling at Central City Community Center twice a week.

4. Work Assignment
Work experience with structural maintenance men at Central City Community Center.

5. Other

V. The Rules and Regulations established for the Program by the Department of Corrections are any Rules and Regulations as amended that the Department shall have established and put in effect and the Rules and Regulations applicable to residents of any facility of the Department at which the Participant shall be lodged during the term of this Agreement. Said Rules and Regulations are hereby incorporated into the Agreement as if set forth in full herein.

VI. Interpretation of this Agreement shall be in accordance with the terms and provisions of the approved California Model, A Proposal for Mutual Agreement Programming and Individual Voucher Referral as amended and in effect. All questions, issues or disputes respecting determination of successful completion of this Agreement by the Participant shall be submitted to the MAP Project Coordinator designated in Paragraph IV herein for his recommendation to the Adult Authority. Prior to this recommendation the Project Coordinator shall consult with both the Participant and the program staff member who made the evaluation respecting successful completion, and, in the Project Coordinator's discretion, he may mediate and consult jointly with the participant and staff member respecting such question or dispute, or with any other person having material factual information regarding such question or dispute. The recommendation of the Project Coordinator shall be in writing and shall set forth the facts on which it is based and shall state the reasons for the recommendation.

IN WITNESS WHEREOF the parties undersigned have hereunto set their hands and seals this 7th day of June, 1976.

(Signed) John Doe (SEAL)
Participant

(Signed) Henry W. Kerr (SEAL)
For the California Adult Authority

(Signed) Curtis Lynum (SEAL)
For the California Adult Authority

(Signed) Charles B. Wilcots (SEAL)
For the California Department
of Corrections

(Signed) Donald McDonald (SEAL)
For the American Correctional
Association Parole
Corrections Project

HALFWAY HOUSES

The halfway house provides services for offenders in a setting that falls between the custodial care and structured programming of a training school or prison, and the relative freedom of probation and parole. The halfway house was introduced into the United States in the early 1800's when religious or volunteer groups opened small facilities to provide temporary shelter, food, clothing, advice and sometimes help in securing employment for the ex-offender.[34] Goetting states that "The utilization of halfway houses as an alternative to more structured institutionalization in the correctional process is on the increase," and he notes that "it is accepted that these facilities are based upon sound correctional theory; in order to ultimately place a person in society successfully that person should not be any further removed from that society than is necessary." [35] When used in conjunction with prison or training school release programs, the halfway house provides: [36]

1. assistance with obtaining employment;
2. an increased ability to utilize community resources; and
3. needed support during the difficult initial release period.

There are actually various types of halfway houses operated by public and private agencies and groups. However, they can be divided basically into those that provide bed, board and some help with employment, and those that provide a full range of services including treatment. The latter includes a variety of methods, from guided group interaction, to psychotherapy, to behavior modification. A halfway house may be primarily for released inmates, parolees, or for probationers as an alternative to imprisonment. Halfway houses may also be used for probationers or parolees who violate their conditions of supervision, but not seriously enough to cause them to be imprisoned.

The *Talbert House* in Cincinnati was founded by Dr. Jack Brown, a professor of psychiatry at the University of Cincinnati, to aid parolees. Dr. Brown believed that an ex-offender needed the security of a

[34] Calvin R. Dodge, *A Nation Without Prisons* (Lexington, Mass.: D.C. Heath, 1975), p. 197.

[35] Victor L. Goetting, "Some Pragmatic Aspects of Opening A Halfway House," *Federal Probation* (Dec. 1974), p. 27.

[36] Bertram S. Griggs and Gary R. McCune, "Community-Based Correctional Programs: A Survey and Analysis," *Federal Probation* (June 1972), p. 12.

homelike setting where he could get professional assistance with reintegration into the community. In addition to the professional staff employed by Talbert House, many staff members are offender ex-residents of the program. The Talbert House program involves three phases:

1. residing under a structured environment;
2. part-time dependence on the house and its staff for assistance; and
3. almost entire independence for the offender, with the house acting only as a crisis center in time of need.

Residents for the three Talbert Houses are selected by the program directors, who visit Ohio prisons. The basic criterion is that a person must be employable and want to change. Inmates are usually released from prison on Thursday and are taken to the police to register, and to meet the parole officer. They settle in during the weekend, and on Monday begin looking for work. For those who have extreme difficulty finding employment, Talbert House has training programs available and is usually able to arrange for employment through its many community contacts. The average stay at the facility is 90 days, although some stay considerably longer. Other than parole rules, there are few restrictions on a resident's freedom to come and go; there is a midnight curfew on weekdays, and a 2:30 curfew on weekends. Residents are charged for their stay at Talbert House and pay according to their means.[37]

Pharos House in Portland, Maine is also a privately initiated halfway house for offenders; however, they must reside within a 25-mile radius of the facility to be eligible for the program, which usually lasts 90 days. Like Talbert House, there is a curfew and a charge for room and board. The program works closely with the resident's parole officer, who is notified of any flagrant program violations.[38]

Ohio has been using the halfway house concept to treat parole violators intensively within their communities at a reduced cost. The centers are located in Cleveland, Columbus, and Cincinnati, the three largest population centers in the state. They have structured programs to change negative attitudes of the parole violators, improve their self-esteem, and raise their levels of aspiration. Each of the three centers uses a distinct treatment model, and the Ohio State University

[37] Dodge, pp. 197–203.

[38] Benedict S. Alper, *Prisons Inside-Out* (Cambridge, Mass.: Ballinger, 1974), pp. 105–06.

School of Public Administration has a contract to evaluate the program to determine the most effective model.

One center provides rigid control. Parole violators are awarded privileges on a progressive basis. This center requires residents to participate in group interaction and motivational achievement training. The residents' time is tightly scheduled.

The second center has minimal custody and control. Treatment and achievement training come to grips with problems such as employment turnover, inability to use recreational time, sexual problems, budgetary problems, and behavioral problems.

The third center uses a *medical model* with medium custody and a structured environment. The focus is primarily on alcohol- and drug-related problems of the residents, as well as the psychiatric needs of this group. In addition, the program includes guided group interaction and maturational achievement programs.

Parole violators are asigned to the centers on the basis of the geographical proximity to their family. For this reason the treatment models in all centers are necessarily flexible, and based on the needs of the resident as determined by the professional staff. The average stay is 12 weeks, but the period varies depending on the needs of the parolee. Extremely violent parole violators are not accepted into the program.

Each center has a staff of 16 including a superintendent, assistant superintendent, a secretary, cooks and correctional counselors. The staff consists of primarily young college graduates whose initial naiveté quickly wears away and is replaced by more realistic approaches to dealing with offenders. Psychiatric and medical services from the community are used as needed, as are community recreational facilities. A study indicated that more than half of the residents have been employed while in the program.[39]

The major difficulty with opening or maintaining a halfway house is community reaction. A Lou Harris poll, for example, found that while 77% of the representative U.S. sample favored the halfway house concept, 50% would not want one in their neighborhood, and only 22% believed that people in their neighborhood would favor a halfway house being located there.[40] Some experts stress the importance of getting community support of the project before opening a halfway house, while others talk of a "low profile," or even "sneaking" into the

[39] "Community Treatment of Parole Violators," *Target* (Nov./Dec. 1973), pp. 1–2.

[40] Yitzhak Bakal, p. 67. *Closing Correctional Institutions* (Lexington, Mass.: D.C. Heath and Co., 1974).

neighborhood as one Ohio official related to the author. Among some of the strategies used in gaining community support is the formation of an advisory board made up of influential community people. Community people may be placed on the board of directors and hired as staff for the facility. Goetting notes that the local citizenry fear that unwanted criminal elements will come into the area, and he suggests two ways of dealing with such fears: first, the facility can be restricted to serve individuals who would ordinarily reside in the community; or, if outside persons are to be brought in, a screening panel can be formed to alleviate some of the fear. The committee can be made up of community persons who work for the police, sheriff, courts, or parole agencies.[41]

Coates and Miller recommend a "low profile entry into the community" when the latter is not an easily organized neighborhood. This type of area usually has a mixed racial population that tends to be transient, and is thus not easily organized to oppose halfway house projects. The authors express caution about the feasibility of moving into middle-class areas where "In most cases in a conflict, officials, because of their desire to be reelected, will probably go with the majority or a very vocal minority of the residents." [42] The authors also address themselves to the question of community control. They state that when a community recognizes the need for a halfway house for its own residents they may present certain demands such as requirements that a certain portion of staff be from the community, and community residents will have priority for entry into the program. Other demands may include representation on the board of directors and other controlling bodies. Coates and Miller state that where there is real community interest "one probably should not resist real 'community-based corrections' by denying *shared control* over the program." [43]

SPECIAL INTENSIVE PAROLE UNIT (SIPU)

Daniel Glaser called this California project "Probably the most extensively controlled experiment in American correctional history." [44]

[41] Goetting, p. 28.

[42] Coates and Miller cited from Bakal, pp. 76–77.

[43] *Ibid.*, p. 81.

[44] Daniel Glaser, *The Effectiveness of a Prison and Parole System* (Indianapolis: Bobbs-Merrill, 1969), p. 311.

From 1953 to 1964, in four phases, caseloads were varied in order to explore the variable of caseload size in the parole supervision process.

Phase One inmates were paroled early and placed under intensive supervision in experimental caseloads of 15 men each. After three months they were compared to a control group of parolees who had been released at their usual time, and who were supervised in the regular 90-man caseloads. Differences in violation rates were negligible, but there was a savings in confinement costs as a result of the early releases of the experimentals.

Phase Two increased the experimental caseloads to 30 men each and the duration of the experiment was six months. The difference between the experimental caseload and the control caseload of 90-men was not significant in relation to violation rates.

Phase Three used experimental caseloads of 35 men, while the control group had caseloads of 72 men. In addition, both the experimentals and the controls were classified into various "risk" categories. Two years of study revealed that the reduced caseloads had an impact on the "lower-middle risk" category, which had distinctly fewer violations than the control group parolees in the same risk category. The smaller caseloads appeared to have no effect on "low-risk" parolees who probably would have succeeded on parole anyway, and there was no significant effect on those parolees in the "high-risk" category.[45]

Phase Four attempted "to explore the affects of parolee and officer types on case outcome. Caseload size was reduced to 30 and 15, and officers were matched on characteristics thought to be favorable to parole outcome. The results of the study indicated that these characteristics did not measurably affect parole outcome." [46]

Martinson, in reviewing the results of *Phase Three* found that the success of the experimental group occurred primarily in Northern California, where agents were more apt to cite both the experimentals and the controls for violating parole at a higher rate than in Southern California. Martinson notes that the success variable in the performance of the "lower-middle risk" experimentals appears to have been the "realistic threat of severe sanctions," and not necessarily the smaller caseloads.[47] Martinson and Wilks state that "there is a slight tendency to tolerate the misbehavior of those deemed good risks," and

[45] *Ibid.*, p. 312.

[46] Benjamin, ed., *Contemporary Corrections* (Reston, Va.: Reston Publishing Co., 1973), Frank, p. 129.

[47] Martinson, p. 47.

that "Considerable variation may be introduced into the tolerance rate by caseload differences." [48] P/p officers with lower caseloads have more time to spend on each case, and are thus more likely to uncover p/p violations. However, at the same time, they may also tend to be more tolerant of violations because they are not under the pressures that accompany large caseloads.

WORK RELEASE

Many states have prison work release programs, and in some instances these programs involve p/p staff. Work release allows an individual serving a sentence to work in the community, returning each evening to the institution. He is still subject to institutional controls and there are usually additional regulations relative to his extra-institutional status. Under this system an inmate is able to earn a salary and pay taxes, contribute to his family's income, repay debts, and even pay towards his keep at the institution. In addition, work release increases an inmate's self-image.

States vary with respect to the criteria used in selecting inmates for work release programs. Some states automatically exclude those serving a life-sentence or who have detainers filed against them. In North Carolina inmates are divided into two groups according to their sentence: if they were sentenced to less than five years, the court may authorize work release; if they were sentenced to more than five years, the Board of Parole has the responsibility. In Arizona, work release must be authorized by the courts no matter what the sentence.[49] However, the final responsibility for selecting candidates is usually under the aegis of the correctional authorities who also administer the program. Most states do not have specific restrictions concerning who may participate in work release programs, but often use such general expressions as "not a high security risk," or "not likely to commit a crime of violence." [50]

Some states combine work release with furlough programs, thus enabling eligible inmates to leave the institution for specific periods of time in order to seek employment. States often set priorities for

[48] Robert Martinson and Judith Wilks, "Model of Field Supervision," *Criminology* (May 1975), p. 11.

[49] Lawrence S. Root, "Work Release Legislation," *Federal Probation* (Mar. 1972), p. 39.

[50] *Ibid.*

disbursing money earned by inmates through work release. Root notes that the priority order is usually:

1. room and board;
2. travel and incidental expenses;
3. support of dependents;
4. payments of fines and debts; and
5. savings for release.[51]

Unfortunately, many correctional institutions are isolated from urban areas where employment opportunities are usually concentrated. Responding to this deficiency, some states operate a variety of facilities for housing work release participants in proximity to areas of employment. These facilities include minimum security prisons or work release centers, halfway houses, or rented quarters in hotels or YMCAs.

Most states have three basic restrictions on the employment situation of participants in work release:

1. the offender cannot work in a skilled area that already has a surplus labor force;
2. conditions of employment must be commensurate with non-offenders; and
3. if a union is involved, it must be consulted, and no work releasee can work while a labor dispute is in progress.[52]

States vary in the number of inmates involved in work release programs. In 1973, Georgia, for example, had 5% of its inmates in such programs, while New York had 6% in that same year.

Research into the effects of work release programs has been inconclusive. A few studies have indicated that those participating in work release tend to do better on parole. However, since the work release group is not randomly selected, and since there were no control groups, the studies are of dubious value. Other studies using control groups report no differences in the violation rates between participants and controls. There would appear to be a need for further research into the effects of work release programs.[53]

[51] *Ibid.*, p. 41.

[52] *Ibid.*, p. 42.

[53] Frank, pp. 231–35.

Work Furlough Program Rules and Regulations

Office of the Sheriff
Jails & Prisons Division
Work Furlough Program
515 Victoria Street
Jacksonville, Florida 32202
Telephone: 633-4084

Inmate's Name ___________________ Release Date ____________

Participation in the Work Furlough Program is a privilege and is designed primarily to help the inmate become re-established in Society.

The intent of the Work Furlough Law is that the inmate be confined except when actively engaged in his work program.

1. The inmate is to go each work day, directly from his place of confinement to the place of his employment, *by the approved method of transportation.*

2. He is to work diligently at his job and is NOT to leave his place of employment for any purpose unless he is authorized to do so by the Jails & Prisons Division, *in advance.*

3. Any unauthorized absences from the approved place of employment will subject the inmate to possible prosecution for ESCAPE as set forth under Florida Statutes 944.40. If the nature of his job requires him to leave his established place of employment or the employer desires to change his time schedule for work, the employer should make prior arrangements with the Jails & Prisons Division.

4. At the end of each work day, or if work ceases before the end of the scheduled work day, he is to return immediately and directly to his place of confinement. If scheduled transportation is not available, the employer or his representative should call Fairfield House (633-4084) for special instructions.

Failure to return at the end of the working day will result in ESCAPE charges being filed. Maximum sentence is FIFTEEN (15) YEARS for ESCAPE, and must be in addition to any other sentence imposed.

5. The indulgence in alcohol or the use of narcotics is strictly forbidden and will result in the immediate removal of the inmate from the Work Furlough Program.

6. A Work Furlough inmate is entitled to the benefits under the Workman's Compensation Act. The method and expense of treatment for an injury should be handled the same as for other workers. If an inmate is injured off the job or becomes ill, on or off the job, and is not covered by Workman's Compensation or other insurance, the Jails & Prisons Division should be notified at once. He will be treated by the Jail Physician or sent to University Hospital. The Sheriff's Office cannot assume responsibility for medical or hospital expenses unless the above policies are followed.

7. Inmates will not be permitted to operate a motor vehicle unless written permission is obtained from Work Furlough. These inmates must have a valid Florida operator's license, current Florida license tag, valid state inspection decal and liability insurance before being given permission to operate a motor vehicle.

8. The Florida Industrial Commission exercises the same supervision over wages, hours and conditions of employment of all persons under this Program, as it does of other workers. Work Furlough inmates shall receive the same wages as other workers engaged in similar work.

9. Inmate's paycheck should be made payable to Dale G. Carson, Sheriff and mailed to: Account Clerk, Work Furlough Program, 515 Victoria Street, Jacksonville, Florida, unless other arrangements are made. The ordinance provides that the entire earnings of the inmate, less only the statutory deductions (Income and Social Security Taxes), are to be turned over to the Sheriff. In addition to checks, inmates will turn in pay stub or comparable statement of deductions (This will be returned on release). The law does not provide for any deductions by the employer for a debt, advance to the inmate, or for any other purpose. When the Sheriff receives the check or case representing wages earned, it will be turned over to the Account Clerk where it will be placed in the inmate's Work Furlough Account. Any disbursements from this account will be made in this order for the following purposes:

A. The board of the prisoner is $4.00 per working day.

B. Necessary travel expense to and from work and other incidental expenses of the inmate (allowance).

C. Support of the prisoner's dependents, if any.

D. Payment, either in full or ratably, of the inmate's obligations acknowledged by him in writing or which have been reduced to judgment.

E. The balance, if any, to the inmate upon his discharge.

10. Inmate hereby agrees to waive extradition to the State of Florida from any state of the USA, the District of Columbia, or the Commonwealth of Puerto Rico.

11. Inmate will not quit or resign his job or substantially change the nature of his job without prior approval of Work Furlough Officer.

12. Lying to any person may result in immediate dismissal from Work Furlough. Inmates will be truthful at all times.

WHEN THE INMATE IS NOT TRUTHFUL OR DOES NOT FOLLOW THE ESTABLISHED WORK SCHEDULE, FAILS TO WORK DILIGENTLY, LEAVES THE PLACE OF EMPLOYMENT, TAKES A DRINK OF ANY ALCOHOLIC BEVERAGE, USES A NARCOTIC, OR IS ENGAGED IN ANY IMPROPER ACTIVITY, THE EMPLOYER IS RESPONSIBLE FOR NOTIFYING THE JAILS AND PRISONS DIVISION AT ONCE. PROMPT REPORTING OF AN INFRACTION FREQUENTLY PREVENTS MORE SERIOUS INVOLVEMENT BY THE INMATE.

Inmates under the Work Furlough Program will be granted the same privileges given to trusties and will abide by the general rules and regulations of the Jails and Prisons Division of the Office of the Sheriff.

I have read and understand the rules and regulations and I agree to abide by all terms and conditions of the Work Furlough Program as prescribed by the Sheriff, and applicable Federal, State and Municipal Laws.

____________________ ____________________

Effective Date Inmate Signature

Subject is authorized $________ per week expense money and will not have over this amount on his person at any time.

He is to be released according to the following schedule:
Days: ______________ Release at ______ and return at ______

TEAM MANAGEMENT IN PROBATION AND PAROLE

The usual supervisory approach in probation/parole practice is to assign each officer a caseload of specific offenders. The services required by these offenders are rendered by the p/p officer. He provides these services, such as employment counseling, directly, or he makes a referral to another agency, such as the state employment service. The p/p officer under this system is sometimes considered a "jack-of-all-trades" and, critics of this approach maintain, "master-of-none." Sullivan states that "it is questionable whether the traditional casework approach (that is, where each probation officer is given his own caseload) is capable of effectively dealing with either the increased number of probationers or with the diversity of probationers accompanying the increased input." He notes that the officer is often unfamiliar with the wide variety of resources available.[54]

Since a p/p officer may be supervising, on one caseload, persons who have problems with narcotics, alcohol, mental illness, marital situations, etc., it is often difficult, if not impossible, to provide each client with the specific service he needs. Team management has been proposed to meet these problems.

The basic team management approach consists of assigning a much larger caseload to a team of specialized workers. A p/p team may, for example, consist of a social worker, an employment specialist, a psychologist, and a paraprofessional. Each team has a supervisor who coordinates (manages) the work of the team. Paraprofessionals are generally used to make field visits for both treatment and surveillance purposes. Perhaps the most extensive use of the team concept appears in the recommendations of the (New York) Governor's Committee on Criminal Offenders:[55]

[54] Dennis C. Sullivan, *Team Management in Probation* (Paramus, N.J.: National Council on Crime and Delinquency, 1967), pp. 4–5.

[55] Governor's Committee on Criminal Offenders, p. 249.

> Under the proposed system, the treatment plan would be formulated by a regional center or institutional panel and approved by the central board. The plan would then be implemented by teams assigned to the regional center. Where casework as such is prescribed, the plan would so indicate and the plan would also furnish an indication of the intensity required. Where surveillance or verification of residence or employment is necessary, such function would be performed by an investigator or a sub-professional. (Experienced professional caseworkers could then devote full attention to therapy.) Indigenous workers would also be used as part of the teams, and storefront offices would be established for such workers in neighborhoods with high concentrations of persons under supervision.*
>
> The exact make-up of the teams would vary in accordance with the patterns of treatment plans and the degree of specialization deemed practicable in the various regional centers. Without going into detail, the team would have a coordinator, and each person assigned to the team would receive copies of reports made by other members, so that each could perform his function in accordance with all information available. There would be case conferences when necessary among the team members, and where treatment changes are thought necessary—prior to normal panel reevaluation—the coordinator would present the case to the panel. Thus, the caseworker—rather than being the vortex of the treatment process—would become an integral part of a team equipped to furnish the whole spectrum of services in accordance with appropriately diagnosed needs.

The team approach has been criticized by many of the author's colleagues in probation and parole. They point out that one of the basic concepts of p/p treatment is the salutory effect of the relationship between the p/p officer and the offender, and they believe that this relationship is not possible with the team approach. Some officers have expressed their belief that the team approach is also confusing to the offender, who is required to deal with several members of staff instead of "his own" p/p officer. Basically, these critics maintain that while treatment and surveillance activities may be more specialized, they are also more impersonal.

CALIFORNIA SUMMARY PAROLE PROGRAM [56]

On March 1, 1976, the California Department of Corrections began an experimental project designed to test the effectiveness of parole

*These workers would be excellent sources for community job vacancy information; and could be used in many cases to supplement or substitute for surveillance. Additionally, properly selected workers could furnish leadership and guidance to reduce the burden of the professionals.

[56] Information from Deborah Star, California Department of Corrections, Research Division.

without supervision. The program is one part of the department's overall plans to reevaluate its parole system. While the main thrust of the research is to provide a test for parole without supervision, the project will also examine the effectiveness of two techniques for selecting cases suitable for summary parole. In order to find these "minimum risk" cases the research will use an actuarial approach and a clinical (diagnostic) approach.

California states the objectives of the program:

> Increase the rate of successful transitions by identifying adult offenders not requiring normal Parole and Community Services Division services and supervision, and placing them on non-supervisorial status and applying the agent time saved to other parolees requiring an increased level of supervision and services.

California notes that "There are indications that some persons released from prison do not require the full range of Parole and Community Service Division services and control to complete a successful transition in the community consistant with public safety." In part, this program is designed to test the effectiveness of the determinants developed to select these persons for summary parole.

There are 1200 parolees involved in the program, 600 controls and 600 experimentals. Of the 600 experimentals, 200 have been randomly selected, 200 have been selected on the basis of the actuarial method, and 200 have been selected by a clinical-diagnostic method. Excluded from the experimental group are sex offenders, those convicted of Murder in the First Degree, offenders with pending court cases, and those with special conditions of parole—abstaining from alcohol or participating in an anti-drug testing program.

For the experimental group all supervisorial contacts have been waived, although when adverse information is received concerning public safety, a parole agent will conduct an investigation.

Success and failure of parole cases within the program are limited to measures of criminal involvement as detected by the police:

1. Arrested
2. Arrested and convicted
3. Arrested, convicted and sentenced to more than 89 days in jail (or equivalent).
4. Arrested, convicted and a new commitment to prison.

The severity of crimes committed or alleged will be judged on the basis of the *Sellin-Wolfgang Index:* "Each event is classified by its effects as involving personal injury to one or more victims, theft of property, property damage, or some combination of the three. The event is then scored in terms of severity weightings reflecting the type of bodily harm involved, the amount and value of property theft or damage, and the number of offenses incorporated into one event." The final "score" represents the gravity of the crime.[57]

The measure of criminal involvement will be done on a six month basis, with one-, two-, and five-year follow-ups.[58]

(It should be noted that California has enacted a new determinate sentence law, effective July 1, 1977. This law, which abolishes the Adult Authority (parole board) and the Women's Board of Terms and Parole, drastically changes the California parole system. Most inmates will be released at the end of their determinate sentence, minus "good time." They will be required to be on parole supervision for one year, and a violation of parole can result in re-imprisonment for a maximum of six months.)

[57] David O. Mosberg and Richard Ericson, "A New Recidivism Outcome Index," *Federal Probation* (June 1972), p. 52.

[58] A similar, although more limited proposal (100 parolees), was submitted in 1975 by the author in New York State; it was rejected because the "public safety would be comprised by unsupervised parolees."

Chapter 20

Special Units

In some p/p agencies there are units that provide specialized services for particular offenders. A characteristic of most special units is the relatively small caseload and the individual treatment that it permits. P/p officers who work in these units are able to develop expertise that enables them to be more effective with their particular clients. Special units include those that service:

drug abusing offenders
alcoholic offenders
young offenders
retarded offenders
gifted offenders
mentally ill offenders
dangerous offenders

New York State parole, which has been a leader in the development of specialized units, has a bureau whose parole officers do not supervise parolees, but, instead, specialize in criminal investigation. The bureau uses two-way radios and sophisticated surveillance equipment.

New York has also been a pioneer in the development of specialized units for drug addicts and gifted offenders on parole.

NEW YORK STATE NARCOTIC TREATMENT BUREAU[1]

For a number of years the Division of Parole has developed specialized casework services for those parolees whose problems were of such a nature that they required special handling. Specialized caseloads have been established involving youthful offenders, mental defective delinquents, and drug addicts under supervision by parole officers specially selected and assigned, and given the opportunity to develop appropriate techniques and methods of approach.

Parole casework, by definition, involves the use of authority when the occasion demands it. One of the main areas to be worked out in the Narcotic Treatment Bureau was the delicate balance between traditional casework techniques and the authoritative approach as applied to addicts. For example, some professional agencies engaged in the field of addiction and treatment frowned upon the practice of arm examination to determine relapses, feeling that such a step would destroy a worker-client relationship. The bureau did not accept that concept, and arms were checked as necessary.

Traditionally, a parole or probation violator who reverts to the use of narcotics is the subject of delinquency action. However, when the bureau parole officer believed it appropriate, with approval, he could take the calculated risk of allowing the parolee to remain in the community. The decision had to be based on the delicate balance between community protection and the offender's sincere desire to help himself. This flexibility was the result of studies that had shown that complete and permanent abstinence was in most instances difficult to achieve immediately despite treatment. A person might relapse several times before he was finally able to display sufficient emotional strength to abstain completely.

The criteria has changed over the years; originally it included an upper age limit of 25 intravenous heroin users, who had used drugs for at least six months and whose main difficulties with the law revolved around drug usage. There is little difference between the

[1] Based on Meyer Diskind and George Klonsky, *Recent Developments in the Treatment of Paroled Offenders Addicted to Narcotic Drugs.* Albany: N.Y.S. Div. of Parole, 1974, and the author's experience in the unit.

casework approach used in the bureau and that utilized in the generalized caseloads. It is a matter of *degree*, not of *kind*. Bureau caseloads are limited to a maximum of 30; thus the parole officer is able to extend more extensive supervision and guidance than a worker with a much larger caseload. An initially released offender is seen by the parole officer weekly for about nine months. Frequent home visits are conducted in order to speak with relatives as well as the parolee. A considerable amount of the parole officer's time is devoted to working with members of the family to get them to modify some of their attitudes so as to insure proper integration of the offender within the family unit.

The problem of the authoritative versus the traditional casework approach comes up routinely when the parole officer discovers that his parolee is using drugs. Should delinquency action be taken; should he be permitted to remain in the community; or should he be compelled to undergo hospitalization? Compulsory hospitalization is one of the techniques used by the bureau. Several alternatives are available. The violator can be returned to the institution; he can be retained in the community; or he may be placed in temporary detention or a hospital for detoxification. If the risk involved appears too great because of indications of serious criminal activities, he is returned to prison. If, however, he is gainfully employed and makes a satisfactory adjustment in other areas of living, no formal delinquency action is taken. If necessary, he is placed in temporary detention or a hospital detoxification program.

Detecting drug usage is a difficult procedure. However, the parole officers see their clients at least once a week for nine months and thereafter bi-weekly. They can note any changes in physical appearance, attitude, and employment patterns. The client's family is also usually cooperative and often quickly reports any suspected reversion to drugs (addicts steal from whomever they can, often from family members). In most instances a parolee faced with the evidence of drug usage will admit to reverting to narcotics.

The bureau works closely with several New York City hospitals that have facilities for drug addicts. Once hospitalized, the parolee is not permitted to sign out against medical advice. Such action will lead to an arrest warrant being issued for parole violation. In addition, any parolee discharged because of his behavior in the hospital is also subjected to parole violation, something he is warned against in advance.

Considerable activity is centered in the areas of vocational guidance and placement. Experience has shown that most drug users have little or no vocational skill or work experience. The first step in rehabilitation is the maintenance of a steady job. Idleness easily leads to readdiction and it is therefore essential that the parolee be employed as quickly as possible. The parole officers utilize the resources of the New York State Employment Services, private employment agencies, and employment resources developed by each parole officer. A special liaison was established with the New York State Division of Vocational Rehabilitation, so that clients who can benefit from vocational training are referred to it for examination, training and placement.

In cases of parolees who have been given one or more prior opportunities to remain in the community after reverting to drug usage, incarceration serves as a reminder that they have parole obligations to live up to, and failure to do so will result in arrest. The value of deterrence remains an important consideration in the treatment process of addicts in New York State Parole.

GIFTED OFFENDER BUREAU[2]

Correctional authorities have long recognized that a small but significant percentage of the inmate population displayed creative skills, talent, and superior intelligence or possessed high, but unrealized potentials in these areas. For years these offenders were normally absorbed into regular caseloads when released to parole supervision. There caseloads were numerically too large to allow for individualization and casework efforts in the treatment process. The heavy volume of work, the need to attend to more demanding matters, the lack of either the resources or the knowledge of the available resources, absorbed so much of the parole officers' time that these promising areas were permitted to lie fallow and unchallenged. Many potentially gifted offenders completed their parole but were ill-equipped to become more socially productive members of society, and concomitantly they were unable to enjoy a fuller and richer existence.

These observations led to the establishment of the Gifted Offender Bureau. The original criteria was a high intelligence quotient or a demonstrated (while in the prison) interest in academic or artistic

[2] Excerpted from George Klonsky, "We Must Be Doing Something Right," *American Journal of Corrections* (Jan./Feb. 1969), pp. 6–10, used by permission of the author.

pursuits. This was expanded to include any parolee who displayed strong motivation and drive to improve or develop a latent ability or skill. The focus on academic pursuits shifted to other fields or areas, including plumbing or printing, for example. Thus, an offender who had demonstrated an interest in an educational or vocational field would be helped with the financial and other arrangements necessary to enter a college or trade school.

The Gifted Bureau parole officer functions essentially in the same manner as a parole officer assigned to generalized units; the difference is in *degree.* The parole officers supervise no more than 30 cases. This allows them to explore and experiment with different methods of motivation. Since he is not beset with a host of other time-consuming problems, the p.o. is in a better position to help his client in the client's expressed area of interest, while exploring areas of potential that the parolee himself had never been aware of or considered.

Chapter 21

Probation/Parole, Success Or Failure?

Is probation/parole successful, and if so how successful? Estimates are that probation is successful in 75% of the cases,[1] while parole is successful in 55 to 65% of the cases.[2] However, what is meant by success, and how do we measure it?

Social work uses such indicators of success as "improved social functioning" or "better reality testing," but they are subjective and unmeasureable in any universally acceptable manner. Vasoli suggests a combination of indicators for deciding failure in probation cases:

1. filing a petition,
2. issuing a warrant,
3. revocation, and
4. recidivism.[3]

For deciding failure in parole cases, the President's Commission used

[1] Hartinger, et al., p. 169.

[2] *Task Force Report:* Corrections, p. 62.

[3] Robert Vasoli, "Some Reflections on Measuring Probation Outcome," *Federal Probation* (Sept. 1967), pp. 24–25.

return to prison,[4] while Glaser emphasizes felony convictions.[5] Some agencies reduce their success-failure statistics into several categories, such as:

1. no violations,
2. technical violations,
3. misdemeanor convictions, and
4. felony convictions.

However, there is obviously no system that can account for undetected violations. Indeed, a more vigorous probation/parole agency will discover violations that would not be detected by a less efficient agency. A higher rate of technical violations will conceivably result in less convictions for new crimes. The technical violation is designed to forestall the committing of new offenses. A system that bases failure only on new convictions, however, might cause an agency to lose its flexibility and become overzealous in invoking the technical violation.

Probation is generally considered successful, at least insofar as it is a mechanism for screening out those offenders who do not require the sanction of prison. Parole is similarly successful, at least insofar as it is able to release (screen out) those who do not need the continued sanction of imprisonment. However, should success-failure be evaluated after the offender is no longer on probation/parole? If so, for how many years? Success-failure may also depend on who is evaluating the particular case. For example, should an armed robber who is discovered shoplifting be counted as a complete failure? A drug addict has stopped using and possessing illegal drugs, but he is now abusing alcohol; is he a success or failure? An offender who has never been legally employed is successful at maintaining legitimate employment, but he is neglecting his wife and children. Is he a success or failure?

Success and failure in probation/parole should be standardized. Probation/parole agencies would then be able to compare their performance with other agencies, and with prior years. A standardized system would require mutually exclusive categories into which each case could easily be placed. These categories would have to be objective and not subject to the extremes of local variations relative to evaluating success-failure.

[4] *Task Force Report*, p. 62.

[5] Glaser, p. 15.

The author presents his own table of success-failure categories as a basis for discussion. In order to be fully operable these categories must be weighted in a standard manner applicable to, and accepted by, all probation/parole agencies. The table utilizes a basic premise: that probation/parole are in existence primarily because they save tax dollars. This is not to say that probation/parole does not have a basic value beyond saving money. But, realistically, if probation/parole were more costly (or even equal in cost) than imprisonment, there probably would be no probation or parole. Lawmakers who provide budgets and raise taxes deal in statistics, and numbers are often cold and devoid of the humanistic dynamic so dear to many of us. In order to relate to this reality, probation/parole agencies should report to their respective legislative bodies on the dollar amount that their services saved by reducing the amount of costly imprisonment.

Of course, the outcome of probation/parole is largely dependent on the input; as has been noted, offenders are younger, the onset of their delinquent behavior has been earlier, and their crimes more serious, than in years past. These are factors that result in a higher rate of failure by whatever measurement is used, and over which p/p systems have no control.

Probation/Parole
Success-Failure

A. No technical violations resulting in imprisonment. No convictions for one year after discharge from probation/parole which result in imprisonment.*

B. Technical violation resulting in imprisonment, or absconding from supervision.

C. Misdemeanor conviction within one year after discharge resulting in imprisonment.*

D. Misdemeanor conviction while under supervision resulting in a sentence of imprisonment.**

E. Felony conviction within one year after discharge from supervision.*

F. Felony conviction while under supervision.**

*As determined by an FBI clearance.

** A special category needs to be set aside for the limited amount of cases where the supervisory officer discovers the crime resulting in the new conviction.

EPILOGUE: PROBATION/PAROLE: PRESENT AND FUTURE

> The crucial question is how do we develop a balance between the dichotomy of service and supervision. In the last few years, Parole Boards and Departments throughout the country have become caught in the same dilemma as all others in corrections. The idea of rehabilitation and treatment has become superimposed upon the old theory of punishment and control. Thus, jurisdictions can be found leaning in either direction and some even attempt to carry out both at the same time. The basic question is whether both policing and treatment aspects can be carried on at the same time or whether they are mutually exclusive. Examples can be found where the theory is treatment and the terminology used is that of a treatment atmosphere but the reality is still control; one has simply been superimposed upon the other and the original emphasis of the ticket-of-leave from which parole is descended is still very much in evidence.*

We appear to have reached a crossroads in criminal justice where critics agree on the problem, but diverge on the solution. Many agree, for example, that the treatment model has failed to reduce recidivism. However, each critic has his own alternative to rehabilitative efforts, and these alternatives often appear contradictory. Some maintain that the only guarantee against crime is incarceration, insofar as while incarcerated the offender is not free to recidivate. Others propose a drastic reduction in the use and length of imprisonment.

The cost of incarceration and the current overcrowding in most prison systems would appear to limit the viability of the increased use of imprisonment, while public opposition or political considerations would probably mitigate against any wholesale reduction in the use of imprisonment. With these considerations in mind, what should be the future role of probation and parole?

A New Orientation

In order for probation/parole to be successful, judges and parole boards must begin to separate offenders who present a serious risk to the safety of other persons from offenders who do not. Offenders who have a history of committing crimes of potential or real violence should be subjected to long prison terms. No pretense is made that prison rehabilitates, and we cannot even be sure that it serves as a deterrent to

*Benjamin Ward, Commissioner, New York State Department of Correctional Services, *Correctional Service News* (June 1976).

crime. However, prison does debilitate and "age" the offender, and experience has shown a direct correlation between the age of the offender and the proclivity to recidivate.

Non-violent offenders should be "diverted," placed on probation, or incarcerated for only short periods of time: days, weekends, weeks, months, but not years. This would place more non-violent offenders into the community where they would come within the *Service-Surveillance Model of Supervision.*

Service to the Offender

In this model, service must be differentiated from treatment; service is *real* help. The officer would be out in the community developing jobs, educational and training opportunities and resources for his clients—those that requested his help. He would be available to accompany clients to prospective employers, schools and agencies, and would act as an advocate for the offender when necessary. The officer would be available to deal with personal problems either through direct counseling or by referral. In any event, help would be provided only when requested. When appropriate, the officer would also assist the offender in the event that the latter is arrested or in jail.

Surveillance

Any system of community supervision must be based on the need to protect the community from potential lawbreakers. In order to provide this protection, probation/parole officers should be trained and equipped as fully empowered law enforcement officers. Surveillance activities, however, should be limited to specific cases where their use can be justified. Many of the routine and often meaningless control functions of probation/parole officers, such as routine visits to homes and places of employment, should be avoided. Surveillance, like service, should be particularized as indicated by the needs of the case.

Conclusion

Within probation/parole agencies there exists the potential for providing activities that can have an impact on preventing crime. The actual level of these service and surveillance activities would depend on the amount of resources allocated to probation/parole agencies. Hopefully, the "New Orientation" would decrease prison populations and result in a diversion of prison funds into probation/parole.

DISCUSSION TOPICS

1. Discuss the interstate compact, its benefits and problems.
2. Explore the problem of offender disabilities.
3. Discuss the pros and cons of pre-trial diversion.
4. Discuss the advantages and shortcomings of special programs:
   a. probation subsidy
   b. shock probation/parole
   c. community treatment program (CTP)
   d. halfway houses
   e. work release
   f. team management
5. Examine the use of specialized units in probation/parole.
6. Discuss probation/parole failure-success.

APPENDIX

Two Probation/ Parole-Related Decisions

Morrissey v. Brewer

MR. CHIEF JUSTICE BURGER delivered the opinion of the Court.

We granted certiorari in this case to determine whether the Due Process Clause of the Fourteenth Amendment requires that a State afford an individual some opportunity to be heard prior to revoking his parole.

Petitioner Morrissey was convicted of false drawing or uttering of checks in 1967 pursuant to his guilty plea, and was sentenced to not more than seven years' confinement. He was paroled from the Iowa State Penitentiary in June 1968. Seven months later, at the direction of his parole officer, he was arrested in his home town as a parole violator and incarcerated in the county jail. One week later, after review of the parole officer's written report, the Iowa Board of Parole revoked Morrissey's parole and he was returned to the penitentiary located about 100 miles from his home. Petitioner asserts he received no hearing prior to revocation of his parole.

The parole officer's report on which the Board of Parole acted shows that petitioner's parole was revoked on the basis of information that he had violated the conditions of parole by buying a car under an assumed name and operating it without permission, giving false statements to police concerning his address and insurance company after a minor accident, and obtaining credit under an assumed name and failing to report his place of residence to his parole officer. The report states that the officer interviewed Morrissey, and that he could not explain why he did not contact his parole officer despite his effort to excuse this on the ground that he had been sick. Further, the report asserts that Morrissey admitted buying the car and obtaining credit under an assumed name and also admitted being involved in the accident. The parole officer recommended that his parole be revoked because of "his continual violating of his parole rules."

The situation as to petitioner Booher is much the same. Pursuant to his guilty plea, Booher was convicted of forgery in 1966 and sentenced to a maximum term of 10 years. He was paroled November 14, 1968. In August 1969, at his parole officer's direction, he was arrested in his home town for violation of his parole and confined in the county jail several miles away. On September 13, 1969, on the basis of a written report by his parole officer, the Iowa Board of Parole revoked Booher's parole and Booher was recommitted to the state penitentiary, located about 250 miles from his home, to complete service of his sentence. Petitioner asserts he received no hearing prior to revocation of his parole.

The parole officer's report with respect to Booher recommended that his parole be revoked because he had violated the territorial restrictions of his parole without consent, had obtained a driver's license under an assumed name and operated a motor vehicle without permission, and had violated the employment condition of his parole by failing to keep himself in gainful employment. The report stated that the officer had interviewed Booher and that he had acknowledged to the parole officer that he had left the specified territorial limits and had operated the car and had obtained a license under an assumed name "knowing that it was wrong." The report further noted that Booher had stated that he had not found employment because he could not find work that would pay him what he wanted—he stated he would not work for $2.25 to $2.75 per hour—and that he had left the area to get work in another city.

After exhausting state remedies, both petitioners filed habeas corpus petitions in the United States District Court for the Southern District of Iowa alleging that they had been denied due process because their paroles had been revoked without a hearing. The State responded by arguing that no hearing was required. The District Court held on the basis of controlling authority that the State's failure to accord a hearing prior to parole revocation did not violate due process. On appeal, the two cases were consolidated.

The Court of Appeals, dividing 4 to 3, held that due process does not require a hearing. The majority recognized that the traditional view of parole as a privilege rather than a vested right is no longer dispositive as to whether due process is applicable; however, on a balancing of the competing interest involved, it concluded that no hearing is required. The court reasoned that parole is only "a correctional device authorizing service of sentence outside the penitentiary"; the parolee is still "in custody." Accordingly, the Court of Appeals was of the view that prison officials must have large discretion in making revocation determinations, and that courts should retain their traditional reluctance to interfere with disciplinary matters properly under the control of state prison authorities. The majority expressed the view that "non-legal, non-adversary considerations" were often the determinative factors in making a parole revocation decision. It expressed concern that if adversary hearings were required for parole revocation, "with the full panoply of rights accorded in criminal proceedings," the function of the parole board as "an administrative body acting in the role of parens patriae would be aborted" and the board would be more reluctant to grant parole in the first instance—an apprehension that would not be without some basis if the choice were between a full scale adversary proceeding or no hearing at all. Additionally, the majority reasoned that the parolee has no statutory right to remain on parole. Iowa law provides that a parolee may be returned to the institution at any time. Our holding in Mempa v. Rhay, 389 U.S. 128, 88 S.Ct. 254, 19 L.Ed. 2d 336 (1967), was distinguished on the ground that it involved deferred sentencing upon probation revocation, and thus involved a stage of the criminal proceeding, whereas parole revocation was not a stage in the criminal proceedings. The Court of Appeals' decision was consistent with many other decisions on parole revocations.

In its brief in this Court, the State asserts for the first time that petitioners were in fact granted hearings after they were returned to the penitentiary. More generally, the State says that within two months after the Board revokes an individual's parole and orders him returned to the penitentiary, on the basis of the parole officer's written report, it grants the individual a hearing before the Board. At that time the Board goes over "each of the alleged parole violations with the returnee, and he is given an opportunity to orally present his side of the story to the Board." If the returnee denies the report, it is the practice of the Board to conduct a further investigation before making a final determination either affirming the initial revocation, modifying it, or reversing it. The State asserts that Morrissey, whose parole was revoked on January 31, 1969, was granted a hearing before the Board on February 12, 1969. Booher's parole was revoked on September 13, 1969, and he was granted a hearing on October 14, 1969. At these hearings, the State tells us—in the briefs—both Morrissey and Booher admitted the violations alleged in the parole violation reports.

Nothing in the record supplied to this Court indicates that the State claimed, either in the District Court or the Court of Appeals, that petitioners had received hearings promptly after their paroles were revoked, or that in such hearing they admitted the violations; that information comes to us only in the State's brief here. Further, even the assertions that the State makes here are not based on any public record but on interviews with two of the members of the parole board. In the interview relied on to show that petitioners admitted their violations, the board member did not assert he could remember that both Morrissey and Booher admitted the parole violations with which they were charged. He stated only that, according to his memory, in the previous several years all but three returnees had admitted commission of the parole infractions alleged and that neither of the petitioners were among the three who denied them.

We must therefore treat this case in the posture and on the record the State elected to rely on in the District Court and the Court of Appeals. If the facts are otherwise, the State may make a showing in the District Court that petitioners in fact have admitted the violations charged before a neutral officer.

I

Before reaching the issue of whether due process applies to the parole system, it is important to recall the function of parole in the correctional process.

During the past 60 years, the practice of releasing prisoners on parole before the end of their sentences has become an integral part of the penological system. Note, Parole Revocation in the Federal System, 56 Geo.L.J. 705 (1968). Rather than being an ad hoc exercise of clemency, parole is an established variation on imprisonment of convicted criminals. Its purpose is to help individuals reintegrate into society as constructive individuals as soon as they are able, without being confined for the full term of the sentence imposed. It also serves to alleviate the costs to society of keeping an individual in prison. The essence of parole is release from prison, before the completion of sentence, on the condition that the prisoner abide by certain rules during the balance of the sentence. Under some systems parole is granted automatically after the service of a certain portion of a prison term. Under others, parole is granted by the discretionary action of a board which evaluates an array of information about a prisoner and makes a prediction whether he is ready to reintegrate into society.

To accomplish the purpose of parole, those who are allowed to leave prison early are subjected to specified conditions for the duration of their terms. These conditions restrict their activities substantially beyond the ordinary restrictions imposed by law on an individual citizen. Typically parolees are forbidden to use liquor or to have associations or correspondence with certain categories of undesirable persons. Typically also they must seek permission from their parole officers before engaging in specified activities, such as changing employment or living quarters, marrying, acquiring or operating a motor vehicle, traveling outside the community and incurring substantial indebtedness. Additionally, parolees must regularly report to the parole officer to whom they are assigned and sometimes they must make periodic written reports of their activities. Arluke, A Summary of Parole Rules, 15 Crime and Delinquency 267, 272–273 (1969).

The parole officers are part of the administrative system designed to assist parolees and to offer them guidance. The conditions of parole serve a dual purpose; they prohibit, either absolutely or conditionally, behavior which is deemed dangerous to the restoration of the individual into normal society. And through the requirement of reporting to the parole officer and seeking guidance and permission before doing many things, the officer is provided with information about the parolee and an opportunity to advise him. The combination puts the parole officer into the position in which he can try to guide the parolee into constructive development.

The enforcement leverage which supports the parole conditions derives from the authority to return the parolee to prison to serve out the balance of his sentence if he fails to abide by the rules. In practice not every violation of parole conditions automatically leads to revocation. Typically a parolee will be counseled to abide by the conditions of parole, and the parole officer ordinarily does not take steps to have parole revoked unless he thinks that the violations are serious and continuing so as to indicate that the parolee is not adjusting properly and cannot be counted on to avoid antisocial activity. The board discretion accorded the parole officer is also inherent in some of the quite vague conditions, such as the typical requirement that the parolee avoid "undesirable" associations or correspondence. Cf. Arciniega v. Freeman, 404 U.S. 4, 92 S.Ct. 22, 30 L.Ed.2d 126 (1970). Yet revocation of parole is not an unusual phenomenon, affecting only a few parolees. It has been estimated that 35–45% of all parolees are subjected to revocation and return to prison. Sometimes revocation occurs when the parolee is accused of another crime; it is often preferred to a new prosecution because of the procedural ease of recommitting the individual on the basis of a lesser showing by the State.

Implicit in the system's concern with parole violations is the notion that the parolee is entitled to retain his liberty as long as he substantially abides by the conditions of his parole. The first step in a revocation decision thus involves a wholly retrospective factual question: whether the parolee has in fact acted in violation of one or more conditions of his parole. Only if it is determined that the parolee did violate the conditions does the second question arise: should the parolee be recommitted to prison or should other steps be taken to protect society and improve chances of rehabilitation? The first step is relatively simple; the second is more complex. The second question involves the application of expertise by the parole authority in making a prediction as to the ability of the individual to live in society without committing antisocial acts. This part of the decision, too, depends on facts, and therefore it is important for the Board to know not only that some violation was committed but also to know accurately how many and how serious the violations were. Yet this second step, deciding what to do about the violation once it is identified, is not purely factual but also predictive and discretionary.

If a parolee is returned to prison, he often receives no credit for the time "served" on parole. Thus the returnee may face a potential of substantial imprisonment.

II

We begin with the proposition that the revocation of parole is not part of a criminal prosecution and thus the full panoply of rights due a defendant in such a proceeding does not apply to parole revocations. Cf. Mempa v. Rhay, 389 U.S. 128, 88 S.Ct. 254, 19 L.Ed.2d 336

(1967). Parole arises after the end of the criminal prosecution, including imposition of sentence. Supervision is not directly by the court but by an administrative agency, which is sometimes an arm of the court and sometimes of the executive. Revocation deprives an individual not of the absolute liberty to which every citizen is entitled, but only of the conditional liberty properly dependent on observance of special parole restrictions.

We turn therefore to the question whether the requirements of due process in general apply to parole revocations. As Mr. Justice Blackmun has written recently, "This Court has rejected the concept that constitutional rights turn upon whether a governmental benefit is characterized as a 'right' or as a 'privilege.' " Graham v. Richardson, 403 U.S. 365, 374, 91 S.Ct. 1848, 29 L.Ed.2d 534, 543. Whether any procedural protections are due depends on the extent to which an individual will be "condemned to suffer grievous loss." Joint Anti-Fascist Refugee Committee v. McGrath, 341 U.S. 123, 168, 71 S.Ct. 624, 95 L.Ed. 817, 852 (1951) (Frankfurter, J., concurring), quoted in Goldberg v. Kelly, 397 U.S. 254, 263, 90 S.Ct. 1011, 25 L.Ed.2d 287, 296 (1970). The question is not merely the "weight" of the individual's interest, but whether the nature of the interest is one within 'the contemplation of the "liberty or property" language of the Fourteenth Amendment. Fuentes v. Shevin, 407 U.S. 67, 92 S.Ct. 1983, 32 L.Ed.2d 556 (decided June 12, 1972). Once it is determined that due process applies, the question remains what process is due. It has been said so often by this Court and others as not to require citation of authority that due process is flexible and calls for such procedural protections as the particular situation demands. "[C]onsideration of what procedures due process may require under any given set of circumstances must begin with a determination of the precise nature of the governmental function involved as well as of the private interest that has been affected by governmental action." Cafeteria & Restaurant Workers Union v. McElroy, 367 U.S. 886, 895, 81 S.Ct. 1743, 6 L.Ed.2d 1230, 1236 (1961). To say that the concept of due process is flexible does not mean that judges are at large to apply it to any and all relationships. Its flexibility is in its scope once it has been determined that some process is due; it is a recognition that not all situations calling for procedural safeguards call for the same kind of procedure.

We turn to an examination of the nature of the interest of the parolee in his continued liberty. The liberty of a parolee enables him to do a wide range of things open to persons who have never been convicted of any crime. The parolee has been released from prison based on an evaluation that he shows reasonable promise of being able to return to society and function as a responsible, self-reliant person. Subject to the conditions of his parole, he can be gainfully employed and is free to be with family and friends and to form the other enduring attachments of normal life. Though the State properly subjects him to many restrictions not applicable to other citizens, his condition is very different from that of confinement in a prison. He may have been on parole for a number of years and may be living a relatively normal life at the time he is faced with revocation. The parolee has relied on at least an implicit promise that parole will be revoked only if he fails to live up to the parole conditions. In many cases the parolee faces lengthy incarceration if his parole is revoked.

We see, therefore, that the liberty of a parolee, although indeterminate, includes many of the core values of unqualified liberty and its termination inflicts a "grievous loss" on the parolee and often on others. It is hardly useful any longer to try to deal with this problem in terms of whether the parolee's liberty is a "right" or a "privilege." By whatever name the liberty is valuable and must be seen as within the protection of the Fourteenth Amendment. Its termination calls for some orderly process, however informal.

Turning to the question what process is due, we find that the State's interests are several. The State has found the parolee guilty of a crime against the people. That finding justifies imposing extensive restrictions on the individual's liberty. Release of the parolee before the end of his prison sentence is made with the recognition that with many prisoners there is a risk that they will not be able to live in society without committing additional anti-social acts. Given the previous conviction and the proper imposition of conditions, the State has an overwhelming interest in being able to return the individual to imprisonment without the burden of a new adversary criminal trial if in fact he has failed to abide by the conditions of his parole.

Yet the State has no interest in revoking parole without some informal procedural guarantees. Although the parolee is often formally described as being "in custody," the argument cannot even be made here that summary treatment is necessary as it may be with respect to controlling a large group of potentially disruptive prisoners in actual custody. Nor are we persuaded by the argument that revocation is so totally a discretionary matter that some form of hearing would be administratively intolerable. A simple factual hearing will not interfere with the exercise of discretion. Serious studies have suggested that fair treatment on parole revocation will not result in fewer grants of parole.

This discretionary aspect of the revocation decision need not be reached unless there is first an appropriate determination that the individual has in fact breached the conditions of parole. The parolee is not the only one who has a stake in his conditional liberty. Society has a stake in whatever may be the chance of restoring him to normal and useful life within the law. Society thus has an interest in not having parole revoked because of erroneous information or because of an erroneous evaluation of the need to revoke parole, given the breach of parole conditions. See People ex rel. Menechino v. Warden, 27 N.Y.2d 376, 318 N.Y.S.2d 449, 267 N.E.2d 239, 239 and n. 2 (1971) (parole board had less than full picture of facts). And society has a further interest in treating the parolee with basic fairness: fair treatment in parole revocations will enhance the chance of rehabilitation by avoiding reactions to arbitrariness.

Given these factors, most States have recognized that there is no interest on the part of the State in revoking parole without any procedural guarantees at all. What is needed is an informal hearing structured to assure that the finding of a parole violation will be based on verified facts and that the exercise of discretion will be informed by an accurate knowledge of the parolee's behavior.

III

We now turn to the nature of the process that is due, bearing in mind that the interest of both State and parolee will be furthered by an effective but informal hearing. In analyzing what is due, we see two important stages in the typical process of parole revocation.

(a) Arrest of Parolee and Preliminary Hearing. The first stage occurs when the parolee is arrested and detained, usually at the direction of his parole officer. The second occurs when parole is formally revoked. There is typically a substantial time lag between the arrest and the eventual determination by the parole board whether parole should be revoked. Additionally, it may be that the parolee is arrested at a place distant from the state institution, to which he may be returned before the final decision is made concerning revocation. Given these factors, due process would seem to require that some minimal inquiry be conducted at or reasonably near the place of the alleged parole violation or arrest and as promptly as convenient after arrest while information is fresh and sources are available. Cf. Hyser v. Reed, 318 F.2d 225 (C.A.D.C. 1963). Such an inquiry should be seen as in the nature of a "preliminary hearing" to determine whether there is probable cause or reasonable grounds to believe that the arrested parolee has committed acts which would constitute a violation of parole conditions. Cf. Goldberg v. Kelly, 397 U.S., at 267–271, 25 L.Ed.2d at 298–300.

In our view due process requires that after the arrest, the determination that reasonable grounds exist for revocation of parole should be made by someone not directly involved in the case. It would be unfair to assume that the supervising parole officer does not conduct an interview with the parolee to confront him with the reasons for revocation before he recommends an arrest. It would also be unfair to assume that the parole officer bears hostility against the parolee which destroys his neutrality; realistically the failure of the parolee is in a sense a failure for his supervising officer. However, we need make no assumptions one way or the other to conclude that there should be an uninvolved person to make this preliminary evaluation of the basis for believing the conditions of parole have been violated. The officer directly involved in making recommendations cannot always have complete objectivity in evaluating them. Goldberg v. Kelly found it unnecessary to impugn the motives of the caseworker to find a need for an independent decisionmaker to examine the initial decision.

This independent officer need not be a judicial officer. The granting and revocation of parole are matters traditionally handled by administrative officers. In Goldberg, the Court pointedly did not require that the hearing on termination of benefits be conducted by a judicial officer or even before the traditional "neutral and detached" officer; it required only that the hearing be conducted by some person *other* than one initially dealing with the case. It will be sufficient, therefore, in the parole revocation context, if an evaluation of whether reasonable cause exists to believe that conditions of parole have been violated is made by someone such as a parole officer other than the one who has made the report of parole violations or has recommended revocation. A State could certainly choose some other independent decisionmaker to perform this preliminary function.

With respect to the preliminary hearing before this officer, the parolee should be given notice that the hearing will take place and that its purpose is to determine whether there is probable cause to believe he has committed a parole violation. The notice should state what parole violations have been alleged. At the hearing the parolee may appear and speak in his own behalf; he may bring letters, documents, or individuals who can give relevant information to the hearing officer. On request of the parolee, persons who have given adverse information on which parole revocation is to be based are to be made available for questioning in his presence. However, if the hearing officer determines that the informant would be subjected to risk of harm if his identity were disclosed, he need not be subjected to confrontation and cross-examination.

The hearing officer shall have the duty of making a summary, or digest, of what transpires at the hearing in terms of the responses of the parolee and the substance of the documents or evidence given in support of parole revocation and of the parolee's position. Based on the information before him, the officer should determine whether there is probable cause to hold the parolee for the final decision of the parole board on revocation. Such a determination would be sufficient to warrant the parolee's continued detention and return to the state correctional institution pending the final decision. As in Goldberg, "the decision-maker should state the reasons for his determination and indicate the evidence he relied on * * *" but it should be remembered that this is not a final determination calling for "formal findings of fact or conclusions of law." 397 U.S., at 271, 25 L.Ed.2d at 300. No interest would be served by formalism in this process; informality will not lessen the utility of this inquiry in reducing the risk of error.

(b) The Revocation Hearing. There must also be an opportunity for a hearing, if it is desired by the parolee, prior to the final decision on revocation by the parole authority. This hearing must be the basis for more than determining probable cause; it must lead to a final evaluation of any contested relevant facts and consideration of whether the facts as determined warrant revocation. The parolee must have an opportunity to be heard and to show, if he can, that he did not violate the conditions, or, if he did, that circumstances in mitigation suggest the violation does not warrant revocation. The revocation hearing must be tendered within a reasonable time after the parolee is taken into custody. A lapse of two months, as the State suggests occurs in some cases, would not appear to be unreasonable.

We cannot write a code of procedure; that is the responsibility of each State. Most States have done so by legislation, others by judicial decision usually on due process grounds. Our task is limited to deciding the minimum requirements of due process. They include (a) written notice of the claimed violations of parole; (b) disclosure to the parolee of evidence against him; (c) opportunity to be heard in person and to present witnesses and documentary evidence; (d) the right to confront and cross-examine adverse witnesses (unless the hearing officer specifically finds good cause for not allowing confrontation); (e) a "neutral and detached" hearing body such as a traditional parole board, members of which need not be judicial officers or lawyers; and (f) a written statement by the factfinders as to the evidence relied on and reasons for revoking parole. We emphasize there is no thought to equate this second stage of parole revocation to a criminal prosecution in any sense; it is a narrow inquiry; the process should be flexible enough to consider evidence including letters, affidavits, and other material that would not be admissible in an adversary criminal trial.

We do not reach or decide the question whether the parolee is entitled to the assistance of retained counsel or to appointed counsel if he is indigent.

We have no thought to create an inflexible structure for parole revocation procedures. The few basic requirements set out above, which are applicable to future revocations of parole, should not impose a great burden on any State's parole system. Control over the required proceedings by the hearing officers can assure that delaying tactics and other abuses sometimes present in the traditional adversary trial situation do not occur. Obviously a parolee cannot relitigate issues determined against him in other forums, as in the situation presented when the revocation is based on conviction of another crime.

In the peculiar posture of this case, given the absence of an adequate record, we conclude the ends of justice will be best served by remanding the case to the Court of Appeals for its return of the two consolidated cases to the District Court with directions to make findings on the procedures actually followed by the Parole Board in these two revocations. If it is determined that petitioners admitted parole violations to the Parole Board, as Iowa contends, and if those violations are found to be reasonable grounds for revoking parole under state standards, that would end the matter. If the procedures followed by the Parole Board are found to meet the standards laid down in this opinion that, too, would dispose of the due process claims for these cases.

We reverse and remand to the Court of Appeals for further proceedings consistent with this opinion.

Reversed and remanded.

MR. JUSTICE BRENNAN, with whom MR. JUSTICE MARSHALL joins, concurring in the result.

I agree that a parole may not be revoked consistently with the Due Process Clause, unless the parolee is afforded, first, a preliminary hearing at the time of arrest to determine whether there is probable cause to believe that he has violated his parole conditions and, second, a final hearing within a reasonable time to determine whether he has, in fact, violated those conditions and whether his parole should be revoked. For each hearing the parolee is entitled to notice of the violations alleged and the evidence against him, opportunity to be heard in person and to present witnesses and documentary evidence, and the right to confront and cross-examine adverse witnesses, unless it is specifically found that the witness would thereby be exposed to a significant risk of harm. Moreover, in each case the decisionmaker must be impartial, there must be some record of the proceedings, and the decisionmaker's conclusions must be set forth in written form indicating both the evidence and the reasons relied upon. Because the Due Process Clause requires these procedures, I agree that the case must be remanded as the Court orders.

The Court, however, states that it does not now decide whether the parolee is also entitled at each hearing to the assistance of retained counsel or of appointed counsel if he is indigent. Goldberg v. Kelly, 397 U.S. 254, 90 S.Ct. 1011, 25 L.Ed.2d 287 (1970), nonetheless plainly dictates that he at least "must be allowed to retain an attorney if he so desires." *Id.*, at 270, 25 L.Ed.2d at 300. As the Court said there, "Counsel can help delineate the issues, present the factual contentions in an orderly manner, conduct cross-examination, and generally safeguard the interests of" his client. *Id.*, at 270–271, 25 L.Ed.2d at 300. The only question open under our precedents is whether counsel must be furnished the parolee if he is indigent.

MR. JUSTICE DOUGLAS, dissenting in part.

Each petitioner was sentenced for a term in an Iowa penitentiary for forgery. Somewhat over a year later each was released on parole. About six months later each was arrested for a parole violation and confined in a local jail. In about a week the Iowa Board of Parole revoked their paroles and each was returned to the penitentiary. At no time during any of the proceedings which led to the parole revocations were they granted a hearing or the opportunity to know, question, or challenge any of the facts which formed the basis of their alleged parole violations. Nor were they given an opportunity to present evidence on their own behalf nor to confront and cross-examine those on whose testimony their paroles were revoked.

Each challenged the revocation in the state courts and, obtaining no relief, filed the present petitions in the Federal District Court which denied relief. Their appeals were consolidated in the Court of Appeals which, sitting en banc, in each case affirmed the District Court by a four-to-three vote, 443 F.2d 942. The cases are here on a petition for a writ of certiorari, 404 U.S. 999, 92 S.Ct. 568, 30 L.Ed.2d 552, which we granted because there is a conflict between the decision below and Hahn v. Burke, 430 F.2d 100, decided by the Court of Appeals for the Seventh Circuit.

Iowa has a board of parole which determines who shall be paroled. Once paroled a person is under the supervision of the director of the division of corrections of the Department of Social Services who in turn supervises parole agents. Parole agents do not revoke the parole of any person but only recommend that the board of parole revoke it. The Iowa Act provides that each parolee "shall be subject, at any time, to be taken into custody and returned to the institution" from which he was paroled. Thus Iowa requires no notice or hearing to put a parolee back in prison, Curtis v. Bennett, 256 Iowa 1164, 131 N.W.2d 1; and it is urged that since parole, like probation, is only a privilege it may be summarily revoked. See Escoe v. Zerbst, 295 U.S. 490, 492–493, 55 S.Ct. 818, 79 L.Ed. 1566, 1568–1569; Ughbanks v. Armstrong, 208 U.S. 481, 28 S.Ct. 372, 52 L.Ed. 582. But we have long discarded the right-privilege distinction. See, e. g., Graham v. Richardson, 403 U.S. 365, 374, 91 S.Ct. 1848, 29 L.Ed.2d 534; Bell v. Burson, 402 U.S. 535, 539, 91 S.Ct. 1586, 29 L.Ed.2d 90, 94; Pickering v. Board of Education, 391 U.S. 563, 568, 88 S.Ct. 1731, 20 L.Ed.2d 811, 817; cf. Van Alstyne, The Demise of the Right-Privilege Distinction in Constitutional Law, 81 Harv. L.Rev. 1439 (1968).

The Court said in United States v. Wilson, 7 Pet. 150, 161, 8 L.Ed. 640, 644, that a "pardon is a deed." The same can be said of a parole, which when conferred gives the parolee a degree of liberty which is often associated with property interests.

We held in Goldberg v. Kelly, 397 U.S. 254, 90 S.Ct. 1011, 25 L.Ed.2d 287, that the termination by a State of public assistance payments to a recipient without a prior evidentiary hearing denies him procedural due process in violation of the Fourteenth Amendment. Speaking of the termination of welfare benefits we said:

"Their termination involves state action that adjudicates important rights. The constitutional challenge cannot be answered by an argument that public assistance benefits are 'a privilege' and not a 'right.' Shapiro v. Thompson, 394 U.S. 618, 627 n. [89 S.Ct. 1322, 22 L.Ed.2d 600, 611] (1969). Relevant constitutional restraints apply as much to the withdrawal of public assistance benefits as to disqualification for unemployment compensation. Sherbert v. Verner, 374 U.S. 398 [83 S.Ct. 1790, 10 L.Ed.2d 965] (1963); or to denial of a tax exemption, Speiser v. Randall, 357 U.S. 513 [78 S.Ct. 1332, 2 L.Ed. 2d 1460] (1958); or to discharge from public employment, Slochower v. Board of Higher Education, 350 U.S. 551 [76 S.Ct. 637, 100 L.Ed. 692] (1956). The extent to which procedural due process must be afforded the recipient is influenced by the extent to which he may be 'condemned to suffer grievous loss,' Joint Anti-Fascist Refugee Committee v. McGrath, 341 U.S. 123, 168 [71 S.Ct. 624, 95 L.Ed. 817, 852] (1951) (Frankfurter, J., concurring), and depends upon whether the recipient's interest in avoiding that loss outweighs the governmental interest in summary adjudication. Accordingly, as we said in Cafeteria & Restaurant Workers Union v. McElroy, 367 U.S. 886, 895 [81 S.Ct. 1743, 6 L.Ed.2d 1230, 1236] (1961), 'consideration of what procedures due process may require under any given set of circumstances must begin with a determination of the precise nature of the government function involved as well as of the private interest that has been affected by governmental action.' See also Hannah v. Larche, 363 U.S. 420, 440, 442 [80 S.Ct. 1502, 4 L.Ed.2d 1307, 1320, 1321] (1960)." 397 U.S., at 262–263, 25 L.Ed.2d at 295, 296.

Under modern concepts of penology, paroling prisoners is part of the rehabilitory aim of the correctional philosophy. The objective is to return a prisoner to a full family and community life. See generally Note, 56 Geo.L.J. 705 (1968); Note, 38 N.Y.U.L.Rev. 702 (1963); Comment, 72 Yale L.J. 368 (1962); and see Baine v. Beckstead, 10 Utah 2d 4, 347 P.2d 554 (1959). The status he enjoys as a parolee is as important a right as those we reviewed in Goldberg v. Kelly. That status is conditioned upon not engaging in certain activities and perhaps in not leaving a certain area or locality. Violations of conditions of parole may be technical, they may be done unknowingly, they may be fleeting and of no consequence. See, e. g., Arciniega v. Freeman, 404 U.S. 4, 92 S.Ct. 22, 30 L.Ed.2d 126; Cohen, Due Process, Equal Protection and State Parole Revocation Proceedings, 42 U.Colo. L.Rev. 197, 229 (1970). The parolee should in the concept of fairness implicit in due process have a chance to explain. Rather, under Iowa's rule revocation proceeds on the ipse dixit of the parole agent; and on his word alone each of these petitioners has already served three additional years in prison. The charges may or may not be true. Words of explanation may be adequate to transform into trivia what looms large in the mind of the parole officer.

"[T]here is no place in our system of law for reaching a result of such tremendous consequences without ceremony—without hearing, without effective assistance of counsel, without a statement of reasons." Kent v. United States, 383 U.S. 541, 554, 86 S.Ct. 1045, 16 L.Ed.2d 84, 93 (1966).

Parole, while originally conceived as a judicial function, has become largely an administrative matter. The parole boards have broad discretion in formulating and imposing parole conditions. "Often vague and moralistic parole conditions may seem oppressive and unfair to the parolee." Dawson, Sentencing 306 (1969). They are drawn "to cover any contingency that might occur," *id.*, at 307, and are designed to maximize "control over the parolee by his parole officer." *ibid.*

Parole is commonly revoked on mere suspicion that the parolee may have committed a crime. *Id.*, at 366–367. Such great control over the parolee vests in a parole officer a broad discretion in revoking parole and also in counseling the parolee—referring him for psychiatric treatment or obtaining the use of specialized therapy for narcotic addicts or alcoholics. *Id.*, at 321. Treatment of the parolee, rather than revocation of his parole, is a common course. *Id.*, at 322–323. Counseling may include extending help to a parolee in finding a job. *Id.*, at 324 et seq.

A parolee, like a prisoner, is a person entitled to constitutional protection, including procedural due process. At the federal level the construction of Regulations of the Federal Parole Board presents federal questions of which we have taken cognizance. See Arciniega v. Freeman, 404 U.S. 4, 92 S.Ct. 22, 30 L.Ed.2d 126. At the state level, the construction of parole statutes and regulations is for the States alone, save as they implicate the Federal Constitution in which event the Supremacy Clause controls.

It is only procedural due process, required by the Fourteenth Amendment, that concerns us in the present cases. Procedural due process requires the following.

If a violation of a condition of parole is involved, rather than the commission of a new offense, there should not be an arrest of the parolee and his return to the prison or to a local jail. Rather, notice of the alleged violation should be given to the parolee and a time set for a hearing. The hearing should not be before the parole officer, as he is the one who is making the charge and "there is inherent danger in combining the functions of judge and advocate." Jones v. Rivers, 338 F.2d 862, 877 (C.A.4 1964) (Sobeloff, J., concurring). Moreover the parolee should be entitled to counsel. See Hewett v. North Carolina, 415 F.2d 1316, 1322–1325 (C.A.4 1969); People ex rel. Combs v. LaVallee, 29 A.D.2d 128, 286 N.Y.S.2d 600 (1968); Perry v. Williard, 247 Or. 145, 427 P.2d 1020 (1967). As the Supreme Court of Oregon said in Perry v. Williard, "A hearing in which counsel is absent or is present on behalf of one side is inherently unsatisfactory if not unfair. Counsel can see that the relevant facts are brought out, vague and insubstantial allegations discounted, and irrelevancies eliminated." *Id.*, at 148, 427 P.2d, at 1022. Cf. Mempa v. Rhay, 389 U.S. 128, 135, 88 S.Ct. 254, 19 L.Ed.2d 336, 340.

The hearing required is not a grant of the full panoply of rights applicable to a criminal trial. But confrontation with the informer may, as Roviaro v. United States, 353 U.S. 53, 77 S.Ct. 623, 1 L.Ed.2d 639, illustrates, be necessary for a fair hearing and the ascertainment of the truth. The hearing is to determine the fact of parole violation. The results of the hearing would go to the parole board—or other authorized state agency—for final action, as would cases which involved voluntary admission of violations.

The rule of law is important in the stability of society. Arbitrary actions in the revocation of paroles can only impede and impair the rehabilitory aspects of modern penology. "Notice and opportunity for hearing appropriate to the case," Boddie v. Connecticut, 401 U.S. 371, 378, 91 S.Ct. 780, 28 L.Ed.2d 113, 119, are the rudiments of due process which restore faith that our society is run for the many, not the few, and that fair dealing rather than caprice will govern the affairs of men.

We do not prescribe the precise formula for the management of the parole problems. We do not sit as an ombudsman, telling the States the precise procedures they must follow. We do say so far as the due process requirements of parole revocation are concerned:

1. the parole officer—whatever may be his duties under various state statutes—in Iowa appears to be an agent having some of the functions of a prosecutor and of the police

2. the parole officer is therefore not qualified as a hearing officer

3. the parolee is entitled to a due process notice and a due process hearing of the alleged parole violations including, for example, the opportunity to be confronted by his accusers and to present evidence and argument on his own behalf

4. the parolee is entitled to the freedom granted a parolee until the results of the hearing are known and the parole board—or other authorized state agency—acts.

I would reverse the judgments and remand for further consideration in light of this opinion.

Gagnon v. Scarpelli

This case presents the related questions whether a previously sentenced probationer is entitled to a hearing when his probation is revoked and, if so, whether he is entitled to be represented by appointed counsel at such hearing.

I

Respondent, Gerald Scarpelli, pleaded guilty in July, 1965, to a charge of armed robbery in Wisconsin. The trial judge sentenced him to 15 years' imprisonment, but suspended the sentence and placed him on probation for seven years in the custody of the Wisconsin Department of Public Welfare ("the Department"). At that time, he signed an agreement specifying the terms of his probation and a "Travel Permit and Agreement to Return" allowing him to reside in Illinois, with supervision there under an interstate compact. On August 5, 1965, he was accepted for supervision by the Adult Probation Department of Cook County, Illinois.

On August 6, respondent was apprehended by Illinois police, who had surprised him and one Fred Kleckner, Jr., in the course of the burglary of a house. After being apprised of his constitutional rights, respondent admitted that he and Kleckner had broken into the house for the purpose of stealing merchandise or money, although he now asserts that his statement was made under duress and is false. Probation was revoked by the Wisconsin Department on September 1, without a hearing. The stated grounds for revocation were that:

> 1. [Scarpelli] has associated with known criminals, in direct violation of his probation regulations and his supervising agent's instructions;
>
> 2. [Scarpelli] while associating with a known criminal, namely Fred Kleckner, Jr., was involved in, and arrested for, a burglary * * * in Deerfield, Illinois. App., p. 20.

On September 4, 1965, he was incarcerated in the Wisconsin State Reformatory at Green Bay to begin serving the 15 years to which he had been sentenced by the trial judge. At no time was he afforded a hearing.

Some three years later, on December 16, 1968, respondent applied for a writ of habeas corpus. After the petition had been filed, but before it had been acted upon the Department placed respondent on parole. The District Court found that his status as parolee was sufficient custody to confer jurisdiction on the court and that the petition was not moot because the revocation carried "collateral consequences," presumably including the restraints imposed by his parole. On the merits, the District Court held that revocation without a hearing and counsel was a denial of due process. 317 F.Supp. 72 (E.D.Wis.1970). The Court of Appeals affirmed, sub nom. Gunsolus v. Gagnon, 454 F.2d 416 (C.A.7 1971), and we granted certiorari. 408 U.S. 921 (1972).

II

Two prior decisions set the bounds of our present inquiry. In Mempa v. Rhay, 389 U.S. 128 (1967), the Court held that a probationer is entitled to be represented by appointed counsel at a combined revocation and sentencing hearing. Reasoning that counsel is required "at every stage of a criminal proceeding where substantial rights of a criminal accused may be affected," 389 U.S., at 134, and that sentencing is one such stage, the Court concluded that counsel must be provided an indigent at sentencing even when it is accomplished as part of a subsequent, probation revocation proceeding. But this line of reasoning does not require a hearing or counsel at the time of probation revocation in a case such as the present one, where the probationer was sentenced at the time of trial.

Of greater relevance is our decision last Term in Morrissey v. Brewer, 408 U.S. 471 (1972). There we held that the revocation of parole is not a part of a criminal prosecution.

> Parole arises after the end of the criminal prosecution, including imposition of sentence. * * * Revocation deprives an individual, not of the absolute liberty to which every citizen is entitled, but only of the conditional liberty properly dependent on observance of special parole restrictions. 408 U.S., at 480.

Even though the revocation of parole is not a part of the criminal prosecution, we held that the loss of liberty entailed is a serious deprivation requiring that the parolee be accorded due process. Specifically, we held that a parolee is entitled to two hearings, one a preliminary hearing at the time of his arrest and detention to determine whether there is probable cause to believe that he has committed a violation of his parole and the other a somewhat more comprehensive hearing prior to the making of the final revocation decision.

Petitioner does not contend that there is any difference relevant to the guarantee of due process between the revocation of parole and the revocation of probation, nor do we perceive one. Probation revocation, like parole revocation, is not a stage of a criminal prosecution, but does result in a loss of liberty. Accordingly, we hold that a probationer, like a parolee, is entitled to a preliminary and a final revocation hearing, under the conditions specified in Morrissey v. Brewer, supra.

III

The second, and more difficult, question posed by this case is whether an indigent probationer or parolee has a due process right to be represented by appointed counsel at these hearings. In answering that question, we draw heavily on the opinion in *Morrissey*. Our first point of reference is the character of probation or parole. As noted in *Morrissey* regarding parole, the "purpose is to help individuals reintegrate into society as constructive individuals as soon as they are able * * *." 408 U.S., at 477. The duty and attitude of the probation or parole officer reflect this purpose:

> While the parole or probation officer recognizes his double duty to the welfare of his clients and to the safety of the general community, by and

> large concern for the client dominates his professional attitude. The parole agent ordinarily defines his role as representing his client's best interests as long as these do not constitute a threat to public safety.

Because the probation or parole officer's function is not so much to compel conformance to a strict code of behavior as to supervise a course of rehabilitation, he has been entrusted traditionally with broad discretion to judge the progress of rehabilitation in individual cases, and has been armed with the power to recommend or even to declare revocation.

In Morrissey, we recognized that the revocation decision has two analytically distinct components:

> The first step in a revocation decision involves a wholly retrospective factual question: whether the parolee has in fact acted in violation of one or more conditions of his parole. Only if it is determined that the parolee did violate the conditions does the second question arise: should the parolee be recommitted to prison or should other steps be taken to protect society and improve chances of rehabilitation? Morrissey v. Brewer, supra, 408 U.S., at 479–480.

The parole officer's attitude toward these decisions reflects the rehabilitative rather than punitive focus of the probation/parole system:

> Revocation * * * is, if anything, commonly treated as a failure of supervision. While presumably it would be inappropriate for a field agent *never* to revoke, the whole thrust of the probation-parole movement is to keep men in the community, working with adjustment problems there, and using revocation only as a last resort when treatment had failed or is about to fail.

But an exclusive focus on the benevolent attitudes of those who administer the probation/parole system when it is working successfully obscures the modification in attitude which is likely to take place once the officer has decided to recommend revocation. Even though the officer is not by this recommendation converted into a prosecutor committed to convict, his role as counsellor to the probationer or parolee is then surely compromised.

When the officer's view of the probationer's or parolee's conduct differs in this fundamental way from the latter's own view, due process requires that the difference be resolved before revocation becomes final. Both the probationer or parolee and the State have interests in the accurate finding of fact and the informed use of discretion, the probationer or parolee to insure that his liberty is not unjustifiably taken away and the State to make certain that it is neither unnecessarily interrupting a successful effort at rehabilitation nor imprudently prejudicing the safety of the community.

It was to serve all of these interests that *Morrissey* mandated preliminary and final revocation hearings. At the preliminary hearing, a probationer or parolee is entitled to notice of the alleged violations of probation or parole, an opportunity to appear and to present evidence in his own behalf, a conditional right to confront adverse witnesses, an independent decisionmaker, and a written report of the hearing. Morrissey v. Brewer, supra, 408 U.S., at 487. The final hearing is a less summary one because the decision under consideration is the ultimate decision to revoke rather than a mere determination of probable cause, but the "minimum requirements of due process" include very similar elements:

> (a) written notice of the claimed violations of [probation or] parole; (b) disclosure to the [probationer or] parolee of evidence against him; (c) opportunity to be heard in person and to present witnesses and documentary evidence; (d) the right to confront and cross-examine adverse witnesses (unless the hearing officer specifically finds good cause for not allowing confrontation); (e) a "neutral and detached" hearing body such as a traditional parole board, members of which need not be judicial officers or lawyers; and (f) a written statement by the fact-finders as to the evidence relied on and reasons for revoking [probation or] parole. Morrissey v. Brewer, supra, 408 U.S., at 489.

These requirements in themselves serve as substantial protection against ill-considered revocation, and petitioner argues that counsel need never be supplied. What this argument overlooks is that the effectiveness of the rights guaranteed by *Morrissey* may in some circumstances depend on the use of skills which the probationer or parolee is unlikely to possess. Despite the informal nature of the proceedings and the absence of technical rules of procedure or evidence, the unskilled or uneducated probationer or parolee may well have difficulty in presenting his version of a disputed set of facts where the presentation requires the examining or cross-examining of witnesses or the offering or dissecting of complex documentary evidence.

By the same token, we think that the Court of Appeals erred in accepting respondent's contention that the State is under a constitutional duty to provide counsel for indigents in all probation or parole revocation cases. While such a rule has the appeal of simplicity, it would impose direct costs and serious collateral disadvantages without regard to the need or the likelihood in a particular case for a constructive contribution by counsel. In most cases, the probationer or parolee has been convicted of committing another crime or has admitted the charges against him. And while in some cases he may have a justifiable excuse for the violation or a convincing reason why revocation is not the appropriate disposition, mitigating evidence of this kind is often not susceptible of proof or is so simple as not to be require either investigation or exposition by counsel.

The introduction of counsel into a revocation proceeding will alter significantly the nature of the proceeding. If counsel is provided for the probationer or parolee, the State in turn will normally provide its own counsel; lawyers, by training and disposition, are advocates and bound by professional duty to present all available evidence and arguments in support of their clients' positions and to contest with vigor all adverse evidence and views. The role of the hearing body itself, aptly described in *Morrissey* as being "predictive and discretionary" as well as factfinding, may become more akin to that of a judge at a trial, and less attuned to the rehabilitative needs of the individual probationer or parolee. In the greater self-consciousness of its quasijudicial role, the hearing body may be less tolerant of marginal deviant behavior and feel more pressure to reincarcerate rather than continue nonpunitive rehabilitation. Certainly, the decisionmaking process will be prolonged, and the financial cost to the State—for appointed counsel, counsel for the State, a longer record, and the possibility of judicial review—will not be insubstantial.

In some cases, those modifications in the nature of the revocation hearing must be endured and the costs borne because, as we have indicated above, the probationer's or parolee's version of a disputed issue can fairly be represented only by a trained advocate. But due process is not so rigid as to require that the significant interests in informality, flexibility, and economy must always be sacrificed.

In so concluding, we are of course aware that the case-by-case approach to the right to counsel in felony prosecutions adopted in Betts v. Brady, 316 U.S. 455 (1942), was later rejected in favor of a *per se* rule in Gideon v. Wainwright, 372 U.S. 335 (1963). See also Argersinger v. Hamlin, 407 U.S. 25 (1972). We do not, however, draw from *Gideon* and *Argersinger* the conclusion that a case-by-case approach to furnishing counsel is necessarily inadequate to protect constitutional rights asserted in varying types of proceedings: there are critical differences between criminal trials and probation or parole revocation hearings, and both society and the probationer or parolee have stakes in preserving these differences.

In a criminal trial, the State is represented by a prosecutor; formal rules of evidence are in force; a defendant enjoys a number of procedural rights which may be lost if not timely raised; and, in a jury trial, a defendant must make a presentation understandable to untrained jurors. In short, a criminal trial under our system is an adversary proceeding with its own unique characteristics. In a revocation hearing, on the other hand, the State is represented not by a prosecutor but by a parole officer with the orientation described above; formal procedures and roles of evidence are not employed; and the members of the hearing body are familiar with the problems and practice of probation or parole. The need for counsel at revocation hearings derives not from the invariable attributes of those hearings but rather from the peculiarities of particular cases.

The differences between a criminal trial and a revocation hearing do not dispose altogether of the argument that under a case-by-case approach there may be cases in which a lawyer would be useful but in which none would be appointed because an arguable defense would be uncovered only by a lawyer. Without denying that there is some force in this argument, we think it a sufficient answer that we deal here not with the right of an accused to counsel in a criminal prosecution, but with the more limited due process right of one who is a probationer or parolee only because he has been convicted of a crime.

We thus find no justification for a new inflexible constitutional rule with respect to the requirement of counsel. We think, rather, that the decision as to the need for counsel must be made on a case-by-case basis in the exercise of a sound discretion by the state authority charged with responsibility for administering the probation and parole system. Although the presence and participation of counsel will probably be both undesirable and constitutionally unnecessary in most revocation hearings, there will remain certain cases in which fundamental fairness—the touchstone of due process—will require that the State provide at its expense counsel for indigent probationers or parolees.

It is neither possible nor prudent to attempt to formulate a precise and detailed set of guidelines to be followed in determining when the providing of counsel is necessary to meet the applicable due process requirements. The facts and circumstances in preliminary and final hearings are susceptible of almost infinite variation, and a considerable discretion must be allowed the responsible agency in making the decision. Presumptively, it may be said that counsel should be provided in cases where, after being informed of his right to request counsel, the probationer or parolee makes such a request, based on a timely and colorable claim (i) that he has not committed the alleged violation of the conditions upon which he is at liberty; or (ii) that, even if the violation is a matter of public record or is uncontested, there are substantial reasons which justified or mitigated the violation and make revocation inappropriate and that the reasons are complex or otherwise difficult to develop or present. In passing on a request for the appointment of counsel, the responsible agency also should consider, especially in doubtful cases, whether the probationer appears to be capable of speaking effectively for himself. In every case in which a request for counsel at a preliminary or final hearing is refused, the grounds for refusal should be stated succinctly in the record.

IV

We return to the facts of the present case. Because respondent was not afforded either a preliminary hearing or a final hearing, the revocation of his probation did not meet the standards of due process prescribed in *Morrissey*, which we have here held applicable to probation revocations. Accordingly, respondent was entitled to a writ of habeas corpus. On remand, the District Court should allow the State an opportunity to conduct such a hearing. As to whether the State must provide counsel, respondent's admission to having committed another serious crime creates the very sort of situation in which counsel need not ordinarily be provided. But because of respondent's subsequent assertions regarding that admission, see p. 258, ante, we conclude that the failure of the Department to provide respondent with the assistance of counsel should be re-examined in light of this opinion. The general guidelines outlined above should be applied in the first instance by those charged with conducting the revocation hearing.

Affirmed in part, reversed in part, and remanded.

MR. JUSTICE DOUGLAS, dissenting in part.

I believe that due process requires the appointment of counsel in this case because of the claim that respondent's confession of the burglary was made under coercion. See Morrissey v. Brewer, 408 U.S. 471, 498.

Name Index

A

B

C

D

E

F

G

H

O

P

Q

R

S

T

U

V

W

Y

Subject Index